Legacy of a Native Son
James Duval Phelan & Villa Montalvo

James P. Walsh

Timothy J. O'Keefe

HE SERVED THE CAUSE OF ART

by Edwin Markham

James D. Phelan is closely identified with fifty years of the history of California. He was always an outstanding personality, an effective platform orator, an untiring advocate of all issues which he believed to be for the public welfare.

He spent many years in politics, but he was always the scholar in politics, always a man eager to serve the cause of Art and especially the cause of Poetry. He not only had a pen that could turn out clever sonnets, but he was also ever ready to give courage and good counsel to all who were struggling up the slopes of Parnassus.

All along the path of life he was sharing with others the bread and wine of the various Arts. He was beneficent in life, and he was also beneficent in death in providing for others opportunities for living more securely and abundantly. Many hearts will remember him into the long future.

Senator Phelan was a great-hearted friend: he was my friend.

Legacy of a Native Son

James Duval Phelan & Villa Montalvo

James P. Walsh   Timothy J. O'Keefe

FORBES MILL PRESS
1993

Cover Design: Jan Janes

Editor & Text Designer: Robin Gold

Photo Editor: Patty Arnold

Photo credits and colophon appear at the end of the book

Copyright © The Montalvo Association, 1993
All rights reserved

Printed in the United States of America

Library of Congress Catalog Card Number: 93-71667

ISBN 0-9636059-0-9

10 9 8 7 6 5 4 3 2 1

Acknowledgments

The research and writing of this manuscript enjoyed an auspicious beginning—a grant from the L. J. Skaggs and Mary C. Skaggs Foundation. The Irish American Cultural Institute of St. Paul, Minnesota provided a grant for publication support through an endowment given by the Lawrence O'Shaughnessy Research Fund. Between these awards came the help of numerous individuals and institutions. The listing that follows is destined to be incomplete. Hopefully, this will be the most noted shortcoming of a satisfying project now concluded.

The authors wish to acknowledge and thank the following: The Montalvo Association, its leadership, staff, and members; the staffs of The Bancroft Library, San Francisco Art Institute Archives and Library, San Jose State University Libraries, Santa Clara University Archives and Library, Henry E. Huntington Library, California State Library, California Room of San Jose Public Library, Manuscript Room of Trinity College Dublin, Archdiocese of San Francisco Archives, San Francisco State University Labor Archives, San Jose State University Foundation, San Francisco Foundation, San Francisco History Room of the San Francisco Public Library; the San Jose Historical Museum Association; descendants of James and Alice Kelley Phelan, including the Doyle, O'Day, Ryan, O'Neill, and Mahoney families, with particular appreciation to Peter Doyle, Sheila O'Day, Brenda Jeffers, Richard Mahoney, and Alice Wetherow. Other individuals who assisted included Jane Maxwell, Frank R. Quinn, Edith Kulstein, Vanetia Johnston, Linda Garcia, Emi Nobuhiro, Romaldo Lopez, Adnan Daoud, Gerald E. Wheeler, Charles B. Burdick, Catherine Ann Curry, Robert J. Brophy, Thomas Boylan, Thomas P. O'Neill, Mary McDevitt, Joan Keefe, John A. Murphy, Peter Buzanski, Jack Douglas, Rowena Mason Myers, Louise Geiger, Louis R. Bisceglia, Thomas Hobbs, Michael K. Tamony, Leo T. Walsh, Gladys Hansen, Jeffrey M. Burns, James Carrigan, Sister Emmanuel, O.C.D. and the nuns of the Santa Clara Carmelite Monastery. The authors would also like to thank Michael Antonacci, Carolyn Hayes, Ruth Payette, Olivia Davies, Margaret Dyer, Helen Metcalf, Jean Kuhn Doyle, Francis X. Duggan, Richard Roberts, S.J., Roberta Sweeney, James Degnan, Katherine Brody, Gerald McKevitt, S.J., Jennifer Skyles, members of the family of George Doeltz (Mary, Mary K., George, David and Anne Doeltz Farrell), and Jeffrey Gunderson, Librarian of the San Francisco Art Institute. The scholarship of William Issel, Robert W. Cherny, and Judd Kahn is acknowledged with appreciation and respect.

An earlier version of "California's Native Son" appeared as "Moving Day" in *Villa Montalvo: 1991 Performing Arts Magazine*. The fully-documented version of "Creating the Fortune, Creating the Family" appeared in the *Journal of the West* (April, 1992). For those interested in further research, copies of the somewhat larger draft manuscript, with references, have been placed in the Phelan Library at Villa Montalvo, the San Jose State University Library, and the Santa Clara University Archives.

James P. Walsh, Timothy J. O'Keefe
Villa Montalvo   •   February 11, 1993

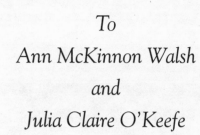

To
Ann McKinnon Walsh
and
Julia Claire O'Keefe

James Duval Phelan

Legacy of A Native Son

	Introduction by Kevin Starr	ix
One	*California's Native Son*	1
Two	*Creating the Fortune, Creating the Family*	5
Three	*Father and Son: Educating Each Other*	15
Four	*Private Life, Public Life*	33
Five	*Campaign for Mayor*	51
Six	*Mayor of San Francisco*	59
Seven	*City Beautiful*	81
Eight	*1906 Earthquake and Fire*	93
Nine	*Graft Prosecution*	113
Ten	*Hetch Hetchy*	119
Eleven	*Construction of Villa Montalvo*	131

James Duval Phelan & Villa Montalvo

Twelve	*Campaign for U. S. Senate*	149
Thirteen	*United States Senator*	163
Fourteen	*World War I Senate Years*	181
Fifteen	*Retired Life and Travel*	195
Sixteen	*Patron of the Arts*	209
Seventeen	*Host of Montalvo*	231
Eighteen	*The Phelan Will and Villa Montalvo*	249
Nineteen	*The Montalvo Foundation*	269
Twenty	*Villa Montalvo at Risk*	287
Twenty-One	*Villa Montalvo: A Community Treasure*	299
	Chapter References	315
	Index	319
	Photo Credits	323

Villa Montalvo

Introduction
by Kevin Starr

For a half century and more, there has been need of a biography of James Duval Phelan. Such a biography, in fact, was long overdue; for the patrician-Progressive Mayor of San Francisco and United States Senator played a major role in such significant enterprises as the reform of the San Francisco charter, the creation of the Hetch Hetchy water system, the commissioning of the Burnham Plan for San Francisco, the organization of the Panama-Pacific International Exposition, and the establishment of the United States as a naval power in the Pacific.

In the private section, James Duval Phelan was equally productive. A connoisseur and patron of the arts, he advanced the cause of California as a regional culture. As the munificent host of Villa Montalvo in Saratoga, Phelan tirelessly promoted a sense of California as a near-magical place, the direct heir to the art-loving Mediterranean cultures of the ancient world and the Renaissance. The Committee for the Adornment and Beautification of San Francisco which he founded brought the City Beautiful Movement to California. The scion of an important Argonaut entrepreneur, Phelan inherited a modest fortune and made it even greater through banking and real estate development in San Francisco and the Santa Clara Valley. Dozens of charities, large and small, knew his generosity.

Not only were Phelan's life and career of significance, the materials documenting his career were available for scholarly research. Throughout his busy life, Phelan kept meticulous records and saved his extensive correspondence, and this collection eventually found its way into the Bancroft Library on the campus of the University of California at Berkeley.

As if all this were not motivation enough for a biography — an important career in the public and private sector, an extensive archive — Phelan continued to enjoy a strong regional reputation. San Franciscans have long since regarded him as one of the best mayors in their history. Scholars of Progressivism in California made frequent mention of Phelan's efforts to reform the politics and governance of his native city. Chroniclers of aesthetic identity in California returned again and again to Phelan at Villa Montalvo as a powerful image of the cultural ambitions of early twentieth century California. From a national perspective, the Senator remained one of the most intriguing public figures of his era: a patrician aesthete, yet a Democrat; an elitist, yet a Progressive reformer; and Irish American, yet very much a member of the national establishment.

Why then, was there no full-scale biography until this elegant presentation of Professors James P. Walsh and Timothy J. O'Keefe? Was it because of certain skeletons in the Senator's closet? His two mistresses, possibly? Or his rabid hostility towards the Japanese? Or were biographers incapable of dealing with the paradox that this paradigm of Irish Catholic civilization, aside from his extra-marital liaisons, was also a skeptic, an agnostic even, in the matter of religious belief? James Duval Phelan, in other words, was encased in one reputation — a regional Maecenas, loyally Catholic, upright and exemplary — while beneath the surface of the public reputation there awaited discovery a much more complex and ultimately more intriguing figure.

Thanks to this biography, we now have insights into both the public and the private Phelan and, more importantly, we can further understand the dynamic tensions within his multiple and complex life. From the public perspective, James Duval Phelan was a Progressive, a reformer, and this story has now been unfolded in its lavish detail. But James Duval Phelan was also an Edwardian gentleman of his time and place and social class. He was an aesthete, a voluptuary, a connoisseur of passion and taste possessed of an instinct for pageantry verging on the operatic. Phelan loved the good life: his clubs, his cellar and table, his social life. (He was known to sweep into a late-night meeting of the Senate in evening clothes, passing from one social event to another.) He knew and collected good books. He adored opera and the stage. Villa Montalvo attested to his exquisite taste in architecture, landscaping, and the arts of hospitality and entertainment. Reserved in manner, he nevertheless found an outlet for his amative life in two dignified liaisons and, towards the end of his years, through a poignant attachment to the tennis star Helen Wills, forty years his junior.

With full detail, this biography presents Phelan and through him the portrait of the late Victorian and Edwardian era, the mauve and yellow *fin de siecle* edging into the sun-splashed marble-white of Progressivism, during which California was recovered, indeed re-founded, as a society and imaginative ideal. From this perspective, James Duval Phelan takes his place alongside David Starr Jordan of Stanford, John Randolph Haynes of Los Angeles, Phoebe Apperson Hearst of San Francisco and the Hacienda del Verona at Livermore, and a host of other prominent Californians of the period who used their financial means and institutional presence to probe and enact the vision of a better California, upgraded in culture, cleansed of the dross of the late frontier. The Ariadne's thread of the labyrinth of Phelan's complex public life can be seen in his persistent effort to assist California in its transition from late frontier provincialism to full maturity as a regional expression of American civilization.

In Phelan's case, this expression was touched dramatically by the Mediterranean metaphor. As ambiguous as he might be in his theology and belief, Phelan revered the cultural heritage of Catholic Mediterranean Europe. For him, California would always be a new Spain and an even better Italy. Sumptuously, Phelan gave this dream a local habitation and a name on the hillsides of Saratoga. He called it Villa Montalvo, naming it in honor of that Renaissance Spanish writer who first envisioned California as a terrestrial paradise.

In urban terms, that California dream was best expressed for Phelan through his native city of San Francisco, which he wooed throughout his life like an ardent suitor. He dreamed of making it a city worthy of mention alongside the urban centers of the American Northeast and Europe. In both fact and psychological identification, Phelan linked his fortunes and identity to that of his native city. Phelan's father had made his fortune in San Francisco and built the family mansion in the Mission district, where Phelan lived until the Earthquake and Fire of April 1906. Turning down the opportunity to attend Georgetown, Phelan chose instead St. Ignatius College and the Hasting College of the Law. Upon graduation, he toured the great cities of Europe, studying their culture and administration, as if it were a certainty (and it was) that he would play a major role in the transition of San Francisco to civic maturity.

Here, then, is a story rich in psychological, political, and cultural significance. Here is an important chapter in the history of California at a most crucial time. Some are born great, goes the adage, and some have greatness thrust upon them. Still others, such as James Duval Phelan, identify most powerfully with great enterprises — the adornment and beautification of San Francisco, the redemption and fulfillment of California as Mediterranean shore — and in that identification, such figures as Senator Phelan achieve a near-greatness (or perhaps something even more) that raises their lives to the level of historical significance. James Duval Phelan is to be measured not only for what he accomplished, but for what he glimpsed in the distance. Throughout his life, James Duval Phelan dreamt of California reformed in politics, celebrated in art. He saw San Francisco gleaming in great architecture alongside the western sea, the Florence of the Pacific. Ever and always there was Villa Montalvo, the deepest realization of his inner life. Set against a cypress and pine-planted hillside, white of wall and red-tiled of roof, Villa Montalvo remains magic in the sunlight, Virgilian in its midsummer peace, its echoes of long lost music, its drowsy murmur of crickets and bees.

Chapter One
California's Native Son

"*...California is full of wonderful things. Mt. Lassen is spouting mud in the North and the Imperial Valley is shaking in the South. If I had the highland and you had the lowland, we would arrive at the same place, and you know where that is [Montalvo]. It is strange that God's country is located over an inferno. I am still, however, stout in my conviction that if I were given Heaven and California, I would rent Heaven and live in California....*" [James D. Phelan to Gertrude Atherton, June 13, 1915]

Years later, in 1930, as spring passed relentlessly on to a final summer, California's most accomplished public figure contemplated his unwilling removal to the rental. A man of worldly achievements, broad interests, and refined tastes, and one who enjoyed loving friends as well as enduring and accomplished enemies, James Duval Phelan resisted. Despite his Irish-Catholic heritage he had lived an abundant life fully for this world — not for the next one. He tolerated all religions and clung to the doctrines of none. So committed was he to this world that he consumed most of his sixty-nine years in laudable struggle to improve the urban environment and quality of life around him.

As each minor seizure gave way to a more serious one, Phelan knew that his niece, a cloistered Carmelite nun, was mobilizing her final assault. Certainly she would intrude upon his courtly life style and attempt the permanent capture of his immortal soul. He anticipated this after she rebuked him for curtailing his philanthropy to within California. Sister Agnes of Jesus disagreed vigorously with her illustrious uncle over matters for which she claimed higher authority. In her view California was not the source of the

James Duval Phelan, three-term mayor of San Francisco, former United States senator, art patron, and humanist. He was California's most cultivated and informed pubic servant. Honesty, progress, and beauty were his gifts to the institutions and people of his beloved state.

The social and cultural life James D. Phelan gathered to Villa Montalvo through the sparkling teens and the roaring twenties had been heaven to him — at least until his first stroke.

Sister Agnes of Jesus (James Duval Phelan's niece Ada) led the conspiracy of love intended to recapture her uncle's soul for her savior Jesus.

family fortune, Almighty God was. Therefore, if Phelan chose to return their wealth to its source, God's work, world wide, should be fostered. Her uncle's wish to disperse his charitable donations mostly among California's institutions, therefore, was misguided. And Sister Agnes told him so.

Phelan had sustained his highly religious niece in her vocation out of genuine affection for her and in fond memory of her mother, his beloved sister, Alice. This support and love, however, did not require his personal acceptance and practice of standard Catholic doctrine.

Throughout his own public and private life Phelan always respected a citizen's freedom of religion and freedom of conscience. The United States Constitution, he remained convinced, offered the best possible guide to church-state relations within a religiously diverse nation. Indeed, advocacy of one's own ultimate convictions was natural enough and was itself protected by the Constitution. But once one's efforts at educating and thereby changing the convictions of others ran its course, good manners, if not respect for the rights of others, should end religious debate. In the presidential campaign of 1928, for example, Phelan flinched at the bigotry directed against his fellow Democrat, Al Smith. But what Phelan privately considered Catholic bigotry in behalf of Smith also repelled him.

Two years later Phelan suspected that Sister Agnes of Jesus held her own church-approved check list for bringing him, her cherished confidant and emotional sustainer, back into the eternal embrace of Holy Mother Church. How she would attempt to ensnare him in her final conspiracy of love remained to be seen.

Death had circled in on California's host extraordinaire and knocked lightly during the first week of May. The master of Montalvo, committed as he was to scientific and medical solutions to human problems, followed his physicians' dictates and death's thrusts drew back. All the while, though, he indulged his lifelong addiction — daily personal correspondence.

To his friends he first made little of his initial stroke. After stopping to pick up a paper, slurred speech and an involuntary contraction of his left hand overcame him, just so briefly. His cousin and confidant since early childhood, George Duval, solicitously responded that the incident must be taken as a timely warning. Phelan should alter his indulgent lifestyle.

As spring advanced into summer and numerous and more debilitating strokes followed, Phelan joked with his nurses, heeded his physicians, and applied himself more diligently to his correspondence. Mail came twice each day then. To those he loved, and as long as his health allowed, Phelan initiated and immediately answered letters in his own hand. He wrote to derive enjoyment from relationships and to celebrate his beloved California. His family origins and the successful fulfillment of the obligations life thrust upon him became his final and comforting companions. Politics and things Irish counted among his life's most engaging and unpredictable companions; they also were most aggravating. As San Francisco's only progressive mayor, Phelan had given a new meaning to the urban classic — Irish Politician.

When Phelan could no longer write, he dictated. His personal secretary, Belle Driscoll, understood him well. In fact, she understood more than he preferred. Mrs. Driscoll was the last of a long line of intensely loyal Irish women who had served the Phelan family since his parents' marriage over seventy years earlier. Phelan could hardly tell her what she should know about his life and what she should not.

Until his last few weeks Phelan had reserved dictation for business associates. Though cold, the practice was efficient enough. Compelled now to resort to dictation for his intimates, as well, he strained for the well-turned phrase, the play on words, the jest that before had always come so easily and gracefully from his pen. When he could no longer form his own sentences, Mrs. Driscoll gathered them. Next, she gathered his thoughts, then his intentions. Thereafter, she shared health reports with his circle and offered Phelan's warm and abiding affections too. His momentary depression she revealed only to George Duval.

From the warm Montalvo nights Phelan absorbed what remained to him of his heaven on earth — the American California his immigrant father helped to form and Phelan helped to reform. He could indulge in reverie now because all obligations had been discharged. His generous, detailed, and thoroughly considered will awaited only his demise. Montalvo, his prized possession, he intended for the citizens of California. The villa and its expansive acreage were to be for public enjoyment and for the advancement of the arts. Lists of extended family members, friends, loyal and devoted employees, lifelong associates in his world of now fading interests — literature, art, politics, religion, education, health care, sports, and more — each in turn received a tangible remembrance along with words of gratitude and encouragement.

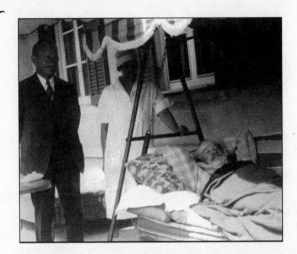

James Duval Phelan with his nurse and Dr. Louis Mendelsohn at Villa Montalvo. During his last summer, Phelan rested on the veranda to enjoy Montalvo's warm summer evenings and watch the shadows lengthen and darkness claim another of his dwindling days.

The only feature of California life that Phelan found distasteful was the prospect of departing it. He resisted as long as possible, fighting with the weapons that science and technology offered the wealthy and the informed. In the end, though, he punctuated an abundant life with a model will — remembering and thanking all who counted and others who did not.

His solitary private concern, which Phelan intended to settle beyond the legal bounds of his last will and testament, required special attention. And Phelan's sense of propriety required that it be settled not by Mrs. Driscoll, even though he could never expunge her knowledge. Before slipping into the eternally solicitous hands of Sister Agnes of Jesus, Phelan beckoned Thomas B. Doyle, his final executive secretary, to Montalvo. Like each of his predecessors Doyle was knowing, prudent, and immensely loyal to the Phelan family. Each of these Irishmen had trained his own successor, and the best, George Welch, had even died while in Phelan's service. Doyle's concluding task, a reenactment of what his predecessors had been called to do, was to convey final and lasting independence upon Florence Ellon. Ellon had been a passion of Phelan's youth, an aggravation of his middle years, and a nostalgic and provocative consoler in old age. Throughout forty-two years she had been a loving, demanding, secluded companion to her "Dear Jimmy."

Once her final "thank you" arrived at Montalvo, no other obligation crowded Phelan's thoughts. Soon enough the Irish women and the Catholic priests would extend their spiritual envelopment. Until then all of California's gifts were his to enjoy, but now in reverie.

Villa Montalvo blended James Duval Phelan's prerequisites for the exuberant celebration of the beautiful and the refined: superior natural setting, architectural good taste, and expansive landscape gardening. When he entertained on the corner veranda Phelan offered hospitality with an unsurpassed visual experience — the blush and fragrance of the Santa Clara Valley. Only splashes of bright acacia delineated the symmetrical orchard lines which, in the distance, stretched off toward Mount Hamilton. Each year Phelan anticipated spring's burst upon the valley floor — a garden of 125 square miles, of ten-million flowering trees. From the terrace he watched — the pinks and whites of spring exploded the drabness of winter, then yield to the cooling greens of so many lingering summers, each bountiful and so serene.

Chapter Two

Creating the Fortune, Creating the Family

James Duval Phelan's father, also James Phelan, never knew the date of his Irish birth and never cared enough about the matter to establish it correctly. To him starting points were irrelevant; destinations and the plans to reach them were the matters that counted. Always a planner, an organizer, and an achiever, the senior Phelan compounded his own results at every step of life's journey. A propensity for responsibility and a meticulousness for record keeping were additional traits of the remarkable, demanding, and abundant provider who fathered James Duval Phelan.

The father's story sprang from the fragile but surprisingly opportune social, economic, and political context of early nineteenth-century Ireland. The grandfather, John Phelan, held land in Queen's County and undoubtedly enjoyed the benefits of some education. The rather complete records of Trinity College, Dublin, do not record John Phelan's attendance, however.

John Phelan's marriage to Judith Brophy produced three sons: John, Michael, and James. Even though he was relatively advantaged within his world, John Phelan, Sr., sailed for New York on an assessment trip. He sought broader opportunities than were available to him in pre-famine Ireland.

Whether his hope for expanding American opportunities or his fear of the contracting Irish ones determined his decision is not known. His wife's death may have firmed his resolve. John Phelan returned to Ireland, disposed of his property, gathered up the two older boys, and set sail permanently for America. Young James (our central figure here, later to be James D. Phelan's father) remained behind in the care of his father's sister in Kilkenny. In 1827, at age six, James was reunited with his father and brothers in Newark, New

When death overcame James Phelan senior two days before Christmas 1892, the seventy-one-year-old Irishman bequeathed an estate estimated to be eleven and a half million dollars. The press of the day considered his final will a proper model for the passing generation of America's tycoons. Unnoticed was Phelan's human legacy, a public-spirited heir who was both to mold and to reflect California's distinctive culture.

By arriving on August 18, 1849, James Phelan senior qualified as one of the original forty-niners. At the time the distinction was irrelevant to him. Phelan reached San Francisco for commercial advantage, not for historical distinction.

Phelan recognized his own talent for divining consumer needs. Also, he knew how to help matters along. While waiting for a shipment of oil lamps he had ordered from the East, he bought up the whale oil that glutted the local market. Once his ship arrived, his previously ordered lanterns raised demand for oil. He then sold for $1.50 to $2.00 per gallon the same oil he had purchased for twelve cents. As for consignments lost on the high seas, he wryly noted that the bills normally sank with the merchandise.

Jersey. Fortunately for the youngster's own future, his father failed in business. Unceremoniously James went from public school directly into retail trade. In effect, then, he started near the bottom and ended by setting the American standard — creating the California Dream. James Phelan played a central role in the establishment of American California.

Gold and the Trip to San Francisco

James Phelan was in Cincinnati in 1848 when he heard of the gold discovery in California. In his mid-twenties, he was an established merchant and looking for opportunities. By waiting for the federal government's official verification of the discovery before moving from planning to action, he demonstrated sophistication not commonly associated with youth, particularly under such exciting and unprecedented circumstances. Unlike most gold seekers rushing into California, Phelan developed a comprehensive plan that increased the value of his resources and assured their best use in the distant and unknown land. Phelan was alert, resourceful, and prudent.

Following government verification of the gold discovery he moved with haste. He converted his merchandise into commodities that would likely be in demand in San Francisco: mostly liquor and iron safes as well as an assortment of wall papers, nails, tacks, beans, stationery, and cooking supplies. Phelan arranged for shipment around Cape Horn and he set out to arrive in San Francisco ahead of his goods, prepared to commence business immediately. His brother, Michael, preceded him from New York in the party of David C. Broderick, an aspiring young politician with ambition and skill that were to carry him far. Broderick later became California's United States Senator, the first Irish-American to reach that height in public office.

Michael Phelan may have been well acquainted politically, but his brother James possessed superior prudence, imagination, diligence, and vision. Rather than consigning all his goods to a single sailing ship for the perilous trip around the Horn, James Phelan divided his merchandise into separated cargoes aboard three different vessels. Some of the lighter, high-value commodities he dispatched by faster transport. All the vessels sailed around the tip of South America. Phelan, calculating the days, sailed to the Isthmus of Panama aboard the schooner *El Varado*, trekked over land through the jungle, and sought passage north on the Pacific side.

Phelan's first crisis, yellow fever, all but overcame him. The port town of Panama had become dangerously overrun by 8,000 stranded gold seekers. Fortunately, he was in the company of Dr. Daniel H. Carpenter, the physician Phelan later attributed with saving his life. Getting out of Panama, as well as remaining, was life threatening. Repelled by disease, attracted by gold, but unable to obtain commercial transportation, some men constructed rafts and launched themselves into the not always peaceful Pacific. Men died in the attempts.

Phelan figured better. He hung on, marshalled his strength, and entered his name in the lottery for five tickets available for the steamship *Panama* whose arrival was imminent. On all three counts he was successful. He drew one of the steerage tickets, thus ensuring his escape and sustaining his hope.

The quality of life below deck convinced him, however, that he would die en route if he could not improve his condition. On board the *Panama*, however, was his own consignment of lightweight goods. Promptly he sold his stock of sodium bicarbonate, a leavening agent needed for the ship's galley, at a handsome profit. More important, he acquired an upgrade to a cabin as part of the deal.

Having renegotiated his most important lease, on life itself, Phelan survived the passage and recovered his strength in what he characterized as San Francisco's bracing and salubrious summer.

The original Phelan Building on Market and O'Farrell Streets in San Francisco. It survived the 1906 earthquake, but was consumed by the post-earthquake fire. In its early days (1882–1906), the Phelan Building was prized as the most handsome and imposing office building in the West.

San Francisco: Building the Business

Prior to his arrival in California James Phelan knew nothing of mining or the creation of the instant city, San Francisco, within which he was to play so paramount a role. The San Francisco he encountered was a temporary society of tents and shacks — a base camp to the Sierra Nevada gold fields. From San Francisco thousands headed off to try their luck, get rich, and go home. Not so for Phelan. He recognized financial opportunities while the gold seekers hardly noticed the city at all. Phelan never prospected for gold or silver, never invested in mining stock, and never mortgaged his property holdings.

From the start his luck held fairly well. Another of the vessels that carried his consignments anchored safely in San Francisco Bay. In the grossly inflated sellers' market, Phelan more than recouped the value of what was lost at sea aboard the third ship, the *Robert Fulton*.

Success in Panama

Just how far the elder James Phelan's entrepreneurial success took him is best illustrated by his return to Panama, where his most profitable venture was a digging and dredging subcontract to the international DeLesseps Company. In a closely held corporation, the American Contracting and Dredging Company, Phelan was vice-president and his New York brother, John, was treasurer. Inspired by the dredging and digging machinery he saw in the San Joaquin River Delta, Phelan had fabricated in San Francisco a second generation steam-driven earthmover. By 1885 seven machines were shoveling 3,000 cubic meters of soil per day, tended by a labor force of 500 men. Each machine cost $125,000 and was towed by barge to Panama where early efforts at a transoceanic canal had begun.

By 1889, however, the DeLesseps engineers who had succeeded in digging the Suez Canal failed in Panama. The company had spent over $260 million and then succumbed to bankruptcy. Phelan, as a paid subcontractor, remained on the positive side of the equation. The American Contracting and Dredging Company earned $6,700,000.

Phelan enjoyed sound personal skills as well as good business skills. The war with Mexico, which brought California to the United States, had ended in 1848, before the gold discovery. Thereafter, the military auctioned its war surplus barrels of pork and beef, rice, and dried fruits. Backed by John V. Plume, whom he met aboard the *Panama*, Phelan purchased the stores for $75,000. This transaction required no Phelan capital risk — the cash was made available through Plume's influence and his banking firm, Burgoyne & Company. Phelan's resale at a handsome profit within the booming, if artificial, mining economy was immediate. In effect, Phelan paid for the government merchandise with income that the sale of the merchandise generated.

As a large scale and successful merchant, Phelan observed the opportunities as well as the problems associated with other industries, particularly banking, real estate, commerce, construction, and insurance. In each he invested and in each he prospered. An added benefit was his growing geographical expansion and financial diversification. In 1871 he organized and became president of the First National Gold Bank of San Francisco. In 1869 he organized and became vice-president of the Mutual Savings Bank of San Francisco. In addition, he developed the First National Bank of San Jose and expanded his urban and agricultural holdings in what has become the heart of Silicon valley. To the south he acquired shoreline property for the family's summer estate on the cliffs above the Santa Cruz beach. His compulsion to purchase land and develop properties sprang from his simple observation that land was limited and the prospect of California's population growth was quite unlimited. Being financially capable of acting on his convictions allowed Phelan to attempt what others might consider an extravagance. In 1882 he was able to give his daughter, Alice, a square block of San Francisco as a wedding gift.

His organizational successes included several insurance companies, the Western Fire and Marine Insurance Company and the Firemans Fund among them. He was a key organizer of and profit taker in California's entry into the wool market and the international grain trade.

The most visible of his investments was the construction and occupation of his own building on Market Street at the corner of O'Farrell Street. The prime location, the imposing size, and the advanced features of the five-story Phelan Building enhanced the family name and offered greater public visibility to the financial undertakings associated with the Phelans. Phelan distributed the half-million dollars in construction costs among fifty subcontractors, all working class entrepreneurs, and he maintained harmonious labor relations through his personal on-site supervision.

Other prominent real estate holdings included the Roos Brothers retail men's clothing store and the White House department store, both major San Francisco landmarks. Smaller hotels and lesser residential and commercial properties were additional holdings. Other urban properties were located in San Jose, towns in Southern California, and New York City. Ranches in Napa, Lake, and Santa Clara Counties expanded his diversified portfolio, which, at one time, included 1,115,000 undeveloped acres in Oregon.

Basically, James Phelan fit the standard Irish-American model: despite rural origins the Irish became urban Americans. In Phelan's case, he became an urban capitalist.

James Phelan's Family

James Phelan's greatest challenge was not early California's unpredictable business environment; in that he thrived. His problem was his older brother, and junior partner, Michael. Both were Irish bachelors. In 1855, James was 33 and Michael was 34. Unlike James Phelan, Michael Phelan was not noted for his steady habits. James realized his financial success and then, and only then, considered marriage. Hardly a romantic, James Phelan engaged to marry Alice Kelly, who still resided in Brooklyn, New York. Their Irish-American circle was quite close; both Alice and James were Irish born, actually from neighboring villages. She was five years his junior. The major difference was her illustrious family lineage. Its genealogy included the Norman conqueror, Strongbow, and was authenticated in 1786 by the Principal Herald of Ireland. Cognizant of this, Phelan was also well aware of her family's more recent political and literary accomplishments in Ireland.

Phelan's trip east to claim Alice Kelly as his bride ended in an abrupt and revealing manner. In his autobiography, Phelan obscured his brother's real role as he shows clearly that money concerns were more important than romance. He wrote that Michael, "by unfortunate investments, practically wrecked our firm; and I had to return to San Francisco and begin over again." In actuality, a friend, W. H. Oliver, sent James newspaper cartoons of his brother rioting at "Irish Mary's" pleasure house. Apparently Michael's invest-

JENNY CORBETT, ONE OF "IRISH MARY'S" PROSTItutes, whose head was broken, some time since, by MIKE PHELAN, of the firm of J. & M. PHELAN, liquor merchants, Front street, "screwing" $150 from Mike, in the County Court, last Thursday. This case was appealed from Justice Austin's Court, and Mike paid $150 and costs, before it went to trial. Why didn't you pay, at first, Mike, and save exposure?

This is one of the cartoons sent to James Phelan about his brother, Michael. Apparently James carried the cartoons back to San Francisco and confronted his prodigal brother. Thereafter, James retained them in his office files, which his son, James Duval Phelan, inherited in 1892, along with the management of the family holdings and enterprises. James D. Phelan rescued the cartoons among the few select family and personal records he snatched as the fire of 1906 approached the Phelan Building. Ultimately this nucleus of family history found its way into the Bancroft Library as part of the extensive James D. Phelan and Noël Sullivan (his nephew) papers. The preservation of Michael's cartoons, through three generations, along with far more edifying family memorabilia, illustrates an enlightened realism that formed the family's sense of self as well as a respect for the integrity of history.

The Battle of the Whisky Barrels: or, J. & M. Phelan's Set-to, on Sacramento street the other day. James deposited, in his own name, $50,000; Mike showed fight; James said Mike had spent in drunkenness, and among bawdy-houses, $100,000. Mike retorted that the firm was in liquidation, and that he (Jim,) had no right to use the firm's funds. Grand set-to; Jenny Corbett, Mike's "bottle-holder," one of the "B'hoys," and *a dog* on Jim's side. Grand flare up. More about it next week. "A house divided against itself cannot stand."

Michael Phelan died young, at age 37 in 1858. His remains were not reinterred with other family members into the family mausoleum later established at Holy Cross, the modern Catholic cemetery in Colma. His successful brother James covered for him in life, but not in death.

ments, or lack thereof, were merely disastrous side effects of a lifestyle not condoned by his younger, more prudent, brother James. The younger Phelan turned on his heels, returned to San Francisco, and began to restore himself to his former position. All this was done in a haste that, for him anyway, precluded marriage at that time. Alice Kelly remained in Brooklyn.

Because of the financial consequences of his brother's behavior, Phelan delayed marriage for four years. In May 1859 he and Alice Kelly married in San Francisco. He was 37 and she was 32. Archbishop Joseph Sadoc Alemaney, the pioneer prelate who bridged the Mexican and American periods in the history of California Catholicism, presided at St. Mary's Cathedral (now old St. Mary's Church in Portsmouth Square). This highly publicized ministry by the archbishop himself recognized Phelan's prominence within both the Catholic and larger civic communities. Alice and James' three children arrived within the next years: Alice in 1860, James Duval in 1861, and Mary Louise (Mollie) in 1862.

James and Alice changed residences several times as their three children arrived. Their homes clustered in what is now the downtown, commercial district of the city. Their last temporary home seems to have been on the site James intended for his flagship property, the Phelan Building. These moves are evidence of the progressive master planning that characterized the accomplishments of the senior Phelan. Before commencing the construction on the West's most impressive and up-to-date office building, however, Phelan completed a permanent residence for his growing family.

As a husband and a father Phelan was an abundant, but not lavish, provider. The Phelans could have constructed their own opulent mansion on Nob Hill beside the other new rich. Instead they chose a family-oriented environment out in the warm and dry Mission Dolores district. Phelan (who was a devout communicant) selected a neighborhood within walking distance of Mission Dolores Church, away from downtown, and away from the ostentatious displays of Nob Hill.

At Valencia and Seventeenth Streets, on a three-and-a-half acre site, James Phelan constructed a large, though restrained, two-story mansion surrounded by an expansive garden. In the beginning, it was virtually a small farm with barns, cows, orchards, and vegetable gardens. The house itself was comfortable and roomy, with a spacious veranda looking out on an expanse of lawn and pepper and willow trees. In time the blossoming bushes and the fruit trees assumed the appearance of a private park in turn surrounded by a gated fence. Although surrounded by the city, entering the home's gates gave visitors the feeling they were going to the country. This home served James and Alice from 1876 through their lifetimes. The fire of 1906 burned out their unmarried children, James Duval and Mary Louise Phelan.

The most frequent dinner guests to the Phelan mansion were priests. Beyond their religious and church concerns, the next most common topics of conversation included Ireland, books, travel, and education. The best insight into the interior of the residence appeared in the social pages at the time of young Alice's marriage in 1882 to Francis J. Sullivan. The picture that emerged was one of refinement. Art works acquired during grand tours befitted the unusual combination of restrained tastes and unlimited means.

James Duval Phelan and his sisters grew and developed in a sheltered home environment. The three were close in age and cared for by warm and generous servants, within a large and well appointed home. The few, faded photographs from the 1870s are within the garden confines. The refined, well-dressed youngsters are at croquette and under watchful eyes as well. James Duval's one recorded venture beyond the garden gate ended in bloody confrontation. A neighborhood bully took his toys. Gamely the diminutive Phelan (he never reached five feet, eight inches as an adult) asserted his

The Domestic Scene

Household help was a natural part of the domestic scene at the end of the nineteenth century. Alice Kelly Phelan's maids were as much companions and friends as they were servants. Like her, they were old-country Irish women. They identified with the family in a bonding common within such homes. The same women were with Alice from her wedding day to her death. If Alice's life had been longer and her mental health stronger, undoubtedly she would have followed another minority Irish tradition: caring for the servants in their declining years.

Less is known of the man servants and grounds and stable men. They were undoubtedly Irish, although the Phelans may have managed through their first generation without any male house servant. A butler or a valet suited the requirements of James Duval Phelan better than those of his father. Ethnic and religious compatibility characterized the household staff just as it did the office staff. Loyalty remained evident through the years. The Phelans and their Irish domestic staff shared the same values and partook of the same heritage. Their degree of comforts and opportunities differed, but their social, cultural, and emotional lives were intertwined.

Harmony and continuity was hardly absolute though. Young Irish women of the household had their own goals that diverged from those of the older women whose companionship was the commitment of a life time. Some younger women sought independence, marriage, and families of their own. Others simply liked moving around, much to the distress of the Phelans.

The Phelan family home at Valencia and Seventeenth Streets, San Francisco

Alice Kelly Phelan is shown near the time of her wedding in 1859. She was thirty-two.

The senior James Phelan's only noted association with romance was the honeymoon he and Alice took in 1859. He brought his bride to the Santa Clara Valley in mid-spring. The valley's blossoms had fallen by May, but that month's mild warmth and dryness of the air remained a pleasant and alluring alternative to San Francisco. That Phelan could have devoted his attentions exclusively to the bride of his delayed marriage challenges the imagination. The locale he chose was sprinkled with the investments of his diversified portfolio. The creator of the fortune cooperated in creating the family. Then he returned to San Francisco and to work.

property rights only to have his hand sliced by the knife-wielding ruffian. Perhaps it was an early lesson in the need for law and order and a duly constituted professional police to do the enforcing.

James and Alice Phelan celebrated their tenth anniversary in 1869, the year that the Transcontinental Railroad connected San Francisco to the East. The family entrained for New York and reunions with Alice's sisters, Mary S. Kelly and Kate Kelly Duval, and with James Phelan's older brother, John. Ireland was next, followed by the grand tour of Europe. This Irish and continental trip bonded the next generation and defined its lifestyle. Young James Duval Phelan met his New York cousin, George L. Duval, for the first time. Their destiny was to manage, expand, and disperse great family wealth, and throughout their lives they remained devoted friends and correspondents. Mrs. Phelan may have remained in Brooklyn with her sisters and the Duvals while her husband took their young brood (Mollie age seven, James age eight, and Alice age nine) abroad.

Alice Kelly Phelan

Little survives about their mother, Alice, other than her impressive Irish genealogy and the military, literary, and political achievements of her illustrious forebears. Her influence is obscured further by her having lived in the shadow of her successful pioneer husband, whose records constitute the bulk of available historical documentation. She may have been a dependent victim of the gender segregation that characterized much of Irish and Irish-American social and emotional life, even within marriage. Irish men had their world, so the women were left to theirs. Alice and James both were Irish-born immigrants, yet she arrived as a young adult who had enjoyed a privileged Irish upbringing. James arrived as a child of six. In the cultural sense, he was virtually second generation and he made his own way early on.

Alice Phelan's middle years were associated with her home and family. From her mansion's garden gate she encouraged the children of the neighborhood with flowers and fruit. She followed their academic progress at the local Catholic school, and recognized and rewarded their academic success. Her life as a mother and wife left no direct historical records other than her interest in the neighbors' children. Her husband's will, to which she consented when it was drafted in 1889, provided amply for her, but it did not place her in any position of influence or distinction within the family. James by-passed Alice in the arrangements for their estate. She was maintained in comfort, with no decision-making role over the estate. Following his death, she became incapable of addressing the modern world and was dependent upon her son and servants.

Her unhealthy and unhappy years of widowhood conditioned the home life for her unmarried, adult children. During these years as a "nervous in-valid" she frequently cried, lost interest in her surroundings, and found the task of expressing herself more difficult. Medical attention in San Francisco and a trip with her family, by private railroad car, to New York for additional help failed to produce change.

Mollie, Alice, and James

Illness, also unspecifically diagnosed, overcame her daughter, Mollie, quite early in life. In fact, Mollie's illness predated her mother's. Two years younger than her sister, less stately and presumably less active, Mollie underwent an emotional crisis in 1882 at the time of her sister's engagement and her broth-er's coming of age. During the parties her only recorded suitor was talked about by the other young women in their circle: they criticized him for being handsome to the point of prettiness. Using the vocabulary of their day, these young women mistakenly considered him to be homosexual.

Even though this singular episode could hardly determine a life's course, it did mark the observable onset of Mollie's unending series of emotional bat-tles with depression and despondency. When she was twenty her older, more determined sister left her, when she was thirty and at home, her dominating father died, and thereafter her withdrawn mother succumbed to her own form of instability. Whatever the causes, Mollie never adjusted to an active adult life. James assumed in turn roles of psychologist, protector, comforter, and loving brother — virtually the same roles he performed for their mother.

Alice elected early departure by entering into what was to be a difficult marriage. In 1882, Alice married Frank Sullivan, the politically active scion of a wealthy pioneer family (Hibernia Bank). To mark the occasion, her par-ents presented Alice with $10,000 in government bonds, a chest of solid sil-ver service (114 pieces), and one square block of San Francisco. She left the home of a dominant, untrusting father and an apparently reserved mother to

In establishing their fortune and their family in San Francisco, James and Alice Kelly Phelan provided San Francisco and California with the most distinguished, independent, political and cultural leader of the genera-tion — James Duval Phelan.

Taken in San Francisco in the early 1860s, this is the first photograph of California's future leader, James Duval Phelan.

create her own home and family. She chose a talented and well-educated husband whose frustrations in life compounded his basically irascible nature. As a result Alice became lodged between her husband and her brother, the two men she loved, the two men who most disliked one another. Her refuge became the solace she derived from religion, its practice, and its commitment to the poor and unfortunate.

Alice's active social life included volunteer work, much of which was under Catholic auspices. She traveled, but family circumstances, including an inflexible and volatile husband and four sheltered children, circumscribed her actions. On political and financial matters she found herself unhappily caught between her erratic husband and her willful and highly successful brother. Further, her husband presumed to speak and act for her in her own family financial matters just as her brother did for their invalid sister, Mollie. The vote on contested issues within their private corporation, Heirs of James Phelan, always favored James D. Phelan by two-to-one.

James Duval's sensitive adjustment to the dynamics of the home life, determined by his parents, and particularly his father, was respectful cooperation, attention to growing responsibility, and privatization of his personal convictions. As the heir apparent his bargaining position was stronger than that of his older and younger sisters. Neither coped as well as their brother.

Except during his United States Senate years (1915–1921), for which he purchased a forty-four-room mansion fashionably located on Washington's Embassy Row, James D. Phelan always lived with his family: his parents and sisters, then his widowed mother and sister Mollie, and finally with Mollie alone. He never married. As the prudent negotiator of his dominant father and the devoted sustainer of his mother and sisters, James D. Phelan compartmentalized his own social life. He minimized any impact that his forty-two-year relationship with Florence Ellon might have created. Beyond his nuclear family, Phelan lavished his devotion upon his city and his state.

But in 1882, his time had not yet come. Besides, he and his father had not yet constructed their own mature relationship.

Chapter Three
Father and Son: Educating Each Other

San Francisco's first generation Irish rich sent their sons abroad to be educated. Stonyhurst College in Blackburn, England, was a frequent choice of the Irish Catholic families who had created new fortunes for themselves and sought better educations for their sons than were available, at least initially, at home in their instant city. James and Alice Phelan, by virtue of their tardy marriage and delayed family, enjoyed an advantage of perspective. They could observe the results and assess the impact of education upon the transitional generation. Their children's generation had to solidify, maintain, and advance the family's fortune and position in the Far West.

Phelan, the forty-niner, undoubtedly was unaware of Thomas Jefferson's democratic distaste for foreign education, but he nonetheless acted upon that view. His personal wealth allowed his bright son access to any institution of higher education, but Phelan chose not to deport his son the way his Catholic Irish cohorts did. Given their wealth, James and Alice lived modestly, if comfortably, and they believed in keeping their son at home during his formative years as well.

Local Schools

James and Alice Phelan rejected foreign schools as an option for their three children. They chose among what they considered to be the best then available locally. Alice, their first child, attended the Presentation Convent School (the girls' school preferred by San Francisco's Catholic rich) in San Francisco and the Convent of Notre Dame in San Jose. She finished her

James Duval Phelan's fondness for dogs started early and remained.

Foreign Education Reflections

During a reflective moment in the twilight of his life, James Duval Phelan reviewed the results of the Stonyhurst (England) experience upon the Donahues, the Murphies, the Barons, and Parrotts: all sons were of well-to-do parents and all were sent off to Stonyhurst. Phelan's conclusion was cruel: all led undistinguished lives. Some became mired in drunkenness, snobbery, and ineffectuality. Some, "while of gentle manners, can hardly be called a success." For others, "Drink seems to be their besetting sin." They "…were rated according to the number of bottles they could consume, principally of Port and Madeira, and were dubbed, 'two, three or four bottle men'."

For "Little" Peter Donahue, heir to an industrial fortune, Phelan reserved his most critical observation. In a 1925 letter to his grandnephew, Fred Murphy, Phelan wrote, "Little Peter Donahue … had a Papal title, and … when I was with him in London, … he considered membership in the Marlborough Club, (of which the Prince of Wales was also a member) the highest distinction he could attain." Peter, Phelan recollected, was a snob.

Apprehensive about his fifteen-year-old grandnephew's enrollment in Stonyhurst, Phelan recommended pride in accomplishment rather than in ancestry. He concluded with the adage from the American West: "One man is just as good as another, and sometimes a d---d sight better!"

education under the direction of Mrs. Colgate-Baker at her Van Ness Avenue Academy. Mollie, the youngest of the three, completed the secondary school conducted by Presentation Sisters.

The Phelan's son, James D. Phelan, who matured into a man of letters and a major patron of California arts, retained a strong, most likely inherited, prejudice against exclusive English schools, those to which other prominent San Francisco Irish sent their sons. His formal education was at the hands of the Jesuits, the earliest by tutor. Even though his father and then Phelan himself were benefactors of the parish school, no records demonstrate James's attendance. The family lived first in old St. Mary's parish where James and Alice were married. It offered elementary education from the 1850s until the 1890s. During those years, St. Ignatius College maintained an upper elementary grade school. As late as the pre-World War I period St. Ignatius offered instruction from beginning elementary school through law school.

Phelan earned his Bachelor of Arts degree from St. Ignatius College in 1881. (Later, Santa Clara College conferred an honorary Ph.D. upon him after his successful progressive terms as mayor of San Francisco.) The undergraduate curriculum in which he was immersed included the standard liberal arts subjects. The classics, languages, history, and literature ranked high in his own interests as well as among the college's offerings. Mathematics and science, and particularly physics and what would become the field of electrical engineering enjoyed a particularly local blossoming that coincided with Phelan's college years.

Jesuit Education and Religious Doctrine

James Duval Phelan's Jesuit educational experience was the best of what was available in San Francisco at the time. His surviving study and scrap books reveal his full commitment to structured learning. Through these years he expanded his interests from celebrities and wrestlers to literature, poetry, public affairs, and applied science. Phelan became a voracious reader, a practiced writer, and a popular orator. He derived satisfaction from each activity and they were to remain his enduring companions.

Phelan's cooperative spirit and apparent acceptance of Catholic doctrine induced the Jesuits to classify him with his fully orthodox parents and his less-reflective classmates. The Jesuit fathers chose him as a commencement speaker in 1881. His address, "The Utility of Classical Study," was in keeping with his interests and tactics. In public he remained on safe ground.

Privately Phelan enjoyed an intellectual life of considerably greater complexity. During the same year his scientific mentor, Father Joseph Neri, was electrifying Market Street, Phelan read and recorded the orations of the nation's most prominent agnostic, Robert Ingersoll. Still in his teens, Phelan noted Ingersoll's words for his deceased brother: "Life is a narrow vale between the cold and barren peaks of two eternities." Elsewhere, "Let us believe, in spite of doubts and dogmas [that death brings return to health]."

As a teenager Phelan lived happily and undisturbed among his own people while detaching himself from their most cherished convictions. He was well on his way to his personal conviction that one person's religious beliefs, politically in any case and perhaps dogmatically as well, were as valuable and true as another's. Always prudent with his parents, his teachers, his friends, and later the voting public, Phelan's religious opinions remained private.

Even near the end of his life, and much closer to home, Phelan advised his niece, Sister Agnes of Jesus, to enjoy to the utmost her birthday. He assumed that vows were suspended among the cloistered nuns and that feasting was allowed. He approved, writing, "…enjoy the fleeting hour because it is the only hour that we are sure of! Birthdays are awful reminders of the procession which ends too soon.…"

Intellectual Interests

During his adolescence and young adult years Phelan gradually focused his intellectual interests upon matters of public concern: immigration, British political and imperial institutions, the place and condition of Ireland within the Empire, American political reform, urban development, and the beautification and functionalism of man's habitat — the city. His artistic interests clustered around poetry, the performing arts, architecture, and landscape gardening. He enjoyed nature but seemed always to prefer its slight improvement by man's touch.

Throughout this period of preparation for a public life, Phelan concentrated on perfecting his substantial talents at writing and public speaking. He enjoyed both, worked at commanding greater bodies of subject matter through his reading, and tested his delivery before varieties of local

Joseph Neri's Influence

At St. Ignatius College, the Reverend Joseph Neri, S.J., distinguished himself as a scholar and scientist by advancing knowledge of electricity as an applied science. During James D. Phelan's school years, Father Neri developed carbon electric lighting in advance of Thomas Edison's breakthrough with the incandescent lamp. During his St. Ignatius years, Neri staged public exhibitions that illuminated the College and adjoining buildings — all located across Market Street from Phelan real estate holdings. Phelan studied physics under Neri's direction and remembered him fondly, visiting him at Santa Clara College during the revered scientist's advanced old age.

Phelan's Religious Views

In 1925, prompted by the death of William Jennings Bryan, the political and religious fundamentalist, James Duval Phelan expressed his personal views. To President Woodrow Wilson's son-in-law and Treasury Secretary William Gibbs McAdoo he wrote: "The trouble with religious people is that they are not content with saving their own souls." As to the recently departed Bryan:

He was so cock-sure about the Bible that, if he still enjoys a conscious existence, he must be greatly gratified or painfully disappointed. I believe, however, that he was so honest that, if he controlled the megaphone in the skies, he would tell us all about it, even if it cost him his 'election'!

audiences. In his college years he began his uncompromising regime of reserved reading time. Every day he allocated a fixed block of hours for reading. His next priority was writing time. In most cases he consumed those hours in initiating and answering correspondence, his happy lifetime addiction.

Throughout Phelan's life, the U.S. Mail provided two deliveries a day in San Francisco. He personally monitored the service and gauged his growing social and business communications accordingly. In time he inherited his father's secretarial staff, along with his father's business responsibilities, and they managed standard correspondence. For his expanding social circle Phelan always offered his personal touch.

Upon graduation from college, Phelan turned rather naturally to writing and speaking on public issues, to poetry, and to the arts. He enjoyed the social company and intellectual companionship of San Francisco's cluster of aspiring writers and artists. He expanded his reading in the areas of political and social responsibility. He also interested himself in the study of the law. All of this took place while his father continued grooming young James to assume management of the extensive family enterprises. James Phelan drew his son into active participation by placing James Duval, as his junior partner, on boards and directing bodies. The son's role, of course, was assured because of the senior Phelan's ownership or majority interest within the diverse financial enterprises. Similarly, James Duval took up memberships within the city's prestigious clubs such as the Bohemian and the Pacific Union. Certainly the son's personal interests as distinct from his father's expectations continued the potential for conflict.

The Grand Tour

As yet, young James failed to anticipate his father adequately. For his twenty-first birthday, for example, James Duval Phelan had expected financial independence accompanied by its symbol, his own grand tour — alone. Instead, his father presented him with gold cuff links and a deferred and alternate European travel plan. The two men would go together, and the son would extend his interests in civic and political affairs. The aging Phelan had plans for his son's future — redirection away from legal and literary interests and into business and public service. The extended residence would constitute an alternate to academic study wherein the son could pursue interests and concerns that would prepare him for a lifetime of public service, a satisfying personal augmentation to the requirement of family management.

Because most family and business records were destroyed when the original Phelan Building burned following the 1906 earthquake, it is uncertain whether the senior Phelan actually accompanied his son to Europe and remained there throughout his year's residence. During the young man's stay, James D. Phelan investigated civic and political conditions in major European cities. From the father's point of view the result must have been satisfactory, perhaps just as satisfactory as from the son's.

The young man's independence of mind and the talent and self-assurance upon which it rested qualified him to be a player, though as yet an inexperienced one, in the world of his father. Both seemed to understand and accept the limits beyond which one could expect to influence the other. The extended European residence, the further indulgence in study, and the preparation for public service that they assumed — all were concessions by the father. Abandonment of legal study, reduction of literary interests from active aspirations to largely passive participation, and full acceptance of the role of family manager — all were concessions by the son.

During his year and a half in Europe, James D. Phelan clustered his interests permanently around matters of urban management, public works and civic art, opera, architecture, and landscape gardening. Through 1883 he provided written follow-up to his personal observations and studies in the form of articles published in the San Francisco newspapers. Upon James D. Phelan's return to San Francisco he commenced life as his father's business partner and as heir apparent. His parents' influences and his father's intervention prepared him for public service, and their fortune freed him to perform that service in the most noble and independent manner possible.

Family Relationships

Undoubtedly James Phelan, Sr., loved his wife and their children. Certainly his care and his generosity and his public pride in them on symbolic occasions attest so. Yet, his son was the only one among them who was able to come to an understanding with the old man. Their rapport sprang from emotional equity. The gender gap was the father's problem, one he seemed unable to bridge. His role and his relationships were traditional, but they seemed

HIRSCH früher WINTER Fot. in CARLSBAD.

James Phelan's habits of consumption illustrated his restraint. His alleged response to an inquisitive tobacco dealer as to why he smoked five-cent cigars while his son enjoyed the best, displayed the old Irishman's verbal restraint as well. "I do not have a wealthy father," he noted.

Frank and Alice Phelan Sullivan, their three daughters — Gladys, Alyce, and Ada (who would become Sister Agnes) — and their son Noël.

In 1933 Noël recorded some critical observations. He concluded in his privately printed family history, Forty Years Remembered: A Letter in the Form of a Memoir to the Children of My Sister Gladys S. Doyle, *that his father "...was an essentially lonely man, with enormous and towering ambition....All of his brother-in-law's many achievements must have represented exactly what he wished for himself." Perhaps unknown to Noël Sullivan, Phelan had a small hand in Frank's political failure. Phelan denied Sullivan political support when he ran as a Democratic presidential elector, and Phelan enjoyed Sullivan's crushing defeat in his non-reform campaign for San Francisco mayor. Besides personal differences, the brothers-in-law shared no common political ideology.*

satisfactory only in the impact they had upon his son's perspective. Though perhaps unintended, the women in the senior Phelan's life who did not escape became casualties. The son, observant and self-assured, chose for himself a non-traditional life, a distinct contrast to what he had experienced at home. Even this perhaps galling aspect of the son's lifestyle had to be tolerated by the religiously orthodox parent. James and James Duval each gave ground, and each gained ground. By the 1890s they understood each other.

Young Phelan's association with his brother-in-law, Francis J. Sullivan, began with the power relationship in disequilibrium. Sullivan was ten years Phelan's senior and even though he had a brother of his own, Phelan (the bride's brother) was his best man when Sullivan married into the Phelan family in 1882. He had preceded Phelan through Saint Ignatius, attended Stonyhurst, and earned an M.A. degree as well as a law degree from Columbia University. Frank Sullivan was a practicing lawyer, state senator, and repeated close contender for the U.S. Congressional seat. Though not as secure in his family's gold and banking wealth as was Phelan in his own diversified investments, Sullivan was well off in his own right.

During the early years of their relationship Phelan confided in Sullivan. Phelan's father appointed Sullivan as attorney for one of his new San Francisco banks, Mutual Savings, in 1889. Sullivan also served as a director. It was to Sullivan that young Phelan first documented his relationship with Florence Ellon. Many years later, well after his father had passed from the scene, at the other bank directors' insistence, Phelan removed Sullivan from his position as bank attorney. Incredibly, Phelan cited his brother-in-law's alleged incurable disability — Sullivan's personality!

Sullivan's personality was the major cause of the family stress. The management and disposition of Alice Phelan Sullivan's own inherited wealth constituted an additional and substantial cause for tension. But their respective relationships with women and the divergent convictions that sustained those relationships drove the breach between the brothers-in-law even wider. Sullivan modeled his behavior on his acceptance of the traditional moral teachings of the Catholic Church. Phelan privately dissented from Catholic doctrine and in his young manhood incorrectly assumed a flexible tolerance on Sullivan's part as well.

The apocryphal story of Phelan's carriage proposal and its hypothetical alternative both assume Phelan's acceptance of romantic love. But because, like his father, he seemed limited in this area, romance would never lead him to marriage. Unlike his father, he intended not merely to defer marriage; he ruled it out. He intended not to create a family. His adult years were spent trying to care for the family created around him. Others who began families received his congratulations and caution. To his favored secretary and Mrs. George Welch he wrote, "The birth of a baby girl… will add to your and the world's troubles, but we only make progress by overcoming such things." Phelan hesitated at the point of concluding that procreation multiplied human problems beyond the talents of the rare genius who occasionally offered humanity the scientific, technological, or social solutions to the problems caused by the many. He lived in hope, but it was guarded.

More personal, though, was his basic reason for never marrying. He was quite unwilling, perhaps incapable of the commitment that marriage required. More important, he understood himself well enough in this regard before tradition and social convention ushered him unreflectively into an ill-advised marriage. His life was one of organization and calculation. He identified his interests among the arts, public service, finance, and travel. Phelan enjoyed the reading, the study, the debates, and the viewings that these essentially intellectual activities assumed. Dilettantism was not his goal; mastery was. All this excluded marriage and the obligations that would follow.

Deep in the twilight of his life Phelan responded to California's most beautiful and internationally celebrated woman. So struck was Phelan by the appearance and grace of Helen Wills, the commanding women's world tennis star of the 1920s, that his description of her physical attributes to his nephew may have dismayed the younger, equally sensitive, though far less passionate man. In apparent response to the reigning young athlete-queen's anticipation, Phelan told Wills why he had never married (and perhaps why he planned not to then either). He would not allocate the time marriage required.

Only in measuring how he spent his time could Phelan be judged miserly. He fixed his daily reading time, he scheduled his daily corresponding time, and he set special times for his artistic and cultural enhancement. He normally blended socialization with his pursuit of art and culture to make better use of time. He invited friends and associates to share in readings, poetry, and all the other refinements he enjoyed as host or patron. He even scheduled his sexual pleasure on Tuesday nights while he was mayor of San Francisco.

Carriage Courtship

Persisting in family tradition is a story that as a young man Phelan had bashfully courted a fine young woman whose parents were about to remove her from San Francisco for a trip to the East. The tale has it that in riding with his love to the train depot the floor of their coach gave way just as James was on his knee about to request the lady's hand in marriage. To save himself from serious injury he had to run as fast as his short legs would carry him, feet on the ground, torso within the carriage. The comic features of the scene overwhelmed the girl whose uncontrolled fits of laughter stifled the power of romantic love.

While amusing, the story has no documentary basis within the vast, highly personal and revealing Phelan-Sullivan manuscript collections. His early and well-developed sense of decorum would not suggest that James Duval Phelan would consider proposing in a carriage in any case. Far more likely, he would have chosen a sensitive, idyllic environment in which to ask the question, which he would put with poetic originality. Undoubtedly in hand would be tastefully impressive jewelry, inducement and then visible symbol of the young woman's response and commitment. Phelan had a fondness for diamonds.

Florence's Family

Born in Los Angeles in 1864, Florence Ellon was, like Phelan, the child of European immigrants. Florence was one of four daughters of Isaac and Sara (Jacobs) Blumenthal. Florence's mother was born in Poland and her father in Germany. Of the daughters, young Sara remained single and lived with their widowed mother and with her sister Mary and Mary's husband, Leon Goldstein. Together, the four shared a substantial flat at 1028 Pierce Street, near Turk, in the Western Addition of San Francisco. Leon Goldstein edited and published the daily official quotations of the San Francisco stock exchange. When he died in 1909 Mary (Blumenthal) Goldstein assumed his position and branched out into printing. The fourth daughter of Isaac and Sara, Annie (Blumenthal) Dettleback, also lived independently in San Francisco.

Florence Blumenthal's early and brief marriage was to an older man, Robert Ellon. They lived together on Webster Street while he maintained a downtown office that dealt in mining stock. Robert Ellon was German and had relatives near Berlin whom Florence would visit later during her European travels. Born in 1845, Robert was nineteen years older than his young wife. Their daughter, Vera Ellon, was born in a boarding house, not an altogether uncommon domestic arrangement in earlier San Francisco. By this time, however, more settled domestic arrangements were enjoyed by those who were better off.

Florence Ellon, the Beginning

On his own terms, but sometimes on hers too, James Duval Phelan and one special woman maintained a forty-two year relationship. It began in 1888 in the suite he occupied in his father's ornate Market Street office building. She introduced herself and explained her problem. Whether she asked explicitly for help or not, the result was the same. Phelan provided. He was to provide liberally, if at times under duress, until his death at Villa Montalvo in 1930 effected their final separation. Even then their parting remembrances one to the other characterized their long, if bumpy, relationship. Ellon provided, thanks to Phelan's comprehensive filing system, 194 letters. They depict a relationship that Phelan kept private during his life. In this way she contributed to his historical record as well as creating her own.

In 1888 the young Mrs. Florence Ellon sought out and was received by James Duval Phelan, the promising young heir apparent to the Phelan fortune. He was twenty-seven years of age and she was twenty-four. When her husband died at age forty-six, the crisis of early widowhood presented Florence with prospects that were both few and, to her, quite unattractive. She felt at home in a middle-class lifestyle. Her formal education is unknown but she wrote clearly, correctly, and well in English. She read French and German as well and wrote passable French. She seemed as inexperienced at physical labor as she was repelled by the thought of domestic service or even tutoring the children of the well-to-do. Further, she disliked her childless married sister, Mary, whose husband was the man of the house. Her mother and single sister, Sara, were more agreeable, but they were socially reserved and led quiet, uneventful lives. Certainly they would take her and her baby in, but would such a life be bearable?

Ellon never recorded how or why she selected Phelan. His name was often enough in the newspapers although she would have been too young to have read and remembered the extensive social coverage of his sister's impressive wedding six years earlier. Throughout her life she displayed a vicarious interest in celebrities and seemed always up on the latest social news. She liked getting out of the house and seeing what was happening, even attending public lectures. It is quite possible that before approaching Phelan at his office she had attended one of his public presentations on some Irish, political, or artistic subject.

Thomas Mahony, *the Phelans' Trusted Aide*

Press coverage and public appearances aside, Phelan was certainly easily located. His father's new office building, the pride of commercial San Francisco, proclaimed the family name. Its premier Market Street location welcomed visitors and in an era before telephone-arranged appointments, callers simply arrived during business hours and waited their turns. The senior Phelan maintained his own office while he directed his son's gradual assumption of management of Phelan enterprises. As partners their names undoubtedly appeared prominently upon the Phelan Building directory.

Thomas Mahony would have been the first of the Phelan Irish staff with whom young Florence Ellon had to negotiate. He was secretary to the father, secretary to the son, and was discharging his final service to his employers. Mahony was integrating young James into the extensive financial and commercial organizations that Mahony had assisted the father in creating. Mahony could not help but know the Phelan family members well because of the close, regular, and intimate nature of his work and his relationship with the creator of the fortune and the family.

From the young mother's vantage point, Mahony was old then, even though his service to the family would continue into his near physical incapacity. Throughout, age refused to dull his wits. Mahony's deep and abiding loyalty to the Phelans and his very close attention to the details of their business were accompanied by his dour appearance and his self-effacing manner.

Apparent in his otherwise disengaging exterior must have been a pair of twinkling eyes. Whatever story Florence Ellon spun in the outer office for the secretary's benefit and for the ears of those ahead of her in the waiting line, Mr. Mahony surely understood. Without a proper calling card to place upon the desk of young Phelan, Mahony would himself introduce the beautiful young stranger to his special charge, the most prominent Californian of the upcoming generation. For Mahony the old Irish adage on the subtleties of shared understandings was apt: you needn't write when you can speak, and you needn't speak when you can nod. Mahony knew young Phelan well and his nod may have been profound. He appreciated the young woman he ushered in and he became her social and emotional protector as long as she remained within that part of the Phelan domain over which he exercised authority. Among the Phelan inner circle Mahony, the old man's subaltern,

James Duval Phelan inherited his father's business enterprises, including the Phelan Building where this bust of the father, James Phelan, stands.

This is the Phelan Building lobby through which Florence Ellon passed on her way to introduce herself to young James Duval Phelan in 1888. In his offices above, Phelan already was expanding his art collection. The Phelan Building itself, its refinements, appointments, and some of the art were lost in the 1906 fire.

cast his relationships in a mold of dignity, with the young Mrs. Ellon particularly. She reciprocated, appreciating greatly the buffer that his protection afforded her in her interactions with the less appreciative Phelan associates. "On my last visit home," Ellon later wrote Phelan, "when I was in the office Mr. F[ay] tried to look in and Mr. M[ahony] shut the door saying, 'He is always sneaking around.'"

An Attractive Companion

Ellon always presented herself at her best. She enjoyed doing so, and her glorious youth of 1888 faded only so slowly. Even during the roaring twenties she blended with the times and laughed at being accused of having undergone one of the newly fashionable face lifts. After enjoying the compliment she chided Phelan for her not being able to afford one. So proud was she of her attractive profile that as late as 1912, at age forty-eight, she believed that if she were pregnant, no one would know through the sixth month.

At age twenty-four though, in 1888, she was not dependent upon such compliments for her personal esteem. Fair complexion, dark eyes, and well arranged (perhaps red) hair marked an attractive and poised young woman. She was quite recovered from the delivery of her child. Because Phelan compartmentalized their life together no photographs of the two together have survived and no accurate estimate of her height is possible. Her single portrait was of her own doing. It captured her in a delicate, perhaps reflective, moment and presents a well-groomed, finely dressed, and carefully coiffured woman. Her features are both refined and strong with prominent, though hardly unbecoming, lips and nose. Her jewelry is decidedly understated, allowing no distraction from her person. The picture is of a woman well prepared and well composed. She thought well of herself.

The photograph, like Ellon herself, remained separate from other sectors of Phelan's life. Within the numerous albums through which he recorded his life's activities no photo of Florence found a place. She always wrote to the Phelan Building, never to his home. He, or more likely Mahony, placed her photo within her file among the office correspondence. Phelan did not (perhaps he felt he could not) bring his lover's photograph into the home he shared with his mother and sister. He never included it in the leather-bound albums over which the Phelans spent quiet moments in prideful reflection.

Travels Together

Whatever the nature of the specific problem she shared with Phelan, he provided the required cash and someone else to attend to the details. The intimate relationship that developed thereafter is more difficult to define in today's terminology than it is to chronicle in its historical development.

Notes, flowers, poetry, and short, local trips together became their opening activities. As part of James's internship in the family businesses he toured Phelan holdings (throughout Northern California) on inspection, get-acquainted trips. Local rail, carriages, and ferry boats were the modes of transport. Except for the summer heat out in the valleys, the tasks could be pleasant and enjoyable — particularly with suitable companionship.

Florence Blumenthal Ellon recorded what she thought of her first trips with James D. Phelan. Her memories were fond and enduring. Her outings to San Jose were one of her two most often recollected romantic experiences with her Jimmy. The others were the intimate New Year's Eve dinners they shared amidst his expanding art collection. Often Flo and Jimmy saw out the old and brought in the new with catered meals in the Phelan Building suite where they first met. For her these were the highlights in a comfortable, exciting, but always guarded life. Of the recollections, San Jose ranked higher. There they were free to move about together openly, if not among friends, at least among convivial strangers and circumspect employees.

For Phelan these events constituted his leisure and pleasure, nothing more. For his part he was interesting, caring, generous, and fun loving. With one bouquet of flowers he included his own original effort:

> Your likeness (yet anothers) thank you,
> Vain with such beauty would I link you!
> Your colors equal but more bright,
> When loving or in mimic flight
> Your eyes dispel the glow of night
> So covet not the day, your realm
> Is either six P.M. or heaven!

Phelan provided more tangible tokens of his affections: books for Ellon's intellectual development, opera and symphony tickets for her cultural enhancement, and diamond earrings just to see her eyes sparkle. When they enjoyed opera "together" in San Francisco they "shared" each other's

The compelling photograph of James Duval Phelan's lover originated as a European holiday postcard that she sent to him in a tasteful, white envelope lined in burgundy. It is the only likeness of Florence Ellon that has been found despite Phelan's addiction to photography, his steady habit of record-keeping, and his sense of order and completeness.

Lovers' Travels

The Chico ranch that the family put in rice acreage was a bit too hot and desolate to be an attractive sidetrip for Phelan and his paramour. Besides, his brother-in-law's cousin, Denis J. Murphy, was the ranch manager. The Santa Clara County agricultural and urban properties were far superior for the purpose of the young lovers. The senior Phelan had a San Jose bank, commercial buildings, hotel interests, and scattered ranch lands. Young James was to develop additional San Jose interests: banking, hostelry, entertainment, and a private club. He also minded the family ranch lands in the north quadrants of the city. His father donated to San Jose those areas that would be laid out into streets and parks once the city expanded to the north. Young James's interests included such locally novel ideas as street design for esthetics — not the near universally accepted urban grid. During his inspection tours, Florence was his companion. A romantic, she often recalled the valley of spring blossoms, their freedom and their youth together.

company from distant boxes, each making merry among separate and distinct parties. In public Phelan's sense of propriety sublimated any more natural desires to proclaim their affections. Florence's beauty, enhanced by all the decorous arts of western civilization, could be admired but at a distance by the man she easily learned to love.

James D. Phelan, in turn, had his own attractions: certainly wealth and power and the eroticism they so often project, plus the spell cast by his gentle sophistication and his private sharing of the public charm and acclaim so respected by those Ellon admired and envied from her distance.

Operas, banquets, civic ceremony, these were the public, symbolic occasions at which his prudence denied open disclosure even in San Francisco. When they "shared" an evening in public they did not touch hands. They arrived and they departed separately. They only shared admiring glances. Once, when Phelan was ill, Florence took the social initiative, and tried to visit him at home. He responded, "I am not displeased at you calling … but would not advise it again. I know it was prompted by your solicitude."

To move beyond such limitations Phelan began meeting Ellon in New York, London, and Paris. They lived separately even when traveling abroad. Phelan required his privacy and his scheduled solitude. Also, he minded propriety and the law. They never shared a domicile. Only when away from San Francisco and his family, could he and Florence meet publicly. When he traveled unaccompanied, as in 1900 during a respite amid his third term as mayor of San Francisco, he wrote from Paris reassuringly: "Last night I was … at the Follies…, a show not as good as the [San Francisco] Orpheum, but there are great promenade foyers where the Coquettes circulate. They are repulsive in paint[,] powder & bad English."

Ellon's sophisticated tastes in opera, symphony, and the theater are difficult to assess because they may have been cultivated after her association with Phelan. Certainly by 1905 her operatic interests were impinging upon his weekly regime: "If you were not so eager to see this particular opera[,] I would have seen you. It is my idle night — that is my night of pleasure & leisure — and — now lost to both pleasure & duty." Obviously, Florence was not on call.

Phelan insured Ellon's comfort as well as little Vera's care. And Phelan, remarkably, seems even to have promised that Flo would always be happy! Throughout, however, Ellon understood that she was never to be any part of his public life. The approach to his family became an intrusion; even his employees were discrete.

No commitment

The fact of the matter is that Ellon fell in love with the man she had chosen to help her and to provide for her. In essence, she was a romantic who aspired to good living and lacked independent means to attain it. Therefore, she made herself dependent upon a generous, refined, engaging, and personally considerate young heir with a magnificent future. She had the additional good fortune to select a gentleman close to her own age who lacked a wife and, if he would never accept her for that role, at least he would not complicate her life by selecting any other woman.

Phelan himself inherited no romantic impulses because none were bequeathed to him. In youth he actually organized a cartoon collection on the subject of romantic love, courtship, and marriage; the conclusions were unhappy. In the organization of his life, Tuesday nights became his leisure and pleasure nights. And as years passed, no matter how shared good times affected Ellon, Phelan's commitment was never in question; he had none.

By 1894 six years had passed since Ellon entered and claimed a sector of Phelan's life. He was between trips to Europe and was clarifying his sense of obligation. His sister Alice had been married twelve years and had four children. His father had been dead for two years. His mother and sister Mollie lived in the family home with him. Both were under the care of loyal and solicitous servants, so he conducted his official and personal entertaining mostly beyond the home.

Within this matrix Ellon had no place. With bluntness, perhaps cruelty, he expressed his relationship for the record: "I have no relations with her [other] than sleeping with her occasionally.... I have treated her well." Also for the record Phelan made it clear that, "Her child is by Robert Ellon born long before I knew her." Phelan even listed the names of those who knew this to be true. Obviously he was concerned about his estate after coming into his inheritance only two years previously and at the prime of life, thirty-three. Ellon was to have no claim on his estate and he wanted to assure himself of that. His loyalty and commitment was to his own nuclear family.

Mixing Business and Pleasure

Business and pleasure were a satisfying mix in the early carefree days for James Duval Phelan and Florence Ellon. Ellon's single responsibility in life was the rearing of her daughter. As a mother she was attentive and responsible, but hardly consumedly devoted. She drew Phelan into friendly and sustaining association with Vera even though the infant did not travel with them. Instead, Florence obtained the services of a middle-aged nurse who cared for her child on a regular basis. "Mother" Frost lived in an old San Francisco house. Phelan became familiar with the residence and sufficiently acquainted with Frost to have observed her devotion to the Catholic Church.

Four decades later, Ellon generously entertained Frost with motor rides in Phelan's chauffeured limousine. Then in her eighties, Frost responded, Ellon wrote, by blessing "me in the names of all the Saints." Still playful herself after the passage of all those decades, Ellon chided her man on the disparity of his religious heritage and his convictions. "I'm passing over to you a big share as I owe it to you Jimmy...."

Dear Jimmy

Below are samplings from letters Florence Ellon wrote to James Duval Phelan:

Jarnac, April 3, 1907: There have been times when I have wanted you! Just before leaving Paris I went slumming.... How I wish that you had been there with me to take me "home!!! I would have made it a night to be remembered!!!

London, July 6, 1909: The Country about London is so green and beautiful and the air delirious and for a time I fell into a day dream and thought that I was motoring to "San Jose" with "Somebody."

Berlin, March 18, 1913: I heard a clever woman of the world lecture.... I have felt very bitter, don't you think I have had cause? Yet I am sorry for you for I feel that you are not happy. You can't be. I have not deserved all this. I have been a good woman and loved you!

San Francisco, July 6, 1915: I am a woman and alone and I have no one but you. After all these years.... If you had not come into my life I would now, no doubt, be the wife of some good man. What a home coming this has been and only last Xmas you sent me a book "Letters of Passion."

Paris, March 11, 1923: It's Spring time in Paris!! Sunshine and flowers. A breath of our California — but only that.... I do want to see you....!! Will you come?

Baden Baden, Undated: My love for you has kept away all temptations.... When I see all the women about me with strings of pearls, I too long for one. But it's the old story.

Yet, when he wrote that he treated her well, he had cause for his remarks. Previously he had conveyed a city lot to her and in 1894 he provided her with $6,000 in cash (in $100 bills) for her to build her own home, or better yet, income-producing rental units. He planned more as an aside, in place of a bequest, in case he should die suddenly or unexpectedly. In 1894 he instructed his brother-in-law Frank Sullivan, "Treat the little girl well & see that she gets what I leave her. I met her in 1888...."

Whether Mahony was amused or exasperated is unknown, but his introduction of Ellon to Phelan added considerably to the office work load, as well as to the fascination for the job. During his tenure as Phelan's chief secretary and those of each of his groomed successors (George F. Welch and Thomas B. Doyle) Phelan attempted to confer lasting financial independence upon Mrs. Ellon, once at her request. Each time he failed because he could not convince her that money and property were for investment first. Consumption, for those who wanted to be secure and comfortable, had to be second. Florence was happiest when she could spend and shop, particularly in Paris, for the pure joy of the experience. She found release in irresponsible shopping and spending. Each time Phelan provided for her future, she consumed. And how she loved to!

In the Phelan Building, the all male, all Irish Catholic office staff maintained financial records on Ellon just like any other account. In the pre-IRS era, Phelan did not always differentiate between personal expenses and business expenses, so where Ellon's bills and receipts were filed would offer no further insight into how Phelan perceived her. In any case, the $100,000 mark was broken as early as 1905, and it was rising fast. That was a particularly expensive year that cost an extra $16,800.

Confrontation

Confrontation in their relationship took place during 1905. Its timing from Phelan's point of view was not particularly awkward. He had completed his three successful terms as mayor of San Francisco without incident. Father Peter C. Yorke, his most vocal public critic, had been ignoring him. As a private citizen Phelan was attending mostly to his own business affairs. His support of the crusade of his friend and business associate, Rudolph Spreckels and *Bulletin* editor Fremont Older to prosecute the resurgent political grafters was a year into the future. So, too, were the unforeseen earthquake and fire that were to devastate the Phelan estate. So, he was out of public view for the moment.

By 1905 Ellon was forty-one years of age and Phelan was forty-four. They had been lovers since 1888, seventeen years. She was at the time living in Paris where he visited her during the previous year. Upon his return to San Francisco, Phelan continued to busy himself with the organization of the California Democratic party. Making the most of rather ordinary days he reported to Ellon, "I am keeping up well & have no surplus energy to waste, bestow, or give away! Love and politics are inimical. I see no one you know. I will expect more letters than I send."

Ellon's response was hardly what Phelan would have desired. She simply returned to San Francisco and served him with this by messenger:

> Jimmy!! Upon the advice of my friends in Paris I have returned home to be taken care of and have the attendance of my own physician. I mean to get well again no matter what the cost….I desire $50,000[.] If I do not hear[,] will put it in the hands of my attorney and shall then tell all from the beginning 16 [sic] years ago until your visit to Paris last year. Oh how I believed in and trusted you and all your promises to me…. I have had the finger of scorn pointed at me all these years in protecting you while you posed before the world as a good and honorable man….I have known for some years that you were selfish etc. but never did I think you would act as you have towards me at such a time! …how you have failed me!! …if compelled to go to Court will not there ask for 50,000 but my just rights….I have told no one[,] not even my sister the cause of my illness or of this matter. It now depends upon you.

Neither left any record of what Ellon was trying to recover from. On the back of her envelope Phelan noted, "Demand 50,000!" He settled, nonetheless, for $16,800 and a formal handwritten statement from Ellon. In it she acknowledged having received an aggregate of over $100,000 since 1888. Further, she stated her purpose to be the refutation of

> …malicious persons who might imply from our relations more than actually exists [and] to state that I have always lived at home and that no promises have ever passed between us….I acquit James D. Phelan of all demands … as he has been a good friend in helping me and … he has done all that reasonably be expected of him.

Flo and Jimmy both had varying forms of leverage that they were capable of using against the other. She had knowledge and evidence; he had wealth and power. Whatever the specific cause, the results of their 1905 confrontation permanently altered Phelan's part in the relationship. Always cautious and guarded, thereafter he became clearly distrustful. Ellon, of course, had her own reaction based upon her own perspective and experience.

By the following spring she was back in Paris, her head filled with visions of "velvet, furs and motor cars," which she accused Phelan of lavishing on other women. Besides, all around her in Paris women were being treated

James Duval Phelan accepted his father's single justification for an office — business and work — as his own prime, but not exclusive reason. Young James learned the value of investment over consumption, yet he created his own pleasing balance. James Duval enhanced the aesthetic qualities of his rooms, which after 1888 also became the locale for intimate New Year's Eve dinners. Those dinners remained among Florence Ellon's most often recollected romantic experiences.

better by less well-to-do gentlemen. Despite her recently acquired financial independence, she used the occasion of her preparation for Vera's first wedding (Her daughter married three times; the first and third times to the same man, G. Selmer Fougner) to ask Phelan for $4,000 and additionally "...that as a *wedding* gift you send Vera a note for $2,000." Regardless of the written statement he extracted from her exactly one year before, Phelan would have behaved out of character by not gratifying her requests. And in fact, Vera thanked him with a gracious note acknowledging his gift. The Ellon-Phelan relationship, however, remained a dynamic one.

Ongoing Relationship

Ellon was back in New York when the San Francisco earthquake and fire created worldwide headlines in April, 1906. It virtually destroyed the income-generating basis of the Phelan fortune, as well as the family mansion Florence had never penetrated. Phelan immediately became central to disaster relief. From her New York hotel Florence addressed her letters of love and anxiety to "Jimmy Dear!," "Formerly" of the Phelan Building. Where they had met and where they had loved and the art they had appreciated, all were in ashes. Like the rest of commercial San Francisco, the once imposing symbol of Phelan wealth ceased to exist.

Ellon's spontaneous reaction was to offer Phelan her surviving properties, real estate he had given to her over the years. "All I have," she wrote, "is yours." Prudent even in crisis, Phelan ushered his extended family to their country homes and rented for himself, and for Mollie, a furnished home at 2555 Webster Street in what survived of San Francisco. He did act on Ellon's offer, though. The temporarily dispossessed Bohemian Club relocated in one of her residential properties on Pacific Avenue.

After Vera's wedding on June 2, 1906, Ellon entrained for San Francisco and an uncertain welcome. She asked, in fact, "Will you be glad to see me and forgive? You see my pride is humbled, and I am at your feet." "If your people are still away and you think it's safe[,] I will come to your house about 8 P.M. either Thursday or Friday." Mahony's understudy, George Welch, could convey Phelan's response. Unsure perhaps of being received at all, Ellon added a post script: "You have never suffered through me and you never will[.] I don't think that you really *understand* me. I wrote that letter [the demand for

Practicing Economy

Occasionally, during James D. Phelan's rare successes at consumer education, Florence Ellon would comply but not silently. Living in Paris in 1911 and watching her funds in anticipation of a trip to London to attend her daughter's second wedding, she reported to Phelan that she was staying at a "small private hotel or boarding house ... practicing economy which you preached! How I hate it!"

In the same letter she added: "I suppose that you will wish to give her [Vera] a wedding gift. If so[,] you can send me what you wish to spend and I will buy something that she would like...." This was pure Ellon.

$50,000] but you too were at fault and after you said that you were glad to have helped me[.] I am certain no other woman would have kept our love story *sacred* as I have."

Phelan relented five months later, not until the night before she was to depart for New York and sail for Bremen and travel on to Nice. Her thank you note saluted Jimmy in French, noted her enjoyment with their short visit and expressed her appreciation: "You were so good in *every* way." Thereafter her letters were of hotels, drives, men, divorces, dinners, balls, and assorted entertainments. Phelan welcomed the correspondence and undoubtedly felt somewhat relieved that he could enjoy it at a distance. They still had more than half of their years together ahead of them, but Ellon's 1905 demand and Phelan's reaction marked the conclusion of the youthful stage of their relationship. Their middle years had begun.

Chapter Four
Public Life, Private Life

At the time Florence Ellon identified James Duval Phelan as her target, he was in command of the basic skills he was to display so well in an active, public career. As her secluded love for him was developing, so too were his preparations for a public life. By young adulthood he had established himself as a highly literate, perhaps literary, personality whose interests and perspectives arose from a deep concern and appreciation of western civilization. Led by obligation into practical matters in a modern, dynamic, post-pioneer urban economy, Phelan struggled through a lifetime trying to reconcile (sometimes compromise) cultural heritage to California utility and growth.

He enjoyed reading and studying diverse public questions and he spoke before whoever invited him, including civic, cultural, patriotic, and religious groups. By the time he assumed family leadership, Phelan had become a featured speaker among Catholic organizations under the sponsorship of Archbishop Patrick W. Riordan and prominent Catholic laymen of his day.

His sensitive understanding and expression were duplicated by no contemporary California public figure and perhaps by none in the nation. Phelan considered such symbolic offerings his contribution to the general welfare. Symbolism and the events in the life and death of the nation were, he felt, the vital means at notable moments to advance civic education and to honor and energize the citizens of the Republic. At this task he began early and he persisted.

Quite frankly, and freely, Phelan would speak to just about any group interested in his ideas. Once he became widely recognized as an interesting personality and an informative and engaging communicator, he was regularly

Gladstone's Influence

Phelan had listened attentively to William Gladstone addressing Parliament when he was in London in 1882. His attention may have been heightened by having had to pay for the privilege, his card having been rebuffed by the usher's remark, "Oh, from California, the land of gold." Not slow, Phelan traded a coin for his own card to be seated. Back in San Francisco, he combined his perceptions of what he had seen and heard with what he had been reading in the press. In a speech to the Young Ireland Parliamentary Club (the organization's title suggests a constitutional nationalist rather than a revolutionary nationalist approach to Irish aspirations), Phelan advanced Prime Minister Gladstone as a promoter of home rule for Ireland. Quite likely Phelan was the only San Franciscan, perhaps the only American, who had seen and listened to Gladstone in person and also made an academic study of the Irish question. Phelan spoke to a receptive audience, and his remarks were printed for distribution by activitists who disagreed. This was his idea of public education on civic questions. His alternate approach was to speak before the groups with whom he disagreed, such as the local Socialist Party.

No Honorariums

James D. Phelan never accepted an honorarium from an interest group and never accepted expenses from any organization. When money arrived at his office with expressions of gratitude, George Welch returned it with Phelan's compliments and a brief statement of Phelan's ideal of public service. Because of his wealth, Phelan enjoyed almost unrivaled, permanent freedom from political fund raising. He paid much of the organizational expense for California's Democratic Party during lean years and was self-reliant for his own campaigns.

before the Commonwealth Club of San Francisco. His local commitments did not prevent him from entraining to Santa Barbara to speak to a high school graduation class or speaking to Friends of Neighborhood Art, the Leagues to Enforce Peace (1919), or eight hundred banqueting Irish Americans in New York on St. Patrick's Day, 1916.

He spoke to all organizations, whether he believed in their goals or not. He joined, however, only those organizations whose purposes he chose to endorse and whose methods harmonized with his sense of propriety.

Phelan seemed never to be at a loss for the right word, either in prepared oratory or in correspondence. He was gifted and became a practiced speaker. He could turn the proper phrase, offer homage to the victor, recognize the scholar, encourage the student, and console the bereaved. Always patient, always precise, often witty, Phelan met and advanced the tastes of his day.

The only disapproval expressed of either his style or his content came from U.S. Senate colleagues who impatiently held the votes and were compelled to await Phelan's conclusion before they could cast them and move the national legislative agenda where Phelan preferred it not go. For all others his wit, his historical allusions, his flights into poetry, when guided by his considerate brevity, prevented him from being a wind bag.

Phelan most often prepared for oral presentations by formalizing his thoughts in written manuscripts from which he made his delivery. He was a good reader and a good speaker, and the two blended comfortably. The result for his listeners was the appearance of easy, if not spontaneous, delivery. The side effect was the existence of a basic manuscript that Phelan frequently polished for publication. His routine began in college and simply continued.

His first general exposure as a writer resulted from his post graduation residence in Europe. Throughout most of 1883 his observations and commentary appeared regularly in the San Francisco *Examiner*. His articles originated from Florence, Monte Carlo, Rome, Vienna, Carlsbad, and Paris. Two years out of college, the senior James Phelan's son was creating his own public identity. San Franciscans were learning who he was, where he was, and a bit of what he thought.

Phelan only released part of his intellectual life through publications, however. Public affairs, immediate and more broadly construed, maintained his permanent interest; his essays focused upon these subjects. His research was thorough enough: popular press, reference works, specialized magazines, interviews with the principals, academic consultations, and examination of scholarly literature at hand or encountered through personal associations.

As his years of preparation for service advanced, his own voluntary memberships increased. He sprinkled his acceptance of leadership positions among the Bohemian Club, Red Cross, the Association for the Adornment of San Francisco, San Francisco Art Association, Pacific Union Club, University Club, and the Olympic Club. Besides the Bohemian Club, he lavished his greatest personal attention in advancing the work and the organization of the Native Sons of the Golden West. As interesting as his list of memberships may be, those that are missing may be even more suggestive.

Prominent among those absent are Catholic organizations and Irish nationalist organizations. He spoke to the Knights of Columbus, the Young Men's Institute (the YMI was a Catholic response to the YMCA), and numerous, short-lived popular Irish groups. But he never sought membership. That was George Welch's domain and one of the many reasons why his incorporation into the Phelan office staff at age 15 became so valuable and why his premature death in the influenza epidemic of 1918–1919 was such a blow to Phelan's political career.

Phelan served as President of the American Historical Association's Pacific Coast Branch and delivered the 1908 annual banquet address at the Faculty Club (for men only!) of the University of California, Berkeley. His interest in the academic papers read before the sessions extended to his seeking permission of Professor E. D. Adams of Stanford to share his paper, "English Interest in the Annexation of California," with the American Ambassador to the Court of St. James (England). What Phelan never did, however, was to adapt the scholarly-academic tone to his own writing.

Audience and Topics

His audience always remained the general voters, the politicians they put into office, and those who influenced the economic decisions of the nation and the community. He wrote for publication with these audiences in mind. His intention was to convince and lead his readers to action. If the city were corrupt, then citizens should cleanse it. If the fire, not the earthquake, destroyed San Francisco, then correctly constructed water mains should rectify the problem. Therefore, rebuild the City!

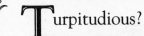

Turpitudious?

In the midst of one speech in 1912 Phelan coined the word "turpitudious." Upon checking his well-thumbed Webster and Century dictionaries he verified his linguistic "creation." Pursuing the matter he wrote to his friend Benjamin Ide Wheeler, then President of the University of California and a noted linguist, and asked "...why should there not be an adjective to enlarge the use of 'turpitude'?" If Dr. Wheeler knew of no authority citing "turpitudious," Phelan playfully offered his newly coined "word to the English language through your department of English...."

Oratorical Self-Indulgence

Phelan guarded himself against oratorical self-indulgence by carrying in his vest pocket a special time piece designed by the Geneva watchmakers Vacheron and Constantin. By means of a small gong it could lightly strike the minutes thus alerting him to the dwindling pool of comfort and attention that he assumed of formal audiences. The striker could be silenced when not needed.

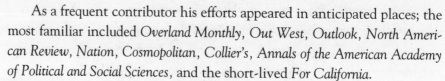

As a frequent contributor his efforts appeared in anticipated places; the most familiar included *Overland Monthly, Out West, Outlook, North American Review, Nation, Cosmopolitan, Collier's, Annals of the American Academy of Political and Social Sciences*, and the short-lived *For California*.

His subjects ranged from "The Growth of Municipal Art in California" to "Why Congress Should Pass the Hetch-Hetchy Bill," and "Why Wilson Should be Nominated." He wrote an article on "The New San Francisco and the Old," for the *Pacific Monthly*, which was forced to suspend publication. Phelan redirected his labor to *International Fair Illustrated* and concentrated on the rise of the city from its ashes, the downtown, his Phelan Building, and the promising future of the city he loved.

Phelan's Library

Phelan personally sought out obscure, privately printed monographs in the fields of California and San Francisco history. As a collector he haunted book stores and perused catalogues of American and European dealers in used and rare books who dealt particularly with the history and historical background of California and the West. His reputation as a local and regional collector attracted researchers who sought library privileges to advance their own scholarship. Among them was Theodore H. Hittell, the noted author of the early multi-volume *History of California*. Phelan's secretaries allowed reading and note taking but drew the line at borrowing.

His sense of discrimination displayed its refinements through his acquisition of the far less famous *Catholic Encyclopedia*. The highly ambitious work constituted the early-century legitimization of Catholic intellectual life in America. Phelan's other book purchases and periodical subscriptions evidenced no interest in theology, philosophy, or Catholic doctrine. His compartmentalized attention to the Catholic Church was exclusively to its history, art, and other manifestations as a conservator and conveyor of western culture. The *Encyclopedia* addressed Phelan's intellectual needs without upsetting his strictly temporal orientation. Phelan recognized the Church's publishing efforts for the success they were and included the multi-volumed set within his growing reference library.

As years passed, collecting brought its own problems. Focusing primarily on California he continued purchases on the state's Spanish heritage. The meeting of the mission system and the indigenous peoples of California, and the military and social history of exploration and conquest all attracted his interest. Regrettably he was not drawn into expressing his views on the missionary versus Indian controversy. His rare perspective regarding the irrelevance of the Christian doctrines of penance, redemption, and salvation plus his commonplace acceptance of western civilization's superiority could have offered additional insight into the quality of his mind. Surprisingly, the historic gold rush of his father's day interested him less as literature than it did as symbol. Saluting and celebrating the California pioneers was more to his liking than reading about them.

By 1911 he drew the line on acquisitions; he resolved not to indulge himself further in the collection of biographies. He relented though in his second area of interests, the history and literature of Ireland. Even with the destruction of his library in 1906, his successful restoration efforts created severe space problems. He could always rent or construct more space, and during his Senate years in Washington he even developed an alternate private California library for the edification of his friends and associates in the Capitol. This alleviated his space problem but did not solve it.

Finally he engaged his first female secretary, Mrs. Rosabelle Driscoll, to create his own card catalogue system. One of Phelan's book agents prompted the tardy decision by having purchased, at the cost of $100, the celebrated *Narrative of Edward McGowan.* Inside the cover Phelan found his own book plate along with the author's autograph. Phelan first assumed that the book had been borrowed or stolen from his library, but later recollected that he had traded it off. This type of confusion he found intolerable, therefore the formal organization and catalogue of his library.

Phelan as Author

Within the creative environment that San Francisco fostered before the turn-of-the-century, Phelan chose the role of an essayist: practical, progressive, and always attentive to public questions. Next, as a eulogist, he was sensitive, eloquent, and reassuring for the living. Noticeably, in both of these fields, the first self selected and the second thrust upon him by virtue of his official positions and retained because of his demonstrated capacity, he had few local competitors. He enjoyed the company of talented young California

James Duval Phelan's bookplate design displays his love for books and for his native city risen from the flames of 1906.

Encyclopedia Endorsement

When *Scientific America* wished to promote sales of the *Encyclopedia Americana* in Europe they turned to Phelan for his endorsement:

> *...thousands of Americans have purchased England's Britannica, France's Larousse, and Germany's Meyer or Brockhaus, but now for the first time the people of England, France and Germany have an opportunity to own an AMERICANA. The people of the two continents are placed under lasting obligations to the Scientific American for the production of this great National reference work, and I heartily recommend it to everyone throughout the world who can read the English language.*

Not only would no other California political figure be asked for such an endorsement, none could have truthfully or convincingly written it. Some could not have written at all.

writers and hosted and honored their work, but Phelan's life was too diverse and his head too fact filled to dream of being a novelist or a playwright. Only poetry he could not resist, and even there he knew how to participate and still protect his ego.

Through poetry, particularly in his formative years, Phelan privately indulged his own quest for beauty and artistic expression. As the demands of a public life closed in on him Phelan redistributed his poetry-writing hours and carefully set aside his poems in scrap books, which were destroyed by the 1906 fire. He confessed to Dr. Aurelia Henry Reinhardt, President of Mills College, that with his poems of young manhood also "perished my dream of immortality." He added late in life that "only poets are immortal, because they leave their soul behind them for careful cultivation by us who come after; at any rate, it is an earthly immortality."

During his post-Senate years, the 1920s, he would return to his early love for poetic expression, but during his most active public years he contented himself with enjoyment of the accomplishments of the acclaimed. These abundant years allowed him a broad forum from which to incorporate their graceful words into his many public presentations and private communications. When rare opportunity allowed or provocative stimulus required, he penned his own.

Phelan's Travel

Travel constituted such an early and permanent part of Phelan's lifestyle that he seemed never to consider it as a terribly important factor in his preparation for life. His travel established a bond with his eastern cousins; later George Duval's return trip to San Francisco further secured the bond. Phelan's trips East and on to Europe acquainted him with the geography, industry, politics, and social customs of his own expansive nation and the civilization from which it had sprung. To him, travel, exposure, and experience were requirements for productive lives for anyone seeking to interpret or to guide human destiny. In Phelan's case he began young and continued as long as his well-being allowed.

Phelan was different even from most others who could afford ambitious travel — from his travels came productive results. Phelan sent home ideas applicable for civic improvement and enhancement that he circulated as broadly as his speaking and writing skills allowed. From his first extended European residence to his around-the-world tour following his senatorial retirement, Phelan shared his learning and experiences with those who would listen and those who would read. Besides the vicarious pleasure from well-composed firsthand experience, Phelan offered practical suggestions.

Phelan wrote only one book, *Travel and Comment*, which he gave to friends as a memento for Christmas in 1922 and published in 1923. Most of the chapters recounted his trip around the world and his political, cultural, and social observations. The remaining chapters originated from his first extended residence abroad in 1883.

Other authors enjoyed his encouragement and more tangible support, particularly if practical benefit might be expected or if public policy might be influenced by publication. Phelan believed strongly that publications brought forward the best new thinking. Intellectual advocacy would advance the more worthy point of view. With his progressive friend, Rudolph Spreckels, Phelan subsidized the writing of Franklin Hichborn's *"The System" as Uncovered by the San Francisco Graft Prosecution*. Once published, Phelan saw that the book was well advertised. He even presented a copy to President Woodrow Wilson, his cabinet members, and each member of the United States Senate.

Toward the end of his life, Phelan advanced the publication of a military work on the threat of Japanese preparedness in aviation. The views of the author, W. Jefferson Davis, were fully in harmony with Phelan's own regarding Japan's growing military strength during the late 1920s.

Phelan also brought out, as *Somewhere in France*, a leather bound private edition of his nephew's highly literary and engaging letters home from World War I. For the moment, they suggested the talent upon which Noël Sullivan might build his own literary career. But that was not to be. Phelan often underwrote private printings of the efforts of local poets or collections that he gathered from aspiring college students. Phelan's personal associations with local poets, writers, and playwrights began early and continued through to generous remembrances in his last will.

His most practical contribution was a pamphlet he wrote for American soldiers demobilized in San Francisco following their service in the Philippines during the Spanish-American War. Phelan offered understanding and practical advice to mostly young and educationally limited young men on

Phelan's Biography?

Another major manuscript that interested James D. Phelan greatly was his own biography. His old St. Ignatius classmate, George J. Duraind, brought the idea to Phelan. Duraind had spent a full career in San Francisco journalism and had observed and written about much of Phelan's public life. Phelan cooperated and encouraged Duraind's work and contributed to the expense, but his own good sense ultimately prevailed. Fond as he was of sponsoring private, limited editions of manuscripts that he found worthy, he could easily have had Duraind's manuscript handsomely printed and distributed as gifts and placed in libraries. Instead, Phelan rejected the result as "too laudatory, albeit too generous." In fact, parts of the manuscript ranged between puffery and beatification.

Later Phelan did print 1,000 copies of a pioneer diary, *How Many Miles From St. Jo?* to which he appended a brief autobiographical statement by his own father. The book remains a primary source on his family history. He brought honor to his father, but he correctly recognized that similar action, through Duraind, would hardly bring the same result to himself.

The Grand Life

So comfortable was James Duval Phelan with travel as education and recreation that matter-of-fact letters such as Gertrude Atherton's hardly raised his eyebrow. From the Algonquin Hotel in Manhattan, she shared with Phelan her indecision for the summer of 1910. Her six options included bringing a party to Europe for the Brussels exposition, summer with musical friends in Paris, fulfill a half-promise to go to Munich, take up residence in an antiquated village in the English countryside and write a play, be smart and write in San Francisco during the summer — "unrivalled for work," or give in to temptation and go to the West Indies with other friends. Phelan's own lifestyle allowed him to read such letters with apparent sympathy.

how to avoid personal trouble and succeed if they intended to remain in San Francisco — the largest city many of them had ever seen.

A major ingredient in Phelan's evolving plan developing and beautifying the city he loved was population growth. Youth and patriotic commitment were proper subordinate ingredients for those he sought, but so too were sobriety, diligence, and reliability. Phelan wanted more San Franciscans who were properly disposed and motivated. He reached out to the best among the new veterans. His wider audience of readers was all of San Francisco and, later, his national and international list of friends and acquaintances.

Monte Carlo and Carlsbad

Phelan's 1883 essay on Monte Carlo reads like a popular short story. In eight pages the reader peeps into a strange and exciting world of the rich and the bold. As an introduction Phelan sketched the land and seascape, the climate and vegetation; he even fixes the economy and politics in his reader's head. Phelan's focus, however, is on the reader's central interest, the casino. Within this mix Phelan explained the games. That roulette became his own favorite he omitted from his published account. That he acquired his own wheel for gaming at home in San Francisco likewise is not included. That he brought it to Montalvo for the amusement of Vice President Thomas R. Marshall and Franklin and Eleanor Roosevelt remained for the future. His explanation of the game conveys a simplicity born of personal observation. Phelan reduced the refinements of roulette to a literary tempo of his short piece.

Despite his personal fascination, Phelan opposed public gambling and favored efforts of international organizations devoted to its suppression. "As a matter of public policy, it should be restrained, for it has a tendency to discourage labor and establish false values." From Phelan's point of view money should not be a subject of public amusement. In San Francisco when his view counted, he advised against horse racing because he knew that the gambling, not the sport, made the events commercially profitable. His opposition to public gambling rested upon his foreign observations. His essay's conclusion was a mild lament:

> *Without gaming Monte Carlo, shorn of its tables, would still be beautiful, and attractive, too.... The gorgeous theater, the unrivaled orchestra, the*

tropical surroundings, might be sufficient to attract, but I doubt very much if the same sportive throng — so representative of Parisian civilization — could be assembled in the Casino after the danger which they loved had passed, and the fruit which was forbidden is no more.

While gambling in Monte Carlo was an excitement Phelan could privately afford to indulge and publicly agree to abolish, Carlsbad was an entirely different matter. The resort was Europe's premier wateringplace. There, between May and October, promptly at 6:00 A.M., Phelan noted that 30,000 season visitors promenaded to orchestral concerts, "…and ladies and gentlemen, with drinking mugs suspended to shoulder-straps … keep without protest these unseasonable hours." They sampled the various natural mineral waters and partook in mild exercise under officially prescribed "medical" regimes. If they stayed more than eight days, they paid a tax that supported the musical programs and gave them the freedom of the mineral springs.

Phelan recognized the water cures as bunk, psychology and improved living aside. "Carlsbad is nothing more nor less than a practical expression of the golden mean. Its panacea is moderation. The first object is simply health, attained by well-ordered life, made pleasant by rational divertissements, far from the wicked world." He partook first with we know not whom. Later, while still in top form, Phelan and Rudolph Spreckels amused themselves and their California party at Carlsbad. Later, Phelan sought his own restoration through modern medical science with technology's assist and not at "the most aristocratic wateringplace in Europe." He noted this misnomer in an 1883 article observing that infirmity was the great leveler. "And what strange admissions must be forced from royal personages who come hither to mend their shattered constitution!"

When Phelan was but twenty-two though, he recognized Carlsbad for the example it offered California enterprise. This Bohemian village

> *…ought to awaken some interest in these natural springs, which, with its climate, entitle California … so well equipped … to be the Sanitarium of America, if not the world.*

> *Why should not a state like California establish about some of its best springs such a community, taxing the beneficiaries for music and service? In a land where Hygeia has scattered her favors, she should not be without a worthy shrine, and taxation is sacrificial, and gold propitiates goddesses.*

Inside the Casino

Once inside the Monte Carlo casino, James Duval Phelan treats us (through his essay) to the physical setting, the lore of the gaming tables (oil lamps burn independently of any centralized gas or electrical lighting system to thwart criminal design and to keep the wheels spinning), their compulsive attraction to brilliantly adorned patrons approaching great risk. Phelan moved gracefully on to the human factors: why and how the attendants eye the patrons, the women (the majority of players) and their sources of the monies they leave behind, humor (the English scion lost, won, and lost again while cabling home at each stage with a contrived story covering each eventuality), the promenaders seeing and being seen and the men (the minority who wager most and, therefore, lose most).

Phelan directed his messages from Monte Carlo and Carlsbad at San Francisco's popular readers of the 1880s, and he delivered it with clarity and grace. One message was negative, the other positive. In preparation for a public career the young heir partook, observed, assessed, and selected. The older, well-developed societies offered much, but not all should be transplanted to his idealized California. His prose was pleasant enough even for San Franciscans wishing only to idle away time over their 1883 newspaper. But Phelan did more than amuse.

Phelan's post-graduation essays, emanating from Europe's major capitols as well as her leisure resorts, enhanced his visibility among a broader sector of San Francisco voters. The essays' contents demonstrated his powers of observation and allowed insights into young Phelan's sense of judgment. Simultaneously readers could conclude that he was enjoying himself in his enterprise but was generous enough to share it too.

Father and Son

The *modus vivendi* between father and son stabilized into their permanent adult relationship. For his part, while preparing for a public life, Phelan cooperated in his father's plan for mastering banking and commerce and developing the management skills needed to preside over extensive holdings in agriculture and real estate. Through the on-the-job training method, he came to comprehend the detail and scope of the family enterprises and to appreciate what personal qualities and organizational abilities were needed to manage them. Young Phelan enjoyed a high level of personal skills, and he worked at applying them in the business environment. Beyond his sincere and successful engagement in his business apprenticeship Phelan read, he wrote, he traveled, and he socialized with San Francisco's upcoming literary and performing artists.

The father's side is equally interesting. By his cooperation in his son's post-graduation trip, James Phelan acquiesced, even encouraged the boy towards a life he himself hardly bothered to understand. His support of the European residence was the father's acknowledgment and approval of the son's broader career ambitions. Given his own more limited, largely commercial interests, this was a great personal psychological concession. Further and far more painful given the pioneer's behavior toward his own wayward brother

James Duval Phelan and his father, James, during the son's business internship of the 1880s. The impact that each man had upon the other was profound. The autocratic father approved of the son who did but a portion of his bidding. The art-loving son adjusted his literary ambitions to manage the commercial world his father had created. The great unknown is still the origin of James Duval Phelan's committment to public service. Commerce, religion, and literature were his primary early influences. Concern for the civic well being ranked much farther down the list.

Michael and his unwavering acceptance of Catholic moral teachings, the senior Phelan apparently extended his tolerance to his son's shadowy relationship with Mrs. Ellon. That he never shared this knowledge with his wife is entirely plausible. That he never acquired it himself is not.

Phelan's trade-off with his father allowed him to create for himself the beginnings of a complex intellectual, cultural, social, and political world that was to extend far beyond the boundaries secured by his father and mother. His father sought merely that Phelan become competent and therefore secure in his assumption of control of the first generation's prize, a California fortune and the functioning financial empire that sustained it. Beyond these, the old man allowed that the boy's life had room for many things that he did not choose for himself and would hardly have chosen for his son were he fully capable of enforcing his decisions. The resulting respect the son retained for the father was immense. With his father's guidance and forbearance Phelan determined his own life. Unlike the little good boy who appeared in his "Monte Carlo" essay, Phelan very carefully minded his demanding and indulging father. By doing so he never missed his heap of fun, too.

Nature started running its unrestrainable course by 1890. James Phelan had advanced James Duval Phelan into full partnership and when the father's health began to fail him he resorted to Harbor Springs in Lake County where he held additional property. His rest cure failing, Phelan senior returned to his San Francisco home to live out his days of diminishing physical capacity. In 1892, on December 23, James Phelan died. The heir apparent had cooperated in his apprenticeship and now succeeded to authority.

The Phelan Business and Staff

The complete transfer of fiscal authority and its desired sequel, continuity, were more easily achieved among the staff than among the family. In the Phelan Building offices the transition had been anticipated and effected. Thomas Mahony was fifty-five when James D. Phelan came to power. Had Mahony a bright son rather than a bright daughter he would have been encouraged to draw the son into the office management. Instead, Mahony accepted the youngest possible threat as a new assistant, understudy, and his ultimate successor. When Mahony welcomed the bright and personable George Welch in 1895, the youngster was only fifteen. Besides Welch's

Portrait of "James Phelan, First President of the First National Gold Bank," by Ossip Permelma. The senior Phelan had organized the bank in 1871. His son advanced to the position of owner-director of all enterprises in 1892. Following World War I, in 1919, James Duval placed this artistic rendering of his father in the First National Director's Room.

Bridging Generations

Thomas Mahony was the senior James Phelan's man first, and Mahony would be recognized handsomely in the old man's will. If he were playful enough to introduce Ellon to young James as well or secure enough to protect her from social slights thereafter, he hardly needed to be foolish enough to conspire secretly against the fully perceived convictions of his employer and benefactor.

Two Speeches Per Day

When he was on the political trail throughout California for Democratic party candidates, James Duval Phelan preferred two speeches per day. In these cases the audiences were different, and he could address the same issues. His record was six speeches in a day for his own Senatorial campaign. For variety and his own intellectual and cultural development he prepared and delivered addresses to cultured audiences on the life and works of Giuseppe Verdi (whom Phelan placed at the head of the Italian romantic school of opera), other masters, and the works of familiar composers. When German American citizens offered San Francisco, as public art, a group of statuary honoring their homeland and memorializing the contributions to civilization by Goethe and Schiller, Phelan delivered the City's acceptance in the form of a public address. His words at the unveiling in Golden Gate Park offered appreciative understanding based upon familiarity with the literature. (His reading here was in translation. He never became a reader of German.) On Irish culture and history, Phelan was at his best.

on-the-job training, the Phelan organization saw him through law school and admission to the California Bar. Mahony prepared Phelan for the position of chief executive officer, then turned to preparing his own replacement. At it for twenty years, the old Irishman drew out the process until the eve of his death in 1912.

Mahony managed Phelan business operations, but not without help. He and the senior Phelan had engaged another young lad, Robert M. McElroy, and charged him with the occasionally challenging job of rent collections. In time he outgrew the job and assumed the position of manager of rental properties. Being young, bright, male, and Irish seemed to be the Phelan office formula for success. Unlike Mahony, McElroy had a qualified son to whom he was able, in time, to assign his own position.

In the McElroy case, the result was much to the young Phelan's liking. When the time came for Robert D. McElroy to assume his father's place, he extended the professionalism of the office. Phelan's confidence in the younger McElroy became so great that Phelan gave McElroy shared power of attorney when he was abroad, and in the end Phelan made McElroy a trustee of his massive estate.

The Phelan offices, then, possessed their own customs and mores. As long as a male offspring was capable, he enjoyed the right of succession. This culture discriminated against outsiders and women and bonded those who were within. For his part, Phelan was the ideal chief executive. His management style included many valuable features: detailed personal knowledge of his own business affairs, close attentiveness to potential problem areas, reliance upon professional advice from within and beyond his own organization, and access to the political and economic decision makers in San Francisco, Washington, and New York. Always he recognized and rewarded his staff for their own precise work, and he encouraged their professional development. Given Phelan's lifestyle, perhaps his most notable sacrifice to his business interests was his foregoing European holidays in the wake of financial downturns. He chose not to be absent when business needed his presence.

When the heat was on, Phelan made the big decisions and guided the implementation policies. He formulated and directed the post-earthquake and fire business strategy that reestablished the Phelan fortune. He personally managed the important renewal of the Roos Brothers lease of their Market Street store. His active hand intervened in all ventures that seemed to be heading into the hands of attorneys and the courts. He redirected them into out-of-court compromises. His personality and sound business sense kept the Phelan enterprises surprisingly free of litigation. This Phelan penchant for avoiding the courts, even when the opposition's nastiness tempted suits of spite, helps explain the personal and professional reserve he maintained toward Garret W. McEnerney, California's premier lawyer and a man with whom he had so much in common. McEnerney was engaged by those who contemplated legal actions against Phelan, but Phelan's personal diplomacy and willingness to compromise kept him out of court with the recognized dean of the California Bar.

Phelan's philosophical position, assisted by the buffer of great wealth, always helped. Rather than taking offense at the business or personal behavior of competitors, Phelan kept money matters at the professional level. He recognized that when pinched, not squealing was difficult. He tolerated the squeals of others and remained silent at his own occasional loss. The bargains he drove were firm, but restrained. He understood that the bargain's longevity depended upon the other fellow's profit margin as well. Phelan welcomed more business, even closely located competition because a city's commercial activities encouraged spin-off success. He enjoyed good times with the best and preached tolerance and endurance during bad times.

Because of his higher political and social standing, Phelan watched commercial indicators from a more elevated perspective. He monitored technological advances, major world developments such as the trade impact of the Panama Canal (not all positive for San Francisco), and shifting world demands on foods and raw materials. Phelan was diligent in his research into the broader economic trends. And like his essays on Carlsbad and Monte Carlo, he always applied his lesson to San Francisco. Phelan brought together within himself the broader view expected of highly placed executives as well as his command of the details of his expansive holdings. The common injunction to Welch and McElroy was to keep nothing from him, and "where is the monthly summary of accounts?"

In gross terms, Phelan inherited a third of an estate that approximated twelve million dollars — an individual total of slightly less than four million dollars. At his death thirty-eight years later he left a personal estate placed at approximately seven million dollars. In between he lived very well and reestablished the fortune destroyed in the 1906 fire. Business was not his sole

James Duval Phelan was the San Franciscan who tendered the citizens' welcome to the touring President William McKinley. Phelan did so in full voice in the grand nave of the City's Union Railroad Depot.

As the chosen articulator of his city's grief he later eulogized McKinley, Warren G. Harding, and Woodrow Wilson. The latter orations he presented over the radio, an invention he welcomed and admired. More sensitive and personal yet was his eulogy of George Sterling, California's disappointed poet whom Phelan loved, patronized, and encouraged.

Mollie Phelan and Alice Phelan Sullivan in the Phelan garden where they had played as children under the watchful eyes of Irish household staff. Two years apart in age, they were in their mid-forties by the time of the 1906 earthquake and fire, which destroyed the mansion and the gardens. Mollie seldom enjoyed sound health as an adult, but outlived her more active sister by nineteen years.

reason for being — an abundant and diverse life was. Business therefore got its due — as much of his attention as he calculated it deserved.

The Phelan Family

After his father's death, Phelan was able to discharge business responsibilities with greater assurance than he did his new family responsibilities. As the new head of the household, he continued the maintenance of ordered daily living through the management of the domestic staff. His mother and his sister Mollie were hardly capable of independent living, not to mention household management. For them he provided the best physical care he could obtain and his personal support and love. The aging mansion in the Mission District belonged to Mollie by their father's will, with their mother Alice retaining the rights of occupancy during her lifetime. In it, Phelan ministered emotional solace to those who had become his dependents. His efforts found no cures, but they were the best available and were well received. Family matters beyond the home were quite the reverse.

Phelan's older sister Alice was coexecutor with him of their father's estate. The old man had understood the inheritance laws of his day and had drawn the children into his own estate planning. Accordingly, he deeded to each of the three children major properties. Though no records of his thinking survive, the results suggest that he started with his Phelan Building for his son. The office building was the flagship of James Phelan's enterprises and should remain with the child who had been groomed to carry them forward. The other major real estate holdings were given to the daughters in as financially balanced a package as he could contrive. What the elder Phelan could not conveniently disentangle from his interlocking assets, he conveyed through his will. The result, after he provided for his wife, was an inheritance for each of their children that constituted a one-third portion in the remaining bulk of a still formidable estate. From this came a family corporation, Heirs of James Phelan, with each child holding a one-third interest and each, officially, holding an equal vote. In practice James D. Phelan acted for his sister Mollie, thus holding two votes, while his brother-in-law, Frank Sullivan, claimed the vote of his wife, Alice.

Phelan's father had drawn Sullivan into the banking activities, and Sullivan served as attorney to the family's Mutual Savings Bank of San Francisco until Phelan and the directors removed him. Had Phelan to deal only with his two sisters, undoubtedly harmony would have prevailed. Phelan was honest and open, as motivated as Alice for a well-managed, productive estate. He and Sullivan could not get along, and his long-suffering sister, Alice, was stuck between them.

Historical judgment of this enduring family turmoil is difficult to make, because the clear records are from Phelan's side. Sullivan's letters are entertaining to read, but quite an indictment of their author. They put into question his emotional stability, his command of his own pen, and certainly basic good manners. The letters to Phelan are tirades, and the longer they extend, the worse Sullivan's initially poor handwriting became. Phelan's standard office practice was to give his brother-in-law's correspondence to one of the office clerks "to be decoded" and typed so he could read it.

There were too many essential differences between Sullivan and Phelan for them to get along. The power differential was one. Its exercise within the 2/3 – 1/3 relationship was intolerable to Sullivan. The getting and spending of money was another basic cause of friction. From Phelan's vantage point, Sullivan's pleasure came in amassing funds. He did so, Phelan thought, through conservation for its own sake. Phelan ridiculed Sullivan among his own friends, wondering if Sullivan expected reincarnation or if he would try to take it all with him. Sullivan's brand of Irish nationalism, likewise, was unpalatable to the more politically conservative constitutional nationalism Phelan accepted.

San Francisco politics also prevented harmony. Sullivan, personally honest himself, supported the Union Labor Party that Phelan and Spreckels literally had removed from office for corruption. Strangely enough, as opposed to his correspondence, Sullivan was a model of personal decorum in Phelan's presence. Yet, because all business matters that flowed through the Heirs of James Phelan Corporation went through Sullivan's hands too, the opportunity for incessant aggravation was perpetual. During his sister's lifetime Phelan persevered as a conciliator, even when Sullivan threatened him with law suits. Sullivan actually brought a gratuitous suit against Phelan when Phelan discharged Sullivan from the bank. It was a suit the press enjoyed, Phelan didn't, and Sullivan finally dropped.

Crisis came when Alice Phelan Sullivan died. Frank Sullivan had entered the Phelan family as a well educated, respected member of a family

Rivalry

When Douglas Hyde, yet to be the first president under Ireland's 1937 Constitution and already chief advocate of the nation's Gaelic revival movement, visited San Francisco, Frank Sullivan and James D. Phelan competed for Hyde's attention and promotion of his cause. Sullivan's militancy, accompanied by a slightly heavier contribution to the cause, determined the contest's result. He did not win by default though. Phelan contributed $1,000 and presented Hyde with a gold knife with his guest's name engraved upon the case, a departure token of appreciation and encouragement. The Sullivans presented Mrs. Hyde with a jeweled broach.

whose history predated the Phelans in California. His wealth was not as great as that he married into, however. At the death of his wife, Sullivan consulted no one, but filed legal documents that conveyed her inheritance to himself without regard for their children, all of whom were of age.

Phelan, in cooperation with his sister's children, contested Sullivan's action. Noël Sullivan, the only son, confronted his father personally and, with Phelan, forced him to back down. From this confrontation came the Alice Phelan Sullivan Corporation with Frank Sullivan serving as president and holding a one-third interest. The children held the remainder. Phelan held one token share in order to serve on the board of directors. Frank Sullivan's independent personal estate was about two million dollars.

Phelan never forgave Sullivan for his action. When Sullivan suffered a stroke in 1925 and remained unable to move or speak for the remainder of his long life, Phelan felt no remorse. To the son Noël he wrote, your father is "a blank." In his memoirs Noël recounted the crisis and, hounded by the specter of debt through the latter part of his adult life, wondered if his father's actions were guided by a financial conservatism that would have protected the capital. Later, perhaps, the children might have become prepared to manage it as prudently as he would have wished. His belated lament was the best explanation Noël Sullivan could offer in defense of his father's actions.

Frank Sullivan had his point of view too. For all Phelan's political and social success, he was sleeping with a woman who was not his wife. What sort of example was that to his own family? When aggravated by being fired from his position as attorney for the Mutual Savings Bank, Sullivan dissipated his anger through an unfocused legal action against Phelan in which he gratuitously named Ellon. He knew her by sight, most likely from her occasional appearance at the Phelan Building where he maintained his offices too.

Charities

The other burden associated with the assumption of authority of the Phelan estate were the obligations of charity and philanthropy. James D. Phelan solved that problem easily. He gave money to everyone who asked and to some who did not. His indoctrination began with the charitable distributions associated with his father's will. An Irish cousin wrote to him, proclaimed her respect and devotion and filed her complaint. When James

Phelan's bequest to the poor of the parish back in Queens County was distributed, she received only one pound! Certainly a man of his stature intended something more dignified.

James Duval Phelan's collected papers include two archival boxes filled with requests for support. The bulk alone suggests that no Catholic fund raiser, from parish bazaars to major building drives, to universities, cultural centers, and restorations of historical cites ever missed Phelan. His approach seemed to have been that he would be happy to contribute if he were never asked to attend. He automatically donated to the Red Cross annually; it was budgeted. He pledged $10,000 toward the restoration of the Santa Barbara Mission to "…give the movement a satisfactory impetus and make up for my refusal of the Chairmanship of the Committee." His original pledge was contingent upon the subscription drive reaching the projected and needed $500,000. When it failed, Phelan illogically reversed himself and gave the Mission the money because they failed rather than succeeded. He found difficulty in saying no.

Phelan served regularly as a committee member of Archdiocesan fund-raising bodies established by Catholic Archbishops. Before World War I he directed a $10,000 check to Santa Clara College from the Heirs of James Phelan. He had to remind the new president of his personal promise to the recently deceased former president. After the War he provided $100,000 for buildings for St. Ignatius College. His exceedingly generous gift seems to have been used for construction of the Jesuit prep school, formerly located adjacent to the college cite on Ignatian Heights in San Francisco. In his letter of conveyance to Reverend Patrick Foot, S. J., he commented ironically on the grandeur of the Jesuits' plans that he expected "will require a disavowal of the vows of poverty."

War charities made Phelan doubly vulnerable. Obligation and patriotism seized him. To various war causes he donated $30,000 in 1918 and 1919. This was in addition to his purchase of an equal amount of liberty bonds, which he considered a poor investment and disposed of soon after the war. Between such major distributions he would provide a new organ for one church and tuition for needy students at other colleges and trade schools. He even bought and donated a London medical practice to a marginally competent Irish cousin who made a failure of it. Phelan saw disaster coming when he learned that while the doctor and his wife were practicing birth control

Still Lacked Good Sense

Years after naming Florence Ellon in a legal action against James Duval Phelan, Frank Sullivan took a solitary trip to Europe. Alice was dead and their children looked to their uncle, not their father, for guidance and companionship. Aboard ship, Sullivan and Ellon chanced to meet. Sixteen years her senior, he apologized for the grief he had caused her, but lacked sufficient good sense simply to lose himself among the crowd.

Catholic Causes

James Duval Phelan's most efficacious contribution to a Catholic cause was a modest $250 in 1915 to Father Richard Collins. Father Collins led a physically vigorous life rather than one of theological study. He was the chaperon and organizer of a historically forgotten Catholic youth group, a paramilitary organization called the League of Cross Cadets. Back when a minority of local Catholics mistakenly assumed that they were threatened by the majority community, the League was organized. It was armed, but it was hardly a quasi-terrorist organization. Patriotism and responsibility to country and church constituted its credo. Fund raising exhibition drills constituted its major activities.

In time, beside its close order drills, the League took summer outings in the Santa Cruz Mountains. Collins rewarded the Senator's generosity by naming their summer encampment Fort Phelan. Collins invited their benefactor to visit the troops in camp, but the press of other business prevented it. What resulted was a fond, non-intrusive relationship between priest and public man that was to conclude under remarkable circumstances in 1930 with Phelan's death.

they had twins. He sustained the doctor's Dublin cousin, a dentist, who was losing his combined home and offices to the bill collectors. The Dubliner and his wife had 11 children and could not meet their expenses. Phelan helped them, maybe because of blood lines, maybe because of their genuinely engaging letters, or maybe for no reason at all. Both medical men were frustrated writers who could not do what Phelan did. Phelan's compassion surely fell short of envy.

Phelan's contributions to Catholic causes were merely the most focused of his donations. They were not his only generosities, nor were they his most generous. Culture, the arts, and artists received millions over his life time. Individual, personal charities displayed Phelan in his most compelling role. No example is more suggestive than his treatment of the widow and two infant children of George Welch. When Phelan's most accomplished chief administrator succumbed to the influenza epidemic of 1918, the Welches, and Phelan too, were unaware that the newborn Welch child was deaf.

Once Phelan discovered the problem, he took a personal interest in the family's welfare that extended beyond any normal sense of duty. He saw to it that his staff unobtrusively assessed the widow's financial circumstances, including an appraisal of her home. Phelan guided prompt and full payment of the life insurance policy and thereafter assumed the support of the family and the special education of the afflicted child. Phelan personally reviewed credentials of schools for deaf children. When one was chosen in St. Louis, he arranged for Mrs. Welch's reception by the Jesuit community, and he imposed upon Missouri's two U.S. senators and a congressman to facilitate her relocation.

No wonder his staff always felt the bonds of loyalty and trust. While trying to tap Edward L. Doheny, the Southern California oil magnate, for one of his charitable fund raisers Phelan put to words the assumptions of his lifetime: "…we who have something, must regard ourselves in the sense of 'trustees'."

Phelan's father was generous and magnanimous in death. The son could afford similar behavior throughout life.

Chapter Five

Campaigning for Mayor

James D. Phelan's family taught him that one's private advancement was associated with the general prosperity of the larger society. Each time the common good advances, one's personal well being improves along with one's investment in the society itself. For the Phelans, banking, insurance, land holding, agriculture, and real estate constituted the investment. Making San Francisco and California more prosperous, better governed, and more attractive to immigrants and tourists constituted the improvements in the larger environment.

This conviction contained one serious point for potential conflict. The family was consummately Irish and Catholic. In San Francisco life the Irish were everywhere. Although social, cultural, and economic diversity characterized the Irish in California, the image to the outside (perhaps to those on the inside as well) was that of working class status, devotion to Catholic doctrine, and acceptance of corrupt political machines.

From the vantage point of the San Francisco Irish voting masses, the Phelans were orthodox and loyal (and therefore reliable) on religion. James and Alice were inconspicuous in politics and generous with their personal charity. The Phelans, without too close a look, appeared just like the other Irish — only with a lot of money.

One additional difference existed within the home that contributed to James D. Phelan's political philosophy. This difference liberated his mind and elevated his commitment. But it also constituted the wedge that was to separate him occasionally from his natural political constituency, the critical mass of Irish Catholic voters, most of whom were working class. Phelan's

The year 1902 was difficult for Mollie Phelan. Her mother died after great and lengthy suffering. Mollie's own emotional life had been fragile since her sister's engagement and marriage twenty years earlier. Her brother, James Duval Phelan, pictured with her, remained the sustaining influence throughout her troubled life.

Bohemian Club

His family's economic and social position in the city (and therefore in the West) made young James Duval Phelan somewhat over-qualified for the presidency of the Bohemian Club that he assumed in 1891. What has since become the world-famous, exclusive club for America's power elite still enjoyed a more artistic, if not riotous, membership. Journalists, writers, playwrights, and gourmets then characterized the Bohemians' public image much as today wielders of national political and international economic and diplomatic power do. Then it was Phelan the poet, essayist, and buoyant host who set the Bohemians' standards for membership. His knowledge, organizational ability, and progressive outlook qualified him for leadership and fit well into the Bohemian Club's slow transition into the gathering place for men of authority and power.

During his second year as Bohemian Club president (1892), Phelan's father died, thus elevating him permanently to the pinnacle of the American West's financial elite. James D. Phelan's own substance had already placed him at this point of social and cultural lift-off.

political formation took place in a family environment dominated by the view that political corruption (and all dishonesty) was intolerable. Public safety, order, and stability took precedence. Without such an ordered society, justice and equity were impossible.

These underlying premises, corollaries to the concept of personal stake within an advancing common good, accompanied young James D. Phelan's political coming of age. The heir apparent to the family fortune was quite well prepared to explore San Francisco's political domain on his own. His resources, besides independent means and integrity, included a gifted and cultivated speaking voice and platform presence. He commanded an academic knowledge of alternate models for urban management. His patience in the pursuit of long range objectives was endless, and he felt comfortable and at ease with himself among individuals and groups from all walks of life. He soon discovered his knack for organizing people and resources to accomplish goals that extended beyond those individuals could reach on their own.

Personally, young Phelan possessed a strong sense of loyalty to his family, his friends, and those with whom he became associated. After his father's death no one directed or restrained him. No one enjoyed a claim on his time and attention. He decided what matters deserved his interest and concern.

James D. Phelan entered politics from the top. His first activities clustered around the civic-social-improvement club nexus. The Bohemian Club was rising to its reputation for exclusiveness and power membership, but literary or artistic talent and some money still sufficed. Phelan enjoyed the city's Bohemian Club facilities and summered at the Grove on the Russian River. At the club he gathered his friends and their expanding circle of business and cultural leaders. In 1891 he became president of the Bohemian Club — not bad for age thirty.

Throughout the 1890s young Phelan tried to help rid his beloved San Francisco of political corruption. As a member of the Citizens' Defense Association he advanced progressive reforms and offered alternate leadership to the notorious Blind Boss Christopher Buckley. Phelan worked within the Democratic party which always claimed his loyalty. Phelan led the young reform element that struggled to establish the secret ballot as a means of driving the Blind Boss from power.

Because of his artistic and cultural interests and free time, Phelan was appointed vice president of the California Commission for the 1893 World's

Columbian Exposition in Chicago. The illness of the president, Irving M. Scott, who was president of the Union Iron Works, allowed Phelan to take charge of California's exhibit and participation. As the capstone to the successful event, Phelan returned $50,000 to the state treasury from his original authorized budget of $300,000. He had come in under budget, certainly a novelty in any age and a point of merit and public notoriety for the young political reformer and patron of the arts. As a continuation of his successful engagement at the Chicago fair, Phelan served as chairman of San Francisco's own Mid-Winter Fair in 1894. Through his contacts in Chicago, Phelan obtained the cooperation of major exhibition directors to relocate in San Francisco for the city's Mid-Winter Fair. The purpose was to extend the Columbian Exposition to San Francisco, particularly to bring national attention to San Francisco and the Pacific Coast. Phelan believed San Francisco should be viewed as an attractive place to visit or a desirable place to relocate permanently. The mildness of the winters was Phelan's primary selling point.

This thinking served as a basis for Phelan's grand designs for San Francisco. Political corruption had to end. San Francisco had to become safe, prosperous, and beautiful. Nothing less was worthy of the physical endowments that nature had conferred upon Phelan's birth city.

Visibility and Reform

Reform politics in San Francisco needed Phelan more than he needed the nascent political movement. He could have remained apolitical like his father and restricted his exercise of power to the economic domain. However, he liked the political arena and derived personal satisfaction from the exercise of his always-improving political skills. He liked thinking and planning, he liked organizing, he liked overcoming opposition, and he liked advancing his dream for a San Francisco unsurpassed in civic order, beauty, and honesty.

In the 1890s, Phelan was the city's best public speaker. He was among the most knowledgeable on the subject of urban planning and reform. Most important, among young reform-minded individuals, he was the only one with the ethnic-religious affiliation of the city's absolute majority: the Irish and the Catholics. Highly politicized, their incidence of voting was high and their preference for their own kind was likewise high. San Francisco was a diverse society: economic power was in the hands of the businessman, and

Chicago's World Fair

The World's Columbian Exposition, more popularly known as the Chicago World's Fair, commemorated the 400th anniversary of the discovery of the New World. As well, it marked the arrival of the United States at the threshold of world power status. The nation's continental boundaries had been secured and its scattered, diverse, and abundant citizenry and resources were fully connected by the most advanced transportation and communications networks of the age. Celebration mixed with self-congratulations and an excited and expectant pause before the American assault upon the twentieth century. Phelan himself was primed for the immediate role he was to play for California and then for San Francisco.

Christopher A. "Blind Boss" Buckley represented what James Duval Phelan detested — corruption of government. Buckley's biographer, William A. Bullough, wrote, "Buckley may have had his own ideals but … they seemed not to get in the way.… Chris Buckley did not corrupt San Francisco. He just took it as it was, enjoyed it, and made the most of it.… By his own standard, he made good on his father's legacy: the state of California to make a living in!"

Phelan did not attend Buckley's lavish funeral in 1922.

political power was rather loosely, and at times absentmindedly, held in the hands of the immigrants and their children. The result was that no one was in charge of San Francisco. From the vantage point of the young reformers, this was among the reasons for the corruption surrounding the notorious political life of Blind Boss Buckley.

Phelan advanced his political visibility and name recognition while advancing the central reform cause of the 1890s: charter revision. The organic law by which San Francisco was governed had been designed in the pre-urban era. The state legislature held legal authority for the management of San Francisco much like California counties held responsibility for unincorporated areas within their boundaries a hundred years later.

The young reformer's charter revision efforts brought him into contact with more and more San Franciscans. The process also became intellectually stimulating. By the time San Francisco finally passed a new charter, the meetings, the arguments, and the reports from experts, business, and labor lobbies all constituted an intellectual ferment that heightened civic understanding and commitment.

Bossism under Buckley had been on the run following a Chinatown killing by one of Buckley's collectors, "Little Pete." Buckley fled to Canada before being arrested for tampering with the judicial system, and San Francisco experienced its periodic outrage at corruption. The immediate political reaction was an anti-bossism, anti-machine surge that brought two nonpartisan candidates into the mayor's office, each for the standard two-year term. Levi R. Ellert and Adolph Sutro were both honest, hard working, and well intentioned. From the viewpoint of the young reformers, both also were totally ineffectual. So poor was the administrative performance of the Grand Old Man Sutro that his lack of political savvy and his proclivity for vainglorious bombast tended to discredit the reform movement itself.

In reality, Buckley's lieutenant, Sam Rainey, re-gathered his chief's dispersed factions, exercised control through the board of supervisors, and waited for Buckley's return following a favorable decision of a higher California court. Rainey controlled a sizable number of Democratic regulars and enjoyed considerable influence within the city's fire department. As the 1896 election approached the reformers and nonpartisan activists still were without the reforms they sought despite having deposed Buckley and having elected two successive reform administrations. Nothing had changed.

The "Solid Nine" on the board of supervisors continued to vote their personal interests and the interests of the "bosses." Fiscal mismanagement remained rampant with merchants being unable to obtain payment from the city because of recurring year-end deficits. Gambling, vice, and more general crime seemed to be growing. The city even plunged itself into darkness, unable to pay its own electricity bill.

Seizing the Moment

James Duval Phelan's moment arrived on the night of August 12, 1896, before the merchant-backed Citizen's Charter Association. Officially, he spoke on behalf of the fourth attempt for a new city charter. Phelan belonged to most, if not all, civic groups whose object was the political reform of San Francisco. The active and well-financed Merchants' Association created the Citizen's Charter Association and Phelan led it. The reformers' objective was to have San Francisco voters approve the reform charter then being debated. The larger political reality was that the reform movement to which Phelan was so committed was at a turning point. The voting public had given reform its chances in City Hall and San Francisco had little or nothing to show for such virtue. Now, with the passage of time eroding the public's outrage at Buckley, older and set voting patterns threatened to reemerge under the guidance of Sam Rainey and his cronies. Also, because 1896 was a presidential election year, the local machines could expect to ride on the coattails of the national parties that always brought regular party support to the polls.

The reformers' anxieties were exaggerated. The two regular parties continued to split. The Regular Democrats (Buckley-Rainey bossism) did not revive sufficiently to extend their control beyond their old power bases. For the fall election they concentrated on opposition to the new charter that, once again, was being considered by the voters. Through charter change, the anti-boss reformers attempted to restructure the city government, and in so doing constituted a serious threat to the old corrupters. Their nominee for mayor, the Regular Democrat, was Supervisor Joseph I. Diamond, who also received the nomination of the Populist party that had evidenced national vitality, though only moderately so in San Francisco.

Phelan received the nomination for mayor from the reform wing of the Democratic party and found his Republican opposition, like the Democrats,

Sutro's Administration

A local journalist and old school friend of Phelan, George J. Duraind, commenting on Sutro's "vast ignorance of municipal administration" concluded, "Administrative ignorance is often worse than administrative corruption, and the creature of a wily but cautious Boss may often be less of a menace to a city than the saint of a reform political party." This was an accurate characterization of San Francisco politics at the moment of Phelan's approach.

Phelan and Yorke

James Duval Phelan and Peter C. Yorke were contemporaries, Yorke being three years younger. Yorke was born in Galway, Ireland, and educated for the priesthood there and in the United States. In San Francisco Archbishop Patrick Riordan recognized him early as the most gifted among his clergy. In 1896 Yorke was the Archbishop's fair-haired boy, with a bright future ahead of him in the Church hierarchy. Only later did the young man's erratic behavior and, perhaps, personality flaws surface.

Like Phelan, Yorke was well educated, more so in the formal sense though within clerical lines. He, likewise, was a voracious reader. Phelan read far more widely in politics, public affairs, science, art, history, and literature. Yorke's focus was Catholic doctrine and Irish culture. From there he extended himself in a practical manner. He gathered his intellectual resources not from English language publications alone. His papers revealed notes from his readings in Gaelic, Spanish, French, Latin, and Greek. His travels, limited by his means and clerical assignments, included Ireland and America. Phelan, of course, was familiar with the art, culture, and heritage of the Western World.

Both men were attractive on the lecture platform: Phelan was compact (5 feet, 7 1/2 inches, and of medium build), proper, and always well groomed and splendidly tailored. Yorke was considerably bigger, powerful in stature and delivery. Both men commanded attention by their presence and held their audiences by clarity, wit, and subject matter command. Yorke was rough and devastating while Phelan was sensitive and accurate.

split between regulars and reformers. The Regular Republicans nominated Charles S. Taylor, a candidate the Irish and Catholic voting block found utterly repulsive. He had been popularly linked with the organized bigotry of the loud, but impotent American Protective Association. Charles Laumeister rounded out the field for the Reform Republicans. Like the leadership of the Republican reformers, he was a popular merchant who enjoyed the respect and support of the progressive element within the Republican party.

Phelan's advantages were numerous. Reform was still on the attack despite the poor showing of the post-Buckley administrations. A central issue of the campaign for mayor was charter revision. This allowed the reformers to attack the structure and organization of urban government that the bosses were able to manipulate. Conversely, the regular wings of the major parties, particularly the Democrats, were required to wage a defensive battle for the status quo. They tried to draw upon traditional working-class and ethnic alliances to protect their interests and to ensure their survival. They tried to include newly organized labor groups and labor's most vocal and dynamic spokesman, Father Peter C. Yorke.

Phelan, of course, was the strongest possible candidate for the Democratic reformers. He was the best thinker on the subject of urban reform, the outstanding articulator of the new ideas of the day, and eloquent herald of San Francisco's destiny. Perhaps the most tangible asset Phelan was able to bring to the reformers was his affinity with the city's largest and most politicized voting block — the Irish and the Catholics. In the upcoming national census of 1900, the San Francisco Irish were to number 95,000, the second largest group in the city, only 6,000 fewer than the Germans. In the religious census of 1906, Catholics constituted 116,000 in number while only 22,000 were Protestants of all denominations. Jews were few in number.

The general public, the Irish masses, and the Jewish and Protestant businessmen supported Phelan at face value: an upper class reformer who sprang from the Irish Catholic community. Father Peter C. Yorke, local Irish Catholicism's self-appointed guardian of tribal membership watched and judged more carefully.

Throughout the 1896 mayoral campaign, Yorke's personal psychological imperative was to destroy the candidacy of Charles S. Taylor because of his past association with the anti-Catholic organization, the American Protective Association. As the popular editor of the Catholic newspaper, the *Mon-*

itor, Yorke ensured that the Regular Republican candidate would receive no Catholic votes. Yorke's gifts for wit, sarcasm, and invective were hardly engaged given the ordinary quality of his target, yet no Catholic readers of Yorke's Catholic paper doubted where their entertaining champion stood.

Even more likely, Yorke's contacts within the Irish community would have known of James Phelan's relationship with Florence Ellon. Yorke was the rising star within the clergy and a highly engaging one at that. His personal company was good fun for the numerous other Irish assistant pastors. His official positions as editor of the Catholic *Monitor* and Chancellor to the Archbishop enhanced his attractiveness. That not one of these friends and aspiring associates ever saw Phelan, the presumed leading Catholic layman, at Sunday mass could not have been unknown to Yorke.

Phelan's own household staff and his office personnel constituted such a close and personally loyal band that they would have felt no compulsion to reveal young James's midnight dinners atop the Phelan Building with Ellon. Those who provided the gourmet meals from the kitchens of the Bohemian Club or the Pacific Union would have known too. And their bonding to Phelan was far less. Yorke and his fellow priests ministered to these men and enjoyed leisure time among them as well.

All else being equal, Catholic priests did not go out of their way to denounce wayward members of their flock. In Yorke's case, Phelan was the candidate running for mayor in 1896 closest to those with whom he identified, if a bit refined and presumably in sin. Phelan was before the voting public for the first time and had a rather empty record. If he wasn't the most ardent of Catholics or even Irish nationalists, his disposition and his affinity were positive. Besides, Yorke's target was Taylor, the man he identified with the bigoted American Protective Association. That misguided hate group had given Yorke his start in San Francisco by allowing the gregarious priest to exterminate it. Yorke's misfortune was that he never rose above the significance of that first public triumph.

Phelan wisely campaigned for mayor without referring to the new charter on the same ballot that Yorke and organized labor opposed. Phelan simply campaigned for good government, as the charter advanced, without referring to the document itself. This allowed Irish Catholics to vote for Phelan and not violate the benchmarks set out on their political landscape by both their political priest and their political labor leaders.

Father Peter C. Yorke distrusted those who were not of his own economic and social class. Anyone who chose to disagree or challenge Yorke's views was, as the years passed, considered by Yorke to be morally loathsome. Unmeasured and uncomplicated devotion to Ireland and Irish nationalism along with hatred of England became Yorke's measure of Irish Americans and, to a lesser extent, all other Americans too. Yorke required complete acceptance of Catholic doctrine.

Yorke had not yet immigrated to San Francisco at the time James Duval Phelan delivered a public address commending the English Prime Minister, William E. Gladstone, as a positive force in Irish affairs. A voracious reader, Yorke may have read Phelan's youthful oration later. Phelan's non-conventional views had been opposed by the San Francisco Irish at the time, however, and certainly would have been brought to Yorke's attention.

Phelan made himself the most distinguished figure of the campaign and the most promising hope for the redemption of San Francisco. He propelled himself onto center stage by his oratorical success. On September 1, 1896, he delivered the opening address to the Mechanics Institute Fair. The effect was electrifying, and his speech received extended coverage in the press. Political observers cited the speech as key to making Phelan mayor. With drama, clarity, and credibility, young Phelan painted for San Franciscans his own imperial dream for the city he loved. Beauty and humanity were the values of San Francisco's future; they were the values that should triumph over the sordid practices of San Francisco's past. He compared San Francisco's opportunities to the achievements of Athens at the time of Pericles and to the transformation of Paris that took place within the lifetimes of many present before him. Deftly he painted a glowing word picture of an incomparable imperial city, the commercial and cultural capital of the Pacific. To attain so lofty a goal all citizens would have to work and act in harmony.

Phelan believed the city should be rich, its citizens a model of civic responsibility — educated, healthy, prosperous, and cultured. New schools and libraries, public utilities, monuments and parks — all of these rested upon San Franciscans seizing their own destiny.

Chapter Six
Mayor of San Francisco

The election returns gave focus and definition to James Duval Phelan's life and fixed his identity in the public mind. "Turn-of-the-Century Mayor of San Francisco" identified him in a manner he appreciated, even though his enduring economic and cultural achievements were certainly equal to those in the political arena. His 1896 mandate was a strong endorsement by the electorate. Nonetheless, it had its collateral limitations. The public had previously voted into office reform administrations with no result. Also, the continuing progressive struggle for a reform charter for San Francisco had not succeeded. Phelan had remained quiet on the issue during his own campaign for mayor. This strategy resulted in his gaining twice as many votes as the charter did. Thus, he ended up in office, but without the reform charter he felt was necessary for the city's regeneration.

Phelan's position was not unlike that of Sutro and Ellert upon their taking office. The most substantial difference was Phelan's superior understanding of the political system in which he was to play his part. Phelan's immediate concern was to alter the structure of that system in such a way that his knowledge and hard work could count for something.

The standard, long-established corrupt prerogatives of the board of supervisors included setting the rates for the utility services and the awarding of franchises to corporations wishing to do business with and within the city. Expansion of water, gas, electricity, transportation, and communications services was critical to a growing city. The services were, as well, highly profitable to the corporations and to the politicians who approved or disapproved of the rates and new construction.

Here is the James Duval Phelan who successfully contended for mayor of San Francisco. In 1896 he was thirty-five years of age, well educated, civic-minded, informed, and inspired with a vision for an imperial San Francisco. To his beloved city he was to bring the most advanced planning of his times. He intended even to replace San Francisco with an idealized version of itself — worthy of its own geography.

San Francisco's Palace Hotel has its own history, as rich as its physical adornments. Before 1900, carriages entered the court, discharged their passenger-guests, and departed. Resident complaints of the smell of horses and their droppings forced change. The court had its garden added, and the carriages remained outdoors.

Under the old organic act Phelan and the reformers wanted to replace, the established practice within the board of supervisors was quite direct. Most of the members simply took private money for their votes. In fact, it was expected that they do so. That was how public business was transacted. They owed their election and therefore their favored position to the community bosses. The bosses or their intermediaries normally interacted with the representatives of the utilities and other franchise seekers and spread their bribes ("consulting fees") among the cooperating supervisors. Phelan opposed this system, first because it was corrupt and, second, because such limited vision blocked the development of San Francisco as the Pacific capital of his dreams.

Boodling Board

Phelan's first major excitement in office and his first chance to exercise his enthusiasm for reform concerned the "Boodling Board of Supervisors." Phelan's energy in this case was exceeded only by that of Superior Court Judge William T. Wallace, an ally of good government who had put Buckley on the run. In a surprise decision Judge Wallace ruled that the board of supervisors had violated the law in their previous fixing of the water rates. His ruling held that by so doing the board had forfeited its very right to the occupancy of their positions as supervisors!

Phelan was convinced that eight of the twelve Supervisors were corrupt, and while his prudence and his position would not have allowed him to initiate this sort of action, he welcomed it and followed up on their removal.

The organic act that Phelan tried to supersede with a new charter allowed him, in consultation with California Governor James H. Budd, to replace the supervisors. Phelan kept the four supervisors who were honest and appointed eight new members to the board, all of whom were more than acceptable to the progressive reform elements of the city. They were men of standing within the community, men with whom Phelan held shared convictions on the question of civic duty and responsibility. Not only did Phelan appoint the new board, he had them seated and doing business at the places of the old members when the discredited supervisors appeared.

The Boodling Board appealed Judge Wallace's decision to oust them, and, on a Saturday night ahead of the scheduled Monday board of supervisors meeting, they entered City Hall, seized the supervisors' chambers, and determined to hold their ground. Outside City Hall an unruly gathering of their supporters, referred to as "The Push," stood by in case of fights.

Inside, the supervisors spent the Sabbath eating, drinking, and holding their chairs. During a make-believe all night session they kept warm with more whiskey and a few blankets. Phelan arrived on Monday morning after consulting with his legal advisers. He brought along the city police who removed the squatting "supervisors." In the words of Phelan's journalist friend George Duraind, "It took the police just ten minutes to root out the whole nasty crowd from the Chambers, bag and baggage, like a porter kicking out into the streets a lot of old ash cans."

Nonetheless, the corruption that had gained such a stranglehold on the political institutions of San Francisco was not easily vanquished. On appeal, the Boodling Board made a successful comeback. Following protracted legal action the Wallace judgment was reversed and the boodlers were back in office. From Phelan's point of view this was another display of what he already knew: corrupt supervisors were not going to roll over with one push, bossism still lived, and corporate influence sustained the corrupt status quo. Also this combination of politics and corporate interests placed the best legal minds within the corrupters camp, and while Judge Wallace provided Phelan with an exciting opportunity, the State judiciary was not in the camp of reform.

Charter Reform

Fortunately for Phelan, life's reversals weighed lightly upon him. In this case he seized the chance to give reform exciting press well beyond San Francisco for he knew of no other chief executive who had replaced the elected Supervisors in a judicially sanctioned action and then used the police to escort the deposed to the streets. Heady stuff for a reformer still in his thirties.

Phelan's academic review of urban affairs taught him that ousting individual grafters might be gratifying, but permanent reform required restructuring the political system. For San Francisco to advance, that long-debated charter had to be engineered past the voters. Until he achieved that success, the most he could hope to do was prevent the grossest forms of public theft.

Phelan's own charter advocacy in early 1896 and his observation of the new charter's defeat during the campaign energized him for one more try at

When James D. Phelan was mayor it became his custom to host annually all the heads of the city departments. After they had dined and refreshed themselves freely he called for their oral delivery of annual reports required under his reform charter of San Francisco. To the Bohemian Club, which he served as president, Phelan gathered the more select, often the literary and cultural personalities of the day and the twenty or so with whom he chose to share their talents.

Reform Attempts before Phelan

James D. Phelan came of age politically amidst the struggles over charter revision. San Francisco was governed according to the Consolidation Act of the City and County of San Francisco passed by the State Legislature in 1856, five years before his birth and when his father was busy establishing the family fortune. When Phelan was completing his college degree at St. Ignatius, the Legislature attempted (McClure Charter) to simplify the organic law by bringing together all the amendments and relevant acts of the legislature so that at least the organic legislation was available in one place. The State Supreme Court declared that practical effort to be unconstitutional.

Three subsequent attempts also failed, the latest one in 1896, largely because of public apathy. The issue itself was always legalistic and quite tedious. The stand-up traditional politicians and their manipulators, in cooperation with the representatives of the corporations, added their weight to the opposition largely because of their own self interests. Also, not infrequently the drafters of the various charters unwittingly offended one interest group or another and thereby ushered their brain child on to political oblivion.

charter reform. He was convinced the job could be done and its success was mandatory for any permanent improvement in San Francisco.

The old Consolidation Act had spawned nearly 200 modifying amendments that were scattered over forty years of legislation. No one really understood the Act, portions were in conflict with one another, and it allowed the State to interfere with the internal affairs of the city. Further, legislative and executive functions were mingled and conferred upon the supervisors. Amidst this confusion thrived the corruptionists, in and out of city government, whom Phelan and his reform colleagues so despised.

The Consolidation Act put no one in charge of city government and as a result no one could really be held responsible for inefficiency or corruption. Corruption bred public distrust and from public distrust logically followed resistance to taxation. The Treasury would be squandered or stolen anyway!

Under the Act, Phelan as mayor was bereft of power. He wanted to be responsible and to have power to act for San Francisco's welfare. Therefore, he threw himself fully into a new charter struggle in 1898. With the Merchants' Association, he initiated each legal step that the charter-creating process required, and en route he addressed each reason why the process had failed during the political campaign of 1896 when the voters placed him in City Hall, but rejected the document for which he actually stood.

First, Phelan called into being the Committee of One Hundred whose task was to lay down the principles upon which the government of San Francisco would be based. Next, the Committee was to draft the actual document. For membership on the Committee Phelan relied heavily, but not exclusively, upon members of the Merchants' Association.

Previous charter attempt failed because of apathy, entrenched interests of the boss-corporate nexus, apprehensions of school teachers, organized labor, and Father Peter C. Yorke's provocative expressions of concern for Catholic and workers' rights. Besides noting the failed charter's inadequate attention to education, Yorke made clear that labor had not been properly consulted. With his usual sharp pen the priest noted for the voting Irish that San Francisco did not belong to the merchants alone. If the merchants wished to construct a document to govern all the people, then they should consult with the people — particularly if they wished the endorsement at the polls of those very citizens.

With the interest of labor, education, and Yorke's Catholic Irish in mind, two high-profile, if self-neutralizing, labor leaders were included among those from beyond the Merchants' Association membership. Walter McArthur was the militant leader of the Sailors' Union and editor of the *Coast Seamen's Journal*. More in keeping with Phelan's thinking on civic matters was Patrick H. McCarthy, head of the Carpenters' Union, a political appointee of Phelan and much later a mayor of San Francisco himself. To many he was more conservative than the merchants themselves.

When the Employers' Association locked out McCarthy's unionized construction workers and denied them the lumber they needed, McCarthy used their treasury to build their own sawmill. He set the union up as an independent business. Then he demanded admission into the very Employers' Association that had locked him out! His objective as a committee member was to have the charter and the city support higher wages and more humane conditions, namely an eight-hour day. The committee met McCarthy's limited objective. When McArthur's more cerebral concerns were not met, the two disagreed publicly. McCarthy spoke for and to the largest city voting bloc (unionized at that), the Irish. McArthur, a Scot, had a smaller union following, of Scandinavians, and a paper that circulated far more restrictively than Yorke's Catholic weekly.

In essence then, what Phelan did was to call into being a charter drafting committee consisting of those who shared his perspective and constituted his strongest support base. Then he added individuals whose views and professional associations would convey the appearance of more broadly based public consultation. Phelan screened out the bosses and the political cranks. The plan worked, and all viable points of view were heard during the extended deliberations of the Committee of One Hundred. In the end, Phelan's views, shared by the Merchants' Association, prevailed.

Phelan and the Merchants' Association were well prepared for the next legally required step: the popular election of a Board of Freeholders who were officially required to present the charter to the citizens for a popular referendum. Phelan and the Association selected a much tighter group, screening out unwanted opinion. Needless to say, McCarthy made the cut; McArthur did not. At this point Phelan had established the ground work, labor was neutralized, and Father Yorke was pacified. Phelan and the Merchants' Asso-

Patrick H. McCarthy, progressive labor leader and Phelan protégé, represented the Irish working class in San Francisco and later he too became mayor. Considered by his destructors to be more conservative than the Merchants themselves, he pursued an agenda to improve the life of the working men in San Francisco. In this he was successful.

Collapsible City Hall

San Francisco's City Hall construction began in 1871 and continued from one partial annual appropriation to the next until 1898. Occupied by Phelan in 1900, it virtually collapsed in the earthquake of 1906. City Hall was a briefly occupied monument to bad management, bad taste, and no planning—fiscal or otherwise. Only the construction company of Shea and Shea seemed to profit, having made the twenty-seven-year construction project a lifetime sinecure, less of course the kickbacks that perpetual refunding through the boards of supervisors had required.

ciation still faced two formidable enemies of the new Charter: traditional voter apathy and the old political-corporate combination.

To overcome apathy Phelan threw himself into the battle to educate the general public on the values of a new charter. City government should be responsible and that responsibility should be fixed on the mayor. The State should not manage city affairs. Civil service, the popular initiative, and referendum should become part of urban political life for the twentieth century.

Phelan wrote and spoke to all who would heed him and to many who would not. Besides that, Phelan and the Merchants set December 26, the day after Christmas, as voting day for their slate of freeholders. Election day was not to be a holiday. Thus, members of the working class would be required to get up an hour earlier or lose part of a day's pay to vote. Later Phelan was accused of closing the polls at 5:00 P.M., one hour earlier than announced. Historical documentation seems unavailable to demonstrate whether Phelan and the merchants were catching on to the methods of the bosses.

The reality was that those who were dedicated to the new charter in-the-making would take the extra effort to turn out and vote for the Phelan-Merchants' slate of freeholders. That meant those who were committed to the charter from the start. They were the activists. Thus, Phelan shifted the apathy problem into the camp of the charter's opponents.

The Phelan Charter

The result was what Phelan sought. The Phelan Charter, or more properly the "1900 Charter" because of its effective date, increased substantially the mayor's powers. It eliminated those previously exercised by the California Governor and Legislature to appoint officials and to enact legislation for the city. The board of supervisors was enlarged to eighteen, elected at large, and not elected according to the old ward subdivision. The supervisors' powers were more clearly delineated as a legislative body with budgetary duties. The mayor became the executive. Civil service was instituted and the functioning departments of the city were rationalized on a businesslike basis with lines of reporting and responsibility.

The Phelan Charter set the pace for progressive urban reform, an academic subject matter that American historians and political scientists have studied ever since. The document also became the guide for San Francisco's civic life into the twentieth century. Phelan had persuaded San Franciscans to expect that their government should be both honest and efficient.

Having matured in a personal environment where large amounts of money were regularly used to create even more commanding resources, Phelan came naturally to big spending by government as an investment in the civic future. The future he saw for a well-governed San Francisco was beautified, safe, secure, and healthy. His vision of the future would draw into San Francisco increased population and an expanded tourist industry.

He therefore addressed what even the bosses had never dared to try: heavier annual budgets and heavier bonded indebtedness. He did not need to look beyond the incredible physical shambles of his own City Hall and its executive office. Phelan scrutinized city expenditures himself until the new supervisors elected under the 1900 Charter came into office. He vetoed extravagant payments, demanded competitive bids with the contracts going to the lowest (not the highest) bidder. All of these actions received good press and with the return of general prosperity and the penetration of Phelan's message on progress, as well as the threat of competition from Los Angeles, the result was greater public inclination to spend city funds. Also, Phelan's personal example hardly hurt.

Throughout, Phelan paid lip service to maintaining the traditional tax limit ($1 per $100 tax evaluation) which has led California historians to question his consistency. The improvements he wanted could not be accomplished without spending more money, which required more taxes or more bonded indebtedness. In fact, Phelan did both. He spent more tax money on an annual basis and he increased the bonded indebtedness of San Francisco.

The bosses did neither, and the city was a disgrace to its setting and an embarrassment to its forward-looking populace. The streets lacked uniform paving, the sewers backed up during flood conditions or at high tide, going to the city hospital was an act of courage or despair, and moving from one place in the city to another was always inconvenient and uncomfortable, sometimes dangerous. Attacking these problems, Phelan increased spending as he could within the set limit. One effort was to set corporate tax rates more in line with the value of their properties. Also, Phelan believed that because improved streets and sidewalks helped business, the businesses should pay half of the improvement costs.

Mayor Phelan enjoyed patronizing young artists and highlighting their accomplishments. To do both and to give the city a taste of what a larger city beautification plan might offer, he commissioned the award-winning Berkeley sculptor Douglas Tilden to create a fountain recognizing California's admission to the federal union. (See Chapter Sixteen for a photo of the statue.)

Art for the City

Mayor Phelan directed additional personal gifts to San Francisco in the form of public libraries. Later he would entice Andrew Carnegie into participation on the grand scale, but on his own Phelan donated libraries to Laguna Honda Hospital (then the Almshouse), Mission High School, Girls' High School, and a branch library in the Mission District. Andrew Carnegie provided three-quarters of a million dollars for a major library. Sugar magnate Claus Spreckels donated the temple of music at Golden Gate Park. Phoebe Hearst funded the architectural competition that sparked the progressive enthusiasm of the next decade in which Phelan played so extended a part. The result was the production of Daniel Burnham's Plan and the City Beautiful movement envisioning the comprehensive physical redesign of San Francisco itself.

To maintain and advance the physical well being of his city, Phelan increased the bonded indebtedness some sixty times over during his three terms in office. When he left office the total was still a modest $11 million. The historical question is really not why Phelan was so conservative in trying to implement his dream, but why the old bosses with a nonresponsive system to manipulate had not figured out how to exact big money through government corruption. In essence, the bosses sold political favors cheaply. Had they been bigger corrupters, Phelan would have had a greater comparative chance to use honesty and efficiency in the creation of a comfortable, healthy, prosperous, and beautiful San Francisco.

By 1899 Phelan induced the supervisors to set two bond elections in which the voters approved multi-million-dollar bond issues. The bonds were approved to cover a new city hospital, an extension of the Golden Gate Park panhandle north to the Presidio and east to Market Street and Van Ness Avenue, a new sewer system, and seventeen new schools.

Phelan had convinced the properly skeptical citizens that government was trustworthy and that progress was so promising that they should pay for it. Unfortunately not every citizen agreed. A taxpayers' suit halted the proceedings when the California Supreme Court ruled that the city's bond elections were void. The elections had been conducted under enabling legislation that had preceded the 1900 Charter, not according to the Charter provisions. To Phelan and his progressive reformers, the decision must have appeared disingenuous. The bond election was conducted before the Charter was scheduled to go into effect. Nonetheless, Phelan's effort miscarried.

The mayor's prestige increased with each initiative under the new charter: civil service, centralized education with an appointed school board (his innovation in appointing a woman was well received), expanded public works, and improved law enforcement. As long as his basic support structure of the merchant progressives and the socially well-to-do retained the acquiescence, if not the good will, of the working-class Irish and Catholics, Phelan and his honest and efficient government remained highly regarded. Phelan could claim a broad and popular mandate for his reforms and fight his opposition as the corrupting bond of bossism and the corporate giants. While his progress in City Hall continued, he was unaware that Father Yorke, the Irish champion of the working-class, watched with disfavor and awaited his chance.

Political Handicaps and Controversy

Throughout his long and active political career James D. Phelan struggled against the weight of two serious handicaps. His support base was always in a minority status, first as a progressive wing of the Democratic party in San Francisco, then as the Democratic party of California. At the time Phelan's career advanced to state and national levels, the California Republican party enjoyed majority status.

His second political handicap was very personal and very close to home: the Catholic priest, Father Peter C. Yorke. Yorke came to hate, utterly, James D. Phelan. Yorke, when removed from his editorship of the *Monitor* by Archbishop Patrick Riordan, established his personal weekly publication, the pro-labor Irish *Leader*. And on its pages Yorke never missed his chance to criticize and defame Phelan before his natural ethnic-religious constituency. Only Yorke's death in 1925 allowed Phelan to live undisturbed. Until then Yorke's attacks had been so vicious, so foul, and so unrelenting that one wonders if Yorke, rather than the issues over which the two differed, was the problem.

The public divergence erupted during Phelan's reelection year of 1898. (Mayoral terms were two years until the 1900 Charter extended them to four.) It stemmed from Yorke's continued preoccupation with the defunct American Protective Association.

On the San Francisco waterfront, a refuge for sailors, the Ladies' Seamen's Home, was an established institution. The women's organization, mostly mothers and wives of seamen, maintained and managed the facility on property leased from the City and County of San Francisco. It had been federal property that was given to the city for its current use. With a lease coming due, the organizers applied to the board of supervisors for renewal.

A small Catholic women's group, the leader of which had been associated with outreach activities directed by Father Yorke, objected. They maintained that the sailor's home was a sectarian institution and was anti-Catholic. It should not be the recipient of advantage from the city: use of the leased property. The Catholic women requested that their organization be considered for the lease of the institution.

The board of supervisors then found itself in the middle at a time when insufficient perspective was available to know that religious antagonisms were actually receding. Also, at the time few power figures in San Francisco

Father Yorke and the APA

Peter C. Yorke's own success in journalism, oratory, and ethnic militancy crested early. He was only 30 when he became the popular champion of religious freedom and ethnic rights in a culturally diverse city. Yorke gained local acclaim over the mangled corpse of the American Protective Association, transplanted nativists who failed to realize in San Francisco that they were trying to convert to xenophobia and anti-Catholicism a population consisting of their intended ideological victims.

The APA led itself to its own political slaughter, and Father Yorke gleefully swung the axe. En route, Yorke also displayed his talent and brilliance as a stand-up combatant. In Yorke's case, perhaps public adulation by his own Irish Catholic working class came to him too soon. He was, then, his Archbishop's protégé: personal secretary, Chancellor of the Archdiocese, and editor of the Catholic *Monitor,* a monthly newspaper that holds the historical record for the San Francisco newspaper with the longest continuous publication. Local historians who have assessed Yorke's uproarious career in and out of the Catholic Church have wondered if his ego had become diseased.

Mayor Phelan is shown with Mrs. McKinley, her niece, and state dignitaries. Phelan officially welcomed President William McKinley and his cabinet on May 14, 1901. In the grand nave of the Union Depot, Phelan saluted the nation's chief: "The people of San Francisco bid you cordial and patriotic welcome. They ... now enjoy the pleasure ... of receiving ... the President of the Republic of which they are a devoted part, and in whose greatness and glory they are proud to share."

Four months later, Phelan was called upon to express the city's grief. The President had been murdered.

enjoyed sufficient acumen to know that in such a culturally diverse metropolis tolerance already had established itself as a significant operating principle of society. In this case, the warm potato landed in the lap of Dr. Charles A. Clinton, member of the San Francisco board of supervisors. He was a Catholic even though Yorke was to lambaste him as an American Protective Association (APA) follower. He enjoyed Phelan's respect because he stood out among his peers for his honesty. Also, he was active in reform politics within the Democratic Party, just like Mayor Phelan.

Phelan, who had veto power over any decision by the Supervisors on renewal, worked with Clinton and Yorke to resolve the problem. The Supervisors heard both sides, Yorke's group and the original lease holders. A compromise emerged that included adding Catholic women to the governing board of the original Ladies' Seamen's Friend Society and terminating Protestant religious activities with a Protestant clergyman at the Home.

At that point, and apparently happy, the challenging Catholic women's group withdrew from the field. The board of supervisors, with a majority Catholic membership, approved lease renewal under the adjusted arrangement. The Irish Catholic mayor allowed the matter to take prompt effect. The only discordant note, not publicly known at the time, was that Dr. Clinton's personal communications with Father Yorke were tart. Clinton did not respect the activist priest and made the political error of expressing his feelings to Yorke. In politics, the priest was unforgiving and unforgetting.

The 1898 Fall Election

When the Democratic Party readied itself for the fall election, 1898, Dr. Clinton agreed to serve as a member of the statewide campaign committee. Phelan was a candidate for reelection and longtime liberal Congressman James G. Maguire was relinquishing his national office to run for Governor of California. Both were Democrats.

Yorke intervened at this point using the old APA issue as his point of departure. He painted Clinton with a broad stroke of his APA brush and covered Phelan with guilt by association. Yorke completed his APA matrix by placing Maguire, head of the State Democratic ticket, clearly within the camp of anti-Catholic bigotry.

Yorke was familiar with Maguire's humanism and his anti-papal writings because the spokesmen of the anti-Catholic American Protective Association, who foolishly tried to debate Yorke, had cited Maguire's work to support their anti-Catholic thesis. In pristine Yorkean style the Catholic champion satirized the congressman. Even if Maguire did not understand the subject of his book, Yorke wrote, at least he showed "...the renegade's virulence against his mother's faith and that turncoat's contempt for people who placed him in office."

Father Yorke's line up became as easily set as the progressive reformers', only it was the reverse. Yorke's chain of logic traveled from the APA-tainted Sailor's Home, to Clinton's role in leasing renewal and Phelan's cooperation, to their political support of Maguire for Governor. To Yorke they were all bigots, and he opposed them publicly and with dramatic effect on the eve of the November election. More dramatic than the very well spoken Phelan, Yorke caused a political sensation in cooperation with the Republican Party. To a packed Oakland auditorium he denounced Clinton, Phelan, and Maguire. The papers had been alerted to have shorthand correspondents present, and the opposition Gage organization printed Yorke's address as a campaign pamphlet, "Father Yorke to Mr. Maguire," and circulated it throughout the state in support of Henry T. Gage, the Republican candidate. In it Yorke's best was held for Phelan and Maguire. Yorke alleged that Phelan and Clinton had not settled the Seamen's Home controversy in a tolerant way because it would have been a politically unpopular decision for them.

> *James D. Phelan stands in the forefront of bigotry and intolerance....approving the action of men who did not hesitate to vote away the public money of San Francisco for sectarian purposes.... James D. Phelan is a moral coward, and he is afraid to be a man, because he is afraid of losing votes.*

Yorke's indictment of Maguire was even stronger. As far as Yorke was concerned the APA (which had been the vehicle for his own triumphal entry to local political life) was still a live issue. He had discussed it in person with candidate Maguire. Yorke maintained that Maguire, in private conversation with him, had admitted that Clinton (a Catholic) stood for the denial of equal rights to Catholics. Yorke further maintained that Maguire promised Clinton would be removed from the Democratic state campaign committee.

Maguire versus Gage

James G. Maguire was born and raised a Catholic and had taught in a Catholic college. However, by the time of his election in San Francisco to the U.S. Congress, he had become quite unorthodox. A free-thinker and a humanitarian, he published a book entitled *The Pope and Ireland: A Brief History of Papal Intrigues Against Irish Liberty* in which he blamed Ireland's misfortunes on the Catholic Church and not on English armies and subsequent misgovernment.

Maguire's Republican opponent, Henry T. Gage, was fine on Father Yorke's checklist of what counted. He was a corporate lawyer from Los Angeles and closely aligned with the Southern Pacific Railroad, the dominating California corporation and the target of progressive anti-corruption efforts. This did not count. Gage had singularly stood and opposed an APA-backed resolution in the State Republican convention four years previously. For his religious tolerance he had been booed from the floor. That counted.

Before the large Oakland audience and for partisan political use, Yorke concluded that Maguire failed to act on his promise because he was "...not man enough to stand with those who have since he was able to walk put bread in his stomach and clothes on his back." To the hushed crowd of Irish Catholic voters the priest delivered the *coup de grace*: "False to your father's people, false to your mother's creed, you needed but this crowning infamy, James G. Maguire, that you should be false to your own pledged word."

Perhaps in Yorke's mind Maguire was the greater transgressor. His public life — free thinking, humanism, his book — these things mocked the church, the institution to which Yorke dedicated his life. So far, Phelan had kept his own personal life, itself a mockery of Catholic dogma, reserved from public view. As far as the public was concerned he was still among California's most distinguished Catholic laymen. Accustomed to a professionally prudent clergy, Yorke's own subculture would not have accepted disclosure of Phelan's private life with ease. The puritanical Irish working-class would have been as scandalized by a priest exposing Phelan as by the exposure itself. Needless to say, Yorke's Archbishop, cooling as he was over his subordinate's unrestrained and undirectable public behavior, would have been outraged had Yorke attacked Phelan on moral grounds.

The practical result was that Clinton was overwhelmed by Yorke. With no effective or timely response available to him, Supervisor Clinton the Catholic was defeated in his reelection campaign. He blamed the Catholic priest for his political demise.

Maguire lost the California governorship and he too blamed Yorke. He could not resist responding in kind, asking Yorke what sort of world he envisioned when every man remained bound by the views of his mother? This post-election retort would not have earned Maguire any added votes from Yorke's Irish Catholic constituents, even if made earlier. If anything, it justified Yorke in the eyes of those with whom he was so closely bound. By asking such a question, Maguire talked back to a priest!

Help from the Archbishop

Phelan was smarter and more diplomatic than Clinton, and he acted with cunning. His job as mayor had hardly begun; the Charter was passed and he wanted to implement it rather than have the corporations negate its intent.

Besides, Phelan liked being mayor. His relationship with Charles K. Mc-Clatchy, editor of the *Sacramento Bee* was secure and in this case quite valuable. McClatchy wired Yorke's superior, Archbishop Riordan, and sought clarification on Yorke's public address. Did Yorke speak for himself or the Catholic Church regarding Clinton, Maguire, and California politics?

The Catholic Archbishop of San Francisco answered promptly with a one-liner: "Father Yorke is alone responsible for his utterances." On election eve Riordan granted a press interview himself, not a common action. The San Francisco *Examiner* printed Riordan's remarks at great length and demonstrated why yet another Irishman, Riordan, was the Archbishop and why Yorke would never be able to claim that rank on the organizational ladder that his own Irish controlled so absolutely.

> *The Catholic Church does not dictate to its priests or its people the policy which they should adopt in political matters….In religious matters they are amenable to the authority of their church and in this connection permit me to say that there is not in this diocese and under my jurisdiction a priest more obedient to his ecclesiastical superior than Father Yorke. He is a man of splendid abilities, untiring zeal and devotion to the interests of his church, and for four years he has defended its doctrines and its practices with an eloquence and learning for which all our Catholic people should be forever deeply grateful….His whole priestly life has been one of great devotion to religion and perfect obedience to the commands of his ecclesiastical superior.*

The interview's purpose was not to honor his troublesome young chancellor. Phelan was the subject. So his excellency continued by characterizing the kind of person he thought San Francisco needed for its mayor.

> *…a man who is largely interested in its prosperity and is capable of giving it that position in the commercial world to which it is entitled by its very location … active, energetic and capable of grasping the advantages which now seem to be within our reach. If the voters of the city feel that Mr. Phelan is such a man, they should vote for him and give him, if elected, their hearty and cordial support.*

The Archbishop terminated the interview with his response to the reporter's question that focused the interview quite neatly: Did he feel that Mr. Phelan was such a man, the man the office mayor of the City and County of San Francisco called for?

Archbishop Patrick W. Riordan was a wise and trusted administrator of Catholic institutions of the San Francisco Archdiocese. Appointed as the city's second archbishop in 1884, he had a successful thirty-year career. Twenty years older than James Duval Phelan, he understood men and institutions. His management ability allowed him to construct the churches, schools, hospitals, and the Catholic infrastructure twice—on both sides of the 1906 earthquake and fire. His institutional wealth exceeded Phelan's

Travel, novelty, and the mental stimulation that follows ranked high among the stimulants James Duval Phelan offered his sister Mollie. Himself addicted to European trips, Phelan brought Mollie when she was able and willing. Once he even arranged an auto trip for her and her companion (professional guides included) from Italy to France. The trip shown here seems to have been taken as a vacation from Phelan's duties as mayor of San Francisco.

Well, I'll be perfectly frank with you. I think he is… Others might think differently, this is a free country in which everyone is entitled to his views. I have given you mine.

What began as a political attack by a priest ended as a political endorsement by an archbishop delivered in such a way that even the remnants of the APA might respect. Were he more sensitive Yorke would have known that his preferment within his church had ended.

Phelan had behaved with restraint and dignity. He was wise enough not to brawl with Yorke in a verbal gutter. He was insightful enough to know that Yorke's preferment with Riordan could not last. The larger interests of the Archdiocese were financial, cultural, social, political, and historical as well as spiritual. Of the three Irishmen concerned, two — Riordan and Phelan — grasped the magnitude of Catholic interests and one — Yorke — did not. Yorke played well in the Oakland auditorium and beneath his newspaper byline. In the archbishop's study he had become an embarrassment.

Yorke had treated Maguire, Clinton, and Phelan unjustly. But only the Mayor's response worked. Astutely Phelan drew in Yorke's respected superior between himself and his adversary in such a way that the politicized Irish Catholic community knew that the priest opposed the head of their church. While they loved Yorke's fire, they respected Riordan's authority.

Yorke effectively ended the political advances of Clinton and Maguire. Phelan survived reelection and thereby kept alive the opportunity to advance his dreams for San Francisco. At the same time he realized that besides the corrupt political manipulators at the ward level and their senior partners in the corporate offices, Phelan had to be ever watchful of Yorke. The priest was most dangerous because his voice and his pen both reached Phelan's natural constituency and carried influence. Round two came with San Francisco teamster's strike of 1901.

The Teamster's Strike, 1901

Mayor Phelan's relationship with labor, organized and unorganized, was quite satisfactory from his point of view. His basic support originated among those who shared his reform impulses, those who were of the upper and upper-middle classes and whose livelihoods were not dependent upon the major corporations. For his election and two reelections Phelan also gathered in the votes of the ethnic working class. As long as no issues arose to separate them on class differences, Irish labor could vote for an Irish capitalist. The economic dynamics of turn-of-the-century San Francisco were changing, however, and settled ways were about to end.

Prosperity had returned in the wake of the war in the Philippines and the discovery of gold in the Klondike. As a result local efforts at unionization were making headway. Union labor in San Francisco always had the advantage of being rather isolated. The importation of strike breakers took time and gathering them was expensive.

Before prosperity returned, Phelan had worked well with delegations of the unemployed. He created public works projects from public subscription and heavy personal donations. He even tried to have the high-standard wage paid for laborers whose projects improved city thoroughfares, but the supervisors reduced the wage. Phelan served as treasurer for funds collected to support noted out-of-state strikes, and he presented awards at public labor celebrations. Without a divisive issue, labor seemed happy with the mayor and he certainly had no ground for complaint.

Prosperity brought expansiveness, simultaneously, to organized labor and employers as well. The employers organized themselves into the Employers' Association and gathered a one-quarter-million-dollar treasury to see themselves through what they anticipated and, in part, provoked—union labor's campaign to make San Francisco a union town by requiring union recognition by the employers and the closed shop. The City Front Federation, as the umbrella organization of well-established unions, represented the agent of economic and political change. Their advanced ideas maintained that rightful union concerns extended beyond simple matters of working conditions, wages, and hours. The union advocated the closed shop; no nonunion person should be allowed to work in a union shop.

The first few skirmishes between unions and ownership were settled rather easily. Then the carmen struck. Their timing was perfect. The owners of the transport system were in the midst of a major stock market manipulation. Not wanting to jeopardize their more profitable dealings, they simply granted the union's demands.

The inevitable conflict that followed began mildly enough with the arrival in the city of a Methodist youth group, the Epworth League, for its

For James D. Phelan in his early middle years, this was casual dress. Later, in the twenties, he did wear sports jackets — often with white trousers and shoes. Contrasting tweed splashes were rare, particularly during his occupancy of City Hall.

national convention. The amount of baggage their members brought over-taxed the hauling capacities of the nonunion Morton Special Delivery Company, which had the contract. At that point a second—union—draying company was engaged by Morton to help complete the job. When this firm ordered its union teamsters to assist the nonunion primary contractor, the teamsters refused under the provisions of their current contract that exempted them from working for nonunion companies.

The objecting teamsters were locked out. Like a domino effect, each succeeding teamster's local that was ordered by its employer to haul the Epworth baggage and refused was locked out. The result was a city-wide teamster's strike in July 1901. More strikes followed immediately.

The City Front Federation promptly organized a sympathetic strike of its friendly member unions: sailors, longshoremen, marine firemen, ship joiners, porters, packers and warehousemen, clerks, pile drivers, engineers, and an assortment of other unions. At the start some 15,000 union workers were on strike and locked out. As more union workers joined in sympathy, the strike force rose to an estimated 25,000. The waterfront closed down except for the movement of U.S. Government goods handled by federal employees. Businesses and industries dependent upon the movement of food stuffs and raw materials were nearing a state of paralysis. The commercial life of San Francisco was about to cease because the Employers' Association and the City Front Federation were locked in combat.

From the start of the conflict Phelan exercised a moderating influence, attempting always to advance toward a just and equitable solution. He threw himself into the work personally, participating in as many as three conferences per day with the interested parties.

During the first month he met with Michael Casey, Teamster's President, and Andrew Furuseth, the Seamen's Union leader who had been a dissenting member of the Charter 1900 Committee. This meeting also included members of the Citizens' Conciliation Committee of the Municipal League. The purpose was to clarify and address the differences that the unions had with the employers over the central issue, the closed shop.

Upon completion of that meeting the Mayor adjourned to the Mills Building and met with the Employers' Association where he encountered the spokesmen of the larger businesses of San Francisco. From the employers, Phelan obtained a document known as the Michael's Letter (signed by their attorney M. F. Michael), which listed their terms. In essence, the employers recognized the rights of labor to organize into unions and promised not to discriminate against union members. But the employers continued to insist on the right to settle problems with employees without dealing with the unions. Until the provisions of the letter were clarified Phelan may have hoped that the standoff in the negotiations might allow work to begin pending a later settlement.

Clarification revealed that the Michael's Letter was as reactionary as Phelan feared. It denied union principles that already prevailed in San Francisco. Obviously conciliation and diplomacy were not going to be enough, at least at this stage, to settle San Francisco's strike. Simultaneously, violence began to play a larger part.

By the advanced stages of the strike, nonunion teamsters had been recruited into the city and put on the drays in place of the striking and locked-out union men. The players in this drama were not delicate men, and they advanced their well being with the skills they had. One skill was physical intimidation and violence. With these came charges and counter charges.

From Phelan's point of view the Employers' Association was worse than reactionary; its members failed to recognize their own self-interests. All citizens had a legitimate stake in San Francisco. The enlightened approach was not to hold down a rival sector, but to accommodate and, together, expand the well being of all. To a better and more harmoniously functioning city would come more tourists, increased population, and more business.

Also, from the Mayor's point of view the unions merited legitimacy. The closed shop was another matter, one that his personal papers as well as public statements seem not to address. He certainly never encouraged it. Perfectly clear, however, was his view on industrial violence. He was opposed to it in all its forms.

What began as the intimidation of nonunion strikebreakers developed into terrorism. By the end of the strike five persons had been killed and 336 persons had been assaulted. Of the latter, 250 suffered seriously enough to require medical attention, including surgery. Employer accusations were met with union denials and even the assertion that anti-union thugs were committing the acts to discredit the strike. Few accepted this. Phelan rejected it outright. More arguable was the alternate union response that, for a strike of such magnitude and with such militant employers, the amount of actual

This festive outing could have been a modest celebration by teamster leadership following their successful strike of 1901. Michael Casey (at center, pouring), was born in Ireland in 1860 and worked as a teamster in San Francisco when it was a grim and exploited way of life. With Father Peter C. Yorke's help and political influence at the state level, Casey obtained a favorable resolution of the general strike after Mayor Phelan had been unable to budge the Employers' Association.

violence was quite limited. Phelan rejected this too. He felt that Casey and Furuseth were winking at the union violence. Not only was it unacceptable, it was losing the unions the support of the general public.

Phelan resisted pressure to call in the state militia. George Newhall happened to be serving both as President of the Chamber of Commerce and President of the Police Commission. He requested that if city police could not control the situation and guarantee law and order, then state troops should be brought in. The Labor Council, as might be expected, demanded Newhall's removal from the commission and castigated Mayor Phelan for not doing so. Phelan, however, remained firmly against state troops.

Throughout this period of charges and counter charges, all of which found their way prominently into the papers, the city police had been riding with the nonunion strike-breaking teamsters and protecting them against abuse. Strikers maintained that they did more, even directing the out-of-towners how to negotiate their heavily laden wagons over the uneven terrain of San Francisco.

Conditions worsened following the outcry that, with the police on the drays, the city proper was unprotected. At that, special police agents were recruited for the driver protection program. Those hired were seen by union labor as a private army at the disposal of the employers. With both sides behaving according to formula, conditions on San Francisco streets deteriorated further.

Watching attentively from the side lines throughout this industrial war was Phelan's adversary, the popular Catholic champion of the rights of the Irish working class, Father Yorke. His entry into this fray coincided with the ebbing of union labor morale. The role Yorke chose was that of fund raiser, inspirational leader, and interpreter of modern Catholic social doctrine.

Yorke's forums included the lecture platforms before the friends of the union movement and the front pages of the San Francisco *Examiner*. The working class had been his bonded constituency since the Charter revision movement and the election of 1898. In the first of numerous speeches on behalf of the strikers, Yorke called for union solidarity, for contributions from those who remained employed, and for boycotting those firms that belonged to the Employers' Association.

Although Yorke cautioned his union listeners against violence, he was far more strident in lashing out at the politicians, Phelan particularly, for their lack of help to the union cause. During one of Phelan's attempts at mediation when union representatives were complaining of police aggressiveness, he asked them why they did not go back to work? Yorke seized the context, paraphrased Phelan, and quoted him as saying (variously rendered), "If they don't want to be clubbed, let them go to work."

The public battle of the affidavits followed. Phelan publicized his, signed by four supervisors who were present at the meeting, all maintaining that Phelan never said what Yorke attributed to him. Yorke responded immediately with Andrew Furuseth's affidavit. Yorke's own biographer Joseph Brusher, S.J., (*Consecrated Thunderbolt*, 1973) assessed the Furuseth document as maintaining that Phelan used "equivalent" language. Phelan's side could add that Furuseth, like Yorke, hardly was a disinterested spectator. Decades later, in private correspondence, Phelan continued to resent what he considered Yorke's calumny that the priest used unjustly to turn labor against Phelan.

Besides being "Jimmy The Rag," Phelan had to try to plow ahead in a life of public service as "Clubber Phelan!" Yorke pursued Phelan relentlessly. The idol of the Irish Catholic crowd attempted to inflict the political *coup de grace* upon their own culture's most promising American son. Instead of terminating Phelan's political career in 1901, Yorke only maimed it.

This time an appeal to the Archbishop would have been of no avail. By now Yorke was beyond the Archbishop's control on political and labor matters. Riordan understood his limits vis-a-vis Yorke as clearly as Yorke knew how far he could push his religious superior. Besides, this time Yorke called down the Pope on his side, so what could an archbishop do?

Whether for raw political advantage or the advanced social concern that also motivated Yorke, the popular priest used this major labor conflict to popularize the teachings of Pope Leo XIII, whose encyclical *Rerum Novarum* had been announced ten years previously by Rome. Yorke interpreted it for the populace and applied it to the San Francisco labor context. In fact, Yorke maintained that Leo XIII's famous encyclical was the reason that he entered the labor war. According to it labor had the right to organize and, indeed, organization was their natural right and the best means of protecting themselves against the power of employers.

In a manner he was to perfect during his journalistic career as editor of his weekly *Leader*, Yorke punctuated his paragraphs with Phelan as his point of reference:

Jimmy the Rag

In Peter Yorke's outpouring of rhetoric the dynamic and engaging priest tossed off a one-liner that he stuck permanently on James D. Phelan. No matter how he tried Phelan was never able to shake it off. The working class Irish always remembered it, remembered Yorke, and smiled at Phelan's expense. According to Yorke, Phelan the politician had professed to be labor's friend. But when it came down to helping in the hour of need, Phelan was useless. He was, as Yorke put it, as useful to labor as "a dish cloth on top of a pole."

The priest rechristened James Duval Phelan and named him "Jimmy the Rag." The name stuck and when Yorke initiated his own popular Irish labor weekly, the *Leader,* he used variations of the line over and over for the amusement of Phelan's fellow ethnics. If Phelan thought he was getting rough treatment at the cleric's hands, this was nothing compared to what was to come.

Could Pope Leo have described the Employers' Association and the situation in San Francisco better even if he were to make a personal examination of Battery, Davis, and Front Streets? Behold the small number of very rich men! That means the executive committee of the Employers' Association. What are they trying to do? They are trying to lay a yoke on the laborers. Can they succeed? They can succeed if the unions are destroyed. What kind of a yoke? A yoke little better than slavery itself. Can you hear the crack of Mayor Phelan's whip?

Workingmen of San Francisco, which will you heed, Mr. James D. Phelan or Pope Leo XIII?

Archbishop Riordan had removed Yorke from the editorship of the Catholic *Monitor,* and the gifted and volatile priest was not to found his personal weekly *Leader* until 1902. During the teamster's strike of 1901, however, Yorke enjoyed free access to the San Francisco *Examiner.* William Randolph Hearst's daily had been solidly in the Phelan and reform camp, but reversed itself over rather small matters and then took Yorke's side in the labor controversy. The journalism of the day made the most of the violence in the streets and Yorke's slant, popularity, and journalistic skills enhanced the *Examiner's* competitive position among the City's daily newspapers.

Throughout the summer-long strike Phelan remained intent upon rational and temperate discourse. He remained prudent and diplomatic in all public statements. Regrettably, almost all of his private correspondence burned with the Phelan office building at O'Farrell and Market Streets after the earthquake of 1906. Phelan's 1906–1930 correspondence shows that he thought infrequently of Yorke. Once, among several thousand letters to a worldwide friendship network, Phelan referred directly to Yorke. He was in Phelan's mind "the Catholic bigot."

At the time the best Phelan could do was to reiterate his convictions on nonviolence and what he considered the basis for responsible life within society. Roy Swanstron's University of California at Berkeley thesis of 1949 quoted him directly:

The present policy is simply to make the streets safe for men, whether union or nonunion, because the law is no respecter of persons; all are alike entitled to its protection and all violators of it shall alike receive punishment. The police have nothing to do with the merits of the controversy between employ-

ers and employees—their duty is to prevent the commission of unlawful acts and arrest offenders.

The end came to the strike not at Phelan's hands, but at the hands of the California Governor, Henry T. Gage, the Republican Yorke had backed during the 1898 campaign. Gage came to San Francisco and symbolically visited Yorke in the priest's rectory at St. Peter's parish in the then-Irish Mission District. The two discussed the possibility of calling in the state militia and declaring martial law in San Francisco. Yorke, as Phelan had already done, opposed such an option.

Next Governor Gage met with the spokesmen of the Employers' Association at the Palace Hotel. He then called in the strike leaders. Gage's message was plain: Agree to the terms then on the table or expect martial law. This was October 2, 1901. San Francisco was exhausted by three months of disruption, tension, and terror. Gage's timing and the city's exhaustion seemed to be greater contributing factors to termination of the protracted strike than the governor's personal involvement. His threat of martial law, perhaps, tipped the balance toward the ending of the strike.

Governor Gage, beholden to Yorke for having detached the San Francisco Irish working class vote from his Democratic opponent three years earlier, greatly enhanced Yorke's local prestige at Phelan's expense. Before he left office Governor Gage expressed his gratitude in an even more tangible manner. He appointed Father Yorke a regent of the University of California, an institution that Yorke had also attacked publicly with his usual ferocity.

Phelan, by trying, impartially, to buffer and to harmonize two discordant elements—reactionary employers and violent unions—suffered a common enough fate. He was blamed by both sides for favoring the other.

Moving On

James D. Phelan did not record his reasons for not seeking a fourth term as mayor of San Francisco. Perhaps he was weary of the stress brought upon him by those who did not share his dream for San Francisco the beautiful.

Phelan also was a good enough politician to know that his prospects of reelection in 1901 were highly questionable. Besides Yorke and union labor, other concerns existed. The San Francisco of his dreams had not material-

James Duval and Mollie Phelan appear at their best in this turn-of-the century portrait. Again, he provided for his sister's happiness by stimulating her environment. Here they visited London during the European vacation Phelan took from his service as San Francisco's mayor.

ized during his administration; a reconstructed, beautiful city still waited. The Charter of 1900 helped the conduct of urban government, but problems always lingered. Phelan and his party of reform had lost the support of William Randolph Hearst's *Examiner*. The cause had been personal and petty, but the result was the same. San Francisco's largest circulation daily became the outlet for Yorke and union labor.

Even the civil service reforms hurt by detaching Phelan reform activists from their crusade and installing them permanently in City Hall. Their motivation shifted its center of gravity. Others, those associated with vice and liquor, did not appreciate the attention Phelan's administration had paid them. Even Phelan's original basis of support, the Merchants' Association, seemed reduced to just another special interest—certainly in the minds of the working class voters.

Phelan had brought San Francisco into the twentieth century with a modern, efficient Charter. He taught the city that efficiency and honesty could be expected from government because he provided them. When San Francisco tired of hope for the future, for efficiency, and for honesty in government, Phelan hardly despaired. Nothing in life was absolute. He had done what was possible, more than many had believed possible, and then he returned to the pursuit of those refinements that life had always offered him. Perhaps after the local world took a spin or two, he might have another chance to advance California's general well-being. His years in City Hall were invigorating, engaging, and even fun.

Chapter Seven
City Beautiful

Continuity characterized the life and interests of James Duval Phelan, perhaps nowhere as dramatically as in his devotion to civic improvement, particularly in bringing honesty, beauty, and refinement to urban life. From the donation of his first sculpture to the City of San Francisco to his final bequest of Villa Montalvo for the encouragement of young artists and the professional development of some not so young, Phelan pursued lifelong goals. His philanthropies and patronage were, in fact, so persistent that isolating and examining them individually contravenes history as it happened.

As mayor of San Francisco, Phelan helped strengthen the authority of government through charter reform. His persistence included moral and financial support of San Francisco's historic graft prosecution that he helped initiate against his unworthy successors in City Hall. Both efforts—strengthening city government and prosecuting the corrupt custodians of the enhanced power he had provided through charter reform—were merely subordinate parts to Phelan's grander goals. Similarly, Phelan's efforts to free San Francisco from corrupting exploitation by the privately owned water providers and to create the Hetch Hetchy water system, though vast in the geographical, social, political, economic, and technological dimensions, still represent but a piece in Phelan's larger scheme. His devotion was to San Francisco, its beautification as well as its glorification as a great city.

Knowingly or not the senior Phelan had prepared his only son for understanding, appreciation, and active participation in what was to become the most significant American urban development of the time, the City Beautiful movement. This thrust to plan and to restyle the great cities of the United

The Overland Monthly *and James Duval Phelan shared common concerns. The editors published his numerous essays from 1885 to 1921 and mourned his death in this commemorative issue.*

The Urban Environment

The boulevards, the centralization of functions and symmetry of locations and compatibility of architecture; the public buildings, the grand fountains, arches, parks, vistas, public order, and social harmony -- in all, the beauty of the physical setting seemed to guarantee tranquil, happy, and prosperous public harmony.

All these elements combined for Phelan into a grand art form, not artificial color affixed to a two-dimensional canvas for the private admiration by the few. Public art certainly included statuary and fountains, but they constituted public art at its most basic level. For Phelan beauty was the grand ennobler. Beauty enhanced the lives of all who beheld it. And those who were fortunate enough to reside within civilization's greatest cities should be exposed to the greatest nobility of all.

Cities of beauty, utility, prosperity, and culture were, for Phelan, the essence of art. And most of all, they were alive. They provided the outlet for all genius, be it aesthetic, artistic, political, social, economic or technological. Even nature, in Phelan's plan, was to serve and be blended with the City Beautiful. All this should be replicated within the city for the refinement and the elevation of the citizenry. It should be made available to all as parks, lakes, and tree-lined streets.

Phelan's informal postgraduate education in Europe allowed his absorption of such notions. His father's ever-present commercial needs and Phelan's positive, if not wholehearted, response to them, molded the young heir into the composite personality that was to guide San Francisco in its best effort at making itself worthy of the setting in which nature had placed it.

States had many contributing causes, many illustrious players, many grand designs, and some successes. At the turn of the century and thereafter City Beautiful was to the urban landscape what the Progressive Movement was to American politics. Phelan was well prepared and properly disposed to play convincing parts in both.

Phelan was more at home in the great cities of Europe than he was in any American city except San Francisco. His longest residences abroad centered on Paris with less time in London, Rome, and Athens. The French capitol was his favorite followed by the sun-splashed cities of the Mediterranean. London offered Phelan linguistic ease, political and legal models, and luxury goods. Dublin alone provided him with what he cherished: the company of literary, cultural, and political leaders with whom he felt comfortable and to whom he offered respect, friendship, and encouragement. Although his ethnic ties were to Ireland, that troubled land offered him opportunities to provide help, not models to emulate. For Phelan, Paris and then Athens and Berlin were the grand cities.

Chicago World's Fair and Daniel Burnham

Phelan's extended education in Europe offered him the leisure and opportunity to study, observe, and examine the glories of Western Civilization. His appointment in 1893 as vice president of the California Commission to the Chicago World's Columbian Exposition introduced Phelan to hands-on experience in converting concept into temporary reality.

With the illness of the commission president, Phelan performed most of the tasks that the state's successful exhibition in Chicago required. Supported by funds the California Legislature appropriated, Phelan organized and managed the state's pavilion. He concluded the committee's work, saw to the construction of the state's pavilion exhibit, dismantled it upon the fair's conclusion, and fulfilled all the objectives of the exhibition as well. And he did so under budget! Then he returned $50,000 to the state's general fund.

More important than returning budgeted but unspent funds was the additional education Phelan received at the Chicago World's Fair. The event attracted the most advanced thinking on urban planning. Dramatic full-sized buildings captivated the imagination of Phelan's American generation. The Chicago exposition marked the acceptance of city planning and the birth of

City Beautiful. In theory, master planning triumphed over uncoordinated urban construction. Phelan then brought City Beautiful to San Francisco and placed the city fully within the progressive urban ferment of the day.

The enthusiastic acceptance of the World Fair model by the learned, as well as by the general populace, sprang from the model's appeal: its dramatic classical lines, enhanced by symmetry, proportion, spaciousness, and unity. Daniel Hudson Burnham created Chicago's Great White City for the fair. His work exerted a commanding influence over his generation in the field of civic design. Those who saw Burnham's near-fantasy city at the Columbian exhibition returned home intent on uplifting their hometowns.

Phelan remained with the California exhibit, imbibed deeply of the city of make-believe, and acquainted himself with those who had made it real, if only for the season. What he saw and what he learned fitted snugly with his European internship. He liked what he saw and assumed a permanent commitment to aggrandizing an imperial San Francisco like Burnham's model.

Specifically, Phelan observed the harmony, order, and grandeur of each edifice — alone, but more important in a balanced harmony of comprehensive design. Burnham's buildings were large and imposing, and all reflected classical inspiration. Their construction materials were identical, and their facades blended in a coordination of design and color. Harmony prevailed.

The placement of the great buildings seemed even more important and impressive than the grand total of the individual architectural statements, even as commanding as each was individually. The comprehensiveness of the plan added a previously neglected dimension. Balance, scale, and symmetry promised a civic dignity and esthetic excellence that Phelan appreciated and that San Francisco lacked. For the Chicago World's Fair, Burnham and his engineers conceived the grand plan and designed its detailed embodiment. Burnham's army of contractors erected the dream for the envy and edification of Americans. At the same time Phelan's developing architectural interests received San Francisco Bay Area stimulation as well.

City Beautiful in California

Phoebe Apperson Hearst became interested in a comprehensive new design for the University of California (at the time that meant Berkeley). Her enthusiasm climaxed in the creation of a competition among an international

The California State Building at the World's Columbian Exposition, Chicago, 1893. The following excerpt is from James Duval Phelan's address at the opening ceremonies:

California has a special reason to join in this Columbian Exposition, inspired as it is by the heroism and achievements of that great type of the Spanish navigator, Christopher Columbus; for only fifty years after the discovery of America, the seamen of Spain, under Cabrillo, discovered the California coast, and subsequently settled the country. And so we Californians join, I say, with special interest in celebrating the magnificent services to civilization performed by Spain.

But in this practical age we are not actuated entirely by sentiment. Californians had also other reasons for coming to Chicago. We came here to show the part we are playing on the great stage of the world. We came here to show the development of the State since the American occupation in 1846. We came here to enlarge our markets and invite a new immigration. These were our objects, and therein you will find the meaning of our building and our exhibits. In the Spanish mission architecture of our building we honor Spain; and in our display, we trust, we honor California.

The Hearst family wealth came from western mining (Anaconda silver and copper) and large-scale ranching. Phoebe Apperson Hearst (seen here) and her husband George ceased living as husband and wife after the birth of William Randolph, the future publishing magnate. Phoebe Hearst lavished attention upon her only son and the University of California.

pool of architects. Hearst's objective was the design of a university that would befit California and the state's children. Stanford University's Spanish ensemble blended with the low contour of the Palo Alto landscape, but did not fit Berkeley. Hearst responded to the more classical preferences then current within international architectural thinking. The classicism Phelan saw so well received at the Chicago Exposition became the Berkeley model.

Phelan monitored the progress of the Berkeley competition and sprang to action as mayor of San Francisco in 1898. The competition's jurors announced the selection of their European finalists in Belgium and, through the continued generosity of Mrs. Hearst, invited all eleven competitors to Berkeley to see how their suggested plans conformed to the terrain. Phelan, behaving in character, hosted the delegation of architects for dinner at the Bohemian Club. At that time he seized his opportunity for San Francisco and announced that Mrs. Hearst wished to do for the city what she currently was doing for the University of California. She would sponsor a new design competition for the city itself. Drawing upon his cherished Paris example Phelan added that the anticipated result would follow the model of what Baron Georges Haussmann had done for Napoleon III. San Francisco could become an imperial city redesigned along grand scale incorporating aesthetic harmony while exploiting its unique location and topography. Imaginatively restored, San Francisco could be without equal among the world's cities.

This opportunity so captivated Phelan's imagination that he followed through when Mrs. Hearst's interests shifted from a comprehensive redesign of San Francisco. Phelan assumed natural leadership in the application of national and international trends in architecture and urban design to his native city. Further, he was more direct, more personally knowledgeable, and better connected than the patrons of the area's major universities.

Instead of holding an international competition in Europe to attract of aspiring continental architects, Phelan already knew what he wanted and who he wanted. Daniel H. Burnham embodied both the *what* and the *who*. Phelan sought his services directly.

Phelan's first step was a public call for the redesign of San Francisco. Understandably he enjoyed press attention given the nature of the subject, his celebrity status as former mayor, and his well-known concerns over the beautification of the city. Also, his connection with the *Bulletin* grew stronger during the editorship of Fremont Older, a public-spirited journalist.

Stanford versus Berkeley Architecture

The two major centers of regional activity were The Leland Stanford Junior University at Palo Alto and the University of California in Berkeley. Leland and Jane Lathrop Stanford founded the former as a living memorial to their son and only child who had died during a European tour just prior to his own college entry. Young Leland, arriving after eighteen years of marriage, had been the joy in the lives of his wealthy but aging parents. His traumatic death proved to be the stimulus that transferred to education the fortune Senator Stanford had accumulated from railroad construction and organization. The bereaved parents converted their loss into love for the children of California.

Architecturally, Stanford University began unencumbered, on virtually clear land. For the spot where the Senator's Palo Alto stud farm had been, Stanford's architects designed the ensemble that resulted in the Stanford Quadrangle and complementing structures. The architecture drew heavily from the area's Spanish heritage, blended to the local environment and graced by dramatically presented biblical references.

Following Senator Stanford's death, the university became Jane Stanford's overriding compulsion. She lived in Palo Alto and the campus' development and improvement became an extension of herself. The expanding architectural scheme was uniform and comprehensive, but certainly not classical.

Across the Bay to the north, the University of California enjoyed its own kindly mother, this one by adoption. Created by an act of the state legislature in 1868, the university began without a master plan. And like San Francisco, it looked like it. Intent on correcting this initial misfortune was Phoebe Apperson Hearst, the widow of George Hearst and mother of William Randolph Hearst, heir to the Hearst mining fortune.

The degree to which Mrs. Stanford and Mrs. Hearst inspired each other to greater philanthropies on behalf of their competing institutions has not been settled by biographers. Sufficient, however, is the fact that the universities were the permanent beneficiaries — particularly in their architectural development.

Stanford University with its Spanish-California building enjoyed the full patronage and attention of Mrs. Leland Stanford following the death of her only son, Leland, Junior.

The Hearst Mining Building, University of California, Berkeley, was a family gift in honor of George Hearst, a self-taught mining engineer who established the Hearst fortune. The family wealth enabled Phoebe Hearst to provide for the education of California's children

Daniel H. Burnham's reputation was already well developed when he came to San Francisco at James Duval Phelan's urging. Burnham was America's most noted master planner. His prestige was as monumental as his designs, and for Phelan to have obtained his services for San Francisco was an achievement in itself. After the Columbian Exposition in Chicago, Burnham headed the commissions that planned turn-of-the-century Washington, D.C., Cleveland, and later, Manila.

Phelan's second step was to respond to his own call. He organized a meeting at the Merchants' Exchange, at which he created the Association for the Improvement and Adornment of San Francisco. Phelan gathered the Association's twenty-six cofounders mostly from the ranks of the city's merchant capitalists. The few exceptions included railroad executives and a college dean. Phelan was comfortable with these men and, indeed, shared membership with many in the city's prestigious clubs — the Pacific Union as well as the Bohemian. One founding member of the organization Phelan created was, in fact, a cousin of Daniel Burnham himself.

Phelan was the prime mover and the critical link between San Francisco and the forefront of American master planning. Phelan's position, his influence, reputation, and contacts were the ingredients that drew Burnham into Phelan's San Francisco orbit. Quite promptly, Phelan announced Burnham's interest in undertaking the preparation of a comprehensive plan for San Francisco. Immediately thereafter, Phelan installed Burnham and his well-trained associates in an office studio constructed atop Twin Peaks. From this vantage point Burnham and associates commanded a panorama of the city. They measured the perspective and balanced it against their more focused examination of the city's individual buildings, streets, and open areas.

The Association hosted Burnham at the Saint Francis Hotel and tendered him a banquet. Phelan, of course, presided comfortably over the elegant and distinguished event. He conveyed at this public occasion what had been agreed upon already. Burnham's charge was to prepare a new, comprehensive plan for the City of San Francisco. Summarizing Phelan's remarks in *Imperial San Francisco*, Judd Kahn noted that "Phelan ... stressed his favorite themes: the riches that nature had bestowed on San Francisco; the new imperial destiny in store for the city; and the need for a new spirit of cooperation and achievement to take advantage of both opportunities, to make San Francisco 'worthy of its position and destiny'." Always a compelling public speaker, Phelan prepared the way for the man who was to redeem San Francisco from itself — his distinguished guest, Daniel Burnham.

Burnham's Plans for San Francisco

Burnham, for his part, welcomed public comments. He shared Phelan's ideas, not surprisingly because they derived from the same mainstream City

Beautiful thinking. Burnham had absorbed the same European influences Phelan had imbibed in his youth. Phelan spent his early career mentally adapting what he learned to San Francisco's unique geographical setting. In Burnham, Phelan reached out and selected a master of urban art in its broadest conception. Phelan drew to San Francisco a master planner who was remarkably open, even solicitous, of the informed opinions of local players, men whose support sustained his planning work and offered the best chance of transforming his completed design into physical reality. Burnham's characteristic assumptions that constituted the essence of City Beautiful embraced the concepts so successfully demonstrated at the 1893 Chicago Exposition: uniformity of architecture, classical design, consistency of construction materials, symmetrical patterns of distributed clusters of major buildings, and harmony of scale.

The destruction of the bulk of Phelan's pre-1906 papers in San Francisco's fire reduces the historian's ability to document the extent and depth of Phelan's impact upon Burnham's plan for the city. Burnham, the leading professional in the excitingly new field of urban planning, certainly had no reason to exclude Phelan, the local patron of artistic as well as political enlightenment. In fact, Burnham wanted Phelan to stop over in Chicago for extended meetings during the summer of 1904 when Phelan would be traveling west by rail following another of his European sojourns.

Burnham's *Report on a Plan for San Francisco* clearly reflected Phelan's influence. Hardly a question of Phelan superimposing his will over the master planner's, Phelan and Burnham simply shared that body of advanced ideas that constituted and propelled the City Beautiful movement nationwide. Both believed that from the city's new physical beauty would rush a new social, emotional, and economic renewal as well. With the new city would come the new society. Measuring the influence patron and planner exercised over one another is difficult when there seemed to be such agreement between them over the fundamentals.

The benefit Burnham sought to derive from Phelan was in the application of the concepts to the local peculiarities. The benefit Phelan sought to derive from Burnham was the opportunity to plant his own enthusiasms within the master's plan. Other than that, Phelan was indulging himself in yet another of life's engaging experiences.

Burnham at Full Career

Burnham's career and reputation were at a professional peak at the time he redesigned San Francisco, so he organized his time, utilized competent subordinates, and made the most of his opportunities. After his measured personal attention to the San Francisco redesign, he left for the Philippines where he accepted a commission for a redesign for Manila and an alternate summer capital.

Burnham's general work pattern was to solicit local comments, determine the broad outlines of the project, and identify its central features, then turn the details over to his associates. He reviewed and passed upon their work. In the end, the urban designs bore Burnham's name. After all, he was the attraction the clients sought. He was, nonetheless, generous in his crediting and lavish in his praise of those who contributed to the finished product.

Burnham's San Francisco Plans

The best and most readily available scholarly examination of the Burnham plan as it relates to Phelan is Judd Kahn's *Imperial San Francisco*. Kahn's analysis of the plan notes Burnham's preoccupation with streets and parks as well as his predominant concern with centralization and segregation of functions, particularly civic functions. According to Kahn, "Burnham's general theory pictured the ideal street plan for a city as a spiderweb of concentric circles intersected by diagonals. The geography of San Francisco, especially the tallest hills near the center of the city and the concentration of population in the northeast quadrant, made a single-centered web impossible." Instead of abandoning his concept, Burnham modified and expanded it to fit San Francisco. The planning result was multiple, dispersed but coordinated circles joined by the diagonals.

Burnham absorbed Phelan's specific enthusiasms quite naturally into his comprehensive plan. One was the extension of the Golden Gate Park Panhandle eastward to the intersection of Market Street at Van Ness Avenue. The second was the connection of Golden Gate Park to the Presidio via a parkway one-block in width. Phelan recognized the merits of both linkages as practical and aesthetic.

The keys to the creation of visible, public grandeur were buildings of epic proportions that would share a uniformity of size, nobility of appearance, and spaciousness of setting. At the turn of the century, San Francisco's most imposing public building was the gaudy, overpriced, over-built, and unsound City Hall. Phelan had been the first mayor to occupy it upon its completion in 1900. The building had been three decades in-the-making and an almost limitless source of graft to the contractors. Architecturally, financially, and certainly symbolically it insulted Phelan's sense of good taste and his basic honesty. Its cornerstone had been set when Phelan was a boy of ten. Yet, no mayor occupied it until Phelan did twenty-nine years later. During construction the edifice grew and grew; some would say uglier and uglier. In 1906 it collapsed from the earthquake and didn't need the fire to destroy it. Its time under construction was five times longer than its time in use.

Redesigning San Francisco

Burnham concluded his labors on the comprehensive redesign of San Francisco in 1905, a timely one year before the city shook and burned to the ground. In his plan he placed the center of civic life and administration at the confluence of the projected Panhandle extension, Market Street, and Van Ness Avenue. There he projected city, state, and federal buildings within his primary circle, mindful of the requirements of space, balance, proportion, and symmetry. San Francisco, still the West's premier city, housed additional structures that extended into the worlds of finance, education, art, and the professions. Phelan anticipated growth and expansion, which were both causes and intended results of his City Beautiful efforts. Accommodatingly, Burnham extended radials from his downtown spider web out in connection to more distant points of distribution. Viewing San Francisco from their Twin Peaks studio, Burnham and his assistants adjusted their stock concepts to the rather cruel realities of San Francisco. In this sense, they were following the University of California plan, not the Stanford one. They were not implementing an ideal on empty land. They accepted the historical self-location of functions where related activities had naturally clustered. Paris and Berlin were Phelan's and Burnham's models, but San Francisco was their reality. They could not start with a clear drafting board.

From the civic circle two broad boulevards already existed. Van Ness Avenue extended north to the bay at Fort Mason. Market Street cut its famous (and troublesome) swath rather diagonally, in what convenience ascribed as easterly and westerly. The true east-west radial was to be the Panhandle extension, beyond Phelan's goal of Market and Van Ness, through the South of Market, and terminate at the bay shore. The broad thoroughfare was to be adorned throughout by plantings, bridle paths, and recreational settings.

The city's financial activities had situated themselves in that portion of the city that shares its name. The Financial District — well known to Phelan's father — extended from California and Sansome Streets. Its relocation, even marginally as in the case of the projected new civic center, was not part of Burnham's plan. Ahead of his time, Burnham advanced the concept of centralizing attention upon the most prominent function among related activities. In San Francisco's Financial District that was the stock exchange. Enhancement of the central structure meant surrounding it with courts or placing it majestically within one central court. Further, and to ensure the exchange's dignity, no vehicular traffic should intrude upon a unique environment secluded within the more dynamic one.

Even within the residential areas of the city, Burnham planned with moderation — for the lower class at any rate. He accepted as desirable and natural the concept of segregation by function. Rather than the convenience of walking towns or small cities where commerce, finance, culture, and personal housing were blended and merged, the great cities required centralization and segregation of functions. No significant population should reside within the circle of the banks, exchanges, and insurance corporations. Certainly cattle ought not to be slaughtered within wind of the mayor's office or any homemaker's kitchen.

The congested areas to the South of Market Street and the poorly constructed abodes surrounding Telegraph Hill were cases in point. For the working class to the south no residential redevelopment as such was planned. Rather, Burnham's plan advanced improved air quality, open space, and safe-

Daniel Burnham's plan was both attacked and embraced as visionary. At first the serious obstacles to implementation included privately held real estate located in the path of sweeping thoroughfares. Then with the 1906 disaster, no building stood in the way of progress, efficiency, and beauty! For the bold, the fire became San Francisco's opportunity to become worthy of its own setting.

guards against street accidents and injuries. The meanness of the neighborhoods was to be mitigated by a pattern of mini parks intended to liberate the spirit by providing recreation for the young and refuge and solace for the aged and infirm. The actual space for such amenities would have to come from land that was being misused or otherwise under used. The attractive concept of clustered dwellings with shared greens had not been previously established in San Francisco.

The reality of the Telegraph Hill environment allowed Burnham greater room for initiative. The value of legally secured property, land, and improvements constituted but a fraction of the more densely populated South of Market district. The sparseness of construction on Telegraph Hill would allow redevelopment and upgrade. But such a goal would collide with Burnham's conviction that San Francisco's mountain tops ought best be reserved as sites for inspirational displays. Some higher elevations might even be topped to erect monuments of imperial proportion for the education and edification of the people. The firemen's memorial, Coit Tower, illustrates this concept on Telegraph Hill. The importance and the impact of public art and civic beauty clearly influenced Burnham as greatly as it did Phelan.

Housing

For housing the city's populace, Burnham intended enhancing the environments of established neighborhoods. High-density, multiple-unit dwellings were to remain on the periphery of the centers of administrations, transportation, culture, education, and finance. New residential developments to the west and to the southwest were natural though. Beyond the Western Addition (bisected by Filmore Street), out onto the sand dunes of the Richmond and Sunset districts were to be the single-family homes constructed upon land more cheaply acquired than the higher-priced real estate of the commercial, financial, and administrative areas. Unencumbered by prior construction, these extensive tracts lent themselves to creative planning. Diagonals crossed at Burnham's precisely located centers that he punctuated with imperious structures of grand design.

In the strictly residential areas where such display would have violated his own sense of proportion and compatibility, Burnham's centers were set off by wooded parks, gardens, and planted thoroughfares. Two intersected at parkways leading to the majestic Pacific; two others joined at the shore itself, the Cliff House site being the more glorious.

The city's hills had always provided the planners with their greatest challenges and their greatest frustrations. The original pre-gold rush city was laid out on the flat lands adjacent to the bay, between high water and the hills. Hardly anticipating the insatiable demand of a major American metropolis for more land, the primary surveyors merely laid out what was useful for their own day. Their successors contrived extensions upon a grid not of their design. The angle that Market Street cuts through the grid illustrates the design peculiarity. That north and south of Market infrequently meet at intersections is another. In effect, the city's major thoroughfare inhibited the flow of traffic and commerce. More streets ended at Market Street than crossed it.

The bay's shore constituting the original site, Yerba Buena, was not the best beginning of the city that was to follow. At first, though, the hills simply were ignored. By the time Phelan and Burnham confronted the problem, the population growth that Phelan's father had anticipated was a reality, and Phelan and Burnham intended still greater growth. Their planning was to provide for that growth and to stimulate it even further. Phelan particularly viewed population growth as a means of stimulating and developing the economy and, hopefully, providing the resources needed to pay for the Burnham Plan's implementation.

The Burnham Plan, called into existence by Phelan, was not one for an industrial city or for one whose function it was to process the products of a hinterland. Phelan saw San Francisco as a great city with diversified, sophisticated functions, a city claiming a large and growing populace blessed with initiative and stamina. The Burnham Plan had to be functional, just as the city they were trying to recast had to be functional. The classicism that permeated the plan displayed itself clearly in Burnham's treatment of life at the higher contours — San Francisco's third dimension, its skyscape.

The Burnham plan crowned high ground with parks, monuments, and vista points — but not fully. Inspired by the hill towns of Italy, Burnham planned for private residences terraced neatly along the rising contours. From positions of such advantage the accomplished in society could see much and, in turn, be seen by many. Terraces were the ideal for the ascent of the Twin Peaks. Those who had elevated themselves above the competition might also elevate themselves above the congestion.

After the earthquake and fire, James Duval Phelan aided and encouraged Mollie in what may have been the single, most important judgment and decision of her adult life — to build her own home, one in which he too would reside (shown in a modern photograph).

Mollie's plans culminated in the construction of a grand Mediterranean style brick mansion on Washington Street at the north edge of Lafayette Park. The site commanded an unobstructed view of San Francisco Bay and its numerous islands. Her brother kept his own council, even though he himself opposed building on the northern slopes, or even northern crests of hills. In a San Francisco so often enveloped by blankets of cool grey fog, Phelan preferred the southern exposures that maximized the available sun. Mollie opted for the unsurpassed view. James D. Phelan had not developed into the sun worshiper he was to become once he built his own villa, Montalvo, in Santa Clara County. This San Francisco home, however, was to be his sister's and the location and construction were, at least, matters which engaged Mollie in the grand world beyond herself. Nonetheless, his architectural tastes found their way into the design, and who but Phelan would keep after the contractors and artisans to assure the quality control that Mollie had bargained for? The grand side entrance and the Mediterranean styling were to find themselves replicated not too many years later in James D. Phelan's personal expression of architectural good taste, Villa Montalvo.

James Duval Phelan rejected the assertion that photography qualified as an art form. Phelan loved snapping pictures from the first time personal cameras became available to the wealthy and the curious. Taking pictures with his Kodak was recording was history-in-the-making; displaying pictures in his leather-bound albums was assuring pleasure to the family, insight to posterity. Nonetheless, he engaged professional photographers to capture the poses and the occasions he valued.

Phelan himself seemed to have had no particular concern about bending the Burnham Plan to his personal and financial interests, not even for the integration of a new palatial residence for himself and his sister Mollie. During his post-mayoral years they continued to live comfortably in their parents' home out on the flatlands of the Mission District. Though the neighborhood had changed greatly from their parents' time, no pre-fire evidence exists to suggest that they planned to build elsewhere in the city. Without the fire, they undoubtedly would have remained longer in the surroundings of their youth. The significance of the building projects that both Mollie and James D. Phelan were to undertake was their total lack of relationship to the Burnham Plan. Phelan's labors on behalf of the beautification and adornment of San Francisco predated his own residential interests and those of his sister.

Daniel H. Burnham created San Francisco's grand master plan at Phelan's behest. His blueprint addressed traffic patterns, separation of functions, adornment and glorification of a unique urban metropolis. The Burnham Plan itself embodied an ideal, diluted sparingly by the demands of practicality. To implement a plan of such majesty and grace in a setting such as San Francisco's would require the creation of a heavenly city. Certainly such a destiny challenged Phelan's best.

For Phelan to have advanced such a plan for living urban art to this level of development was admirable. He persevered at this task through his middle years as a private citizen. His leadership ability, his cultivated tastes, and his love of San Francisco propelled him to the moment of promise when Burnham presented his formal plan before the board of supervisors, September 27, 1905. Unfortunately, by then the supervisors, once again, were corrupt.

Phelan was the most appropriate San Franciscan to attempt the task of directing the Burnham Plan toward implementation despite the baseness of the Eugene Schmitz administration. Even Phelan, however, had not anticipated the debilitating effects and subtle impact of the two most dynamic events that were to take place in the history of San Francisco: the earthquake and fire and the famous graft prosecution, both in 1906.

Chapter Eight
1906 Earthquake and Fire

City Beautiful — the Burnham Plan — topped Phelan's agenda for San Francisco. Next, came the massive Sierra water project — the Hetch Hetchy Plan. The corrupt political combination of Mayor Eugene Schmitz and his advisor, Abraham Ruef, aggravated Phelan's efforts to advance these ambitious projects for San Francisco and California. The corruption, in fact, caused Phelan to extend his agenda. Hetch Hetchy and City Beautiful acquired a prerequisite — graft prosecution. Phelan's fourth agenda item, the San Francisco earthquake and fire, Mother Nature added. And it overshadowed each of his other plans, complicating them immensely.

On the eve of San Francisco's earthquake and fire, Phelan's life was what might be expected. At age forty-five he had been a private citizen for four years. His relationship with Florence Ellon was relatively tranquil, and her complaint that other women received better treatment from gentlemen who were less well to do hardly constituted more than a minor irritant.

Phelan and his sister Mollie had occupied their season's seats at the Tivoli Opera House on Tuesday night where they enjoyed Enrico Caruso in *Carmen*. Retiring at the usual late hour following such evenings, Phelan slept soundly in the master bedroom that he occupied in the family mansion. At 5:15 A.M. the earthquake shook Phelan from his slumber. The jolt he felt was one of the 120 separate shocks recorded on April 18, 1906. The Ferry Building's clock, two miles away, at the foot of Market Street and several blocks beyond the Phelan Building, stopped. Its time, 5:16, established the official minute of the San Francisco earthquake. Phelan was hardly interested in the precisions of history, the accuracy of his fine Swiss watch, or in the rolling

Enrico Caruso performed his popular role as Don José, in Georges Bizet's Carmen, *at the Tivoli Opera House on the evening of April 17, 1906. The next morning, he awoke in haste because of the earthquake, bade San Francisco farewell, and never returned.*

Matter-of-Fact Reporting

For a man given to fine literary expression, James Duval Phelan recorded his firsthand observations of the earthquake and the subsequent fire in matter-of-fact prose. What caused other writers to reach for expository effect, Phelan played down quite intentionally. Rather than glorify the drama of quake and fire, thereby enhancing the perception of danger, risk, and loss, Phelan addressed the subject with dull, factual understatement.

Here is Phelan's account:

Going to the Valencia Street gate, I met three men and two women who were weeping. I asked what was the matter; and they pointed south to a five-story wooden hotel building on the west side of Valencia Street, south of 19th, which had fallen across the street and crumpled. All they said was, "Everyone is killed!"

I immediately went there, and could see men and women imprisoned by the fallen timbers; and, returning to my stable, I got my men, with axes and saws, and took out the family carriage, a vis-a-vis with two horses, and Barry, the coachman, (My automobile being garaged in some other part of town) and went to the scene of the hotel disaster.

repetitions of the geological experience he underwent. A practical man interested in assessing the magnitude of damage and addressing whatever danger, injury, and loss remained, Phelan sprang to his feet.

By 1906 the aging mansion had been fitted with parallel illuminating systems, electricity and gas. His damaged bedroom chandelier captured his attention immediately. The quake had broken its normal anchoring and it swung violently, suspended merely from a single wire. Even more ominous, though, was the escaping gas. Phelan exited his room, crossed the hall to Mollie's room, only to discover her at the window looking into the west garden. What they saw were the mansion's chimneys, dispersed in rubble below.

Phelan dressed hurriedly and organized the men servants. His directions blended common sense and his understanding of disaster precautions. Familiar with the Chicago Fire, he directed his men to turn off the gas at the street meter where the line entered their property. Next, he directed that no cooking whatever take place in the home. If other San Franciscans had possessed similar presence of mind, San Francisco's rendezvous with its destiny would have been far less devastating.

Assured that the household was safe, Phelan walked to the Valencia Street gate, beyond which he encountered a man and two women. All were weeping. To his inquiries they pointed two blocks to the south, to Nineteenth Street, where a five-story wood-constructed hotel had moved from its foundations and crumpled into the street. The distraught trio assured Phelan that "Everyone is killed!" Actually the mangle of timbers was so pronounced that when local firemen, Phelan, and his servants with their saws and axes cut into the broken structural remains, they found living as well as dead. Throughout their labors, Phelan assumed that the quake had been a localized problem. The hotel had collapsed and his home stood because the hotel had been constructed on what Phelan recalled as "the old Willows," filled land. The quake's shock waves, resounding through and enhanced by the land fill, shook the hotel from its foundation and deposited the twisted remains onto Valencia Street.

Phelan persisted in his limited comprehension of the disaster until a city employee of his acquaintance, Peter J. McCormick, appeared and explained the extent of the quake. Only much later did Phelan learn of the truly mammoth damage along the extended length of the San Andreas Fault. For the moment, though, McCormick told Phelan that "the city is wrecked, and fires have broken out...." At that Phelan had his carriage readied, and he and McCormick set out for downtown San Francisco. By then the morning was well advanced, the day was mild, and the sky, as yet, was clear.

As Phelan and McCormick made their way out of the Mission District, through the South of Market, and approached City Hall they observed the damage and devastation. Everywhere they saw the evidence of the quake; chimneys and cornices lay wrecked in the streets. Phelan wrote,

> *But, not until we reached the City Hall, did we realize the magnitude of the calamity. The City Hall was completely wrecked, large parts of the dome having fallen, leaving the cap in the air and the brick structure, on every side, ruined, with here and there a column standing, resembling the ruins of the Temple of the Dioscuri in the Forum in Rome.*

A recurring question over which historians have disagreed is: What destroyed the city? The quake or the fire? Or both? The business and commercial interests of the city had a stake in establishing that as much damage and loss as possible be tied to causes that could be prevented in the future through science, technology, and improved urban planning. In Phelan's case all of his observations and his personal experiences actually sustained the view that he preferred. Quake losses resulted from a combination of inferior construction and unstable sites. The greatest losses, however, were not from the earthquake itself; they were from the series of massive fires that followed and destroyed buildings that had survived the initial quake and all its aftershocks.

The Valencia Street hotel had been on soft ground; City Hall had been a shoddy monument to graft. In between Phelan observed variations from collapsed structures to simple cosmetic blemishes. He would attribute them to the variations of construction upon secure ground and his inspection of the Phelan Building fortified his analysis.

The Phelan Building

First he climbed four flights of stairs to his fifth floor office of his premier property at the intersection of Market, Grant, and O'Farrell Streets. Thomas Mahony, dutiful and loyal secretary to both Phelan and his father, was already on the scene. Also present, and accompanying Phelan and the older man on their inspection, was General Frederick Funston. The General was

The pre-quake City Hall and Hall of Records was a classic example of pre-reform politics: pure graft. Its construction enriched the contractors and the city fathers who took kickbacks from the annual appropriations. The building collapsed with the earthquake; the fire was unnecessary.

The Phelan Building after the earthquake and fire.

Historians still argue over what destroyed San Francisco. Was it the earthquake or the fire? Those with property losses and building plans blamed the fire. They could, thereby, file claims against their current insurers. In Phelan's case, this argument was true. The Phelan Building survived the earthquake but was consumed by fire.

James Duval Phelan had been able to enter the family office building after the earthquake, inspect, and remove those possession that he valued most: art, jewels, family history, and "certain papers." By the next day what his father had built was gone—destroyed by fire.

commanding troops already formed on the O'Farrell side of the building, not a surprising action since the military headquarters were located on the fourth floor of the Phelan Building, rather than at the Presidio of San Francisco.

Inside his own office Phelan noticed that all of his books that had lined one wall now were cast about on the floor, covered "with a mantle of snow"— plaster that had fallen from the ceiling and the walls. While the three men inspected the damages the building quivered slightly in a mild aftershock that caused General Funston to head for the street below. More secure in his conviction that well-constructed buildings on solid ground had little to fear, Phelan looked to the security of the possessions he valued most. By making selections and recording them he provided insight into his priorities and his values.

He could not predict when, or if, fire would engulf the building his father had constructed in 1882. The obvious threat to the family's building itself was one major source of anxiety, but it was magnified by the realization that his father's business records and their family history — materials dating from the Gold Rush — were in jeopardy. When he took over management of the family enterprises in 1892, Phelan accepted the established office practice of using the garrets beneath the building's roof line for storage. By 1906 dry wooden boxes held the records of a past that he so cherished.

Besides his own disgorged library, Phelan's files, his personal papers, and his art collection awaited rescue. He had the manpower. Building janitors were loyal and willing, and considerably more nimble than Mahony. Labor was not Phelan's constraint, transport was. For an unexplained reason Phelan had chosen one of his horse-drawn carriages on that historic morning rather than either his Mercedes or Renault automobile. Of all of his conveyances the one immediately available was small and slow. Therefore, he moved carefully among his valued possessions.

First, he directed the janitors to remove all his oil paintings, including a portrait of his father. He had always worked, and occasionally loved, beneath this somber rendering of the most significant person in his life. Other paintings included a large William Keith and several by contemporary French artists, including Benjamin Constant. Next, he chose a marble piece sculptured by Auguste Rodin purchased at the artist's Paris studio in 1905, two Russian bronze pieces, and a sampling of lesser works. Tentatively, Phelan directed the men to transport the art works to Union Square and await further instructions. He then turned his personal attention to light weight, valuable, and perishable items to which he attached great importance.

From his office safe he removed bonds and a jewel collection. From his locked desk drawers he removed the documentary record of his relationship with Florence Ellon: the letters they had exchanged, receipts he had retained from successive payments to her, and his early summary memorandum addressed to his brother-in-law, Frank Sullivan. This last document detailed the relationship itself from Phelan's perspective and instructed Sullivan how to treat Ellon in case he should die unexpectedly. In recording his movements of the morning and enumerating what he chose to save from his office, Phelan understandably glossed over such personal documents as "certain papers." He deliberated with himself as to what else to save "as the space in the carriage was limited." He decided to abandon his library and the business archives of two highly successful generations, in part because duplicates could be secured of the books, even limited editions. The collected volume of paper was too bulky and an extended effort to save it would be impractical and potentially dangerous. Instead, he instructed the janitors to "carry down all the scrap books to the waiting carriage at the door, with instructions to bring them home." From this decision came the Phelan and Sullivan family papers presently at the Bancroft Library, University of California at Berkeley.

Downtown

All this took place before mid-morning on the day of the quake. Phelan had assured himself of the safety of his sister and their household, staff included. He exercised rapid and critical judgments regarding those aspects of his business and personal life that revolved around his office. These responsibilities dispatched, Phelan walked to the financial district to inspect his own bank, Mutual Savings, and others in which he held interests. He found the greatest confusion at Bush and Sansome Street where firemen were attempting to save the First National Bank building from the advancing blaze.

Phelan encountered several of his friends, including John Downey Harvey, who sought him at the behest of Mayor Schmitz. Together they went to the Hall of Justice to organize a Committee of Fifty and try to take control of the deteriorating situation. Though perfunctorily offered, Phelan's promise to assist placed him at the vortex of the city in crisis.

The Spreckels-Call Building started to burn about the time James Duval Phelan was walking toward downtown.

Once the numerous small post-quake fires gathered into a roaring inferno strange things happened. Embers and sparks from exploding buildings ignited new structures at the top which then burned from the roof down—floor by floor. The result was total destruction.

Following this organizational meeting, he returned to the Phelan Building for a more thorough inspection, which was encouraging from the structural point of view and served to fortify further his convictions on earthquake damages versus the ravages of fire. Phelan ascended to the roof and from there saw "a splitting on the extreme south west wall." The split was on a portion added to the original structure, "an afterthought for the accommodation of the enlarged premises of Theodore Marceau," as a photographic gallery. Phelan's conclusion was that, "the old part of the building did not seem to have suffered any damage at all, except the shaking down of plaster here and there." Clearly though, his prime property was hardly secure. Just across Market Street, fire raged through the South of Market, moving from east to west, and consuming every building in its path. Phelan saw the fire take Claus Spreckels' Call Building; the Flood Building followed, as did all others of note and those of no distinction whatever. The wild fire raced along consuming the urban horizon of those viewing from the Phelan Building, who were, momentarily, protected by the prevailing winds and the expansive width of Market Street, which served as a natural fire break.

The original fires began as fifty-two individual incidents that expanded and merged into major conflagrations. Confronted with cracked and broken water mains, the authorities turned in desperation to blasting away the buildings that stood in their paths, attempting to deny fuel to the fire. This too failed. By the time Phelan left downtown the South of Market had been devastated and the north side of the thoroughfare was burning, though not at the same fast pace. The Financial District had been afire since the morning, but how far it would extend up Phelan's side of Market Street he did not know. There being little else he could do to safeguard the Phelan Building or his employees, Phelan redirected his concerns back to his sister Mollie and their home. On his route home, back out through the Mission District, his anxiety increased. The Mission was on fire too.

Here again, Phelan's assessment was uncertain. He wondered if the South of Market-Mission fire would extend all the way to his home. Certainly the chances of the North of Market fire reaching the Phelan Building were far greater. But, given the events of the day, anything was indeed possible. Perplexed, Phelan turned to the common chores, purchasing some potatoes, bread, crackers, and coffee at Goldberg Bowen & Co. shortly before the premises disappeared from the San Francisco landscape.

Mission District, Home and Friends

During the day, Phelan's chauffeur, James Mountford, caught up with him. Mountford had spent the morning impressed into service driving the injured and dying to temporary hospitals. Later, Phelan had heard that his own death had been reported in San Jose, where he was well known as a local property holder and banker. Evidently a body in his car had been mistaken for his own and reported to the press. By evening Mountford had completed such responsibilities, joined his employer, and was guiding Phelan through "lanes of fire" as he negotiated the Mercedes back to the Mission District.

At home Phelan found more people than he had shopped for. The servants, loyal and reliable, kept matters under control as long as the environment in which they were comfortable remained reasonably unaltered. Dinner was served without incident even though the fire line burned closer and closer. By nightfall the household had attracted additional unexpected callers and guests. Three Southern California friends of Mollie's who had been burned out of the Palace Hotel were in residence. Phelan servants also felt free to offer the shelter of their employer's home to their friends who had been burned out of their own dwellings. Then came the parade of callers.

John Downey Harvey arrived first. He informed his best friend, Phelan, that on the nomination of Garret McEnerney, dean of the California bar, Phelan was elected Chairman of the Finance Committee of the Citizens Committee of Fifty. Because the functions and powers of the committees were as yet unspecified, Phelan did not know that he would be the central figure at the policy-creation level for the relief of San Francisco. Shortly, he would be officially identified by President Theodore Roosevelt as the private individual to whom almost ten million dollars of relief funds were to be consigned. As yet, however, the significance of his appointment was unclear.

Next, Alice Phelan Sullivan and her husband Frank stopped at the Phelan home. Traveling by carriage, they were striking out for Santa Cruz, seventy miles away on the coast where the family had a country home and their children were already. Robert McElroy, Phelan's properties manager, visited at the same time as the Sullivans, and both relatives and business associate received equal attention from Phelan: he ignored them all and slept through their visits. Phelan's only special precaution was to open his bedroom windows as a safeguard just in case any unaccounted for gas found its

This Arnold Genthe view of the city's downtown commercial-financial district as seen from the residential district is among the most famous photographs of the earthquake and fire. Destroyed homes, damaged track, burning office blocks, and stunned residents constituted San Francisco in agony.

San Francisco's Tivoli Opera House after the earthquake. James Duval and Mollie Phelan had applauded Enrico Caruso's performance on the evening. The earthquake collapsed the ceiling, the fire destroyed the structure. Phelan's devotion to opera and its proper staging eventually led to his successful support for the modern San Francisco Opera House, a major component of Phelan's comprehensive city planning.

way to his chambers. Mollie, suffering from anxiety, declined to sleep indoors at all. Instead she comforted herself as best she could within the garden.

A man of steady habits, Phelan slept fully, awakened, and descended to the garden. Before encountering Mollie, he first met her maid. Knowing that they and the home were still among the present, he asked what news circulated about the Phelan Building. During the night had the fire destroyed it? While explaining that no additional news had arrived, the maid stooped and picked up a canceled bank check that had alighted at Phelan's feet. The scrap's arrival documented the destruction of the Phelan Building. His father's creation was gone!

The check, slightly scorched, was four years old and had been in the Phelan Building's garret storage. Phelan noted that, "The fire must have burst the boxes, and the contents scattered. The building was about two and one-half miles from the garden, and it has always been regarded as a curious thing that one of these telltale checks should have been deposited at my very feet." Phelan did not quite attribute it to divine providence, but more generously to "a messenger from the skies!" Calling his chauffeur he headed downtown, but was halted at Sixth and Market Streets, obstructed by the spreading fire. Retracing his path Phelan noted the fire's advance south to Mission and Fourteenth Streets. It was moving ever so surely toward their home. At that point, he decided to pack, even though "I was not convinced that my residence would be destroyed. The house was entirely surrounded by a close barrier of cypress trees."

Camping

Hopes aside, it was time to go. Phelan hailed a passing wagon and engaged the driver for two loads for sixty dollars — a goodly sum under normal conditions which these were not. The home was Mollie's and he gave first priority to the possessions she prized: a richly carved Swiss bedroom set she had purchased abroad, her wardrobe, some books, and then small art objects, and his scrapbooks — the ones he had rescued the day before from his office. Young George Welch was on the scene by then too. As fire and more apparent destruction approached, Phelan put Welch and an older Irishman in charge of the two loads of cherished possessions. The men guarded them faithfully for days on a secondary street farther to the south out of harm's way.

To Phelan fell the task of picking the site on which the household would spend the night. Most hotels had been destroyed, and no one could say for sure which buildings would survive the second night of San Francisco's inferno. Nothing man could do was deterring the great fire's advance.

Phelan's choice was Golden Gate Park. Far to the west and separated from the built up parts of the city, the park would be safe. Phelan's choice of accommodations was camping. Momentarily blessed by fine, mild days and nights, sleeping under the trees would be as comfortable as one might expect. In Phelan's case, he did not expect much. He had never joined the Sierra Club and never allowed Teddy Roosevelt's enthusiasm for the strenuous life to infect him personally. Phelan's ideal was civilization, and that meant sleeping up off the ground if at all possible. The night of April 19, 1906, might make this impossible. Phelan gathered and directed his household caravan to a restful spot near the Japanese Tea Garden. They appeared well turned out in contrast to their fellow refugees. Phelan noted that the cross section of humanity that clogged the road made an "endless procession of wagons and trundle carts, men and women of all descriptions carrying various objects and seeking places of safety." Even in disaster Phelan retained his habits of maintaining appearances. He did adjust to the circumstances, though. He kept Mollie's jewelry in his pockets. He had not replaced the pieces in any of his downtown bank vaults after their last evening at the opera. For Mollie to wear the jewels would have been worse than provocative. It would have been poor taste.

His driver, Barry, led the procession in what Phelan described as his "vis-a-vis carriage," a light horse-drawn conveyance in which the passengers sat face-to-face. Behind Barry came Phelan's four-wheeled coach. Phelan's regular coachman, James H. Robinson, drove the buggy. As if to splash the sad but necessary caravan with a touch of humor Phelan impressed into service the house dog. From under the cobwebs formed since his youth, Phelan extracted his old dog cart and had its harness made ready. In emergencies all should pull their own weight, even the pet. With Mollie's carriage and driver concluding the party, all was in readiness — transport, personnel, and supplies. Phelan's last act as the line pulled from the confines of the garden and passed through the gate was to induce a distraught woman with a child to accompany them. She did, but only for a while. Later her baby died, and Phelan obtained a burial permit for the infant's interment.

The San Francisco Admission Day statue commemorated California's entry into the federal union. Commissioned by James Duval Phelan and designed and created by Douglas Tilden, the piece survived the city it was intended to adorn. Tilden's public art enjoyed international recognition. Phelan continued to seek out Tilden's talent, patronize his art, and encouraged his creativity. En route, Phelan did his best to ignore Tilden's personality.

Saint Ignatius Church and College, located at Hayes Street and Van Ness Avenue, survived the earthquake, but not the fire. In this case, a neighbor lit her morning fire intending to cook breakfast. Sparks from the damaged chimney ignited the wood structure. The result was the "Ham and Eggs Fire" that destroyed much of the Hayes Valley.

Phelan and his sister chose to travel by automobile and, en route, he directed his driver to stop at Robert McElroy's house, which was safely located behind clear ground and stone walls at the corner of Haight and Buchanan Streets. Phelan wanted to place Mollie with the McElroys, but his scheme misfired when Mollie, atop the McElroy's front steps, turned and viewed the burning city below. She refused to remain. Reconciled to what he could not control in human nature as well as the physical environment, Phelan pressed on and rendezvoused with Barry's horse-drawn party. As planned, they met at the Golden Gate Park Lodge, where the Panhandle joined the park at Stanyan Street. There they refreshed themselves and rested their animals in anticipation of occupying the cite Phelan had staked out just beyond the Museum. Phelan selected the spot because it had piped water, enjoyed the protection of trees, and bordered a grain field where the stock could graze.

An obvious alternative to Phelan's plan would have been simply to discharge the domestic staff and use his available transport to save more of the family's tangible possessions. He not only did not choose that alternative, it never seemed to have crossed his mind. Later, when the losses sustained by San Francisco's notables became common knowledge, the press singled out Phelan as an exception for his loyalty in retaining his then-burdensome domestic staff. The same was true of his office staff.

Unfortunately, San Francisco's already colorful lore cannot be enriched further by documentation of James Duval Phelan sleeping in the park, not even in a quiet, sheltered spot rather than on a hard wooden bench. Such was not to be. A comfort seeker with few peers, Phelan drove back to Valencia and Seventeenth Street to retrieve a grand marquee tent he had used for his outdoor receptions and lawn parties over the years. Phelan's timing was critical. He rescued the tent minutes before he witnessed the line of "cypress trees ignite and send their fire brands over the place, setting the house on fire and destroying everything in it."

Working rapidly and alone, he had removed several paintings from the home and placed them face down several hundred feet away from the house. But to no avail. They, too, were ruined by the shooting sparks. Even his marble sculpture, a copy of Apollo and Daphne by Bernini, suffered from the fire and heat. "Badly spalled," it looked as if it had been worked over by a hammer, having lost numerous chips. What was left, Phelan recorded, was later destroyed by marauding squads of small boys who threw stones at the unprotected target in the then abandoned garden wasteland. Always learning a lesson, particularly when the tuition was exorbitant, Phelan noted that, when faced with impending disaster, valuables ought better be buried. He turned and watched the incineration of his parents home. Laden with his last momento, the tent, Phelan returned to the Tea Garden encampment and reassured himself of the safety and reasonable comfort of the staff and friends.

Reconstruction

Through the days that followed the initial quake Phelan was engaged in a nonstop series of meetings of the Committee of Fifty and related groups and officials. Personally designated by the Committee and by President Theodore Roosevelt as the sole individual to whom relief funds were to be entrusted, his responsibilities extended well beyond his own household to embrace San Francisco at large. His contact with his friends and associates, even in this drastically altered environment, allowed him to place Mollie in more comfortable and settled surroundings and to accept friendly hospitality for himself as well. The heirs of James Phelan did not sleep in the park.

With the cooperation of his school friend and lifelong confidant, John Downey Harvey, and his own club membership, Phelan lodged Mollie and her personal maid, Agnes Curran, at the Burlingame Country Club. Of his nighttime return from Burlingame to Harvey's secure San Francisco residence Phelan wrote: "The Peninsula was so brilliantly illuminated by the fire, that one could read the newspaper out of doors." Harvey's wife, Sophie, was in Europe and their daughters were among the women in Burlingame. So Harvey made his residence on Webster at Broadway available to Phelan. He provided a room for Phelan's use and meals when he was not about the city on official business. Around his table gathered the men of wealth, talent, and power who were to assist Phelan in guiding the relief of San Francisco. Garret McEnerney was among the heavy weights who came to dine. He was the commanding figure who selected Phelan as the individual to control $10,000,000 in relief funds. Phelan, in turn, respected McEnerney, but he never warmed to him. Phelan was always cautious with attorneys.

John S. Drum, another committee member, and Phelan were a bit closer. Both served as directors of the California Pacific Title Insurance Company and they shared memberships in the Burlingame Country Club. Drum was a

John Downey Harvey

John Downey Harvey had been James D. Phelan's friend since school days with the Jesuits. Harvey's widowed mother, sister of California Governor John G. Downey, had married a second time and into a great fortune. Throughout her advanced years, she commanded a central place in San Francisco society. Her son "Downey" did not marry as well as his mother. Yet, accustomed to a life he could not himself afford, he first struggled to qualify for full membership, and in 1906 his financial fate was irreversibly tied to the construction of the Ocean Shore Railroad Company that was attempting to link San Francisco to Santa Cruz. Harvey's speculative venture was struggling at best and the effects of the earthquake and fire were, as yet, unknown. Amidst all his personal travails, Phelan's friend played the perfect host.

Garret W. McEnerney and James D. Phelan

The dean of the California bar, the most powerful and devoted regent of the University of California, and the permanent counsel to the Catholic Archdiocese of San Francisco, Garret W. McEnerney commenced his dynamic legal career by trying and winning the first case brought before the International Court at The Hague. His so-called McEnerney Act was the measure that reestablished title to property following the destruction of records in the 1906 fire. In his will, he divided his fortune equally between the University of California and the Catholic Church.

McEnerney's successive regencies gave him the opportunity to bring Dr. Benjamin Ide Wheeler to California to be president of the University of California and create the modern university system. McEnerney watched Berkeley flourish, first under his autocratic appointee, Wheeler. Then, as California and its university matured, McEnerney set Wheeler aside. Thereafter Robert Gordon Sproul, with McEnerney's support and approval, finished what McEnerney had set in motion — creation of a university worthy of the state.

James Duval Phelan had been appointed to the University Board of Regents himself, but the Legislature failed to approve the Governor's action. Therefore, Phelan never enjoyed the honor or the opportunity for the service that McEnerney so dignified. Phelan and McEnerney cooperated in civic enterprises, but they were hardly one in the spirit. McEnerney's devout Catholicism, likewise, may have created some distance, reduced somewhat by Father Peter C. Yorke who publicly abused McEnerney as viciously, though less frequently, as he did Phelan.

Garret W. McEnerney

Frank Sullivan, Phelan's brother-in-law, once retained McEnerney to sue and harass Phelan. By then, McEnerney was already moving comfortably within a California characterized by corporate growth and complex organizational development. He was a professional whose legal and personal skills were the reasons for his agreeable functioning in this regional society in the making — and the basis for his wealth. His banking connections rivalled Phelan's.

Catholic and a Democrat and was to receive federal appointments during World War I and Phelan's U. S. Senate term. His career was capped in the 1920s as president of the American Bankers Association.

M. H. de Young also enjoyed a place in the inner circle. Owner of the San Francisco *Chronicle*, he could not be relied upon, certainly not taken for granted, by Phelan. Independent in thinking and subscribing to no comprehensive body of thought on public subjects, de Young was unpredictable. In the long run, his public spirited impulses, which were to culminate in the creation of the de Young Museum in Golden Gate Park, won out. The presence of Rudolph Spreckels, however, was more than sufficient to provide adequate ballast at meetings of the Committee of Fifty and even meetings of its Executive Committee. Spreckels and Phelan fully agreed regarding relief of San Francisco as a preliminary, though not as a prerequisite, to the prosecution of the officially elected, corrupt administration.

Elsewhere within the Committee of Fifty were those with whom Phelan maintained professionally proper relationships and little more. William F. Herrin was the chief council and political boss for the Southern Pacific Railroad in California. He was recognized as immensely powerful and, thought Phelan and other would-be prosecutors, immensely corrupt. Mayor Schmitz, by virtue of his official position and his having called the committee into being, served as an ex-officio member.

Solicitation of relief funds was the first priority. One hundred and thirty-one San Franciscans who, like Phelan, had owned much and lost much contributed $413,000 to the Committee during its solicitation campaign. Phelan did not enjoy dunning his friends for money, but he recognized its necessity. His efforts to get the United States Congress to stand behind San Francisco bonds that would have an extended maturity period failed. But Congress did contribute $2,500,000 to the relief effort. Recollecting later, he noted that those funds largely reimbursed the U. S. Army and Navy for the supplies and the services they had provided immediately after the disaster. Somewhat similar in restriction were the contributions of John D. Rockefeller and Standard Oil Company — $100,000 from each. After news of these contributions were conveyed to the local attorney of the Standard Oil Company, E. S. Pillsbury, he retained the funds for special disbursement by himself. In conveying to Phelan his intentions to restrict the funds Pillsbury declined to admit Phelan and his colleagues to his home. Instead, Pillsbury delivered his message to the Relief Committee members through his door.

More substantial amounts came in from throughout California, the nation, and abroad. Phelan centralized in himself a major function normally the responsibility of the American Red Cross (an organization to which Phelan was also a major contributor), which also was on the scene. Joint incorporation of the Red Cross and the local Relief Fund avoided any possible legal problem, and Phelan's cooperative, professional approach avoided

Theodore Roosevelt, Michael de Young, and Eugene Schmitz at the Cliff House, May 13, 1903. The President, the Chronicle *publisher, and the (as yet unsuspected) mayor paused for a moment during their luncheon. Roosevelt came to California to assess the merit of conservation versus development. De Young associated himself with all public issues. And Schmitz merely endeavored to appear worthy of his city and his president's attention. With Abe Ruef as his speech writer, Schmitz succeeded admirably and emerged with a greatly enhanced local reputation. Three years later, Roosevelt cooperated in Schmitz's arrest and removal from office.*

Irish Contribution

One of the most spontaneous and heartfelt responses was that of Douglas Hyde, the Irish language booster and future president of Ireland. Hyde had collected $6,000 during his fund-raising trip through the Bay Area earlier in 1906. About half of his purse had come from Frank Sullivan and Phelan. Hyde had been deeply touched by San Francisco's hospitality and generosity, particularly by the personal attention of the Sullivans and Phelans. Hearing of the disaster, Hyde returned $1,000 to the relief fund.

friction at the operational level between local committees and the relief professionals who gathered in San Francisco.

Of the nearly $10,000,000 Phelan received and dispersed, $300,000 arrived unsolicited from foreign countries. The largest infusions of capital, distinct from relief funds, that came into the destroyed city were from the insurance companies in the form of payments to property owners. Phelan calculated that this total was about $190,000,000. Most companies lived up to their policy commitments and met their losses, some with five- to twenty-percent deductions. "The German insurance companies," he wrote to a friend, "repudiated their policies."

Seventeen years later, in a comprehensive review, Phelan addressed the matter in a way that relates to the continuing controversy over what caused such great damage, the earthquake or the fire. Some insurance companies attempted to reject claims for fire loss on buildings they alleged had already been destroyed or seriously damaged before the fire reached them. The local courts prevented companies from prevailing in their appeals to the policies' "fallen building" clauses. To protect themselves in the future, the companies required a premium of twenty-five percent for coverages that negated the "fallen building" provision. As with most historical controversies there are data that lend themselves to both interpretations. Perhaps that is why controversy remains: both alternatives seem to have been true at the same time. In the Phelan cases, structurally sound buildings were destroyed by fire.

Once the financial situation stabilized in San Francisco, financial institutions in the East advanced mortgage money for the construction of modern new buildings at rates from five-and-a-half to seven percent per year. Individual loans of six to seven million dollars were not uncommon.

Personal Losses

Phelan's own losses were staggering. His lifelong confidant was his cousin George Duval, the New York merchant and Catholic philanthropist, and to him Phelan revealed his precarious situation. "We have lost all our income property here and about half in San Jose. San Diego was not affected....The calamity is overwhelming but everybody is game and making a good fight." To a London friend, Edgar Carolan, he added: "All your friends are well and have a superabundance of health, good appetites and low diet, and attenuated purses.…There is a splendid spirit among the people to rebuild on better lines.…[It] is something to have lived through the tragedy and the fall of a great city in a few hours and to take part in its reconstruction."

Phelan was fully convinced that the fire caused most of the city's damage. The earthquake damaged poorly constructed buildings and those erected on unstable, filled ground. The broken and failed water mains were of rigid construction and unsupported as they extended through filled land. They had no flexibility at their joints and had no support structures that extended to bedrock. For the remainder of his life Phelan waged a personal war against the insurers of the reconstructed Phelan Building for what he considered grossly excessive earthquake coverages required by his eastern mortgage holders. So convinced was Phelan of the durability of well-constructed buildings on solid land that he was prepared to forego earthquake insurance altogether.

By 1926, he had repaid one-half million dollars of an original loan of two million that allowed him to rebuild the Phelan Building on a far larger scale and in keeping with the latest and safest design specifications. Then, with his increased equity having reduced the equity of the lender, the Metropolitan Life Insurance Company, Phelan sought a full waiver of the mortgage clause requiring any earthquake coverage what so ever. "It is so manifestly unjust," he protested, "that I should be mulched, under these circumstances, by an insurance combination, that I appeal to your sense of fair play."

He was direct in his appeal to Frederick H. Ecker:

Personally, I do not want, nor would I have, any earthquake insurance, so confident am I of the stability of my building.…The foundations … are laid upon bedrock, every brick is laid in pure cement, and the amount of steel in the structure — which is of battleship construction, upon a gore [a small, triangular piece] of land — is in excess, by twelve hundred tons, of the amount stipulated by architects and engineers.…I also wish to emphasize again the fact that California earthquakes, so far as is known, have only seriously damaged buildings of inferior construction, and not at all buildings of modern steel construction.

The life insurance company evidenced scant enthusiasm for enforcing the tariffs exacted by the property insurance industry. His lender, Metropolitan Life, allowed Phelan to assume the full risk of earthquake to his modern office building. His judgment has demonstrated its correctness throughout the city's subsequent quakes. Phelan's theoretical convictions did not cause

The San Jose Phelan Building did not burn. In fact, San Joe had no post-quake fire. The structure merely collapsed, much to the curiosity of the neighbors.

The San Jose Mercury of April 21, 1906, estimated selected Phelan losses:

Louise Building, San Jose	$50,000
Alice Building, San Francisco	12,000
Rucker Building, Warehouse, San Jose	10,000
Spring Building, San Francisco	15,000
Williams Building, San Francisco	15,000
Phelan Building, San Jose	40,000
Theater Building, San Francisco	8,000
Theater Victory, San Francisco	7,000
Total	$157,000

James Duval Phelan rebuilt his father's office building on modern lines, with even greater structural integrity and user-convenient features. The larger and enhanced structure came complete with roof garden and dining and entertaining facilities. His motivations for prompt construction were two: show a battered city an example and reestablish Market Street as the commercial avenue of town. The threatened relocation of commercial and retail activities to the Western Addition jeopardized the land values of all who had lost their downtown buildings.

him to throw caution to the winds, particularly when he became the lender on commercial and apartment buildings that were not Class A, concrete and steel. For buildings constructed to lesser specifications and "on account of earthquake conditions," Phelan advised his manager in 1913, "we should get closer to the German rule, and loan but little more than the value of the lot."

Public Responsibilities and Corruption

The former mayor's reputation for scrupulous honesty and the complete and exact discharge of public responsibilities placed him in the center of the relief matrix. San Francisco was, indeed, well served. Two raids, both unsuccessful, were made upon Phelan's relief treasury. One was unexpected; the other was blatant and anticipated.

The Southern Pacific Railroad had dominated California's economic and political life throughout the state's history and would continue to do so until the election of Hiram Johnson in 1910. In 1906 the corporate concern over the local disruption and damage seemed so grave that the railroad's president himself, Edward H. Harriman, entrained by private car for San Francisco. Harriman's elegant train car served as his private hotel at a safe distance — at the Oakland Mole. Because of Harriman's status among persons of influence and power, Phelan invited him to attend a conference of the Committee of Fifty. Following some general discussion, Harriman recommended that a treasurer be elected for the Committee. A banker, he thought, was preferable. Further, the funds should be decentralized. They should be placed in banks throughout the United States and thus not deplete the deposits of small communities that were subscribing funds.

Next, Harriman's chief legal counsel, Herrin (who Phelan anticipated trying for bribery), converted his employer's remarks into a motion whereby Isaias W. Hellman, a banker with state and regional financial interests, would be elected treasurer. The prearrangement of this maneuver was so obvious that checking it was hardly a credit to Phelan. Presiding over the meeting, Phelan ruled the motion out of order. The meeting was a conference and, Phelan recorded in his memoir statement of the events, "whatever action ... to be taken should be taken by the Finance Committee," not this group.

At that the man who controlled Southern Pacific rose and left so abruptly that Benjamin Ide Wheeler, President of the University of California, told

Phelan that he had made an error in alienating Harriman. Phelan overtook a hostile Harriman on the lawn. Phelan's approach was to restate the nature of the meeting and the responsibility assigned to him. Phelan, as the custodian of the funds, had placed them in the undamaged United States Mint. Further, because President Roosevelt had named him personally, Phelan felt obliged not to transfer funds without the President's approval. Finally, and politely, Phelan noted that he agreed with the reasoning for depositing money in diverse banks, that he was a banker, and that he could take that action.

The point that carried the evening was dropping of Roosevelt's name. Harriman, not to be out done, asserted that Roosevelt was his friend, too, and that he had "constant communication with him by telephone between our offices." Thus Phelan averted confrontation with a man of substantial power. Harriman's organization provided highly desirable service to the distraught community, including free transportation to anywhere in America for anyone who could not afford to escape from the San Francisco earthquake and its disastrous aftermath. The result greatly lightened the relief rolls that Phelan otherwise would have to meet.

Still, Herrin, Harriman's local representative, remained marked for prosecution. Clearly, Phelan and his gentlemanly colleagues could respectfully conduct business at one meeting with those whose destruction they planned at the next. Harriman's gracious invitation to Phelan to dine in his private car not withstanding, the prosecutors would try to work from Mayor Schmitz's political manipulator Ruef, through Herrin, to Harriman — prosecuting them all or offering the lesser corruptionist immunity for testimony against those of greater position and power.

Another Challenge

Mayor Eugene Schmitz's run for the purse was more direct. Evaluated by historians as either incompetent or dishonest, or both, Schmitz created Phelan's committee. That action may be *the* singularly significant, unblemished act of his three administrations. The realization that his administration was incapable of meeting San Francisco's needs in the city's hour of loss may have motivated him. Or he may have risen to the occasion, above the sad standard of his proven mediocrity. That he made the appointment through stupidity would be unlikely because Ruef would have intervened. Once the situation

Like James D. Phelan, Abraham Ruef was a San Francisco phenomenon. Both were sophisticated, educated, and refined. Ruef, the 1883 University of California class valedictorian, was also corrupt. Fascinated by political power and manipulation, Ruef was in the game as much for the amusement as the loot.

San Francisco's Mayor Eugene E. Schmitz offered a compelling public presence. He was a popular and attractive orchestra leader whose nomination Abe Ruef finessed through the convention of the new and politically naive Union Labor Party. Schmitz's charm and Ruef's cunning ensured Schmitz's election. Schmitz carried his father's name and practiced his mother's religion when the German-Irish-Catholic combination claimed sixty percent of the city's total population.

clarified and the amount of money Phelan would control also became apparent, Schmitz made his move.

The Mayor invited Phelan, McEnerney and others from the executive committee to his home for an elaborately prepared and elegantly presented luncheon. Promptly, Schmitz addressed his challenge of the moment. Yes, the committee seemed to have moved efficiently enough forward on all fronts, therefore, the city's legislative and deliberative body, the Board of Supervisors, should reenter the mainstream. And, simply, the committee could best accomplish this desirable result by placing the collected relief funds in their official hands. After all, the Supervisors were the representatives elected by the citizens of the city. The reactions of McEnerney and Phelan were predictable. Schmitz (or Ruef) had prepared his ground thoroughly. So Phelan had to do more than merely decline politely. The timing of Mayor Schmitz's initiative coincided with Phelan's scheduled departure for Washington D.C., on the following morning. Phelan was to seek Congressional aid for the reconstruction of San Francisco. His transportation east had been arranged by Schmitz who, with Ruef, certainly understood the importance Phelan placed upon this mission. For Phelan relief, restoration, and City Beautiful were all tied to Washington. His models — Paris, Berlin, and Athens — each had enjoyed access to broadly gathered wealth, and each with but slight accountability by those who spent it to those who had it.

When Burnham had completed and submitted his plan he had estimated that $50,000,00 would have put the plan substantially into effect. Phelan had multiple copies of the Plan printed just days before the fire. He agreed that $50,000,000 would do. Further, the city's freedom from bonded indebtedness, along with the enhanced property values and tourist income the City Beautiful would create, would liquidate the debt. The $50,000,000 was an investment, not an expenditure. The disaster of earthquake and fire greatly affected Phelan's efforts to implement the Burnham Plan. Initially some even felt that the destruction was heaven sent. The Burnham Plan could be more easily implemented because where obstacles once stood, now lay ashes.

Phelan knew that with or without earthquake and fire San Francisco would need to go beyond its own limited resources to create the ideal city. He looked to centralized sources at a distance as the most comparable to his classical models. The Federal Government or Eastern-based finance capital might be induced to provide the needed revenue. His scheduled trip to

Washington and the Eastern financial markets had this objective in mind. Schmitz, however, and his gang of corrupters were threatening the one bird Phelan had in the hand while sending him off to look for more in the bushes. Phelan consulted with McEnerney and decided to remain in San Francisco, on guard against the corrupt administration. No transfer of funds took place and Phelan remained vigilant as he presided over the disbursement of funds.

By June he was confiding again to his cousin George Duval: "Were it not for the responsibility which this work has entailed upon me, I might possibly have gone East to help to get money for the rebuilding of San Francisco. …My own affairs have been neglected by me for the same reason — that the work of the Finance Committee is very absorbing."

Others took up the difficult tasks in Washington and failed while Phelan advanced the investigations of the Schmitz Administration, safeguarded the relief fund, and presided over the relief and rehabilitation of San Francisco. He had to accept the serious modification of the Burnham Plan, largely because he was a vigilant outsider who could not control the political process by which it might best be implemented. From the outside he cleansed San Francisco politics for the second time. But first he fulfilled his responsibilities as chairman of the Finance Committee of the Committee of Fifty and in doing so revealed more clearly his social philosophy.

Relief Funds

Phelan subscribed to the relief ideology that denied that each sufferer was entitled to an equal share of the relief fund. Instead, the fund was to help individuals restore themselves to the status and condition they enjoyed before the fire. Phelan, with imported relief and welfare professionals, sought to stimulate self-help. They shared an aversion to public dependency. The relief funds were used to obtain tools for workers and start-up money for those who had been home owners. Particularly concerned with the business life of the city, Phelan intended that the fund stand behind the reestablishment of small businesses. Throughout, the fund managers avoided competition with private sector activity and endeavored to restore the previous social and economic order. The one area where these priorities were bent was the provisions made for women, particularly single parents struggling to provide for their children. These women received a disproportionate share of the fund.

Well dressed, well groomed, and well fed were James Duval Phelan's prerequisites—even when roughing it. Fresh air and the out-of-doors were the limits to his compromise of civilization. Camping in Golden Gate Park during the 1906 fire could have been endured — if absolutely required. Camping at the Bohemian Grove was something else altogether.

Even though the records are not exact enough to demonstrate that this was due to Phelan personally, it was in keeping with his concept of private charity and philanthropy. Certainly, he could have blocked such relative largess and redirected the funds into other unmet demands.

Phelan, in essence, presided over an extraordinary historical event. He collected, distributed, and accounted for ten million dollars and no San Francisco politician stole any of it! Phelan also continued to encourage the investigations of the corrupt office holders. By attending personally to these matters, Phelan relinquished his advanced position in the quest for federal or eastern money to implement the Burnham Plan as the basis for the restoration of San Francisco. At the time a modified Burnham Plan appeared to have some hope of implementation except for one major stumbling block. Mayor Schmitz's silent partner, Abraham Ruef, emerged as the only individual sufficiently bright, sufficiently energetic, and sufficiently well placed enough to manipulate the financial, constitutional, and political variables.

The rights of property owners and the requirements even of the modified Burnham Plan were not compatible. And the right to personal property was so fundamental to American values that not even a plan as noble as Daniel Burnham's would easily prevail. Only Ruef's blend of wisdom and cunning seemed worthy of the challenge, divesting San Francisco property owners of their valuable frontages. Simple and ingenious, Ruef's scheme was for the government to condemn the less expensive rear, under-used spaces within the major property lots of downtown San Francisco, compensate the owners at lower prices, and then trade the back footage for the frontage. In essence, the owners would be required to construct their new edifices a bit further back on their lots, thus allowing the public space envisioned by the modified Burnham plan for the expanded boulevards and public places.

The greatest tragedy of the era was not the earthquake and fire itself. San Francisco's greatest tragedy was that men as talented as James D. Phelan and Abraham Ruef were propelled by such incompatible motivations. Phelan could not trust Ruef or Schmitz in any activity, least of all in control of San Francisco's reconstruction. So, rather than helping them gain control of the distribution of untold new contracts and risk reconstruction of a gross and shabby city, Phelan allowed Ruef and Schmitz to fail in that effort. Instead, he guided their removal from power and office. Then Phelan watched their incarceration, trials, and convictions.

Chapter Nine

Graft Prosecution

In keeping with his theory of civic improvement, Phelan chose caution and patience after 1906. His judgment was that greater things would not be accomplished through the hands of Schmitz and Ruef. They had to be removed and honesty restored to the politics of San Francisco. Only then would progress come.

Phelan and his close friend and progressive ally, Rudolph Spreckels, agreed that Phelan's successor to the office of mayor should be indicted, prosecuted, and (they hoped) sentenced to prison. Spreckels took the lead, though, in what they both anticipated would be their greatest joint contribution to San Francisco's political health. From Phelan's vantage point, he was in the process of blending several agendas: Hetch Hetchy, City Beautiful, and graft prosecution.

Phelan's other concerns, Hetch Hetchy and City Beautiful, advanced without significant assist or early opposition from the new mayor, Eugene Schmitz, titular leader of the city's new Union Labor Party. Schmitz and his political manipulator, attorney Abraham Ruef, focused their attentions upon more limited and more immediately remunerative opportunities that their control of office allowed. Both enjoyed their own claims to culture: Schmitz was an accomplished musician, Ruef a linguist and an intellectual. Both viewed the beautification of San Francisco and its mammoth water project with benign neglect, at least until Phelan's plans reached the stage of development where greed sensed opportunity. Money attracted Ruef's and Schmitz's attentions and gradually drew city hall into opposing Phelan's plans. The competing, established corporate interests would pay for political

Mayor Eugene Schmitz had an easy manner that at first charmed the voting public. Engaging appearances had their limits, however, particularly when James Duval Phelan and his progressive friends increased their vigilance.

Spreckels and Phelan

James Duval Phelan and Rudolph Spreckels were well-matched collaborators. Both had been born to extraordinary wealth. Spreckels could not endure his own father's autocratic personality. He broke with him and succeeded admirably on his own in Hawaiian sugar planting, banking, finance, and real estate. Younger than Phelan and happily married, he still enjoyed Phelan's company and shared his progressive ideals. Believed to have been the two richest San Franciscans of their day, both men were committed to the implementation of progressive reforms. Both millionaires, in fact, were keen on the adoption of a national graduated income tax. They were convinced that the funds needed to create the activist, progressive government they believed San Francisco and America needed and deserved, must come from those who had the wealth.

help. Phelan would not. As early as January, 1906, Abe Ruef had entered into a confidential agreement with the president and chief stockholder of the Bay Cities Water Company, William S. Tevis. The Tevis company held water rights in the Lake Tahoe area and intended to construct a water system not to supply water to San Francisco, but rather to unload the entire system on the city at a vastly inflated price. Tevis offered Ruef, Mayor Schmitz's political brains and confidential advisor, one million dollars if the scheme succeeded. Ruef's implementation plan was simple, spread the money liberally where it was likely to have the desired effect.

He drew the mayor, the most prominent member of the board of supervisors, and the chair of the board's water committee into the plan. Ruef's distribution scheme allocated $75,000 for the lead supervisor and $25,000 for each of the other supervisors who would vote favorably on the measure when it came before them officially. For the remaining half-million dollars Ruef earmarked a quarter million for himself and the other quarter million for Mayor Schmitz.

This corrupt scheme demonstrated that the public interest simply was for sale. Further, this example was merely one of the numerous corrupt activities in which the Schmitz administration involved itself. The administration's pattern was to accept bribes from the well-to-do. Most often the bribe givers were corporate executives searching for franchises, utility rate increases, or other actions within the authority of the Union Labor board of supervisors. Socially and culturally, Phelan could identify quite comfortably with the corporate bribe-givers. Yet, these same men repelled Phelan on ethical, political, and economic grounds. Even worse from Phelan's point of view, it was he who had strengthened the executive functions of the mayor through his new Charter of 1900. Anyone who wished to make the observation could accuse Phelan of having placed greater power into the slippery hands of Mayor Schmitz and, as a result, the sure and corrupt hands of Ruef.

Ruef had been secretly on the payroll of the United Railroads as a consultant since 1902. With eastern capital and under the direction of Patrick Calhoun, grandson of the South's noted political leader John C. Calhoun, the United Railroads had purchased the San Francisco lines and was attempting to put them on a paying basis. Those efforts included driving down the cost of labor in a pro-union city and modernizing operations through conversion of cable driven cars to overhead trolley lines. Overhead lines and the poles they hung from were ugly, and they obviously conflicted with City Beautiful.

As the trail of corruption became broader and easier to observe, the battle lines formed: Phelan and his progressive friends versus the corrupt allies in City Hall and their corporate bribe givers. Thus confronted, Phelan integrated his public agendas. The more deals Ruef cut for himself, Schmitz, and their equally corrupt tools on the board of supervisors, the more Hetch Hetchy and City Beautiful interests became jeopardized. Understandably, Phelan's cooperation with Rudolph Spreckels increased at the same time Spreckels was motivated by the crusading zeal of the editor of the San Francisco *Bulletin*, Fremont Older.

Phelan's three terms as mayor had illustrated that political corruption was not inevitable; it was not a natural part of the urban process, even in San Francisco. From Phelan the informed public learned that honesty was possible. Then, immediately on the heels of the Phelan administration, the corrupt Schmitz-Ruef regime called into question this precious lesson. Perhaps Phelan's honest and responsible administration was an aberration not to be visited upon San Francisco a second time. Ironically, San Francisco's best administration was succeeded by its worst.

The first person to vent his outrage was the *Bulletin's* editor. Fremont Older had been one of Phelan's most reliable newspaper supporters. He shared many of Phelan's early political views. On the pages of the *Bulletin*, Older continued to advocate honesty and propriety in the political life of the city even after Phelan's retirement from City Hall in 1902. Confronted by Ruef and Schmitz, however, Older made himself into the conscience of the city. His howls merely sounded in a journalistic wilderness. Undaunted, the frustrated editor took his case to Washington D.C. and actually obtained the sympathetic ear of President Theodore Roosevelt who himself had tilted with corrupt city politicians during his formative years in New York.

Roosevelt struck a bargain with Older. If Older could attract sufficient financial support to underwrite an investigation and prosecution of Schmitz, Ruef, the Supervisors, and the corporate bribe-givers as well, then Roosevelt would help. The President promised Older that he would make available for service in San Francisco America's most successful detective and the federal government's best special prosecutor. They were William J. Burns and Francis J. Heney.

Once news of the inside graft schemes became public, Mayor Schmitz ceased being portrayed as the sophisticate who dined and conversed with President Roosevelt. He became a cartoon figure.

Throughout, Abe Ruef retained his sense of humor. At the start, he assured Schmitz that his commanding personal presence was enough to win in politics: "The psychology of the mass of the voters ... is like a crowd of small boys...." Ruef even chose Union Labor candidates for supervisor because some looked like familiar comic strip characters. Later, as a San Quentin prisoner, Ruef hyped reporters about living in a "modern Utopia." Schmitz remained an engaging superficiality.

Gathering to review their battle strategy are those who organized the war on graft and those who executed the campaign. From the left, Francis J. Heney, William J. Burns, Fremont Older, Rudolph Spreckels. Heney, who as a young attorney had killed a client's husband in self-defense, carried the prosecution's case until he himself was shot in open court. Burns ranked among the nation's most accomplished detectives. Son of a Columbus, Ohio, police commissioner, he grew up interested in crime detection. His brilliant career with the United States Treasury Department prompted Theodore Roosevelt to conclude that Burns assumed someone was guilty until proven innocent. Burns and Heney had, together, obtained major federal convictions. Older supplied the press coverage. Spreckels provided (with James D. Phelan) the money that a private action against a constituted government required.

Older's success was remarkable in the light of the pre-trip views of his wife, Cora, and his publisher, R. A. Crothers. Both had encouraged Older to travel to Washington because of their concern for his mental health. A growing sense of futility and depression settled in on Older as he tried and failed to hold back the surge of political corruption. His success with Roosevelt dispelled his gloom, but it also placed huge new demands upon Older as well as upon those who joined him for the new crusade for honesty in government. Quite obviously the Schmitz-Ruef administration could not be expected to pay for an honest investigation of its own corruption. So immediately upon the conclusion of his highly therapeutic trip to Washington, Older sought out Rudolph Spreckels and James Phelan to interest them in underwriting such a prosecution. Older had to do little persuading because Spreckels was personally aware of the Ruef-Schmitz corruption. Two of Ruef's very limited number of indiscretions included a thinly veiled offer of corrupt influence to advance Spreckels' interests in the utilities industry and an offer that he would deliver to Spreckels the complete bond offering of the City of San Francisco which, legally, was open to competitive bidding. Presumably Ruef operated on the assumption that all men in the public utilities and financial industries were corruptible. Phelan, a confidant of Spreckels, hardly required even this illustration to oppose actively the corrupting of the government he had worked so diligently to cleanse.

When Older unfolded before Spreckels and Phelan the results of his White House conference, with the prospects of a presidentially approved investigation and prosecution spearheaded by Burns and Heney, he could hardly have approached more willing and more interested philanthropists. Spreckels, with less experience in political and civic affairs than Phelan, proposed that a few of San Francisco's most prominent citizens be invited to join and subscribe to a prosecution fund. These men would be San Francisco's select, those civic leaders who would return their city to honest, efficient, and progressive government.

In his award-winning history of the graft prosecution Walton Bean suggested that the Spreckels idea was akin to an unarmed vigilante committee. To Spreckels' surprise, though perhaps not to Phelan's, there were no takers. Phelan and Spreckels were the only men of substance willing to support the prosecution of the most blatantly corrupt administration in the history of San Francisco. Ethically isolated from their own economic class and socially isolated from the mass electorate, Spreckels and Phelan remained resolute. As a result the judgment of history is all the more approving. Phelan's three terms as mayor established the model of honesty in local government. And his cosponsorship of the graft prosecution reestablished honest municipal government that has endured through twentieth-century San Francisco.

This was a privately organized and sustained prosecution of a democratically elected, corrupt government. Phelan and his younger, more enthusiastic associate set in motion actions that ended by superimposing private and personal honesty of the few (Older, Spreckels, and Phelan) over institutionalized, democratically sanctioned corruption. The corrupt included democratically chosen representatives of the citizenry: the mayor and supervisors.

Professor Bean correctly identified this dimension as vigilanteeism revisited in San Francisco history. Basic differences, however, are easy to identify. Phelan and Spreckels, the 1906 men of action, were armed with private money rather than with private guns. Also, their motivation and record of civic commitment were more attractive than those of the vigilance committees of the 1850s. Further, their targets extended beyond the corrupt office holders of low social and cultural status to include men of their own class. Perhaps the most significant difference between the vigilantes of early San Francisco and the twentieth-century activists was that Spreckels and Phelan pursued the corrupters through the legal institutions of the day, not through intimidation, exile and murder. Granted, on occasion this self-constituted, self-appointed minority of three and the high powered, highly motivated professionals they engaged, manipulated the legal and political structures of San Francisco. Phelan, Spreckels, Older, Heney, and Burns mobilized their pooled resources of wealth and acumen to dispatch the corrupt officials they had marked for political execution.

Because Burns and Heney accomplished all this by incontestable proof of the supervisors having accepted bribes, the prosecution forced these limited and uneducated men to provide evidence against those higher up on the political ladder. While Phelan and the prosecutors were in such a position of temporary power they used it to exercise absolute control over the corrupt supervisors for their own private, enlightened and heavy-handed control of city government.

Controlling the supervisors with promises of immunity, Phelan and the prosecutors were, in fact, able to exercise the powers that Phelan's Charter

Succeeding Mayors

The man selected to succeed Mayor Schmitz, friendly to Phelan and to his civic objectives, was eminently respectable and honest — Dr. Edward R. Taylor. Both a physician and attorney Taylor had been president of Cooper Medical College, as well as current dean of Hastings College of the Law. Later he served as a trustee of Stanford University. Like Phelan, he enjoyed dabbling in poetry rather than attending religious services on Sunday mornings. In fact, Taylor (1907–1910) was as unrepresentative of San Franciscans and their elected office holders as was his undemocratic selection process. With him, though, Phelan saw honesty restored to the political life of the city.

When San Francisco's more natural leadership reasserted itself, the constitutional, democratic process brought Irish-born Patrick H. McCarthy into office (1910–1912), succeeding Taylor. Then followed the ever popular "Sunny Jim" Rolph (1912–1931), but corruption never returned. McCarthy was rough, honest, and certainly educable in the American political process. Rolph was a unique San Francisco phenomenon, a natural in the new city hall he built to rival the grandeur of the national capital in Washington.

As part of his massive building program, Rolph developed the San Francisco Civic Center in a way Phelan approved. That approval included a major contribution to the construction of the San Francisco Opera House. The total center was classical in its architecture, imperial in its scale, centralized in its functions, and uniform in its construction materials. Rolph's Civic Center illustrated the principles of the Burnham Plan.

Fremont Older was the nervous energy behind the initiation of the graft prosecution. So nervous was he at the start that his wife and physician encouraged him in what they though would be an unrewarding — but distracting — trip to Washington. Older insisted on bringing San Francisco's problem to the President. To Cora Older's surprise, not only did her crusading editor husband meet Theodore Roosevelt, Older enlisted the President's tangible support.

of 1900 had reserved for the board of supervisors. So empowered, and extralegally, the prosecutors actually determined whom the supervisors appointed to the vacated office of mayor.

Before the Spreckels-Phelan prosecution concluded it claimed many successes: removing Mayor Schmitz from office and his mentor Ruef from power, holding the bribe-taking supervisors powerless through their individual needs for immunity from prosecution, dictating the selection and empowerment of the prosecution's own private selectee as the replacement mayor, and placing behind bars (at least temporarily) the central figures in the most corrupt episode in the history of San Francisco. Further (and more heroic in political, social, cultural, and economic terms), the Spreckels-Phelan prosecution identified and tried men of their own class who had corrupted San Francisco.

Perhaps this is Phelan's greatest legacy to his city. Phelan and Spreckels were unique in San Francisco's turbulent turn-of-the-century history. They believed that criminal acts by the rich, just as by the poor, should be punished. And they acted upon their convictions while faced with the hostility of wealthy associates who preferred exposing only their social inferiors.

Chapter Ten
Hetch Hetchy

The damming of Yosemite National Park's Hetch Hetchy Valley and its conversion into a massive water storage lake providing fresh water and hydroelectric power to San Francisco constituted the first national political battle over an environmental issue. James D. Phelan began the twelve-year war. His goal advanced conservation for the greatest use for the greatest number. He recruited and placed progressive experts into their critical battle positions to wage the day-to-day political and technical battles against both monopolists and environmentalists. The utility monopolists wished to maintain corporate control over available water resources to maximize profits. The conservationists wished to preserve the wilderness as a goal in itself. Together in purpose, both groups constituted a powerful counter balance to Phelan's conviction — conservation for use. Besides offering policy guidance to the planners and engineers Phelan lent his own reputation to the cause — a person of refinement and a lover of beauty. In so doing Phelan met America's most prestigious nature worshiper, John Muir, head on.

In 1901, and as San Francisco's mayor, Phelan signed the declaration of war. In 1913 in Washington D.C., as a private citizen, Phelan witnessed the signing of the terms of submission whereby Yosemite's little sister valley, Hetch Hetchy, became the property of San Francisco. This action allowed the construction of the O'Shaughnessy Dam to contain the Tuolumne River and provide a flow of 400 million gallons of water per day. Phelan accepted the military terminology associated with this political, environmental, and economic conflict, not because he had intended it to be a war, but because it turned out that way when his plans were opposed.

James Duval Phelan was an urban person who respected and enjoyed nature's beauty. He understood why those who backpacked into the Sierra wished to retain the wilderness as they found it. If pressed, he might add that they wished to retain it for their occasional, personal enjoyment. His commitment was to conservation for use, and for use by the greatest number. The photograph shows the Hetch Hetchy Valley before dam construction began.

Phelan's Views of Nature

James Duval Phelan came upon his views as naturally, if not as directly, as John Muir obtained his. Muir found beauty mostly in the nature his writings celebrated and glorified. When he observed natural beauty he concluded that, having been created that way, it ought to remain so. Phelan appreciated the "outdoors," but as the term suggests, his orientation was from the perspective of what man created. For Phelan, architectural refinement was the starting point from which civilized persons viewed nature in all its majesty. His idea of roughing it was a beef barbecue in his secluded Montalvo ravine, complete with chilled wine, linen, and uniformed staff. Lunch for ten among the redwoods was right for him. Also right for Phelan was the Ahwahnee Hotel from which, in the 1920s, he could drink in the unsurpassed scene along with a glass of Jameson Irish and a splash of the pure spring water that all the political and, to Muir, spiritual fuss was about.

En route to total victory, Phelan endured four city administrations (one of which he helped jail), three national administrations (one of which he was to join), three city engineers (one of whom he reprimanded), and as many secretaries of the Interior as he could recall. Phelan located the battle site (Hetch Hetchy), preceded his illustrious antagonist (John Muir) into the field, and emerged as the sole survivor of the environmental duel. Muir perished in the contest though his refined and forceful views of preservation for wilderness indeed live on. Phelan's role in the local and national struggle to dam the Sierra's Tuolumne River and assure an abundant water supply was to provide continuity. He was the only significant player who both began and concluded San Francisco's struggle for a clean and sufficient water supply to meet its current needs and anticipated growth and development.

Water for the West and San Francisco

Water, and access to it, always was a problem for the American West. San Francisco, surrounded on three sides by water, still was a semiarid peninsula. Its own lakes, springs and wells were adequate at first for the indigenous population and even the first Gold Rush influx. The increasing population, however, taxed the immediately available sources beyond their natural capacities. Next, entrepreneurs used waterboats to bring in fresh water from springs in Sausalito and peddled it from door to door through the city for a dollar a bucket. In 1858, the year before James and Alice Phelan married, the San Francisco Water Works Company tapped a fresh water stream that ran in the Point Lobos hills in the northwest corner of what was to become the Richmond District.

The Lobos Creek provided 2 million gallons per day through an elaborate system of flumes, a tunnel, pumping station, and storage tanks. Unable to keep pace with the insatiable demand, the Water Works Company surrendered its system in 1865, which was absorbed by a more successful competitor, the Spring Valley Water Works. Spring Valley, which was to become young Phelan's nemesis, recognized the limited water available within the borders of San Francisco and turned to the development of the watershed to the south in San Mateo County. The Spring Valley company delivered water thirty-two miles into a reservoir at Laguna Honda, near the city hospital that currently bears its name. Extending the system for the incessantly growing demand, the company completed the Upper Crystal Springs dam in the 1870s and the Lower one in 1890. In 1878 the system inaugurated a pumping station at Lake Merced. Thereafter, the Spring Valley Company developed its holdings and system in Santa Clara County and in the East Bay.

Accentuating the problem of ever-expanding demands against lagging and inadequate supplies was the fact that early San Francisco burned down somewhat regularly. The fire that followed the earthquake of 1906 was merely the most spectacular. For Phelan as mayor, one more factor made the situation absolutely intolerable: the water monopolists held San Francisco for annual ransom. Even further, the water monopolists corrupted the ransom payers (the board of supervisors) while holding their citizens captive.

If this set of circumstances were not aggravating enough for someone with Phelan's anti-monopolist, ingrained honesty, his political impotence as a pre-reform charter mayor made matters even worse. Before his reform charter of 1900, Phelan was constitutionally incapable of addressing the problem, not to mention solving it. The new charter provisions that freed the city from the control of the state legislature and provided for municipal ownership of public utilities were tailored for Phelan to confront the Spring Valley Water company. Once he had his opportunity, Phelan took it.

Hetch Hetchy Plan

Phelan began the unending political debate over the propriety of damming Hetch Hetchy Valley and creating the massive water and power system that transformed beautiful wilderness into a manmade lake to sustain and expand San Francisco. On July 29, 1901, Phelan filed an application with the Federal Government for rights to construct a reservoir and a water delivery system at what has become Lake Eleanor and Hetch Hetchy reservoir. Phelan did this as a private citizen, not in his capacity as mayor of San Francisco. Locked in political and economic combat with the water monopoly, he acted in secret to forestall the expected intervention of the Spring Valley Water Company. Once knowledge of the matter seeped into the public domain, Phelan assigned his claim to the City of San Francisco.

Phelan's personal selection of the actual water source and the controversial dam site illustrates his approach to problems. The scheme was highly ambitious, forward looking (perhaps to an extreme at the time, though hardly

James D. Phelan's challenge and results were acknowledged by the Hetch Hetchy construction engineer, Michael Maurice O'Shaughnessy, in his personal history of the project that took an additional twenty years at a cost of seventy-six million dollars. In the foreword to his 1934 Hetch Hetchy: Its Origin and History, O'Shaughnessy noted that he had never been associated with a project "where the engineering problems were so simple and the political ones so complex." James Phelan was the single individual the celebrated engineer acknowledged by name, grateful that Phelan's "services and sympathy were always at my command...."

so a century later) measured against other options, and based upon expert scientific and technical opinion. Phelan consulted his newly constituted public works board. Available to them at the time were the first recorded map of a proposed Hetch Hetchy water project prepared by J. P. Dart, a Sonora engineer in 1882, and a 1891 report by John Henry Quinton. Quinton had prepared his report for the U.S. Geological Survey and recommended the Hetch Hetchy Valley as an appropriate source for San Francisco water.

President Theodore Roosevelt's secretary of the Interior, Ethan Allen Hitchcock, denied Phelan's application in December, 1903. Hitchcock concluded that his obligation to the preservation of scenic beauty of Yosemite took precedence over San Francisco's water development plans. Concurrently the new city administration of Eugene E. Schmitz abandoned the project, not for ecological reasons but for the pursuit of alternate opportunities — graft. Based upon a paper scheme designed by the Bay Cities Water Company, the corrupt board of supervisors, under the direction of Abe Ruef, agreed to a 10.5 million dollar proposal. The scheme was to build a water system originating near Lake Tahoe. The estimated cost was 7.5 million. Of the extra 3 million, Ruef was to get 1 million, half of which he would distribute among the supervisors who approved the plan. As Walton Bean pointed out in *California,* "This project, if it had been consummated, would have been far the largest of all Ruef's corrupt transactions."

The arrest and prosecution of Ruef, Schmitz, and members of the city administration ended this diversion and allowed Phelan's initially rebuffed Hetch Hetchy initiative merely to languish in temporary oblivion.

San Francisco Politics

Phelan's most significant contribution to the thirty-three year process that brought clean water to San Francisco may not have been as prime mover, or even as the ever present force for continuity amidst constant changes in personnel and politics — local, state, and national. More broadly viewed, Phelan helped mold and implant San Francisco's new reform charter of 1900. Through it, San Francisco became empowered to act in its own interests for water and to establish its own public works, board, which, at its best, would guide municipal administrations to technically feasible policy decisions. Phelan's role at each stage was critical.

Phelan helped design and institute the political system that allowed Hetch Hetchy's creation. He appointed the significant players, intervened when asked, and brought forward new talent when the old had worn down. Phelan did this while in and out of public office, in cooperation with both major political parties at local and national levels, and largely at a distance, which allowed him productive engagement, policy input, and peace of mind.

To the first Board of Public Works, Mayor Phelan appointed George H. Mendell, Marsden Manson, and Carl E. Grunsky. All were professionally competent, and all were civic minded and honest. Mendell was associated with the Army Corps of Engineers and Grunsky was the city engineer. Manson was to be Phelan's work horse. Deceptively mild and ordinary in appearance, he was to carry the burden of implementing the Hetch Hetchy proposal. He did so over the best years of his career; he did so with cunning and a diligence that came to border on zealotry. Phelan put Manson in place in 1901, assisted and guided him through the tumultuous decade of lobbying and public confrontations, restrained him during his vitriolic lapses, and undoubtedly regretted the engineer's apparent nervous breakdown in 1912.

Phelan began the technical-political phase with Manson in 1901 and concluded this phase in 1913 with his own friend and former City Attorney Franklin K. Lane in the key Cabinet position of secretary of the Interior. By then the matter required federal legislation and the President's signature, and Woodrow Wilson was President. Phelan had been Democratic State Treasurer and organizer of Wilson's California campaign. Apparently, Phelan touched all the right bases — at home and in Washington. Exactly how this took place over the genuinely outraged opposition of good, respected, vocal opponents (as well as several venal ones) adds a dimension to understanding Phelan and his dream for California.

Upon his own initiative and while not employed by the City of San Francisco, Phelan's former appointee to the Board of Public Works, Manson became the chief proponent of the Hetch Hetchy plan. With only the mildest of encouragements from the City, he traveled to Washington and acquainted himself with members of the executive branch of government. Particularly he obtained access to Gifford Pinchot, the nation's chief forester, and James R. Garfield who was shortly to become secretary of the Interior. Through them, Manson met President Theodore Roosevelt and explain San Francisco's water problem and the proposed Hetch Hetchy solution.

Whenever a lobbying trip to Washington to advance Hetch Hetchy was required, James Duval Phelan made himself available. These transcontinental trips were always at his own expense, and he never complained of the days that the train rides consumed. His intellectual and cultural interests allowed him to read, to write, or to observe America as his mood directed.

Marsden Manson reflected the dichotomy within the conservation issue in America. He was an accomplished professional, an outdoorsman and, like Muir, a Sierra Club member. Manson believed in conservationism, except he and other Sierra Club members had a different understanding of the concept than did Muir and his co-believers. Cruelly, Hetch Hetchy divided Manson from Muir and exhausted them both.

Manson, unlike Muir, came from a comfortable professional family. He enjoyed a sound formal education with degrees in both science and civil engineering from the Virginia Military Institute. He also earned a doctorate at the University of California (Berkeley) in chemistry and physics. He was published and well traveled. For most of his professional career as a civil and hydraulic engineer he served varying levels of government in California. Manson possessed extensive firsthand experience of the Sierra Nevada. Besides his California encampments he extended his outdoors activities to travel in Alaska and Russia. Always, he enjoyed the beauty of nature. The Sierra Club and Manson were made for each other when he joined in 1895, three years after its creation. Favoring Hetch Hetchy did not endear Manson to most colleagues.

National Conservation Policies

Conservation as a matter of public concern simply was new to the American mind. Among progressives, certainly, the preservation of natural resources for intelligent, planned use, perhaps not by them but by posterity, was an attractive notion. By the turn-of-the century, the primitive American idea that resources were limitless and that the land needed to be attacked and exploited to make the nation civilized, was distinctly out of fashion.

The Hetch Hetchy controversy became a national issue of epic proportions because for the first time it redefined conservationism so that all its previous advocates could no longer agree. Before Hetch Hetchy conservationists opposed waste, consumption, and destruction of natural resources. The creation of Yosemite as a state park and then a national park was a response to such basic agreement.

Phelan's Hetch Hetchy proposal divided those conservationists who could support conservation for use from those committed to aesthetic conservation. The San Francisco engineers reported that to dam the Hetch Hetchy Valley was an efficient method to conserve a major natural resource, water. Doing so, fellow advocates argued, would provide the greatest benefit for the greatest number. Conversely, John Muir and leaders of the influential Sierra Club revolted at the idea of flooding "Little Yosemite." To intervene was to destroy. Conservation should not be for use; it should be for nature as it was found to be.

By 1895, Manson had been drawn into San Francisco politics and accepted the progressive interpretation of the urban problems as well as the progressive recommendations for change. His investigation of the sewerage and water problems led him to Phelan's conclusion. The charter had to be revised to give San Francisco the authority to determine its own destiny. Once that was accomplished Phelan appointed Manson to the new public works board. He was just fifty, eleven years Phelan's senior and at the peak of his professional stature.

Yosemite and National Politics

Yosemite Park, within which the Hetch Hetchy Valley was located, was given to California by the federal government during Abraham Lincoln's administration. In 1905 the Park was returned to federal control and management. The final determination on San Francisco's request, therefore, rested with the federal government. Manson's Washington exploration trip and contact with Pinchot and Garfield revived the matter to the point where Roosevelt obtained a legal opinion as to who had the authority to answer the request. His attorney general concluded that pertinent acts of Congress placed the matter in the hands of the Interior Department. The Tuolumne River that ran through the Hetch Hetchy Valley could be dammed at the discretion of the secretary of the Interior. By then Garfield had replaced Hitchcock and he and Pinchot had the President's ear on conservation matters. Both Garfield and Pinchot shared utilitarian views on conservation. Pinchot, the forestry expert, endorsed the idea and Secretary Garfield viewed the issue in the light of his concepts of regulated use. He would not, however, reverse his predecessor's decision on the matter without presidential approval and for the moment Roosevelt's reputation as a naturalist made it unclear how he would see the issue.

John Muir and the Sierra Club officials viewed the valley damming as stark exploitation of the nation's resources and callous destruction of God-given beauty. Muir's prestige in questions such as this was substantial and growing. Also, his insight and mastery of public relations were hardly deficient. In 1903 he had taken Roosevelt on a guided camping tour of Yosemite Valley and had created strong rapport. When the issue reached another critical stage Muir lobbied the president with a personal letter. Nonetheless, Roosevelt the political realist triumphed over Roosevelt the nature lover. The President's return letter was unpromising. At that stage then, the Sierra Club leadership and Muir inaugurated a broad, national public education campaign.

At home in San Francisco the 1906 earthquake and fire attracted worldwide sympathy and a national outpouring of assistance and good will. Even though the City's distribution system, not the sources and quantities of water, was a major impediment to fighting the massive fires, water and the need for more of it permeated popular thought. The rectified political situation also helped the Hetch Hetchy cause.

When Secretary Garfield arrived in San Francisco on a fact-finding trip, Mayor Edward R. Taylor appointed Phelan and Manson to present San Francisco's case. They were the best informed, most knowledgeable throughout

President Theodore Roosevelt enjoyed roughing it with John Muir in Yosemite. He craved these experiences as much as Phelan craved the galleries and museums of Europe. Even though Muir held the undistracted attention of the chief executive, himself an outdoorsman and a self-proclaimed conservationist, Muir could not deliver Roosevelt and the national government to the cause of preservation for its own sake.

Roosevelt and Muir pose in 1903 at Glacier Point, far above the Yosemite Valley floor.

John Muir was, perhaps, more critical (even vicious) toward James Duval Phelan than he was toward any other person. To Muir, Phelan was a wanton developer lacking totally in an appreciation of natural beauty. To Phelan's credit, he could receive such criticisms and yet appreciate all the clear contributions that Muir and his Sierra Club made to America. Phelan even commissioned Muir's bust and placed it amid the beauty of his own managed and controlled out-of-doors, the gardens at his country estate, Villa Montalvo.

the process, and offered the best blend of technical understanding, humanistic sensitivity, and political aplomb. Also, Phelan had already acquainted himself with Theodore Roosevelt through Phelan's key position in the relief of San Francisco in 1906. Roosevelt's trust in Phelan's honesty was absolute.

Politics again, this time at the national level, determined the outcome. Garfield's chief, Roosevelt, had come under fire for his conservation policies. His critics denounced the President's actions as removing resources permanently from the public domain, thus excluding them from use instead of reserving them for planned development later and for the public welfare. Hardly coincidentally, Garfield announced his approval of San Francisco's Hetch Hetchy request at the time of a White House conference on conservation to which the state governors were the prime attendees.

John Muir and the Sierra Club leadership, though disappointed by the Roosevelt administration's reversal, were not vanquished. To avoid the impediment of that portion of the Sierra Club membership who subscribed to the principle of conservation for use rather than pure aesthetics, they resorted to the creation of a subset of themselves, the Society for Preservation of National Parks. Under that organization Muir's followers reached out to kindred organizations across America to mobilize public opinion and force the re-reversal in national policy. En route they claimed the higher ground of aesthetic preservationism and abandoned the utilitarian argument to Phelan and the "damned" dam supporters.

For his part, Phelan traveled again to Washington at his own expense to lobby the legislators in person. He added his own agile pen to the task through articles in the *California Weekly, Outlook,* and *Out West,* as well as in his extensive private correspondence. Unlike the Sierrans, Phelan conceded no ground whatever. He argued that the project had immense practical value, presenting it in such a way that the completed work would revitalize the regions it touched. The famous and glorious Yosemite Valley would not be affected. "The Hetch-Hetchy Valley, a smaller valley in the reservation," Phelan wrote to an influential friend, "is the site granted. The reservoir will enhance its natural beauty, and make it more accessible." To his chief secretary, George Welch, Phelan wrote home from Washington in a less buoyant vein, updating him on progress in the U.S. Senate and the House. He lamented that the "Spring Valley [Water Company] & the Nature fakirs are strong in this dying Congress."

The change of national administrations from Theodore Roosevelt to William Howard Taft (both Republican, both self-assertively progressive and conservation-minded) allowed Muir to try for reversal once more. The Society for the Preservation of National Parks formally petitioned Richard A. Ballinger, the new Interior secretary to withdraw Garfield's approval to commence construction of the water system.

Phelan's own lobbying within the Interior Department and before Congress convinced him that his task was difficult, but Ballinger would not reopen the case. Nonetheless, Muir provided Ballinger with a personally guided tour of the Hetch Hetchy, much as he had done for Roosevelt in Yosemite. The national political scene was disturbed again over conservation policies, now those of the Taft administration.

Taft

The public disagreement constituted a political crisis for the Taft administration and public question of Taft's carrying out of Roosevelt's conservationism. The follow up included Pinchot and Garfield openly siding with the San Francisco cause, Taft siding with his beleaguered secretary and firing Pinchot, and Ballinger meeting with Sierra Club members and subsequently issuing to San Francisco a new requirement to show why he should not reverse the Garfield permission to proceed in Hetch Hetchy.

Historians who have speculated on the timing of the events and counter-events have noted how Roosevelt's response to public criticism in the conservation arena was followed by Garfield's permission to proceed and how Taft's response to reverse criticism in the same arena was followed by Ballinger's "show cause" reversal.

Phelan studied and charted the unsteady course and set his own course. By now Mayor Taylor had recognized Phelan's original appointee, Manson, for his devotion to the San Francisco cause and appointed him to the position of City Engineer. Manson dug in and did his own research and detective work independently of Phelan.

While preparing for the Interior Department hearing in Washington, at which San Francisco was to show cause why the previous construction approval should not be rescinded, Manson confirmed his prejudices. Interior Secretary Ballinger, pressured by Muir and assaulted by Pinchot over alleg-

By the time San Francisco's Hetch Hetchy water system was dedicated and the water started to flow, all of the original prime movers were dead. Marsden Manson had long since passed on — hurried, no doubt, by the stress of his commitment. James Duval Phelan died during the latter phase of construction. Even the city's chief engineer for whom the dam is named, Michael Maurice O'Shaughnessy, failed to see his work concluded. Each had given his share to San Francisco.

The Burden of Advocacy

Manson was predisposed to believe the worst of the opposition he just disliked. He considered the nature writings of John Muir as "verbal lingerie." Muir's followers in the Sierra Club he characterized as nature lovers, mostly "short-haired women and long-haired men." He reserved his best sarcasm for the lawyers who represented the Spring Valley water monopoly and the distinguished national conservationists who rallied to Muir's appeal for congressional testimony. To Manson they were "a number of prominent eastern gentlemen, some of whom were actually acquainted with the subject."

Manson's admirable restraint, given his natural disposition, seemed to have marked the final strain upon a man who had carried the San Francisco's burden on a daily basis for a dozen years (on and off the payroll). After his finest hours before the Interior Department he gave vent to his more primitive impulses, striking out at anyone he believed conspired against San Francisco's efforts to rid itself of monopoly and to obtain pure and abundant water for its people.

Phelan, no stranger to emotional disturbance among loved ones, tried to advise Manson. He used the occasion of one of Manson's intemperate letters. Phelan offered Manson friendly advice, suggesting that Manson was antagonizing well-placed Washington friends with his vexing letters. After this brief attention step, Phelan concluded: "So I take the liberty of suggesting a more conciliatory epistolary correspondence."

edly liberal conservation policies, assigned two engineers from the Bureau of Reclamation the task to review the Hetch Hetchy plan. They in turn farmed the task out to a willing Berkeley engineer, Philip E. Harroun, who prepared the highly damaging report that the Bureau of Reclamation submitted as its own. What Harroun declined to reveal was his concurrent employment with the Spring Valley Water Company and that material in the damaging report came, in part, from materials supplied by the Bay Cities Water Company. The one time the preservationists reached out for technical help, they chose very poorly. The Sierra Club expert was indeed guilty of conflict of interest.

Professor Kendrick A. Clements, in his article, "Engineers and Conservationists," concluded that Manson used "subtle blackmail" on Interior Secretary Ballinger. Manson did not lead off with a public denunciation of Harroun's conflict of interest and the Reclamation Bureau's representation of Harroun's report as its own. Instead he allowed Ballinger to proceed with the hearing. When the proceedings had sufficiently advanced, Manson privately conveyed his position and his knowledge to Ballinger, and in the process also told Ballinger that he reserved the right to raise his concerns openly later. That said, Manson merely observed Ballinger's conduct of the proceedings and awaited his conclusion. All of this was unknown to the Sierra Club leadership, which appeared to have no clue why Ballinger concluded by ordering San Francisco to prepare a new study to be reviewed by a special advisory board of army engineers.

Approval

The upshot of all the interplay was victory for Phelan's water plan. Technical expertise was to determine the outcome. By fixing the question within this domain, Ballinger critically damaged the chances of John Muir and the preservationists to save their beautiful valley. Caught in a most unattractive situation, Ballinger delayed the inevitable and arranged to share its announcement from among a committee of experts.

Health matters, physical as well as mental, wore heavily upon the key players. Manson may have suffered a nervous breakdown. Ballinger resigned because of ill health and loss of the emotional edge required for such demanding service. John Muir himself passed away in 1914. For the final engagement, Phelan and the San Franciscan advocates of conservationism for use brought in a fresh new team. Their new consulting engineer, John R. Freeman, provided a masterful and readable report that was technically sound and conceptually exciting. It sailed through the Army Corps of Engineers committee and served as the blueprint for the Hetch Hetchy's expanded hydroelectric system. The new Democratic President, Woodrow Wilson, was beholden to Phelan's political leadership in California. Phelan himself relinquished any claim to cabinet appointment and, instead, ushered into the pivotal position, secretary of the Interior, his friend and former city attorney, Franklin K. Lane.

As a last gasp Ballinger's timid successor, Walter L. Fisher, declined to approve the Hetch Hetchy project without legislation. With Wilson and the Democrats in control after the 1912 election and Lane in the cabinet to

During the public exchanges with John Muir, James Duval Phelan maintained that a lake could be as beautiful as a valley.

Beauty aside, the Hetch Hetchy Reservoir freed San Francisco from reliance upon corrupt combinations of private water companies and public officials. Once the water flowed from the Sierra to San Francisco, the city and much of the Bay Area was assured of sufficient fresh water through the twentieth century. The system is vast, 155 miles of aqueduct that includes twenty-eight miles of tunnel beneath the coast mountain range. In 1934, this creation was the longest tunnel in the world. All for water.

The Hetch Hetchy Reservoir is shown filling behind the O'Shaughnessy Dam.

By 1912 James Duval Phelan was at the height of his powers. The successful resolution of the dispute over Hetch Hetchy was indicative of the benefits San Francisco received from her favorite son. His ability to initiate and complete large, complex, and controversial projects with efficiency and grace was Phelan's hallmark.

watch and guide, Phelan continued to travel to Washington and lobby, but he started to enjoy it a bit more. Also, he incorporated his work into self-education and prepared for his own assault upon a California seat in U.S. Senate. At this stage his Hetch Hetchy water and power scheme was assured.

Phelan hosted thirty-five guests for Thanksgiving dinner at the Metropolitan Club in Washington in 1912. He had gone to the capital on California Democratic Party business following the Wilson election victory. At the request of San Francisco Mayor James "Sunny Jim" Rolph, he remained to testify for Hetch Hetchy. At the dinner, Phelan included Taft's last Interior secretary before whom the matters were pending, representatives from both Houses of Congress, the Judiciary, and of course Jim Rolph himself. Sunny Jim and James Duval got along well together despite their membership in opposing political parties — Phelan enjoyed giving parties and Rolph always enjoyed attending them.

Phelan's next Washington trip on behalf of Hetch Hetchy was to monitor and guide, if needed, the federal legislation authorizing the construction of the complete Hetch Hetchy dam and system. Attentive and responsive to the end Phelan remained in Washington from early November through mid-December, remaining until President Wilson signed the bill.

Back home in California the new City Engineer, Michael Maurice O'Shaughnessy was gathering the tools and the legions of workers for the construction that would take two decades, completed finally in 1934 at the cost of 75 million dollars. The result was an engineering masterpiece that met and exceeded San Francisco's material needs for water through the twentieth century. Phelan created what he thought San Francisco needed. He was successful because he persistently advocated America's still insatiable demand for progress and development over spirited and talented opponents who offered an abstract aestheticism that failed to compete for approval among the jury that Phelan put in place — the technical experts.

Phelan's victory did not silence the national debate between those who would conserve for improved and delayed development and those who would preserve forever the remaining beauty spots in nature. In effect, Phelan began the debate that will not end.

Chapter Eleven
Construction of Villa Montalvo

In the early years of the twentieth century, the Santa Clara Valley was a land rich in bountiful soil and historical tradition, but lagging well behind other areas of the state in its development. In the heart of the valley, Mission Santa Clara was one of the largest and most prosperous of the chain of Franciscan foundations stretching up the coast of Spanish Alta California. After American annexation, San Jose served briefly as capital of the new state. Although it was the largest city in the valley and the county seat, San Jose retained its distinctive character as the market hub of an extended agricultural area until after the Second World War.

When James Duval Phelan decided to build a country home, the Santa Clara Valley attracted him because it offered a different way of life from the bustle and pressures of urban San Francisco and an ideal climate with warm

The palatial homes of California's early millionaires were scattered throughout the state, from San Marino (Henry Huntington) to Belmont (William Ralston). James D. Phelan chose the foothills near "salubrious Saratoga" overlooking the millions of blossoming fruit trees that covered the Santa Clara Valley. In terrain reminiscent of the countryside of Tuscany, Umbria, or Provence, Phelan cultivated the Mediterranean life he so thoroughly enjoyed during his repeated trips to the European continent. In the foothills of the Santa Cruz Mountains, not far from redwood groves that he helped preserve as a distinctive feature of his beloved California, wealth, leisure, elegance, and discriminating taste created the good life for San Francisco's cultivated bachelor. There, above the Santa Clara Valley, he wrote his sister, "I will build a villa and bask in the eternal sunshine.

Saratoga's Attractions

James Duval Phelan was not the first San Franciscan to look to the foothills between Los Gatos and Saratoga as a site for his relaxation and comfort. The warm climate and rustic charm of the area had been sufficient inducement to attract numbers of visitors, some of whom built houses scattered about the hills. Saratoga, which had begun as a lumbering community called McCartysville, was for a number of years a fashionable spa after the discovery of a mineral spring above the town and the development of resort facilities. The gateway to an increasingly popular redwood park and the home of the Blossom Festival, which attracted thousands of visitors every spring, Saratoga was still primarily agricultural, but it was already beginning to change into one of the most desirable residential communities in the Bay Area. Shortly after the turn of the century, it was linked to other valley towns by an electric railway line, and it became popular as the home of many of the valley's leading professional and business people. By the time Phelan started to build on his newly acquired property, some of his old San Francisco friends, Charles and Kathleen Norris and Fremont and Cora Older, among others, already had homes nearby.

days for relaxed weekends and pleasurable summer holidays. In the tradition of other wealthy Californians, Phelan, a man of almost unlimited means, was able to acquire a princely estate.

Phelan knew the area well. Late in life, he recalled nostalgically two idyllic summers spent in the nearby hills during his childhood. Phelan liked the valley's unspoiled rural character, as well as its convenient location near San Francisco. He had various properties in San Jose, and the diary he kept fitfully over the years records frequent visits to that city on business matters, as well as automobile journeys through the valley on pleasure trips to Santa Cruz and Monterey.

When his sister later built her house on Lafayette Square in San Francisco after the 1906 earthquake, Phelan was unhappy with the location, since he disliked the damp fog that often blanketed the area. He maintained rooms at his sister's home, but when he decided to build a home to meet his needs and delight his fancies, he looked to the sun-filled Santa Clara Valley, the "Valley of Heart's Delight." Pleasant memories of his home as a youngster, as well as tastes acquired through prolonged exposure to Mediterranean culture, could be harmoniously combined in a spacious rural estate. Simple, uncomplicated domesticity could blend with the best of European elegance in a perfect California synthesis.

Finding the Property

The rebuilding of San Francisco, including his own Phelan Building, and the reestablishing of public confidence in his native city occupied Phelan for the years immediately following the earthquake and fire. By 1911, at the age of fifty, he was able to turn his attention to plans for his own future comfort and pleasure. Through his trusted business agent, political lieutenant, and friend, Charles Fay, he began to search for a site for his country home. Fay scouted the available properties throughout the Santa Clara Valley, but was especially attracted to the Bonnie Brae Ranch, less than a mile south of the road connecting Los Gatos and Saratoga. Located on a hillside some eight hundred feet or more above the valley floor, the ranch was described without exaggeration in an advertisement, carefully preserved among the Phelan papers, as "one of the most beautiful and scenic properties in Santa Clara County, elegantly located in the foot-hills … overlooking the Bay and Valley." Bonnie

Brae, or the Cody Place as it was called, was a working ranch of 137 acres, part of it planted in the valley's staple prunes, apricots, and cherries, and maintaining a small vineyard. In addition to a large ranch house, it contained a barn, tank house, and the usual farm buildings. Because the location was close to the village of Saratoga, the owners were hoping to find a purchaser interested in parcelling the land into "high-class subdivisions" and asked $45,000.00 for the property.

The Bonnie Brae Ranch became the core of Phelan's Villa Montalvo. Phelan authorized Fay to purchase the property for a little more than half the asking price in June, 1911. Before the sale, with his usual meticulous concern for important details, Phelan made a careful legal search for title to water rights. As one who spent years of his life struggling for an adequate water supply for the city of San Francisco, he realized that an abundance of water was necessary to carry out his designs for the Saratoga property. With the water titles guaranteed, he turned to acquiring another half dozen contiguous pieces of land, some mere corners or fingers, others fairly substantial parcels, to round out his new property and gain secure access to the main highway. In separate transactions, Phelan also purchased another large amount of land he later deeded to his sister, Mollie. For his own estate, he kept about 175 acres, for which he paid a little over $50,000.00.

The poet, Henry Meade Bland, who was to be a frequent visitor to Phelan's home, described the geographical setting of the site in language that captured the boosterism that was so much a part of the California identity of the period. "It is bounded on the north by 'the healing waters of Saratoga,' on the east by the 'gardens of the Santa Clara Valley,' on the south by Los Gatos, 'Gem City of the Santa Cruz foothills,' and on the west by ferns and 'Sequoia Sempervirons of the blue coast range'."

Part of Phelan's newly acquired property spilled down a steep, wooded hillside covered with oak, madrone, bay, wild cherry, birch, and stands of redwood, but there was also a large section of gently sloping land that contemporary photographs show cleared of most of its natural vegetation. In that ideal location, which enjoyed an unobstructed view across the valley to the eastern hills, Phelan decided to place his private retreat. During construction the various residential buildings on the property would house his gardeners and agents, but then they would be gradually cleared away to provide room for the spacious lawns and gardens Phelan envisioned. The practical ranch

The photograph above shows James Duval Phelan's property as it looked when he purchased the Bonnie Brae Ranch for $25,000. Five other sections were purchased at prices varying from $1,000 to $13,700 (totalling $28,000). The owners and acreage of these parcels were as follows:

Cunningham	*18.90 acres*
Richards	*13.00 acres*
Cushman	*6.15 acres*
Coates	*1.85 acres*
Perkins and Boyden	*1.00 acre*

Classical Cities

A keen student of architecture and civic construction, James Duval Phelan was enamored of the beauty of the villas and palatial dwellings of southern Europe. As a young man he had spent many months in Rome, then still a relatively small city almost unspoiled by modern development. Later, during one of his last trips to the continent, Phelan told the Italian king, Victor Emanuel III, that as a youth one of his greatest pleasures was to spend leisurely mornings riding his horse through the gardens of the Villa Borghese. In that quintessential Mediterranean environment, dotted with the estates of the princely families of church and state, he had refined his artistic tastes. The classical elements of architecture found throughout the Mediterranean world appealed to Phelan's sense of tradition as well as his love of elegance and order. Even the large buildings blended effortlessly into the landscape of the Mediterranean, and the materials and colors remained those of antiquity. Now, as he built his own villa, bathed in sunlight and etched against a cloudless Santa Clara sky, Phelan could fulfill his dream of evoking the beauty he had relished in the warmth of the Mediterranean sun.

land of the foothills would turn into an evocation of the dignity and elegance of an aristocratic villa of the old world.

Planning Montalvo

All accounts agree that Phelan was the principal designer of Villa Montalvo. Although better traveled and more cultivated than most of his contemporaries, in his architectural taste Phelan was very much a man of his times. The desire to establish enduring links with California's past reinforced an existing penchant for adapting European cultural models to local needs. The state's Hispanic past found expression in new towns that were often given conspicuously Spanish names such as Los Altos, Sierra Madre, and Monte Vista. The popular literature of the day, including Helen Hunt Jackson's tale, *Ramona*, and Gertrude Atherton's rambling novels of life in early California, provided a romantic and fictionalized context for an architectural evocation of a lost past. California, in reality, had no architectural roots in the classical past and no particular architectural tradition of its own, but its origins as a Spanish colony, its Mediterranean climate, and the decaying remains of the Franciscan Missions seemed to many to dictate a "natural" style of architecture modeled on the traditions of southern Europe. An architectural pattern, combining genuine elements of Spanish, Mexican colonial, and a somewhat ill-defined Mission style, became the vogue in turn of the century California.

Thick textured stucco walls, overhanging red-tiled roofs, bright colors, and even enclosed patios became the desired trademarks. Bungalows, shops, schools, and public buildings incorporated these Hispanic elements with varying degrees of logic and success. The 1914 Panama-Pacific Exhibition, which followed closely on the construction of Phelan's Saratoga home, reinforced and sanctioned this increasingly popular California style.

Always a man of discrimination and taste, Phelan did not slavishly imitate prevailing notions in planning his home, but did adapt elements of current California taste to his classical predilections. As far as it is known, there is no particular building in Europe or America that served as a model for his Saratoga house. Although it incorporated Spanish elements, there were also structural features that seemed to reflect classical Rome more than Spain, and various details of ornamentation that embodied the refinement of the early Italian Renaissance. Villa Montalvo can never be mistaken for an early California rancho, but it seems perfectly suited to the terrain on which it is built and it does justice to Phelan's devotion to California and its traditions, whether romanticized or real. Independent and individualistic throughout his life, Phelan reflected that individualism in the only home he ever built.

Before the end of 1911, Phelan had chosen an architectural firm and awaited a bid for the construction cost. He had extensive experience in selecting and working with architects. Early in his career, he had been a close friend of Arthur Page Brown, later serving as a pall bearer at the funeral of that talented and eclectic architect. He chose Brown to design the Sainte Claire Club in San Jose, which remains one of that city's most striking historic buildings. Phelan had spearheaded the movement to redesign San Francisco and had been the personal patron of Daniel Hudson Burnham. Phelan's reputation for artistic taste, as well as his honesty and shrewd business dealings, earned him a position on architectural selection committees for many public buildings. For the construction of his Santa Clara Valley home, he selected the distinguished architect William Curlett.

Curlett was assisted by his son, Alexander, who did most of the actual direction at Montalvo, while much of the later work was carried out by the San Francisco-born architect, Charles E. Gottschalk. Gottschalk had practiced in Southern California and Illinois before returning to his native city, where he maintained his office in the Phelan Building. When the elder Curlett's health declined and other commissions kept Alexander Curlett occupied in

The Architects of Montalvo

Like James D. Phelan, the Curletts were Irish, the father a native of County Down. Educated in Belfast and Manchester, William Curlett had come to America as a young man and quickly felt the lure of California. He worked throughout the state erecting public buildings, including the Los Angeles and Fresno County court houses. In San Francisco he was a partner of Augustus Laver, the architect of the City Hall destroyed in the fire of 1906. Curlett was equally adept at laying out civic parks and designing elegant private residences. He established a reputation as a favored architect of the wealthiest of San Francisco patrons. Mrs. William H. Crocker commissioned him to build her Nob Hill home, a victim of the fire like many of Curlett's earlier works, and the Floods engaged him for their mansion in San Mateo County. In Southern California he built a home for former state governor Henry Markham.

As mayor, Phelan had given Curlett responsibility for a number of public buildings, and after the fire, eager to give clear evidence of his confidence in San Francisco's future, he commissioned Curlett to build the new Phelan Building on Market Street. When he decided to build his country home it was natural for Phelan to turn to the Irishman, Curlett. A member of the Bohemian Club, former president of the State Board of Architecture, and a Fellow of the American Institute of Architects, Curlett was a distinguished figure in California's architectural establishment. On Phelan's part, the selection of Curlett, a Protestant, a 32nd degree Mason, and a Belfast Unionist, to carry out his private commission was symbolic of Phelan's loyalty, open-mindedness, and commitment to artistic excellence.

Building Villa Montalvo

The photographs show Villa Montalvo in various stages of construction. James D. Phelan insisted that his local agents keep a close watch over subcontractors and expenditures.

Los Angeles, Phelan relied increasingly on the managerial and architectural skills of Gottschalk. It was the latter, for example, who laid out the open air theater behind the main villa. As late as 1924, a dozen years after the actual construction of Montalvo, Gottschalk was still advising the Senator and supervising improvements at the villa.

The contract for what Phelan called his "little box in the country" (according to his friend Cora Older) reflected his business acumen and experience. Phelan's correspondence in the Bancroft Library makes it clear that the Curletts agreed to build Montalvo for a fixed price under penalty of forfeiture of half their fee. They relied on local contractors and craftsmen who, even as far south as San Jose, were still in demand repairing local damage from the 1906 earthquake. The plan called for the construction of a two-story frame building of some nineteen rooms, plus servants' quarters, and a separate guest house. By the prevailing standards of California's millionaire builders, this was a modest structure. Phelan built it for use, not for ostentatious display of wealth. Its scale was to be human, its embrace welcoming. Phelan's home might be as elegant as an aristocratic European villa, but it was also to be as warmly hospitable as a traditional California rancho.

Building Montalvo

Through most of the construction on his estate, James D. Phelan was an enormously busy man. As head of Woodrow Wilson's California campaign for the presidency, Phelan was constantly on the road, crisscrossing the state, making speeches, organizing local constituencies, raising money, and drumming up support for the Democratic candidate. He occasionally visited Saratoga and inspected the work being done for him, but he relied mainly on Charles Fay to carry out his plans. "I want you to take charge for me at Montalvo and keep in close touch with architects," he instructed Fay in November, 1912. "Do everything necessary to protect my interests and if necessary employ expert advice." Phelan was a just but demanding employer, and he expected fair value for his money. On one occasion he told George Welch to go down to the construction site on pay day to make sure each workman collected only his own pay. Like anxious home builders of any era, Phelan was concerned about cost overruns and delays in construction, and he demanded that a watchful eye be kept on subcontracts, shipping receipts, and "extras."

Captivated by the fictional griffins described by Garci Ordonez de Montalvo in his novel, James Duval Phelan used them as a motif throughout the grounds of Villa Montalvo. This watchful guardian is shown soon after construction in 1912.

George Doeltz obtained a variety of trees and shrubs from Golden Gate Park, Stanford University, Phelan Park, and the old Hotel Vendome in San Jose. One of his most successful landscaping achievements was the transplanting of a number of full grown cypress trees from a San Jose cemetery to frame the Italian Garden at Villa Montalvo.

James D. Phelan always closely watched the developments at Montalvo, and from San Francisco, Washington, Europe, or wherever he happened to be, his head gardener received brisk notes with suggestions, advice or corrections. Always professional, Phelan's directives were frequently disguised as consultation. Uniformly considerate, Phelan sent a handwritten note congratulating Doeltz on his marriage and a check for the new bride. When Doeltz was injured in an accident, Phelan was solicitous about his recovery and gave Doeltz one of his own canes. For Doeltz, as for the rest of the Montalvo staff, Phelan was a respected and admired employer, always referred to as "the Senator."

By letter and telegram, Phelan was kept fully informed of building progress, and he intervened on more than one occasion to give specific directions and order changes in the construction. Despite his other political and business obligations, he negotiated personally for the steam laundry, conducted inquiries about the best brand of elevator, ordered marble ornaments, cautioned his new neighbors about excessive water use, told his employees which vendors to patronize, and corresponded with his architects about the exact tint for the paint and the choice of the proper "sanitary seats for toilets." Little escaped his scrutiny in the building of his home.

Despite a number of unanticipated delays, by October, 1912, Phelan was already shipping cases of wine to Saratoga in anticipation of occupying Montalvo. But he did not wait for the completion of construction to enjoy his new property. When he took a brief respite from his political whirlwind, Phelan enjoyed coming down to Saratoga accompanied by a party of friends and inspecting the progress on his estate. He and his cultivated companions stayed overnight in the two ranch buildings on the property. Years later, wandering through the impeccably manicured gardens of his stately villa, he recalled the fun of it all with a touch of nostalgia. Before the end of 1912, Fay reported that the main house was nearly completed, and Phelan was soon able to move into his Villa Montalvo.

A discriminating architectural critic, who would himself be a guest at the villa, singled Phelan out from the other wealthy Californians who built country homes. At Montalvo, Phelan made a conscious effort to link the present with the past, and, according to Porter Garnett, attempted to evoke "a tradition purely Californian." Mediterranean influence prevailed throughout. The main structure, with its tile roof and pale stucco walls was in many ways reminiscent of an Italian villa, generously incorporating the traditional overhanging eaves, arches, and broad porches, particularly on the main facade laid out to overlook the valley. The gentle hillside required the architects to construct the villa on a series of terraces. From the gardens below the house, broad stairways ascended a grassy slope interrupted by a series of landings that extended beyond the front of the villa itself. The steps led up to the level of another broad terrace and to the main building. This formal entrance to the villa looked with stately serenity across sloping lawns to the agricultural valley and the distant bay. Gertrude Atherton later described this view in *Adventures of a Novelist* as "the most superb, it is quite possible, of any country place in America." Three huge arches led the visitor through French doors into the main room of the house. This was rarely used as the actual entrance, since the ornate Spanish doors on the north side of the house proved more convenient and accessible for welcoming visitors. The richly shadowed triple arches surmounted by a shallow loggia, the expansive red-tiled roof, and the stately positioning of the villa above vast sloping lawns and against the dark greenery of the hillside beyond, creates an indelible first impression of Villa Montalvo. When a group of visitors approached Montalvo in the late 1930s, soon after the abdication of Edward VIII, one remarked that this was an entrance fit for a king. "If the Duke of Windsor chose to live in California here's the place for him."

A central feature of the plan was a Spanish style patio in the rear of the house, enclosed on three sides by the building and its two wings. While the lower colonnade may have been Tuscan in inspiration, other features, including the protruding second story, were characteristically Iberian. The back of the patio was formed by another raised terrace reached by two sets of stairs. A central fountain in the patio, another against the terrace wall, and palm trees added further authenticity to this Spanish courtyard. The upper terrace contained an oval swimming pool, sixty feet in length, framed by spacious colonnaded pergolas ending in a tile-roofed pavilion. Contemporary

Watered by two fountains and originally covered with grass, the Spanish patio was one of Senator Phelan's favorite place to enjoy informal lunches with his guests. Unlike her host, Gertrude Atherton, one of Montalvo's most frequent visitors, was no sun worshipper and quickly retreated into the cool interior of the villa.

Montalvo offered a variety of opportunities for pleasant exercise. Senator Phelan and a companion would frequently take a vigorous early morning hike in the hills, then join his guests for a swim in the pool.

Some distance from the main building above the creek running through the property, Phelan built a guest cottage that contained a number of small apartments for overnight guests who could not be housed in the villa itself.

The public rooms were given additional warmth and character by the generous application of wood paneling of a variety of types and colors. Phelan brought an Italian woodcarver to the villa to add ornamentation to fireplaces, cabinets, and stairways. He furnished these rooms with the accumulated treasures garnered from years of extensive travel and tasteful collecting. Moorish chests, heavy leather chairs, inlaid cabinets, and an escutcheon with the arms of Castile and Leon heightened the Spanish atmosphere of the architecture.

photographs of construction show that this was integral to the original conception of Villa Montalvo. The vertical lines of the colonnade and the marble Hermes placed under the arches of the pavilion gave it a classical Roman character. The rear of the pavilion became the backdrop for a small stage, and a grassy slope formed a natural outdoor theater ending in the steep, wooded hillside beyond the villa.

Montalvo Inside

The plan of the interior of the house called for a very spacious living room in the center of the building. This was the largest room in the villa and opened onto the terrace facing the eastern hills. None of the other rooms on the first floor — the entry hall with its exquisitely carved Spanish door, billiard room, library, dining room, and sun porches — were of extraordinary size. Each was commodious, but of a size as comfortable for a solitary reader as for a crowd of holiday makers. In the library, Phelan housed his valuable collection of books, many dealing with the history of his beloved state and the literary achievements of Californians.

The upper story was divided into comfortable suites for Phelan and a few select friends. Each of these apartments was decorated by the fashionable designer, Elsie de Wolfe. A large enclosed gallery occupied the center and overlooked the patio below. The service rooms of the house were capacious and appointed with the most advanced dishwashers, electric cookers, ice makers, and steam laundry presses. They were also handsomely paneled from floor to ceiling in dark wood. Every detail was looked to, including a wheeled library ladder for servants to reach into the tallest cupboards. A servants' wing extended from the south side of the house along one side of the swimming pool and also contained changing rooms for guests.

Phelan's plan for his estate called for a house sufficiently spacious to entertain in the expansive style he enjoyed, but above all it was to be his home. Large enough to accommodate a few particularly close friends, Montalvo, even with its detached guest cottages, was not meant to be a kind of West Coast Versailles.

Before Phelan ever stepped across the threshold of his country house, he had determined that its name, like its eclectic architectural style, would be linked to California's romantic past. The popularly accepted explanation of the origin of the name 'California' was based on an essay by Edward Everett Hale. Probably quite correctly, Hale attributed it to the early sixteenth century Spanish writer, Garci Ordonez de Montalvo. In his *Las Sergas de Esplandian*, a continuation of the universally popular chivalric novel, *Amadis of Gaul*, he invented a utopian island inhabited by pagan Amazons. He named the gold-rich island 'California' and placed it near the terrestrial paradise. Its majestic black queen, Calafia, was both beautiful and a formidable warrior, and among her arsenal of war weapons were fierce griffins capable of killing enemy soldiers by lifting them high into the air and dashing them to the ground. Phelan had his agents search for an original copy of Montalvo's book in Europe, and he corresponded with the secretary of state in Sacramento to make sure there was no other country home of that name in the state. He called his property in Bohemian Grove 'Camp Esplandian' after the title of the romance, and he consciously embraced the fanciful myth of California by naming his new home Villa Montalvo.

On the entry road, Phelan placed a series of tall pillars surmounted by seated griffins, considerably more benign than the ferocious men-destroying creatures of Montalvo's story. The griffins, which protected California's gold-

To commemorate the first use of the name California by Garci Ordonez de Montalvo, Senator Phelan commissioned an ornate fountain from the artist J. J. Mora. This delightful conceit, on the back wall of the patio, incorporates the warlike Amazons and griffin of the sixteenth century Spanish tale and includes more delicate figures of wood nymphs. Phelan himself composed the poem honoring the Spanish novelist:

Know
Ordonez De Montalvo's
Fame
Did He Not See
In Fantasy
Our California Grow
Out of Old Spain
Conferred Her Name
Foretold
Her Gold
A Paradise
For Eager Eyes
His Dream Came True
For Me And You

Among the many Iberian decorative elements integrated into Villa Montalvo are the elegant sixteenth century doors imported from Granada, Spain, decorated with heraldic devices. Below, Queen Isabella.

en treasure in the sixteenth century Spanish romance, became symbols of Villa Montalvo — friendly guardians of Phelan's treasured estate.

He commissioned the Carmel artist, J. J. Mora, to design an ornamental wall fountain embodying the elements of Montalvo's story. Phelan was very proud of this young California sculptor, sponsored him for membership in the exclusive Bohemian Club, and supported perhaps his major work, the cenotaph for Father Junipero Serra at Mission San Carlos Borromeo. The fountain on the back wall of Phelan's Spanish patio boasted woodsprites, a pair of watchful Amazons, and a griffin spouting water through its beak. Its figures, whether heroic or fanciful, were in keeping with the romantic tone of the novel. Above the fountain Phelan mounted a plaque on which he penned a tribute to the Spanish author who coined the name 'California.'

Phelan's penchant for recalling California's Spanish roots found another impressive expression in the carved entry doors he brought from Granada. In their aged panels the images of Queen Isabella of Castile and King Ferdinand of Aragon were accompanied by those of clerics, conquistadors, poets, and scholars of old Spain. Above these doors, lighting the entry hallway, Phelan installed a window depicting Cabrillo's ship, *San Salvador*, which first brought the Spaniards to California's coast. As visitors approached their smiling host standing by the elaborate entry doors, they could not mistake the pride Phelan took both in his native state and this exquisite corner of it, in which he evoked California's connections with the old world.

Montalvo's Gardens

In planning the gardens of his new estate, James Duval Phelan could call on the best advice possible in the western part of the country. Every San Franciscan knew of "Uncle John" McLaren, who had served as superintendent of the city's parks since 1887 and was to retain that position until his death nearly sixty years later. As mayor and park commissioner, Phelan had worked closely with McLaren, and it was natural that, when he turned to the layout of the Villa Montalvo gardens, he would invite his longtime associate to advise him. However, the actual design and execution of Montalvo's gardens were the work of George F. Doeltz, who for a time had worked for McLaren in San Francisco. Perhaps it was McLaren who suggested that Phelan make Doeltz the head gardener of the Saratoga property, but it is even more likely that Phelan selected Doeltz because of an already established family connection. When Phelan's father acquired Phelan Park along the Santa Cruz coast, the landscaping had been entrusted to Louis Doeltz, George's father. The elder Doeltz continued to develop Phelan Park when the property was inherited by Alice Phelan Sullivan and her family. As a young man, George Doeltz worked under his father's supervision at Phelan Park. Trained by two master gardeners, the younger Doeltz was now given the responsibility for transforming the orchards and scrub land of James D. Phelan's newly acquired property into a pleasure garden for its discriminating owner.

The basic landscaping plan of Montalvo called for a gently sloping lawn of more than three acres leading from the villa's broad terraced steps, guarded by a pair of sphinxes, to an Italian garden. English laurel, sweet olive, holly, bush germander, and other ornamental trees and shrubs framed the lawn, the broad expanse of which was occasionally broken by a solitary magnolia, redwood, or bunya-bunya tree. The surrounding land, virtually denuded of vegetation when Phelan purchased the property, was patiently planted with pine, eucalyptus, bay and other trees, both native and imported.

To the north and west of the villa, between the main house and the guest cottages, Phelan laid out another garden marked off by Camperdown elms and horse chestnut trees. One wooded path through the shrubs and flowers led to a small white gazebo in which Phelan enjoyed being photographed with his distinguished guests. In this area he placed the weighty mementos of his travels through the old world, including Roman statuary and an Egyptian obelisk. Elaborately carved stone benches, some decorated with curving griffin legs, tucked in shaded nooks among the trees, provided pleasing solitude for Phelan and his guests. Above this garden and the guest cottages were

In George Doeltz, James D. Phelan had a dedicated employee, a skillful horticulturist, and a talented garden architect. Living in a small trailer on the property, Doeltz's supervision of the grounds at Montalvo began even before the construction of the villa. Without power equipment, Doeltz began the arduous work of removing old trees and planting new ones, laying out paths, building a greenhouse, and taming the rough hillside terrain. Doeltz hired local gardeners and laborers and supervised a dozen or more men. In the evenings, sitting on the concrete foundations of the main house, he would sketch plans for the various gardens Phelan envisioned for the estate.

When Phelan visited the property, proposed designs were carefully inspected and new ventures planned. The resulting gardens of Villa Montalvo were the product of a discriminating and involved patron, the inspiration of John McLaren and the elder Doeltz, and the creativity and constant labor of George Doeltz. At first, Doeltz would consult landscape designers about layout, or botanists about the suitability of certain plants, but as his expertise grew, he experimented with hybridized plants and grew prize-winning dahlias and chrysanthemums in his hothouse on the estate.

George Doeltz's work was so successful that, a few years after the founding of Montalvo, the local school trustees petitioned Phelan to allow them to consult Doeltz about landscaping around their school buildings. For forty years, until his retirement in 1952, Doeltz supervised the planting of every tree and shrub on the property.

The formal Italian garden, which originally commanded an uninterrupted view of the valley below, was laid out with carefully manicured boxwood hedges, shrubbery, and flowering plants along the pathways.

Symbolic of the natural mildness of the climate and the fabled abundance of California, as well as the Mediterranean inspiration of Villa Montalvo's architecture, were the citrus trees integrated into the landscaping of the formal gardens.

The admonitions of John McLaren, who disliked having garden statuary of any kind, were not heeded at Montalvo, but the statues were rarely obtrusive and were placed carefully to be in harmony with the surrounding landscape. Statues such as the Venus in the Love Temple, or the Adam and Eve before their fall, and the Three Graces also reflected Phelan's honest sensuality and love of the beauty of the human form.

tennis courts for the more athletic visitors. Still beyond these was a reservoir constructed to collect, from springs farther up the hill, the thousands of gallons of water needed daily to irrigate the gardens at Villa Montalvo. Not all the statues on the grounds were classical relics: in a circle of redwoods Phelan placed busts of three of his illustrious California contemporaries, Joaquin Miller, Edwin Markham, and John Muir.

Phelan loved the gardens of his villa and devoted many hours to detailed plans for planting and maintenance. His guests, too, occasionally suggested decorative touches, such as Cora Older's insistence on borders of bright pink geraniums. When Phelan traveled, he stored up ideas for improvements on his estate. During his visit to Rome on his world tour in 1922, he sent back additional statuary to place in secluded alcoves and along the walkways of his garden. His well-known humor manifested itself even in his choice of "garden furniture." During a visit to Italy Phelan bought an ancient Roman sarcophagus "to enhance, if possible — by contrast — the beauty of living things." But, as he noted in his account of his world tour, "It might be equivocal to say I did not purchase it for my own purposes, but for the pleasure of my friends." He also sent Gottschalk and his head gardener photographs of the great Roman gardens and the entire plan of one Italian garden he had admired and wished to replicate at Montalvo. Fascinated by the exotic as well as the traditional, he built a special cactus garden and delighted in rare species of plants that might thrive in California. From half way round the world in Ceylon, he wrote his secretary, "I have seen so many beautiful palms here that I may plan a palm garden some where at Montalvo — high-growing palms, like the date palms in the patio & others will grow well there."

The orchards that already existed on the grounds were given careful attention by George Doeltz who planted hundreds of additional fruit trees. Phelan looked upon the property surrounding Villa Montalvo principally as a pleasure garden, but it was also an economic resource to be carefully cultivated. He kept close account of the harvest from his fruit orchards, and he directed that the servants keep a poultry yard and vegetable gardens. The produce of these could supply not only his own table but that of his servants, and he wanted to send Montalvo's fresh berries, vegetables, and fruits to his sister and other favorites.

Phelan as Landlord

Phelan was no careless absentee landlord of Villa Montalvo. He took pains to make sure it was maintained in perfect condition, even when he was away due to his political responsibilities or his extended travels. As if he were expecting to descend momentarily on Montalvo with his customary retinue of friends, he wrote to Thomas B. Doyle from Agra, India, "Have the rugs all beaten on the lawn and the floors polished & cleaned in the two main rooms." Mrs. Downey Harvey, the wife of Phelan's longtime friend, acted as an unofficial hostess and manager of Montalvo. Even before the villa was completed, she and her husband took up temporary residence in one of the ranch dwellings, and from there she supervised the details of furnishing and moving into the estate. Phelan relied on Soffie Harvey to fulfill the domestic roles the age assigned to the wife or daughter of prominent and wealthy gentlemen. Although she maintained her primary residence in San Francisco, for nearly two decades Mrs. Harvey tended to the innumerable details at Montalvo, supervising the ordering of supplies, engaging servants, preparing dinner parties and overnight accommodations for guests, constantly keeping Phelan and his secretary in San Francisco apprised of conditions at the estate. A telegram of March 19, 1915, from Harvey to Phelan, gives some idea of her responsibilities at Montalvo as well as the style of hospitality. "Received wire from Cheyenne," she replied to his telegram. "Am at Montalvo.

The woman pictured is believed to be Soffie Harvey, wife of John Downey Harvey. Mrs. Harvey served as James Duval Phelan's household manager.

Rowena Mason, a frequent visitor to Villa Montalvo, recalls that the estate's idyllic reverie was occasionally broken when the fiery-tempered Soffie Harvey, who was impatient with any mistake or inefficiency, vented her frustration on erring servants. Phelan would often come to their rescue. "The Senator was as kind and considerate to a servant as to a guest. I've seen him seek out a weeping upstairs maid to tell her that she was still employed despite being fired by Mrs. Harvey."

The Phelan vegetable gardens were the responsibility of the household staff and gardeners of the estate. The Senator expected Montalvo's own fruit and vegetables to appear on Soffie Harvey's meticulous menus. Fresh strawberries from the service garden were a particularly prized dessert at James Duval Phelan's table.

A permanent staff of gardeners, cooks and maids maintained Villa Montalvo throughout the year. When Senator Phelan entertained on a large scale, or when special projects were undertaken, the staff would be supplemented by local labor. Some of Phelan's staff lived in servants' quarters on the estate, while those with families often resided in nearby Los Gatos.

Everything will be ready Sunday twentieth for twenty or twenty-four for luncheon and fourteen to stop over night. Soffie."

The servants at Montalvo were numerous, and temporary or seasonal help was also employed. Although Phelan entrusted his important business dealings primarily to people of Irish descent who shared his background and values, he did not seem inclined to the same favoritism in his domestic staff. His butlers were usually of continental background, with names like Zumpe and Garces. Irish names, such as Garvin or Cleary, appear in the employee roster, but these were generally not the highest ranking servants. More typical were Doeltz, de Sloovere, Egli, Andersen, Stellhoff, and the like. As in any other house employing numbers of servants, there were the usual frictions and irritations "below stairs." House staff and gardeners occasionally quarrelled over the right to pick fruit from the orchards, kitchen maids annoyed the cook, a young servant complained he did not get enough "sustaining food," and the butler was suspicious of servants trafficking with the local bootlegger. But Villa Montalvo was a desirable place to work, and the estate was smoothly and efficiently run. Phelan set high standards, but he was a reasonable and understanding employer. Working for Mayor, and later Senator,

Phelan was a prestigious position, and he inspired the same loyalty among his domestic staff that he did among his political and business associates.

Phelan Hospitality

Phelan's hospitality was legendary and he enjoyed nothing more than playing host at Montalvo to guests of diverse types and backgrounds. For most residents of the surrounding foothills, however, Phelan's villa remained a world apart, the elegant conceit of a distinguished outsider, which engendered both local pride and boundless curiosity about activities in the big house. Cora Older, another San Francisco intellectual who owned property not far distant from Villa Montalvo, described to one of her friends the distance separating the newcomers from the older residents.

> *Here in the Country if we set out a rosebush it is known to everyone for several miles. Part of the neighbors are city people, but most of them are country people whose occupation is gossip. The city people are objects of the greatest curiosity and subjected to close scrutiny.*

The weekly procession of famous guests entering into Phelan's garden of delight must have given these onlookers rich material indeed for speculation and gossip. Phelan sometimes allowed neighbors to use his tennis courts, and once a year he sponsored a picnic for them. His chauffeur would occasionally delight a couple of local children with a breathtaking ride along the twisting entrance road in one of Phelan's powerful automobiles, but gave strict orders not to tell the Senator. Even more rarely, the butler allowed a few wide-eyed youngsters to walk with their hands clasped tightly behind them through the downstairs rooms cluttered with the absent owner's *objets d'art*. Despite Phelan's well-deserved reputation as California's most gracious host, he did not tolerate abuse of his good nature and generosity. When he learned that people were using the swimming pool without permission during his absences, he ordered it drained, and he also told Doeltz to put up a sign to keep strangers from swimming in his reservoir. But Phelan must have heard with amusement the suggestion of one of the more militant of his staff that he post a warning that anyone found around the house after seven in the evening would be shot without warning.

To accommodate his own and his guests' automobiles, James Duval Phelan constructed an octagonal garage against the foot of the hillside. This beautifully crafted redwood structure in the Federalist style could shelter a dozen cars, thanks to a large, manually operated turntable built into the wooden floor.

James Duval Phelan presided over his table at Montalvo with his legendary charm and good humor. Conversation was at a premium, and wit paid dividends. One of Phelan's occasional guests, the actress Ina Claire, was asked by a more conventional visitor, "Miss Claire, what color would you say your hair is?" "Peroxide, my dear," she retorted, "pure peroxide." Not to be outdone, Gertrude Atherton shared the secret of her particular shade of blond hair: six eggs as a shampoo and a rinse with Irish whiskey.

Rows of towering cypress led to a distant gazebo, an open classical structure supported by columns, which Phelan fancifully called the Love Temple. The view at left looks toward the villa from inside the temple.

Here in his elegant country home, which Gertrude Atherton, one of his most frequent visitors, described as the "Open House for the World," Phelan welcomed poets, musicians, artists, soldiers, politicians, explorers, film stars, and school children. In a brief poem written at the time of the Senator's death nearly two decades after the completion of Villa Montalvo, a local writer captured the spirit of his achievement.

> The Master of Montalvo dreamed a dream,
> A waking dream as Wonder-workers do.
> A dream of home, with wide doors widely hung
> With hospitality — and made it true!

Chapter Twelve
Campaign for United States Senate

"United States Senator" was the single, expressed career objective in James D. Phelan's life. He wrote the title following his signature in one of his youthful copy books. Never did this goal become an obsession, never did it overshadow his productive civic activity, and never did it receive undue attention through Phelan's developing years. That often troublesome relationship of ego to ambition never made Phelan an unattractive human being. Nonetheless, he wanted that title.

Following his terms as mayor, Phelan assumed a natural, larger statewide role within the Democratic party. He enjoyed the activity, enjoyed the travel, the social interactions, and the informal talks to special interest groups or major addresses to large gatherings. As the richest political activist in the state of California he naturally found his way into the position of party treasurer. In fact, as often as not, when the party could not pay the bills, Phelan helped; sometimes he helped greatly.

Highly politicized, Phelan understood the mechanics of the political process. He augmented the employees inherited from his father with those he groomed as modern replacements. All were politically sensitive. Not only did these Irish Americans tend his properties and arrange his business correspondence, they also minded his political fortunes.

Several serious obstacles inhibited his rise to higher political station: Father Peter Yorke, the weakness of the California Democratic party, method of selection of United States senators, and his relationship with Florence Ellon. Yorke would remain a constant, always capable of the low blow; the other variables fluctuated.

Phelan's Motivation

James Duval Phelan did not reform the Charter, advance Hetch Hetchy, or prosecute his successor Eugene Schmitz for the purpose of becoming U. S. Senator. He did not serve as mayor of San Francisco for three terms to create a stepping stone to the Senate. Yet, no one knows for sure why he did not seek a fourth term. He had unfinished work that a fourth term, possibly, could have advanced. To have been turned out of office, though, would have been quite different than stepping aside when a higher place remained his objective.

"THE MAN WHO CAN HELP CALIFORNIA IN WASHINGTON"

JAMES D. PHELAN
(FORMER MAYOR OF SAN FRANCISCO)

CANDIDATE FOR
UNITED STATES SENATOR
ELECTION, NOV. 3, 1914

James Duval Phelan's election cards (front and back) were standard business-card size and were broadly distributed by Phelan's friends, relatives, employees, and supporters.

Progressive Politics

The progressive political reforms that had taken hold, first within the more advanced states, began sweeping the nation. This Progressive movement greatly improved Phelan's Senate opportunities. From California's admission into the union in 1850 until 1914, the state legislature chose the two individuals California sent to Washington D.C. as senators. This is how David C. Broderick made himself senator. The friend and patron of Phelan's uncle Michael commanded the political skill in the 1850s to manipulate the legislature. Leland Stanford did the same, with the advantage of great wealth and industrial prestige.

Phelan never controlled the Legislature. In his lifetime the Democratic party remained strong in San Francisco, but it continued to lose ground as the remainder of the state grew and outdistanced and outpopulated Phelan's urban base. Minority party status and the more limited ebbs and flows of political trends and personalities did not assure Phelan preference in Sacramento. National and state progressive reform changed this, however, and allowed Phelan his opportunity.

In 1910, both major parties agreed that the state's U. S. Senators should be elected directly by popular vote, and by 1913 the Seventeenth Amendment to the U. S. Constitution made this progressive reform national law. The practical effect for Phelan was that the route to the Senate no longer went through the naturally partisan, Republican state legislature. Instead it went through a perhaps more negotiable Republican electorate.

To Phelan, the new and innovative national and California progressive trends were encouraging. The progressive reforms he had fought for as mayor were finding widespread acceptance. Other national reformers were advancing progressive notions that had true national impact. More important for Phelan personally, though, was the side effect progressive reform spread through the major political parties: realignments that offered opportunity.

Both the Democratic and Republican parties contained reform wings intent on updating the nation's political institutions. Many saw this as the opportunity to create a more just, humane, and efficient society. Both parties also contained conservative and even reactionary elements that resisted progressivism. This powerful political trend threatened the well-established national and California political structure and offered Phelan and other

Democrats the chance to escape their minority status. If California progressives of both parties voted together, Phelan could win statewide office.

At the national level the Democratic party's big chance came in 1912. Phelan's friend, former President Theodore Roosevelt, returned to public life and challenged his own party's incumbent President, William H. Taft. Taft was completing a reasonably successful first term, but it was not up to Roosevelt's standards. Both Taft and Roosevelt were Republicans. Roosevelt enjoyed immense personal prestige and vast name recognition. Impulsive and egocentric, he had concluded that his handpicked successor was not adequate as a progressive reformer. When Roosevelt was unable to strip Taft of renomination at the national Republican party convention, he bolted the party, took his personal and political followers with him, and created his own party. He sought the presidency as a stand up Progressive candidate. The formerly dominant Republican party was torn apart as it approached the then formidable challenge of reelecting its incumbent president.

Phelan admired Roosevelt's progressive politics and enjoyed personal rapport with him. Phelan's rock solid loyalty, however, was to the Democratic party. Conveniently, the Democrats nominated Woodrow Wilson, the former President of Princeton, who had established his own enviable agenda as a progressive reform governor of New Jersey. In essence, the Democrats were able to contain the divergent elements of opinion and stand with unity behind their highly attractive progressive reform candidate.

Phelan and Woodrow Wilson

Phelan had aligned himself with the candidacy of Woodrow Wilson long before the Governor of New Jersey received the Democratic nomination. During the previous fall Phelan obtained the consent of the Democratic party county leaders in California to be chair of the state finance committee for the Woodrow Wilson League. Immediately thereafter, he began his correspondence with Governor Wilson, guiding and financing the Governor's California campaign. In January, 1912, Phelan went East and made himself better acquainted personally with the national leadership of the Wilson for President organizers. That summer, following Wilson's Democratic convention victory over three-time unsuccessful Democratic standard holder, William Jennings Bryan, Phelan joined the National Democratic Committee as a

Phelan and his sister, Mollie, escorted Theodore Roosevelt when he visited former Rough Riders whom he commanded in Cuba during the Spanish American War. Some veterans were cared for at Laguna Honda, the city's alms house.

Taft and Roosevelt

The Republicans as well as the Democrats were disrupted by the Progressive movement. President Taft was the candidate of those who controlled the party apparatus. He was the Republican establishment's candidate at the time insurgent reform was cresting within and beyond the party. Theodore Roosevelt, the ever popular, reforming ex-President, was the candidate of Republicans in revolt against the incumbent Taft. Watching from far off California, Phelan liked the Republican split and moved closer to the action.

James Duval Phelan's first contacts with William Gibbs McAdoo began in 1912 when, like Phelan, the progressive businessman advanced Woodrow Wilson for the Democratic party's nomination for president. McAdoo served as secretary of the Treasury in Wilson's cabinet when Phelan was U.S. Senator. In 1922 the McAdoos relocated in California. Eleanor Wilson McAdoo was Wilson's daughter.

In 1924 Phelan delivered the nominating address for McAdoo at the Democratic convention in New York City, even though Governor Al Smith was McAdoo's opponent. Further, Smith sprang from Irish Catholic urban America, but Phelan considered McAdoo the better-qualified candidate. Phelan supported Smith in 1928 and would have supported Franklin Roosevelt for the Democratic nomination over Smith in 1932 had Phelan lived.

member of the party's finance committee. This was Phelan's first major step into party politics at the national level.

California was a long way from Washington, and national political figures hardly considered the state to be vital to their efforts. Nonetheless, Phelan did his best to entice big name figures to tour the state. The national campaign managers could not be induced to schedule a Wilson swing around the Pacific coast despite Phelan's encouragement. Instead, they sent the runner-up, Bryan. Phelan did his duty and made the most of Bryan's presence. Phelan met Bryan in Los Angeles and accompanied the puritanical, prohibitionist future secretary of state to Sacramento and San Francisco. The pleasure-seeking Phelan must have waved happily when the tiring old Democratic war horse of campaigns past turned home to Nebraska.

On the heels of the November election, Phelan wired his congratulations to Wilson, convinced that the close California count would go to the Democratic candidate by 3,000 votes. The next week, depressed and offering a reward for evidence of the ballot fraud that he suspected, Phelan admitted California's final count went against Wilson. Wilson's landslide national victory over the disrupted Republican party, however, demonstrated how close even the vast majority of California Republicans could be moved toward electing a Democratic candidate. Since no Democrat had been elected to a statewide office and no California Democrat had been made U. S. Senator during the twentieth century, Phelan needed all the encouragement possible.

Phelan's position in relation to the National Democratic party and the incoming Wilson administration was quite clear. He had been the key party functionary in California, been in the Wilson camp even before Wilson won the nomination, contributed financially to the Wilson campaign at the nomination and election stages, and secured limited additional financial support from the California Democratic party. As the most prominent party activist for Wilson in California, Phelan clearly associated himself with the major movement of the Democratic party — almost within the winner's circle, but not quite. Phelan claimed ballot fraud kept Wilson from winning the state vote in 1912, but the facts remained that close (even in a disputed election) was not the same as winning. Also, California in 1912 contained neither the population nor the economic prowess to command center stage in national political matters. Neither embracing nor rejecting California, the Wilson administration looked to the state with limited enthusiasm.

The options before Phelan, as the key Democratic party player in a marginal state, were either to seek a suitable appointment within the Wilson administration or to play a role in distributing federal patronage in San Francisco and California. The former mayor advanced along both lines simultaneously. Given California's fringe position in national and party affairs and given Phelan's personal distinction, a secondary seat in the Wilson Cabinet or a substantial ambassadorship were the best posts to which the Westerner might aspire. The position of Interior secretary normally called forth a Westerner, in part because the barren West constituted so much of the interior and such an appointment gave balance to Cabinets.

Phelan's long time political supporter, attorney Sidney McMechen Van Wyck, Jr., who served as chairman of the San Francisco Democratic Campaign Committee, lobbied Woodrow Wilson on Phelan's behalf. Van Wyck noted that Phelan "...unlike many Americans of great inherited wealth,... devoted his time neither to pleasure nor to increasing his fortune. Highly successful and respected in the business world, his chief interest has always been in public matters, matters of government."

The best Democratic competitor for the post of Secretary of the Interior was a personal and political friend of Phelan, Franklin K. Lane. Phelan believed his friend was most appropriate for the position: Lane had the personal and political skills, and he shared Phelan's sense of civic responsibility. On Lane's appointment to the new Cabinet, Phelan warmly congratulated his friend and displayed pleasure in knowing that California was, indeed, to have a capable and strong voice within the administration. Their friendship became stronger as a result of Phelan's backing away from the appointment. From then on, Phelan enjoyed Lane as a conduit into the Wilson administration and, through his friend, conveyed to the President's official family matters that concerned Phelan — California's well being.

At the same time Wilson was carefully, and slowly, assembling his cabinet, the newspapers and Phelan's family were abuzz with talk of his impending appointment as ambassador to a major European capital. Because the former Democratic mayor was assumed to be a prominent Catholic layman, a posting to one of the remaining Catholic courts was assumed. President Wilson, his personal advisor, Colonel Edward E. M. House, and longtime secretary, Joseph P. Tumulty, discussed Phelan's appointment as U. S. Ambassador to Austria-Hungary. The State Department followed up when the new

Franklin K. Lane

Lane had served James Duval Phelan as San Francisco City Attorney during Phelan's years as mayor. Lane was immensely capable, honest, devoted to progressive reforms, quite personable, and a highly engaging speaker. Phelan liked him and took a special interest in his family, lavished him with gifts of good taste, and even prompted the local auto club to show Lane's teenage son a good time. The boy liked "motoring" at a time when driving regulations had yet to be formalized.

Defeated for governor of California in 1901, Lane accepted a post on the Interstate Commerce Commission in Washington. His career interest was in public service, his devotion was to the reforms of the progressive era, and he simply was (unlike Phelan) in need of steady employment.

Phelan's Reputation?

It was to Joseph P. Tumulty that Phelan discretely inquired if his personal reputation had in any way been diminished in the President's eyes. Tumulty, an Irish-Catholic Democrat, an attorney, and a New Jersey political activist, served Wilson since his days as governor. Undoubtedly, Florence Ellon and the irregularity of his domestic life caused Phelan's concern. Wilson, the strict Presbyterian in the White House, would hardly be expected to be sympathetic. As his administration continued, Wilson's propensity for making political and foreign policy decisions based upon personal morality would become more pronounced.

Sister Agnes' Views

Even James Duval Phelan's niece, the cloistered nun, Sister Agnes of Jesus, anticipated his appointment as ambassador to Austria-Hungary. "If the report is true," she wrote her uncle, "there is special pleasure to me … that you will represent the United States to 'His Most Catholic Majesty'." Sister Agnes' concluding remark most likely left her worldly patron cool. "Austria and Spain are the only great powers in the world at present loyal to the Vatican."

Her indulgent uncle "Didden" appreciated the Catholic Church in its historical importance and as a cultural force. He felt no loyalty to the Vatican; neither did he feel that political loyalty should be directed to the Vatican. Phelan certainly understood the history and culture of Spain and Austria. He could not embrace them as innocently as his devoted niece did. His full devotion was to democratic institutions.

secretary of state, William Jennings Bryan, sounded Phelan out. Phelan was personally known to each of the principals in the process.

Phelan, enjoying Tumulty's confidence, had a well-placed filter between the periodically circulating gossip and what crossed the President's official desk. Wilson's own social limitations further curtailed his exposure to such talk. The result, in the case of ambassadorial consideration, did not adversely affect Phelan's chances.

In fact, Phelan did not embrace the opportunity at all. His inner motivations for not pursuing the ambassadorship remain unclear. He simply announced to the press that he intended to seek a seat in the U. S. Senate.

Phelan's Agenda

During November and December of 1912, Phelan advanced his political interests in Washington. He made a second trip in May 1913. His purposes were to promote his Hetch Hetchy water project, to secure administration support of Asian immigration restriction, and to obtain patronage jobs for loyal Democrats in California. Phelan was a strong advocate of the civil service system. Nonetheless, he sought appointments for loyal party workers to those positions that remained uncovered by the merit system. A political realist, Phelan understood fully that the federal government had not had a Democratic president since the Grover Cleveland second election in 1892, which meant that the Republican party had made California's federal appointments for two decades. Certainly new appointments and replacements rightfully belonged to the Democrats. Because California had no Democratic senator, Phelan felt entitled to serve as a clearing house for federal appointments, particularly to San Francisco and to Northern California. In addition, any new group of federal office holders would constitute a cadre of political activists to advance Phelan as California party leader and as senator apparent. Wilson's election as a progressive Democrat changed the entire California political outlook. Federal appointees grew to include over 300 local postmasters throughout the state as well as over 1,500 other officials.

Phelan had his own political intimates for whom he wished to secure advantageous places. The key to his political organization was Charles W. Fay. Politically capable and astute, Fay was cut from the same mold as Phelan, only he was not rich. The second indispensable agent within the Phelan organization was George Welch, another Irish-American.

Fay and Welch constituted the right political combination to support the most compelling, significant man in their lives. They liked the association and, ethnicity aside, they were naturals for the work. Phelan and Fay worked out political strategies, and Fay and Welch determined the best tactics to implement them. Neither Fay, as a federal appointee, nor Welch, as a private business employee of Phelan, counted against their chief's maximum campaign spending limit set by contemporary legislation. To attend to the detailed work of the ensuing statewide campaign, Phelan and Fay brought in two professionals: John T. Waldorf and John S. Irby.

Waldorf was a San Franciscan with editorial experience from the *Bulletin*. His primary responsibility was coordination with the statewide party. As Phelan's advance man, Waldorf traveled the state and lined up local leaders and local newspapers. He estimated potential Phelan support, rented halls for Phelan's subsequent speeches, and prepared the way.

Irby brought a mix of newspaper and political experience, plus a local connection, to the Phelan campaign. He was a lawyer, journalist, and politician. Irby had been a newspaper manager in Virginia. Later, in mid-career, he was a member of the Colorado state senate. Irby took charge of Phelan's campaign office and met with contributors. He reported directly to Phelan with carbon copies to Fay.

Primary Campaign

Phelan's primary election campaign was, in actuality, pro forma even though the former mayor and his staff had to take the opposition seriously. Thomas F. Griffin, a member of the State Assembly from Modesto, declared for the Democratic nomination when Phelan was away in Washington advancing the patronage claims of his supporters and lobbying for the Hetch Hetchy project. Griffin was respected in Democratic and progressive circles and had been a Wilson man from the start. He and what organization he could call into being were not, however, a significant threat to Phelan's efforts for the Democratic party nomination for U.S. Senator. Operating under the new California election law, Phelan and Griffin contested in the August primary election for the greater number of statewide votes among registered Demo-

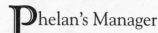

Phelan's Manager

James D. Phelan's father had set Charles W. Fay's father up in the contracting business in San Jose. The sons attended the same college, St. Ignatius, where Charles Fay served on the faculty during the 1880s. Fay managed Phelan's mayoral campaigns and remained his lifelong confidant. He became Phelan's personal secretary in City Hall and even became the clerk of the Board of Supervisors upon the end of Phelan's last term as mayor. Little wonder that Phelan remained well informed as the Board sank back into corruption before the earthquake and fire of 1906.

As was so often the case, Phelan's "employees" also were his comfortable friends, and the bonding extended to their families. Phelan served as patron to Fay's sister, Maude Fay, during her career in grand opera. For his friend Phelan obtained the postmastership in San Francisco and, through Tumulty, was able to tailor the announcement for maximum political impact. From then on, Fay became Phelan's political broker at the new, national arena. Fay grew with the job and on the side tended Phelan's major property acquisitions.

George Welch

James Duval Phelan had inherited his first secretary-office manager from his own father in 1892, just as he had inherited the business enterprises. Young George Welch came into the Phelan employ later, as a teenager, and was the bright, personable young man who would succeed Thomas Mahony. Phelan fostered Welch's education, including law school, and employed Welch as chief secretary and as political advance man. Later, Phelan cared for and guided Welch's young family following the talented employee's death during the influenza epidemic of World War I.

Welch developed into Charles Fay's complement. Younger, more jovial, and more conversant with the neighborhood working people, he was Phelan's eyes and ears in the neighborhoods. Welch was a joiner of Catholic and Irish community organizations. He knew how to get along and to stay on the right side of just about everyone. He even served as Phelan's monitor of Father Yorke. Welch lived in Yorke's parish and as a model, practicing Catholic owed his personal loyalty to Phelan. Not from him did the priest learn of Phelan's liaison.

crats. Phelan won by a greater than two to one margin, and looked stronger than Woodrow Wilson's Democratic showing in 1912.

Analysis of the election results clearly shows Phelan's strength lay in the northern part of the state, even though he campaigned more heavily in the South. His real chance for victory in November, though, was directly related to events within the Republican party, not his own Democratic party.

Phelan and Griffin together received only 123,000 votes in the Democratic primary. The two Republican contenders for their party's nomination, Joseph R. Knowland and Samuel M. Shortridge, received a total of 240,000 votes — almost twice the total Democratic vote. Under normal circumstances within the two-party system, Phelan would have been doomed. Yet Phelan and his intimates were anything but glum as they planned for the fall campaign. The Republican-Progressive split was appearing in California for the Senate campaign, just as it had in the national presidential election two years earlier. In 1914, Phelan stood as the progressive Democrat enjoying the undisputed senatorial nomination of this minority party.

The Republican primary campaign consisted of a bitter competition between conservative and reactionary elements of California's majority party. The state Republican party was so dominated by the right-of-center elements that its own progressive reform element simply left the party. The result for Phelan was promising indeed. He actually expected Shortridge to defeat Knowland in the Republican party primary election because Knowland had personally offended President Wilson in the Congressional debate over the Panama Canal tolls. The President's popularity was very high and rose further during the honeymoon phase of his progressive administration.

Knowland's defeat of Shortridge surprised Phelan and required some limited change in his own campaign strategy. Rather than berating Shortridge for his connections with the political corrupters of San Francisco, Knowland's connections with the corrupt corporations of years past became the alternative. To his credit, though, Phelan waged a positive campaign. The divisiveness of the Republican primary campaign suggested that Knowland might not be able to gather back the Republican primary votes that had gone to Shortridge. Instead, Shortridge votes could go to Phelan, even though the two lived in different political worlds. Symbolically, Shortridge had been the defense attorney for the corrupter, Abe Ruef, when Phelan was privately supporting the prosecution.

Even more promising than this Republican division among the conservatives was the Republican party status versus its own progressive membership. California's leading and most substantial progressive reformer was Governor Hiram W. Johnson. Highly popular and highly effective, Johnson delivered on his own campaign promise to kick the dominating California corporations out of politics, particularly the Southern Pacific Railroad. Through comprehensive legislative programs and vigilance and energy from the executive office, Johnson was transforming California government.

Governor Hiram Johnson also had an ambition — to be senator. He chose to seek reelection as Governor in 1914 rather than run against Phelan for national office, in large part because his revitalizing progressive reforms needed a bit more implementation in Sacramento. Also, California's second U. S. Senate seat would be contestable in 1916. What this vacuum of progressive reform presence on the Republican side of the political spectrum allowed was the candidacy of Francis J. Heney, an avowed radical progressive reformer. That meant a three-cornered race, the Phelan-Democratic ideal.

Heney, independent of Johnson, had declared himself a candidate for U. S. Senator in the Progressive party primary and actually rivaled Phelan in capturing votes — over 75,000. The result was beneficial for Phelan. In November, Phelan, as the Democratic party candidate, faced the Republican Knowland and the Progressive Heney in a three-cornered race, with victory going to the one candidate with the highest number of votes — no run off.

From campaign headquarters atop the Phelan Building, the outlook was indeed bright. For the first time since Grover Cleveland occupied the White House a Democratic President set the national political agenda. Woodrow Wilson was approaching the height of his popularity as effector of comprehensive progressive reform, and he was realigning American institutions with the demands of a modern industrial society. Wilson's legislative package was being enacted into law to the satisfaction of America's leading political thinkers, as well as to that of the laborers, whose contentment and devotion were to remain mainstays of the Democratic party.

Wilson had made progressive reform, which Phelan had advocated before the turn of the century, the new American standard. Wilson, in effect, co-opted progressivism for the Democrats. This split the Republicans against him in 1912, and the same was taking place in California in 1914. Phelan, Fay, and Welch perceived this and campaigned accordingly. They wrapped

How to Mold Public Opinion

James Duval Phelan's lifelong conviction was that public opinion is molded in two ways: oral presentations of substance, delivered with grace and charm to target audiences; and written coverage of such presentations as well as editorial and essay-type articles well placed in the press. Given Phelan's views and the men he engaged to publicize them, it's no wonder that the California press received ample opportunity for political coverage of his campaign. Phelan loved motoring, he loved public speaking, and he loved writing. He and his well-selected campaign team blitzed the state.

Heney versus Johnson

James D. Phelan knew both Hiram Johnson and Francis Heney personally. Both had been intimately involved in the San Francisco Graft prosecution. Heney, in fact, had been the chief prosecutor until a rejected juror shot him in the face for having exposed his criminal past. Of the two, Johnson was somewhat less flamboyant and a bit more calculating. Certainly, he was better organized and appealed to a broader spectrum of voters. Heney's flamboyance, commitment, and impulsiveness were undeniable, and of the two Phelan simply liked Heney more than he liked Johnson. Phelan provided Heney, his November opponent, campaign office space in the Phelan Building, often conveyed his admiration and respect, and remembered Heney generously in his will for the acts of political cleansing Heney had performed for their beloved San Francisco.

Were either Phelan or Heney men of lesser integrity, the question of collusion might have been raised. It was not at the time, and it has not been by historians who have reviewed the period with great care. Also, the Phelan papers bear out the concurrence of appearance and reality. Both Phelan and Heney sought the Senate. Each used the constitutional mechanisms available to advance that ambition in an honest and straightforward manner. Had either man not been in the race, he would gladly have campaigned for the other. In the end, when the ballots were counted, the ever gracious Phelan immediately wrote Heney: "I am sorry that we cannot both share the honor of office. Under other circumstances, I would have been delighted, as you know, to have supported you…." He greatly admired Heney as a political fighter.

themselves in the progressive reform mantle of Woodrow Wilson while maintaining independent positions on issues of specific concern to their individual California constituencies.

Phelan enjoyed what was even better than a Wilson coattail effect. Two years earlier Wilson had converted a huge California Republican registration majority into a very close loss in his three-cornered race for the White House. The national vote elected him. Wilson's administrative and legislative success during his year and eight months in office increased his popularity in California. What Phelan had was the coattail identification with Wilson, plus the recognition that Wilson's Democratic administration was redeeming the nation.

California Women and Phelan

Throughout his political career Phelan exercised caution regarding California women. He established his record early and soundly. As mayor of San Francisco he appointed the first woman member of the San Francisco Board of Education. Early in the movement for Wilson Phelan welcomed women activists into the progressive ranks with men, particularly Grace B. Caukin, who joined the executive committee of Californians for Wilson.

Given his cultural and social contacts, Phelan enjoyed an extensive and well-established correspondence with local professional women of the day, as well as harmonious relationships with the wives of his friends and business associates. He also provided Phelan Building offices, gratis, to women's organizations. He rented other office space to women who experienced discrimination in their business enterprises. His financial contributions to feminist publications may not necessarily be cited as evidence for his forward-looking public views, simply because he seemed to subscribe to almost every publication that could be carried by the United States Postal Service.

By 1914, his mother had long been deceased, and his sister, Alice, had died, too. His remaining sister, Mollie, was incapable of assisting him in any capacity, and his nieces were young. To attract the female vote, he addressed the same issues as with men. Women were Americans, too, and equally capable of understanding and correct action. He advertised, gave interviews liberally, and instructed his staff to provide photographs and all the background information that women editors might wish. In the end, though, he called upon the woman beyond his own family for whom he felt the greatest respect because of her independent achievement — Gertrude Atherton.

The California novelist already commanded a national literary reputation for her relentless production of popular fiction. Her commercial success and personal reputation were to continue for more than another quarter century. It was to Atherton that he turned when Mary Foy, a Southern California political activist and Democratic elector in 1912, told Phelan to obtain and publicize the endorsement of a prominent woman. His Progressive opponent, Heney, already obtained a strong letter of endorsement from Jane Addams, the famous Chicago settlement house reformer.

Phelan's letter to Gertrude Atherton tells much. In the midst of a political campaign for the U.S. Senate, he composed a thorough reply to factual questions put to him by a highly successful writer-friend. Also, that Atherton would put Phelan to such chores at such a time, spoke of her security in their relationship. The letter constituted a mix of knowledge, comfort, efficiency, sociability, and good connections — perhaps name dropping. If Atherton treated Phelan as a research assistant, he enjoyed the role. For him to request political endorsement seemed incidental.

On primary election day, August 25, 1914, Phelan wrote to Atherton. He had more answers to her persisting questions. He explained the role of President Theodore Roosevelt in the San Francisco earthquake relief in 1906 and the committee system that he and his friend, John Downey Harvey, managed. Atherton was not politically astute, so Phelan was elementary, but not insulting. He appreciated her skills, but not in politics:

> …I expect to survive the primary, after which the real battle will begin between possibly myself, Heney and Shortridge…. The primary held today is an elimination contest, as you are aware.
>
> I have been in almost every county…explaining and expounding the policies of Woodrow Wilson and his splendid record of achievements, and have made the plea that the people must sustain the President on account of his good works, especially in the midst of his administration, when he has so much more to accomplish, and of course, it follows that the only way to sustain the Administration is to elect a candidate who will defend and uphold its policies.

Without scientific opinion sampling, Phelan erred in anticipating Shortridge, rather than Knowland; beyond that Phelan was quite correct and quite successful.

November Optimism

Entering the conclusive campaign in November, James D. Phelan was rightfully optimistic. His three permanent political liabilities were as well managed as possible. Father Peter C. Yorke was quiet. He disliked Phelan's Progressive opponent Heney as much as he disliked Phelan, having satirized him as the self-seeking prosecutor of the Catholic Eugene Schmitz. Yorke and his weekly *Leader* had opposed the graft prosecution back in 1907. Yorke had no personal contacts with Phelan's Republican opponent Knowland and no reason to offer his gratuitous support to the Republican party, particularly when his own Irish constituency identified naturally with Heney and Phelan. Therefore, Yorke sat out this election.

Likewise, Florence Ellon remained silent. She had been living in Germany where her daughter had married. Greatly preferring France and England, though, she relocated in London, busying herself with relief work for Belgian refugees after World War I began. The candid opinions she sent Phelan were that the press treatment downplayed German viciousness and Belgian suffering. As to his Senate campaign, she wished her Jimmy well. Two weeks after the election she wrote from England, miffed that he had not written her the results. Still, she asked, "Do you want to see me?" In April she returned to San Francisco, announced her presence, and asked Phelan to call. "I must see you about a matter of importance," she noted on her rich, personalized stationery. By then Phelan was safely elected.

James Duval Phelan to Gertrude Atherton

Phelan's letter of June 17, 1914, requesting Atherton's political endorsement is unique. It reveals a cultural life that separated Phelan from all other politically active Californians. Responding to Atherton's literary inquiries when she was in residence at Columbia, working on her history of California, he wrote

My dear Mrs. Atherton:

…You seem to be very happy in your University environment. Give my kind regards to President and Mrs. [Nicholas Murray] Butler.

…Today, I asked Mr. Franklin Hichborn [California political analyst and author of The System on the San Francisco graft prosecution] to send you a resume of the Graft Prosecution, dates, and episodes, and he promised to do so. He, like myself, is interested in having the public, through your pen, understand the facts, although he has a book on the market himself….[Phelan and Rudolph Spreckels had helped support its creation and publication.] I do not feel quite confident to give you offhand information of [John C.] Fremont. Mr. Zoeth Eldredge, who has given much time to research work in California history, and who has written "The Beginnings of San Francisco" does not take much stock in Fremont. I have always felt that he had assurances from persons high in authority that he would be protected in any work looking to the acquisition of California. I have just come from Sonoma where I spent the night with the Spreckels, and attended the dedication of the monument in honor of the Bear Flag party. The Vallejo family protested against the monument on the ground that the Bear Flag party treated General Vallejo with great severity and indignity. I have always suspected that Fremont encouraged this movement. A short time afterwards the American flag was raised at Monterey, when the Bear flag was hauled down. A Stanford Professor made an interesting search of the London Archives, and published an article on England's attitude towards the American occupation of California, which probably you have seen. If not, I can get it for you. [E. D. Adams, "British Interest in California," American Historical Review, XIV (July 1909), 744-763.] The diplomatic correspondence showed that the English consuls urged the British government to take possession before the Mexican war, and the foreign office replied that they would not commit an act of that kind towards a friendly country, and that they were more concerned in the movements of the French in the South Pacific, but at the same time, they said they would not tolerate any other government taking California….You could here introduce the visit of Drake, and how he failed to discover the Bay in 1579…. You are so familiar with these things that I hesitate to go further except to suggest the dramatic episodes. Yes, [John W.] Marshall [the discoverer of Gold in California] died poor….I have written to Father Mestres, parish priest of Monterey, who, in conversation, told me he had discovered the origin of the word "California": meaning in the Catelonian dialect, "imaginary land," derived from two words something like "Cala" (place) and "fornia" (pertaining to the imagination or romance), hence in creating a fabulous country Montalvo called it California. This seems to me a very reasonable derivation. If I get his reply in writing, I will send it to you, because nowhere has this derivation been published that I know of.*

Phelan did not have to solicit Atherton's help. All she needed was informed direction. Not only did she endorse Phelan for senator, she took time out from the writing and social schedule that she took so seriously. Beyond, that, she amply rewarded her research assistant by dedicating her romantic history of California to the senator-apparent. Harpers published it in a timely manner, one month before the November election. Atherton considered Phelan California's most accomplished gentleman for whom she felt the deepest of respect.

Far less personal, but far more politically significant was Woodrow Wilson's endorsement. Wilson's, perhaps, may not even have been sincere. Phelan drafted it and sent it to his friend Tumulty for the President's approval. Phelan's attempts to induce President Wilson to take a campaign swing through California and the West failed. His own motivations were propelled by a mixture of hard work toward desired goals and enjoyment of California's abundant life. His invitations to the guilt-driven Wilson got nowhere. The responsibilities of the presidency would not allow Wilson to take such a trip. California still remained remote and somewhat unreal; the President had no time for such indulgence.

More genuine official endorsements flowed from Wilson's Cabinet members: Secretary of State William Jennings Bryan, Secretary of the Treasury William Gibbs McAdoo, Secretary of Labor William B. Wilson, and best of all, California's favorite son, Interior Secretary Franklin K. Lane. Lane toured California on Phelan's behalf, delivering three major addresses for his patron, all highly successful, and in Southern California drew more enthusiastic listeners than Phelan himself.

Next in practical value was the influence of Labor Secretary Wilson. Phelan also corresponded personally with tradesmen, explaining the numerous pro-labor actions during his terms as mayor. And, in the end, Phelan successfully contained Yorke's old charge: Go back to work or be clubbed.

Phelan's basic campaign themes had been California's need to support the highly popular Woodrow Wilson administration, Phelan's connection with the administration, and how that connection would help the state's development and well being. Phelan's personality and role allowed his enthusiasm for this approach to exceed the enthusiasm of Wilson himself.

The President's reaction to Phelan's considerable electoral success was a note of cordial congratulations. Phelan's symbolic revitalization of the

Women's Right to Vote

California had preceded the nation in granting the vote to women. California women voted in the 1912 Wilson election, and James D. Phelan solicited their votes himself in 1914. He and the California Democratic party provided recognition for women in politics through appointive positions within and beyond the party. Phelan accepted women's right to vote as a California reality. President Woodrow Wilson, having different roots and a different perspective, opposed the Nineteenth Amendment to the Constitution.

By election day in November James Duval Phelan had made three circuits of California, speaking as often as six times per day in as many locations. He traveled mostly by car—his own Mercedes, chauffeur driven. He loved his state, he loved motoring, he loved speaking. His senatorial campaign of 1914 constituted his favorite mix, pursuit of pleasure and business, with the prospect of success at both. Gertrude Atherton sent Phelan this cartoon.

Democratic party in California received as hardy a recognition as Wilson's personality allowed, but it remained to Phelan's response to spell it out. "…it was a rather remarkable victory, on account of the political complexion of this State." Then the senator-elect itemized the official registered voting strength of each political party:

Republican..............................510,000
Democratic..............................277,000
Progressive..............................217,000

The election results gave Phelan 280,000 votes. Knowland, the Republican received 251,000, and, surprisingly, Heney, the Progressive, received 252,000. Phelan declined to add that he had been the beneficiary of the opposition split that had allowed Wilson's entry into office two years previously.

Somewhat playfully, Phelan did add: "I have been in the field since last February, and canvassed the entire state, urging the voters to approve your foreign and domestic policies, and with as much grace as possible, put myself in the position of being the beneficiary of my own advice.…My slogan was, 'With Wilson for California,' and I believe that the large vote I received — nearly thirty thousand plurality — was meant by the people as an endorsement of your Administration."

In a more businesslike manner Phelan reminded the President that California also returned to the Congress its three Democratic incumbents and augmented the state's delegation with an Independent, a Democrat Prohibitionist (which in time Phelan would consider a contradiction in terms), and a Progressive who replaced the anti-Wilson Knowland who had relinquished his congressional seat to challenge Phelan for the Senate. Phelan assured the President of their support of his administration's programs, too. Respectfully, Phelan concluded this letter by noting that private business would take him to New York and Washington during December at which time he would seek an opportunity to greet President Wilson personally.

James D. Phelan's response to the President's somewhat routine congratulations constituted an informative and respectful offer of additional service within the bonds of Democratic party loyalty in support of shared progressive objectives. Also, it offered an open hand of friendship and personal association that was a hallmark of Phelan's life style. However, the two were not to become close despite Phelan's overtures and his potential usefulness to Wilson and his administration.

Chapter Thirteen
United States Senator

Joining America's most elite and powerful club, for Phelan, was hardly intimidating. Perhaps it should have been. On the surface he appeared well enough prepared for the years ahead of him. He was well educated, formally and through self study and travel. He was highly regarded as a speaker. He grasped issues easily and well. He related well to the progressive reform movement, the propelling political force of his time. His personal and political acumen, if judged by the way he marshalled his various assets and balanced them against his liabilities, was acute.

Two concerns should have given Phelan pause for reflection. First, his organizational experience was limited to an executive role. Phelan was comfortable in this role and accustomed to reflectively reviewing problems, exploring available options, and then making prudent decisions within a familiar and somewhat controlled environment. That was not a description of the U.S. Senate.

Next, Phelan had always functioned comfortably as the host. In his beloved San Francisco, he organized the program, he picked up the tab, and as a result, he determined the agenda.

Given the blended life style of California and the European continent to which he was accustomed, an easy fit into America's millionaires' club, the U.S. Senate, should have been expected. His gift giving, hosting, and celebrating style caused unanticipated problems with his colleagues, however.

Phelan's erudition, which a wide spectrum of Californians appreciated and genuinely admired, stuck in the craw of other hard working Senators who preferred brevity and precision to embellishment and allusion.

Gathering Friends

The Bohemian Club's Red Room was James Duval Phelan's favorite for hosting those whose company he enjoyed. The Pacific Union Club was right for those he wished to influence. For the many, he chose the Palace Hotel. His creation of Villa Montalvo allowed him to host just about everyone.

Formal attire was Phelan's ordinary dress for functions after 6:00 P.M. The importance of the event determined which of his tuxedoes and matching accessories, pince-nez spectacles included, his valet laid out. And, of course, the household laundress labored to save his personal linens from the "common mangle" of the commercial laundries, which he deplored.

With a six-year term of office before him that would include extended, yet part-time, residence in the national capitol, James Duval Phelan rather naturally looked to rent a substantial home that would serve his needs and still minimize his financial commitment. His notion of his needs and comfort and what the rental market allowed simply never met. Instead he purchased a modern four-story city mansion at 2249 R Street, at Sheridan Circle. The thirty-four-room, well-furnished, stately home was properly located in the growing embassy row neighborhood. And, in keeping with the family tradition, it appreciated greatly by the time Phelan sold it off to the Ambassador from Sweden for whom he had to arrange comfortable terms so that Sweden could acquire the Phelan property. (Subsequently, the property has become the Embassy of Kenya.)

Staffing his Washington residence became a problem he was never able to resolve. He recruited staff locally, checked references, hired away household servants from congressional colleagues, and even brought reliable and trusted staff from San Francisco and Montalvo. His standard and his quantitative needs were never satisfied.

Phelan's dinner parties reached banquet proportions, and he hosted formal balls and musical presentations. In time, some of his less cultured, less affluent, and less interested colleagues became privately peeved. Hiram Johnson, who joined Phelan as California's second Senator in 1917, confined to his personal letters his displeasure of Phelan's insatiable demands for others' servants. Some complained that they only saw Phelan in evening dress, an accusation that was inconsistent with his average attendance at committee hearings and roll call votes.

Phelan's household entertaining continued along his California democratic social pattern. He liked hosting the well placed and the accomplished, but the interesting and the attractive also found a place. Unlike at Montalvo, however, he did not have Soffie Harvey to arrange his social calendar and manage the details. His young niece, Gladys Doyle, served as his hostess during occasions when she was in Washington. Her youthful presence, however, had its limitations.

Agnes Tansill

Phelan's companion during most of his senatorial years was Agnes O. Tansill. She was a young civil servant when they met, perhaps in her late twenties or early thirties, with black hair and a light complexion, and from an established family in Connecticut. Apparently a member of the working side of the family, Tansill had lived in Washington all of her life, residing with her mother and a sister. Unlike Florence Ellon, she found living at home satisfactory, and she contributed to the joint expenses through her employment. Other than her occasional fantasy of marrying a millionaire California Senator, she seemed otherwise content with her life.

Tansill's image was that of a somewhat liberated working woman in a new age of improved employment opportunities. The federal government was expanding its bureaucracies and drawing female staff into its orbit. Tansill saw herself as one among many in such a category. She had her own work colleagues — contemporaries who shared their experiences and their gossip. She lived a middle-class life on the edge of political glamour and power. To add excitement and romance she would "…arrange taking the afternoon off as lots of girls do." Even in her relationship with the Senator she still viewed herself in the "lots of girls" pool.

Phelan was far more open with Tansill than he had ever been with Ellon, perhaps because of the younger woman's open and respectable position in society. Tansill maintained herself; Phelan maintained Ellon. When Phelan and Ellon enjoyed opera "together," it had been from separate boxes with separate friends, though at the same performance. Tansill and Phelan met at receptions, moved together in public, and dined in the company of his friends and associates. They, too, enjoyed theater, undoubtedly at Phelan's initiative. In telegrams he signed himself "Prince," and in her letters Tansill became "Ophelia." And her mild and infrequent requests of Phelan hardly constituted demands or burdens.

Tansill objected to what she concluded was Phelan's California disregard for prudence. In Washington, Phelan was away from the care and observation of his sister, the one who had never recovered from the engagement and marriage of their older sister. Thirty-five years had passed, Alice had died, yet Mollie was hardly a functioning member of her brother's world. In Washington, Phelan remained responsible for his own private behavior and contented himself to allow Tansill to follow her own sense of propriety to the degree that it did not curtail his own actions. Never marrying was his fixed position. Although Tansill made her best effort to change his mind, she never considered his position a breach of promise.

When the two first met, Tansill was employed at the International Red Cross Commission. Through Phelan's intervention, she transferred to the San Francisco Office of Collector of Customs, which was directed by his intra-party rival, John O. Davis. She alerted Phelan that Davis was fishing, trying to determine their relationship. Thereafter, Davis extended himself to make her feel welcome in the office. His purpose, Tansill suggested, was to improve his communication with Phelan.

Tansill brought her mother along with her to what was to be a temporary posting in San Francisco, sort of an extended and working vacation. Because Phelan remained in Washington and the two were separated by the continent, the frequency of Tansill's letters increased. Phelan, true to form, filed

Modern Romance

The greatest contrast of James Duval Phelan's more open behavior toward Agnes Tansill was her inclusion in the social life of his home. Ellon never was asked to his home and never was introduced to his social circle. Tansill, in contrast, suffered from role confusion. She dined at Sheridan Circle, remained over night, and felt distinctly uncomfortable because they were among company. Worried about her reputation in Washington society, she reversed herself and ceased staying over when Phelan entertained other house guests simultaneously. Later she even objected to the presence of the servants. "Personally," she wrote, "I think it is anything but dignified to have *women* staying where servants spread news like wildfire…. However if you think it looks proper we won't discuss it … I'm beginning to think … its a case of each to its own kind."

On another occasion, the lover reminded her blue-eyed Irishman of their evening together enjoying Hamlet. Too bad Shakespeare's Ophelia and the legendary Prince of Denmark never enjoyed a post performance gourmet supper helped along by fine champagne. And, of course, how well she remembered their night riding along the Potomac drive. Phelan recited Shakespeare, then they danced, and "then the place was full of spangles…." During this phase of their relationship her letters were uniformly encouraging and graphic.

Disagreement over Marriage

James D. Phelan and Agnes Tansill's overt disagreement over marriage took place after they had known each other for well over a year. Tansill became argumentative at Phelan's assertion that single men are able to do a great deal for their country. Her rejoinder was, "The President and all the other successful men think entirely *just the opposite,* and so I think you stand quite alone in your decision." She omitted that Wilson remarried, some thought hastily, following the death of his first wife.

She added, "I agree with them, so of course I think you ought to belong to me. Of course, if you do not adhere to any of our decisions, there seems to be no way out of it, only that I want my way...."

everything — from water bills to love letters — much of which ended in the Bancroft Library.

The Senator exercised caution in his relations with Tansill. At the time of his death he pointedly noted in his will that he had never been married and fathered no children, in or out of wedlock. His near exclusive commitment was to the family into which he was born; he intended to create no other. So while he remained fully responsible for his own behavior with Agnes Tansill, he did not intend to become responsible for any other man's behavior. As a result, his memos in the Tansill file do not make for innocent reading. His memos for the record held names, places, and occasions associated with his companion's alleged relationships with other men.

Tansill's objective was to entice the middle-aged Senator into marriage. His objective was to continue the lifestyle he had always preferred and to which he had long ago committed himself. Perhaps he had inherited a bit of his father's distrust, too. He did not know to what lengths the young woman who flattered him a bit too much would resort. He treated her with honesty, but his trust was slight.

Following Tansill's return from San Francisco, Phelan used his friendship with Joseph Tumulty to have her reinstated in her previous position. Thereafter, he supported her promotion with a standard letter. Transfer into the yet small but already growing Internal Revenue Service was the next step in her career path. All movements appeared standard. All were modest. And all but reinstatement after the San Francisco odyssey seemed to be accomplished without any special consideration.

Upon Phelan's return from a European holiday he paused in New York amid press reports that he was ill. Ophelia wrote to him at the Hotel Ambassador. His return telegram hardly gladdened her heart: "Thanks for inquiry am feeling much better spent three days in country and go west Friday to get well in best climate on earth hope you are enjoying summer am very sorry i cant go to Washington this trip Prince"

Tansill's response: "I sorry to return this, but I feel that our brief acquaintance has come to a close." To which Phelan noted on the envelope for the file, "Finis Ophelia."

Only it was not the end. Well into Phelan's retirement Tansill arrived in San Francisco and impulsively wrote Phelan from the Fairmont Hotel. Ophelia wanted him to call.

Phelan's executive secretary, Thomas B. Doyle, knew how to cover for his boss. He explained that the Senator was away for some days. He lavished her with attention and consideration. Phelan's personal secretary, Belle Driscoll, the first woman (still Irish though) to serve in that capacity, likewise rose to the occasion. She flattered Tansill by insisting on having her photograph. Unfortunately for historical record, Driscoll succeeded too well in protecting her beloved employer. Tansill departed without leaving a photograph either for her Prince or his biographers.

Phelan and the Wilson Administration

Phelan's major claim during his senatorial campaign was his closeness to the Wilson Administration. He downplayed their shared Democratic party affiliation because of the vast number of California voters who were registered members of the Republican party. He was perceptive, however. Rather than being rock solid party members, Californians shared tendencies, inclinations, or biases in one political direction or the other. This was the point he communicated to national party leaders in explaining his strategies.

Yet, being close to the President, for the good of California and the good of the President's domestic and foreign policies, remained a key to his voter appeal. At least Phelan acted as if it was. In actuality, Woodrow Wilson was hardly a person anyone, except his immediate family, became close to.

First Phelan sought close association with Wilson and his administration. When his overtures failed, Phelan contented himself with the public illusion. The problem was not Phelan's personally, it was the President's. Wilson's personality did not allow non-familial associations that could be confused with friendship. On the other hand, Wilson had no political or psychological reason, as yet, for public rebuff of any Democratic senator.

Wishing to cooperate, Phelan acquiesced to Wilson's request that he investigate corruption charges lodged against James M. Sullivan, a Tammany Hall-type appointed as U.S. Minister to Santo Domingo. The mission required Phelan to hear testimony in New York and Washington and even to take a trip to the island. In his January 26, 1915, letter to his friend Rudolph Spreckels, Phelan admitted that "I tried hard to avoid the service, but I was forced in a position to be either obliging or disobliging to our very excellent administration....I could not but accept a thankless task." The matter

Traveling, But Not Enjoying

As for the required trip to Santo Domingo, it "will be the only rest I shall have had for a year; so I look forward to tropical life with no particular aversion."

He reported to George Welch in mid-February that his augmented traveling party was "in high spirits and are enjoying every minute." Being a U.S. Senator had its perks. "I never had such comfort traveling. As my staff is so efficient I have nothing to do but observe and read." He even brought one of the Duval youngsters from New York in the capacity of "photographer and first asst. courier." The only untoward development was a quarantine because of an outbreak of tropical disease. To C. C. Moore, director of San Francisco's Panama Pacific Exhibition, Phelan cabled "Greetings from Santiago De Cuba the oldest large city to the youngest great city of the western hemisphere both of Spanish origin...." As was his way, Phelan turned what was required of him into a positive experience. In this case, it was his first sample of life in a tropical environment. He found it interesting, but never returned. The real challenge was his conclusion and report for Wilson and Bryan.

Neither Wilson nor Bryan could have liked the truth, even so varnished. For Phelan, the entire pre-Senatorial episode became a forgettable experience.

constituted a minor scandal within the administration and any resolution would be delicate. The administration's tactic was to stick the new boy in the Senate with it and see how he handled it. Among Phelan's other "qualifications" was his presumed adherence to Catholicism. Sullivan was a Catholic urban Democrat with machine support. Santo Domingo was a Catholic country. If Sullivan had to be done in, it best be done by one of his own.

Phelan moved into an apartment in the Waldorf Astoria and commenced his hearings there. He arranged for commission counsel (Charles H. Strong, "a high class man and able counselor"), a secretary (John S. Irby), and stenographic reporters. It was an open, but highly comfortable hearing. The press covered it well and, according to Phelan, "On account of the dislike for Bryan by the New York press, the Secretary of State is made the central newspaper figure." Phelan's New York friends and relatives came to see the senator-elect in action and, undoubtedly, add to the after-hour festivities.

The problem centered on allegations of corrupt influence in a contest between two banks over the Dominican loan of $1,500,000 at seven percent. The rate was lucrative, but the investment was risky. Phelan's conclusion skirted the corruption issue, finding Bryan's appointee, Sullivan, instead to be unfit "temperamentally" for his diplomatic assignment. Sullivan should either resign or he should be removed from his post.

Phelan was the first senator from California to have been elected by a direct vote of the people, and he visualized his role as a senator to be primarily service to his home state. California was his fixation. He wished to use his affinity with the Democratic administration to California's benefit, and he wished the administration and the nation to recognize the emergence of the California commonwealth as a substantial player with a unique style and an exceedingly bright future. As the junior senator, his first task was support of the Democratic legislative agenda, in committee and on the Senate floor.

As expected, his committee assignments were modest. He was pleased with the location of his Senate office, close enough to the elevator so that he could respond to the roll call bell and vote to approve administration bills. He engaged another young Irish American, John D. Costello, as his secretary, and had John S. Irby installed as a committee counsel. Fay remained in San Francisco as postmaster, and Welch continued to oversee the Senator's San Francisco business office. After the campaign, Welch redirected his efforts to Phelan's commercial and financial enterprises, which, by 1915, required the business acumen of additional middle level management and an expanded office staff.

From his California experience, Phelan's position would be expected to be advanced and progressive. His solidarity with the President, though, created disharmony. He was quite comfortable with women voting in California and thought it proper. Yet, he outdid Wilson's argument that women should obtain their vote through state action, as California did. Maintaining his solidarity Phelan supported Wilson by arguing that the southern states would not ratify a constitutional amendment that would extend the vote among Black women and that the national government should not disturb the social arrangements within states.

His argument was similar to his concern over federal policy interfering with California's efforts to restrict the influx of Asians and to curtail their economic and social action in the state. His soft pedaling at the national level of women's rights may have been tolerated by most California women because, just like their male counterparts, they accepted an Asian menace as a reality. Phelan's near obsession on the subject of Asia and Asians was fully accepted by the vast majority of his fellow Californians.

Nonetheless, when President Wilson changed his mind about supporting the suffrage amendment, Phelan followed. In fact, in a major speech before the Senate, he rejected the states' rights argument he had previously accepted. In doing so, Phelan distanced himself from southern colleagues who otherwise would have been more sympathetic to his position on Asian exclusion. In one position shift he rejected the South's concern for maintaining its social order while holding fast to his own version of race prejudice.

Anti-Asian Views

Phelan's racial views were those peculiar to California of his time. Anti-Asian hostility permeated the area since the days of the Gold Rush. Phelan accepted popular thought and became its most articulate and highest placed advocate. He considered the southern Blacks as equally unassimilated, but he never envisioned massive Black migration out of the South to other parts of the United States. He sought the votes of Blacks who already were in California and presumed that they did enjoy and should enjoy full voting rights. His outreach to Black voters included engaging a Black press agent. Likewise, he modified his campaign literature so as not to offend Hispanics. He understood the cultural history of California, Mexico, and the Southwest, and he had a deep and abiding appreciation of Spanish contributions to the New World. He would extend none of these gestures of acceptance to the Asians in California. As the years continued Phelan, in full harmony with the constituents he represented, became even more adamant in his expressions of California's exclusionist mentality.

Phelan's earliest political-economic efforts were directed toward making the rest of America notice California and appreciate its numerous advantages. Even by 1915, when Phelan took his seat in the U.S. Senate, the eastern establishment considered California a distant outpost located somewhere between St. Louis and Hawaii. In Phelan's mind the Pacific rim should have commanded more of America's attention than it did. He believed that the federal government should create a defense presence on the Pacific Coast, in California particularly. Not uncommon in American history, the Senator presented valid reasons why defense spending should be in his state. The Pacific needed protection.

With the onset of World War I in Europe, Phelan had the opportunity to become a leading national advocate of military preparedness. Friends urged him on this course, but his correspondence with Gertrude Atherton shows that his heart was not in it. His love of European civilization hardly encouraged the preparation for its mutilation, if not utter destruction. His political chronicler, Professor Robert E. Hennings, attributes Phelan's failure to become a national spokesman for the military to his limited California perspective. According to Hennings, "There was in his eyes only one potential enemy — Japan — and all his efforts for preparedness were geared to awakening the nation to the danger of Japanese aggressive intentions."

Phelan identified a Japanese expansionism that the next American generation would, indeed, regret. His warnings carried less weight than they otherwise might have because of his attributed motivation. He easily appeared to oppose Japan because of his, and California's, prejudice against all Asians. As the main power in Asia, Japan appeared to attract Phelan's animosity because he was unalterably opposed to Asians in California. His southern colleagues, among others, had become less receptive to his arguments.

Phelan advocated a permanent Pacific fleet to guard the coast and to pursue the nation's interests in the Pacific. While he did not get everything he wanted, he obtained more for California than might otherwise be expected. Hennings pointed out that the naval appropriation bill of 1916 included many California projects, among them: construction of one battleship, twelve submarines, and four destroyers at California naval yards. Also provided for were improvements for harbors, expansion of the coast guard, and added construction of land facilities. Phelan, then, was delivering the goods to California, even if he was not filling a niche in leadership of a national movement that others projected for him.

Oil and Wine Industries

Phelan's commitments to the oil and wine industries of the State met with mixed results. Confusion and contention between Southern California oil producers and the federal government preceded Phelan's tenure in the Senate. The disputes resulted from executive action taken by the Taft administration and subsequently acted upon by Congress.

In an attempt to settle the matter and recognize the producers' claims, Phelan added two amendments to pending legislation dealing with mineral rights more generally. His amendments would settle the protracted dispute by providing legal recognition of private oil leases and by establishing a maximum level of oil royalties for the government. When Phelan intervened, no one seemed interested in the rather limited and isolated dispute. Thereafter, however, conservationists interested themselves and roundly abused Phelan for his amendments. The matter became one of national public interest.

Rather than resolving the matter by compromise, Phelan instead appeared to be serving the oil industry. Franklin K. Lane's proposal was the next step. His compromise emanated from the Interior department and received support from Phelan and the California congressional delegation, as well as the California state legislature. No one in California seemed opposed to the settlement.

Nonetheless, the oil leases eluded settlement. Phelan allowed the noncontroversial parts of the pending legislation to be enacted into law during the press of business before the Christmas holidays. When he returned in the new year the bill was transferred to a new committee and thus consideration was ended. It was dead. That maneuver illustrated Phelan's junior status and peripheral position to the Senate's internal power structure.

James Duval Phelan thought well of himself, comfortable and assured as he was in his own birthright. His natural assumption of destiny allowed him to subordinate acquisitiveness, to celebrate civic virtue. His wealth, education and, most of all, the California environment molded him, his political perspectives and cultural imperatives. Elected by the people, this patrician in politics never allowed mass opinion to determine his actions.

Phelan's Investment Interests

Senator James Duval Phelan's portfolio included agricultural holdings located throughout Northern California. His attention to the state's agriculture and his study of the broader economic context sensitized him to the tenuous nature of the industry. Phelan's personal enjoyment of fine wines and champagnes also led to his personal commitment to the state's historic wine industry at the very time when the production of all alcoholic beverages was under serious attack by prohibitionists. He saw the forces of temperance gaining the upperhand everywhere. This he considered a menace to the California economy and to personal liberty.

His efforts to protect the California wine industry got off to a splendid start, preceding even his actual election. During his campaign, a revenue bill pending in Congress threatened to raise the tax on wine, which was almost exclusively a California product. Alerted to this possibility Phelan used his personal contacts within Wilson's Cabinet and with Tumulty. The resulting legislation considerably reduced the anticipated tax increase.

Once in the Senate, though, the task became increasingly more difficult — aggravated, too, by Phelan himself. His enjoyment of life's refinements allowed his enthusiasm to overcome his political sensitivity. Undoubtedly his Washington guests more than tolerated his lavish provision of California's best. Less likely was their enjoyment of his persistent and predictable advocacy of the benefits of wine drinking. Simply put, most politicians preferred old fashioned bourbon.

Sharing his enjoyment of wines at table extended to explanation on the Senate floor of the healthful intricacies of the art of winemaking. He employed the latter as an appeal against the legal adulteration of wine through the addition of water and its fortification with brandies. Few listeners then shared the educational level of latter-day Californians on the subject of wine. Phelan was ahead of his time on this subject.

Even Phelan's potential allies from whiskey-producing states turned a deaf ear to his pleas for consideration for a valuable and unique industry. The "Whiskey Senators" already saw the encircling forces of total prohibition and felt little concern for the protection or temporary consideration of wine producers. So Phelan's proposed amendments to pending legislation were soundly rejected in the roll call vote. Persistent, though, Phelan successfully reinstituted his measures when Senate and House members conferred to reconcile the specific differences between their respective bills. Professor Hennings concluded that Phelan was more effective "in his behind-the-scenes activities than on the Senate floor."

Profitable, taxpaying, and reputable California industries were being outlawed by the government. Worse, the private rights of individuals were being invaded, and, through legislation, personal and cultural habits were being regulated on moral and religious grounds. As for the argument that American soldiers risking their lives on the battlefields of France deserved munitions that function as a result of sober assembly back home — Phelan saw that as opportunism of the temperance-dry advocates and simple hooey.

Unable to hold back the dry tide in the Senate, Phelan voted against the administration's implementing bill. Only five Senators joined him as the popular, organized political enthusiasm for Prohibition engulfed him. In concluding his report to the California wine and spirit industry he wrote:

> *It seems to be that prohibition can not long be deferred because the constitutional amendment will doubtless prevail....more than two-thirds of the Senate and House were in favor of bringing the liquor traffic to an end. But 'The storm which rends the oak, uproots the flower', and our California wine industry, which is guiltless of any serious offence or even interference with the production of foodstuffs, is in danger of extinction....I therefore have advised the growers to prepare for that contingency which would naturally suggest itself to men of business prudence.*

This was a grim conclusion following his legislative efforts. When the wine industry responded to his efforts by canceling his bill for the shipment of wine Welch had ordered for him, Phelan instructed his secretary to express his appreciation, but the bill was to be paid. Even in defeat, he adhered to his strictness in financial and conflict of interest matters.

Phelan's next step, however, was dramatic. He prepared himself to oppose the American madness — the Prohibition era — by stocking his own homes with sufficient quantities of wine and spirits. All residences were to be stocked: Washington, Montalvo, and San Francisco.

All of these actions were within the letter of the impending constitutional amendment and even its enforcement legislation. Phelan entertained on the grand scale and in a manner consistent with Irish and Northern California tradition. He had Montalvo located, designed, and constructed to give expression to this heritage and to the advancement of the California lifestyle he cherished and cultivated. If the nation had gone wrong, he and his guests did not have to go wrong too. And, indeed, when the Democratic National Convention gathered in San Francisco to nominate their 1920 candidates for President and Vice President, the party's illustrious Senator fulfilled his most accustomed role. Undoubtedly, the politicians who flocked to Montalvo at his invitation welcomed his enlightenment.

As a private citizen, Phelan ceased to offer public statements on Prohibition's follies. He simply maintained his own maximum freedom of action within the restrictions of law. Obviously, his wealth and circumstances allowed him options denied to fellow citizens and to the industries for which

Prohibition

National Prohibition was enough to bring the stereotypical Irishman to tears. Indeed, had it been the law in California during the Gold Rush, the Phelan family fortune would have had a considerably less diversified base. In the Senate, Phelan opposed the national prohibition enthusiasm on numerous grounds, especially that it singled out and attacked a major California industry (wine). Ninety percent of America's wine production, he noted in his report for the *Wine and Spirit Review,* came from California grapes. Likewise, ninety-five percent of the hops for beer production came from the Pacific Coast and fifty percent from California.

Phelan's Wines

James Duval Phelan had been accustomed to laying in stocks of local California wines such as Mount Hamilton Vineyard's Johannisberg Riesling, 1902 vintage, at $9.00 per case. Even at that price Welch inquired of the San Jose winery, "Is there a cash discount?" Phelan also was partial to Golden State Champagne. From there, he branched out across California, the nation, and Europe for wines, whiskeys, and gins. For public announcements, he maintained that he was exclusively a wine consumer, and then in moderation. His "Inventory of Wines and Liquors on Hand at Montalvo," dated May 11, 1919, reveals far more comprehensive holdings.

Though partial to California wines and champagnes, Phelan stocked everything for his guests. Among the heavier alcohols, he utterly rejected the sweet, after dinner-type liqueurs such as Benedictine. However, perhaps out of a sense of ethnic solidarity or simple fondness for a unique product, he did indulge in Irish Whiskey. Orders for five star John Jameson are sprinkled through his records. One, for five cases at $50 each, requested John J. Caffrey to freight the shipment from Dublin to Phelan's sister's residence at 2150 Washington Street, San Francisco.

he had spoken. Occasionally, the protagonists in the moral combat intruded into his life. When, for example, Richmond P. Hobson of the American Alcohol Educational Association for Total Abstinence solicited Phelan's membership, he received polite disagreement and rejection.

"I have been accustomed," Phelan responded, "to drink wine at meals, and am convinced that such beverages, taken in moderation, do no particular harm.… I am very strongly against the use of hard liquor and public bars."

When William H. Metson solicited his membership in the Association Against the Prohibition Amendment, Phelan declined with even greater restraint. He stated his approval of reinstituting beer and wine, but opposed enlargement of the anti-Prohibition movement.

His full and unvarnished views were never made public, even following public criticism of him that resulted from news coverage of major and brazen thefts from his Montalvo cellar. He had the foresight to insure his stock before raiders cut through the door and took 88 bottles of Lacey Bourbon, 20 of Waldorf Astoria Gin, and an undetermined quantity from his 150 cases of Golden State Champagne. The news despatch from Saratoga characterized the loss: "Only the rarest and most precious liquors were taken."

An obscure Southern California publication, *The California Voice*, picked up the item and used it as the basis for denouncing Phelan as "…simply an ordinary bootlegger and is entitled to less respect … than the back alley snipe who peddles bootleg from a hip pocket bottle." On route to its editorial conclusion that Phelan should have been arrested for having had the stock in his possession, the *Voice's* editor denounced Phelan's social class, his political identity, and his religious affiliation.

Being rich and a Democrat suited Phelan. Attacks like this one reminded him of his Catholic connections and aroused a response akin to protecting an unworthy father from an abusive neighbor. After reviewing the allegation Phelan responded in detail:

> I once knew in San Francisco an agent for a society for the suppression of vice.…He also lived on vice and is now in the State Penitentiary. Your business, apparently, is very much of the same kind, to defame the characters of public men … in order to win the favor of your deluded supporters. It is a dirty business.

> I judge you are a fanatical believer in the efficacy of prohibitory laws and a mortal foe of personal freedom. You are, apparently, not appalled by the

orgy of disease and death, crime and murder, law-violation and the dishon-
oring of the flag brought about by the Volstead Act. You should know that
bootleggers, in the awakened public opinion of the country, are now the
ones who are consistently in favor of the Volstead Act, which enables them,
with enormous profits, to traffic in the prohibited commodities. So the hard-
er you work for the Volstead Act, the more certainly you forge the chains of
the Nation's shame. A premium should not be put upon vice. Temperance
may be promoted by moral suasion, but never by legal prohibition....

You will observe that it is the 'sale' that is prohibited by the Constitution and
that by no construction can a person who buys wines, even now, be desig-
nated as a bootlegger....

So please come off your high-horse and do not regard your vocation as any
more honorable and useful than that of other bigots and fanatics ... and be
careful not to call your brother by names which can only imply your own
perversion and iniquity. In the interest of temperance, because all sin is ex-
cess, I beg of you, also, to devote your columns to the evils of intemperance,
which imply a certain freedom which every American should enjoy, against
the abuse of which he should be charitably and convincingly persuaded. Let
yourself become a 'fisher of men' and not a fish-wife.

Irish and Catholic

Throughout his life Phelan enjoyed greater personal harmony with the
Catholic dimension of his heritage than he did with the Irish one. He fully
accepted the Catholic Church as a historic, social, and cultural institution.
He chose from his early years not to live by its theological and philosophical
doctrines and, thus, ceased being a communicant. This action never included public rejection of Catholicism. Had he been invited to convert to any
other faith, he would have considered the option utterly preposterous. He
was convinced that religious beliefs were personal and private, the same as
no beliefs at all. His personal inner circle consisted mostly of the Catholic
Irish with whom he had associated since youth.

Being Irish was as much a part of Phelan's culture as being Catholic, only
coping with this dimension of his heritage was far greater a challenge. He
could not just set his Irishness aside as he did his Catholicism. Yet, he adhered neither to Irish standard views nor accepted Irish practice.

Preparing for Prohibition

Confronted with national Prohibition of
the manufacture and sale of spirits, he instructed
his agents to act with dispatch. They did, to
include: thirty cases of "best Golden State
Champagne," ten cases each of Gordon Gin,
bourbon, scotch, and vintage champagne for
Montalvo, also, ten cases of good foreign light
white wines, like Hackheime, also French clarets
like Chateau Leorille, best California dry white
and red, "in the wood — it will age better ... and
I can bottle it later."

Panicked by Prohibition, Phelan instructed
Welch to stock an additional thirty to forty cases
more of Golden State Champagne, "best vintage,
for I have large storage in Montalvo & fire proof
for it is all concrete.... I think the idea of wine
in the wood in quantities is good as against the
day when the Constitution amendment will be in
force, & if not drunk ... wines will be a good
asset, always increasing &, better than 6% if
bought right & quality assured. Don't let them
palm poor stuff. I want the best California."

In November, 1918, Phelan authorized payment of $1,453 for forty-five cases provided the
shipment to Montalvo did not contain any
liqueurs. After Welch's sudden and unexpected
death, Phelan instructed his successor, Thomas
B. Doyle, to order an additional five cases of
scotch, three of California sherry, two of French
vermouth — all for storage at Mollie's home.

Phelan and Catholic Practices

From the point of view of San Francisco's successive Catholic Archbishops, James D. Phelan's nonpracticing Catholicism was less than ideal, but hardly a disaster. To the public, Phelan remained California's leading Catholic layman. In part, this was why Wilson and Bryan sent him to investigate the U.S. Minister to Santo Domingo. The Archbishops themselves turned to Phelan on public occasions and in symbolic ways to advance various church projects. The nuns and parish priests seldom held a raffle or a festival without sending him tickets. Phelan never turned them down. In fact, he was often an initiator in the advancement of Catholic education and even the Catholic ministry provided, of course, that he was not expected to proclaim his belief.

Even Father Yorke hesitated at denouncing the Senator because of his nonpracticing religious status. The reason for not violating that boundary was hardly respect for Phelan. Even Yorke's primary, self-defined mission was saving souls — including Phelan's. And the Catholic Church, ranking among the world's most enduring institutions, played for the long haul. In this case, straying sons were to be endured over their lifetimes. Fundamentalist denunciation of backsliders was not the Catholic way. The Church outlasted all of its errant children and remained at hand, extending an understanding and benevolent consolation of final reconciliation. Faced with this organized framework, Phelan chose and lived his own moral and ethical life. Religious conviction was not part of that life.

In California the Irish were welcome, integrated, and successful from the start. Largely because of San Francisco's instant major city status and the history Phelan's father helped create, no one else was established in the Far West any sooner and, therefore, no one else was able to assign the Irish inferior status. One major result was that, as an ethnic group, the California Irish always lacked the self-conscious militancy that propelled their comparatively deprived cousins elsewhere in America. California's Irish did not have to validate themselves through Irish American nationalism. An independent Ireland would not change their already suitable integration into the California main stream.

Phelan's Irish-American environment, therefore, was less confrontational than other such ethnic enclaves within the larger eastern urban centers. Phelan was even less militant than the local norm. As advocates of Irish nationalism from the East or from Ireland toured through the Far West, they encountered a rich and giving community — often an excitable one, but never a radical one, and only rarely a militant one.

Phelan had begun on the conservative side even of the San Francisco norm. His interests had begun in Irish literature, poetry, and history. Instead of being highly politicized first, he had been intellectualized. His first transcontinental trip in 1869, when he was eight, extended to Ireland. As a young college graduate he addressed Irish cultural groups on poetic subjects, only shaded with anti-British sentiment. He had followed the example of both of his parents and sent remittances to relatives in Ireland. Through numerous trips and extended correspondence he acquainted himself with Irish literary personalities. He sustained, financially, Irish professionals who were marginally competent and whose careers were hardly successful.

Woodrow Wilson also had his heritage, Scotch-Irish, that touched Phelan's, but was incompatible. Wilson came from a strict Presbyterian upbringing that he accepted and perpetuated. Religion aside, he saw himself suffering from some sort of ethnic dualism. In 1912, upon receiving the Democratic nomination for President he confessed to Tumulty that he felt at war with his own personality. The Irish in him, Tumulty wrote in his reminiscences, waged constant warfare with the Scottish in him.

Both Wilson and Phelan felt concern for Ireland and Ireland's age-old nationalist struggle against England. Both were Irish, but of different persuasions. During Wilson's Presidency no political division existed between

North and South; the British controlled all of Ireland. And that, precisely, was what Irish and Irish-American nationalists wished to change; some wished to do so by force if necessary.

The respective responses of Senator Phelan and President Wilson to renewed and aggressive Irish nationalism constituted their most serious area of disagreement. Phelan couched his views in polite and respectful expressions and symbolic actions. Wilson privately fumed, and his lack of personal openness delayed and distorted Phelan's insight into the President's true views.

When World War I erupted in Europe, Irish Americans viewed England's preoccupation and then full commitment on the continent as Ireland's opportunity. As long as America maintained her intended role as bystanding neutral and supplier to the warring powers, the Irish in America could enjoy England's travails and Ireland's opportunities. Some took vicarious pleasure from Germany's infliction of punishment upon Great Britain.

The Irish seized their moment by revolting against England during Easter Week, 1916. Their doomed uprising in Dublin and the ferocity of the British response sent sympathetic shock waves through the extended Irish community worldwide. Pro-Irish sympathy extended well beyond the ethnic communities, and for a while England's image was seriously tarnished internationally. The aftermath of Easter Week constituted the low point of England's propaganda struggle for American support in the war effort.

Phelan had looked with hope in 1912 upon England's pending Home Rule Bill, which would have provided a major degree of self government for Ireland. He had enlisted the support of Archbishop Patrick W. Riordan in his petition from prominent Californians. Following the Easter Rebellion in Dublin, however, Father Peter Yorke moved to the head of the energized Irish nationalist movement in California and the West. Yorke became the California Irishman of the hour, a role Phelan would not play even for votes. As befitting the priest's personality and inclinations, Yorke approved of the action in Ireland and aroused support in Phelan's constituency for revolutionary nationalism. He became the natural leader of the awakened Irish nationalism, even among the comparatively tranquil California Irish. In Washington, though, Phelan became the nation's most highly placed, active political personality associated with the Irish cause. Montana's Thomas J. Walsh outranked Phelan in the Senate, but Phelan became a more expressive conduit of Irish views to Woodrow Wilson and the administration.

Phelan and Wilson — Both Irish

James Duval Phelan's voluminous Irish-related correspondence offers an image of the Irish as gifted, charming failures. Phelan seems to have accepted this stereotype. When he provided a full scholarship for a young student at the University of California he was pleased to learn that she was the granddaughter of an old friend, Daniel O'Connor. In responding to the letter of Professor Eugene Neuhaus at Berkeley, Phelan wrote that her grandfather was a poet "who, doubtless, left her a large heritage of talent and little else."

President Woodrow Wilson, the former Princeton political scientist and university president, even characterized himself in stereotypes: "...the Irish in me, quick, generous, impulsive, passionate, anxious always to help and to sympathize with those in distress." To this his Irish secretary Joseph Tumulty added balance: "...I saw the Scotch in him — strict, upstanding, intractable, and unrelenting."

Phelan's final analysis of Wilson depicted the world leader as "...an idealist with a mental grasp of great questions to be solved in a great way. He would have set the world right if he were given his way, but was not equipped to deal with obstructionists....He did not know the wisdom of cultivating the good will of necessary men."

Phelan's clear insight into the major leader of the twentieth century reflects as well upon himself — his heritage and his California culture.

Phelan addressed the Senate eloquently on behalf of Irish freedom and for clemency for the unknown numbers of Irish prisoners held by the British. His Senate proposal was that President Wilson request such clemency of the British. This was, perhaps, Phelan's most powerful oral presentation, one that captured the admiration of his Senate colleagues and focused national attention upon him as a worthy articulator of Ireland's lofty goal — freedom.

Events move quickly, though. As America's bonds of finance, industry, and agriculture, as well as basic human sympathy gradually leveraged American public opinion from neutrality to a strong pro-Allied posture, German Americans became less assertive and Irish Americans became more confused. For German Americans this marked the start of their acquiescence and actual encouragement of identity loss in America, a welcomed anonymity that Hitler and the Holocaust finalized.

For the Irish, confusion became psychic crisis following Germany's unrestricted submarine warfare that violated American neutral rights and claimed the lives of U.S. citizens. The American response was President Wilson's war message and Congress's declaration of war on Germany and the Central Powers. This turnabout linked the United States with Ireland's oppressor, Great Britain, as comrades in arms. Previously Yorke was unfettered in his denunciation of England. With the British-U.S. cooperation in a common war against Germany and the Central Powers, not only did his perspective become untenable, his weekly newspaper the *Leader* was seized and denied use of the mails. Anti-British, pro-German commentary had suddenly become seditious propaganda. The mental world of Phelan's most volatile antagonist had turned upside down.

Phelan's basic commitments left him quite unaffected. For him America's national interest as defined by the federal government was always paramount. He valued Ireland and his Irish heritage, but Ireland's interests were not to be considered when apparent conflict with American interests arose. But having been subjected to Yorke's ire in the past, he understandably chose not to confront the local Irish champion on this subject. He remained open and active, but stayed in Washington attending to Senate business.

As long as World War I continued in Europe, Phelan supported the American war effort as a Senator and as a citizen. Uninspired by the destruction of the civilization he loved, he did his patriotic duty at home and advanced Ireland's interests only as a lessor priority and only when that

Yorke, McEnerney, and Phelan's Irish Views

Senator Phelan's growing political caution over the Irish issue was evident. Into this vacuum innocently walked Garret McEnerney, the University of California's historically most significant Regent, California's most noted attorney and, next to Phelan, the state's most prominent and successful Irish American. When, during early World War I, the dean of the California bar offered the San Francisco Irish a somewhat more polished version of "America: Love It Or Leave It," Father Peter C. Yorke responded in character — with journalistic execution. In an anti-intellectual outburst, he denounced the "learned self" for having distinguished himself from the common people by study and success. Through a contrived set of syllogisms, Yorke turned McEnerney's logic against him, so that McEnerney was made the traitor. Yorke's printed denunciation attracted such notice within the Irish American community that it remained for years as a staple for logic instruction at the archdiocesan seminary.

McEnerney, having learned Phelan's lesson of 1901 the hard way, returned to the creation of the modern University of California and to the service of the state's unhyphenated population.

Father Yorke (shown at right), Irish born and bound to Irish nationalism, found himself in a far more complicated position than either of the second generation Irishmen, Phelan or McEnerney. As an immigrant, Yorke was compelled to be more patriotic than the Americans themselves, while at the same time he had to sustain Ireland absolutely. Not only did his behavior have to be right, his actual thinking had to conform to his imperatives too.

Yorke's mental adjustment included justification of America at war, a war for none other than — IRELAND. He blessed Irish America's sons as the draft drew them off to warfare on the western front. He comforted parents when their boys never returned. When President Wilson released his peace goals, the famous Fourteen Points, Yorke seized upon Self-Determination for Subject Nations as his logical and psychological lifeboat. Yes, the Great War was being fought for Ireland. Didn't the President say so? Join up and serve so Ireland can be free! These became Yorke's adjustments to America and Britain waging war together against Germany.

country's well being clearly did not conflict with America's national interest. Phelan voted for the administration's measures designed to organize and support the American Expeditionary Forces. He subscribed handsomely to the War Bond drives, once during a Washington night at the theater when the program was interrupted to sell bonds. He purchased an added $10,000 to boost the California total subscription. Financially, he considered the bonds to be a poor investment. Setting the proper example motivated his actions.

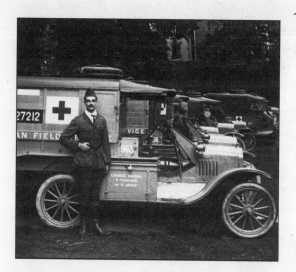

Noël Sullivan was his uncle's heir apparent, only their relationship became kinder, more mutually considerate than that of James D. Phelan and his own father. Sullivan served in the Ambulance Corps during World War I, and Phelan had his letters home printed and bound as Somewhere in France. *Respectful of each other, neither man made an important impact upon the other. Sullivan resisted business, or any calling for that matter. He was a gifted dilettante, a humanitarian, a charming and sincere companion, a consumer.*

For his adventuresome, young nephew, Noël Sullivan, he offered advice on how his active duty might best assist the national war effort. For Californians whom he knew to have lost their loved ones in France he composed, through several redrafts, sensitive and gentle words of soothing compassion. Death in youth, in promise, and in violence was hardly an acceptable reward for patriotic valor. But no California political leader in any age endeavored more artfully to offer such refined tenderness to the bereaved. He took no pleasure from war, and to those who suffered its pain, James Phelan dispensed what solace his considerable talents allowed.

At war's end, with America victorious and the militarism of the Central Powers destroyed, Phelan returned to San Francisco. As President of the St. Ignatius College Alumni Association (now the University of San Francisco) and presiding over its black tie annual banquet he offered his own lines characterizing the end of the war and with it the end of what had remained of America's youthful innocence:

> There are gains for all our losses,
> There is balm for all our pain.
> But when youth the dream departs,
> It takes something from our hearts.
> And it never comes again.

Chapter Fourteen

World War I Senate Years

Historians periodically rank the presidents in terms of "historical greatness." Washington, Jefferson, and Lincoln lead the poll with moderns such as Franklin D. Roosevelt and Woodrow Wilson challenging but not overcoming them. The stature of Woodrow Wilson rests upon his leadership in fulfilling the promises of the progressive reform movement. The laws he ushered through Congress recognized the modern, urban, industrial status of the nation and conform with that modern reality.

Next, and equally important, Wilson educated the American public on the importance of world events: first, he promoted the advantage of strict neutrality to America as the First World War spread through Europe; second, the President, with no other alternative, guided the nation into the conflict itself. Wilson educated the Congress of the United States as well. The result was America's new position of world leadership and power that determined victory for the Allies in World War I.

Phelan had provided his senatorial vote as part of the Democratic and often bipartisan support which allowed much of Wilson's success. Throughout the war years, Phelan served diligently within the Senate.

In 1918, the end of the war and its military success marked the pinnacle of Wilson's political success. When he toured Europe he was hailed by the survivors of war as their savior. At home, however, he had made critical mistakes. In order to advance his ideal democratic world through the impending peace treaty, he brought with him to Paris a massive delegation of academic and technical experts. He included those who agreed with him, and those whose input he could accept or reject.

Wilson's Ideals

Wilson even elevated the American people to his own level of idealistic commitment. Subsequent generations of American cynics have used the slogans, "Make the world safe for democracy," and the "War to end all wars," without even knowing their coinage. These were Wilson's words which summarized the insight, rationality, and idealism of America's best ever academically prepared chief executive.

In the end, however, Wilson's idealism became more than most Americans, and most Senators, could tolerate. Wilson's means for ensuring a future world without wars was his idealized League of Nations. Wilson chose to go personally to the Paris Peace Conference in order to write his cherished League into the peace treaty establishing the new world order.

To have his treaty accepted at home, he had asked the American voters to elect a Democratic Congress in 1918. America declined. When he found himself confronted with a Republican Senate, the body the Constitution authorizes to approve or reject treaties, he took no Senator — Republican or Democrat — with him to Paris. When Wilson sailed for France, the still popular former President, Theodore Roosevelt, announced to the world that Wilson spoke not for America but only for himself.

Compounding his problems, Wilson may have suffered a minor stroke while in Paris. Yet when he returned with the highly complicated, highly detailed, and highly controversial Paris Peace Treaty in 1919, Wilson expected the Senate to sign, not really to read and study, but just to sign. Even Phelan, a Democratic Party regular, was hardly prepared for that. Even less tolerant, though, was Phelan's new junior senator from California, former progressive Governor Hiram Johnson.

Now a Republican, Johnson joined forces with Senators Henry Cabot Lodge of Massachusetts, William E. Borah of Idaho, and Robert M. La Follette, Jr., of Wisconsin. Together they constituted the nucleus of the "irreconcilables," those opposed to Wilson's League of Nations and the Paris Peace Treaty. They disliked Wilson's work; they disliked Wilson's party; they disliked Wilson.

By the time the Senate Foreign Relations Committee, which Lodge chaired, began its hearings, the mood of America had changed. Idealism had

Phelan never felt at liberty to invite Wilson to his Washington mansion for any suitable event. He had arranged for Wilson to be his overnight guest at Montalvo in 1915 when the President was to participate in the Panama Pacific International Exposition in San Francisco. However, the war in Europe allowed Wilson to send his vice-president, Thomas R. Marshall (former governor of Indiana), and Assistant Secretary of the Navy, young Franklin D. Roosevelt, in his place. Phelan never dined at the White House because senators did not dine there with Wilson.

Bronze for Golden Gate Park

James D. Phelan was instrumental in commissioning copies of life-sized bronze statues of the Irish patriot, Robert Emmet, who had been executed by the British in 1803. Emmet was the symbol of Irish youthful valor and oratory. When given the right of the condemned to speak from the dock, the 25-year old rebel delivered a spontaneous oral essay on Ireland's right to freedom. The classic rebel speech remained a mainstay within Irish nationalistic lore, to be recited from memory by all Irish American boys who aspired to oratorical excellence.

Phelan presented one bronze to the people of San Francisco, by Eamon de Valera, dedicated in Golden Gate Park in 1919. Father Yorke's response was that Phelan could not hide his insufficient Irish nationalist posture behind all the statues in the park. Phelan presided over the dedication of a second Emmet bronze in Washington. President Wilson was present and the event was a success. Thereafter, Phelan presented the President with a "miniature" of the statue that stood over 18 inches tall. On that occasion Wilson took exception to Phelan's pro-Irish remarks: Emmett represented ultimate sacrifice for ultimate expression — the desire to be free. Phelan's gift of art embodied

his Irish message to the President of the United States. Wilson accepted and retained it as he did no other comparable input from Irish Americans. Phelan's Emmet miniature may be viewed in Wilson's Washington D.C. home. Full-sized statues are located near Phelan's Washington residence at Sheridan Circle, in Dublin, and in San Francisco.

run its course. Wilson had become tedious. The Europeans were avoiding their repayments of huge American war loans.

James D. Phelan stayed in Washington when President Wilson toured the West promoting his Treaty and his League of Nations. When Wilson spoke at the San Francisco Civic Auditorium, Phelan was prudently missing. Phelan had invited Wilson to San Francisco on three previous, happy occasions, occasions in which Phelan could have set the ground work for sympathetic bonding between Californians and their President. Wilson hadn't come. This time, Wilson had to stand alone.

On the evening of September 17, 1919, San Francisco citizens booed their President for 23 minutes as he attempted to address them from the Civic Auditorium stage. Even the popular mayor, James Rolph, could not quiet them. Finally, when the crowd exhausted itself and Wilson spoke, he

The Phelans' California

The California of the Phelans was a variation upon the theme. Gold's discovery brought the world rushing in spontaneously. San Francisco, the Gold Rush metropolis that dominated California and the West, was populated immediately by those who elsewhere would have been classified as respectables or undesirables by those who were already present and well established. In California no one was established, so the classification and assignment of groups to categories and roles evaded the otherwise accepted national formulations. The business success of James Duval Phelan's father is a vivid illustration. Historians have interpreted the Vigilante movements as illegal efforts to impose eastern notions of hierarchy on an uncooperative city. In California, too many Irish, among others, seemed not to know their place. Social confusion prevailed, however, and with unusual side effects.

The sense of racial superiority, and the irrational fear and hatred of those who were different, arrived in the cultural baggage of the state's new citizens. When those who considered themselves the real Americans discovered that they could not easily discriminate against "white" foreigners, they learned to relax their xenophobia and accept the new mostly-Europeans as members of their own group. European emigrant behavior merged with that of the "Americans." Feeling that they were on trial in the new country, immigrants and their children tried to out do their hosts in patriotic, and then exclusionary, behavior.

was eloquent in behalf of the idealism for which he had brought America into and through world war. His League of Nations, he promised his listeners, would ensure that their grandchildren would not be called again to war by any subsequent president, that their sons' lives had not been lost in vain.

The Irish present wondered how Wilson's League would hinder Ireland's revolutionary efforts for independence. Article X of the Charter seemed to guarantee the possessions and boundaries of the subscribing powers and, therefore, caused Irish Americans to pause. Would the President who did nothing for Ireland's claims at the Paris Peace Conference now effect a League whereby America as a member would be required to assist England against Ireland? Following on Wilson's heels, the "irreconcilables" swept through California and the West, challenging each of Wilson's points. In San Francisco the Republican Senators received the greatest amount of anti-League coverage from Father Peter Yorke's *Leader*.

After Wilson's train left California he spoke once more, in Pueblo, Colorado. That evening Wilson collapsed, suffered a stroke, and never fully resumed his functions as the nation's chief executive. Thereafter, his wife and his physician determined what he saw, and they limited it mostly to good news, of which there was little to interrupt his protracted and ultimately unsuccessful convalescence.

Phelan's Senate Efforts

Phelan busied himself throughout these months with the Senate's consideration of the Paris Peace Treaty and the League of Nations. Bereft of effective Presidential leadership and exercising an independence of judgment, Phelan participated in the detailed, comprehensive, and confused analyses of the specific clauses of the massive treaty. He and his California colleague, Johnson, virtually canceled each other out when voting on proposed reservations, conditions, and amendments to treaty provisions.

The Democrats were the Senate minority. The minority leadership still looked to the incapacitated President for their directions in face of the Republican assault upon the Wilsonian document. When they were able to obtain any hint of direction from Mrs. Wilson or Dr. Carry Grayson, the message was always the same: accept no revisions to the chief's handiwork!

Phelan had never been drawn into the Democratic inner circle and didn't consider himself honor bound to vote the party line when it violated his comprehension of the national interest. He offered only one reservation of his own creation, an amendment to the Treaty that would reserve for the United States the right to interpret its Treaty obligations in light of the Fourteen Points. Always concerned with Japan and Asian immigration, Phelan supported an additional reservation that explicitly declared that America, not the League of Nations, would determine what was a domestic question and what was proper jurisdiction of the League itself. Also, California's senior senator supported his junior colleague's amendment to equalize the number of League votes the United States would have in comparison with Britain and her oversees dominion. Toward the end of the debates, negotiations, and preliminary votes that continued through the year, Phelan supported the reservation that recognized the claim of Ireland to its self-determination. By this time reservations to Wilson's original document were numerous.

Critical to interpreting Phelan within the mix of American ethnic history is his far western environment, liberal education and great wealth, and acceptance of the racial mania of his state and time. While he did what he could on behalf of Ireland, he was more concerned with Japan and the Japanese in California than he was with Ireland and the Irish. When the showdown came and the United States Senate had to vote, Phelan abandoned the rigidly loyal Democratic leadership that followed its incapacitated President to oblivion. These Democratic loyalists refused to accept a peace treaty with any Senate reservations. The Republican "irreconcilables" refused to approve a peace treaty without reservations. The result was that the nation that had determined the outcome of World War I became incapable of participating in the new world settlement, the settlement its President had written. The vote was forty-nine for (including Phelan) and thirty-five against and failed by seven votes the two-thirds majority required for approval of treaties.

Though Phelan didn't shared Wilson's lofty ideals of humanity's capabilities, he did recognize America as a world power. The United States should participate in the international arena. His vote with the unsuccessful Senatorial majority demonstrated his commitment to America as an active participant in a real world beyond national borders. Ireland was one part of his California perspective.

"The Deliverance of the California Electoral Vote, January 1917." This was James Duval Phelan's high tide politically. In 1915 he became California's first popularly elected U.S. Senator, a Democrat in a Republican state. Two years later Republican California supported the reelection of the Democratic President, Woodrow Wilson. Among the Washington group gathered to receive California's vote for Wilson were (right to left) Phelan, John S. Irby (Phelan's campaign organizer and his Washington secretary), Vice President Thomas R. Marshall, U.S. Congressman John E. Raker (author of Hetch Hetchy legislation), and Francis J. Heney (the graft prosecutor). The last man is unidentified.

The integration of immigrants into American society remains an active social, political, and economic issue and constitutes a rich theme for historians. At one time, Phelan's own Irish were perceived as threats to the life of the Republic. Most politicized Californians including European ethnics focused their animosity upon Asians. Blacks were too few to constitute any perceived threat. (In the early days Californians had considered slavery, publicly argued the issue, and rejected it.) Though Blacks were hardly welcomed, for the most part California tolerated the few who came. Anti-Mexican sentiment, however, dated from the early mining days around Sonora. Through legal manipulation and extra-legal coercion, Mexican miners were largely driven from the fields. Native Americans fared even worse.

Mindlessly at best, calculating at worst, the new Americans joined the old Americans in anti-Asian discrimination and violence. All were not active participants, yet the fixed weight of public opinion in California was absolutely anti-Asian; first, anti-Chinese and, later, anti-Japanese. In Phelan's young manhood Irish workers of the city killed a Chinese fish peddler by throwing him out of an upper story window. The Irish port commissioner of the day, E. L. Sullivan, at his own discretion, returned Chinese women to Hong Kong by labeling them prostitutes. Officially classified as wives of Chinese men in California, they may have been "picture" brides.

Violence was not Phelan's way. These outrages were what his society inflicted and accepted. Phelan and his arch foe, Peter Yorke, fully shared the common anti-Asian prejudice. Both accepted the prejudice of their time and place and made it part of their world view. Yorke, in a historically insightful editorial, listed all the reasons why Asians could never become Americans. This Irish immigrant's litany was a transfer onto the Asians of all the historic accusations that nativists earlier had heaped upon the Irish.

Refined in its expression, Phelan's conclusion remained the same for the Japanese as for the Chinese. Assuming the absolute right of those who then were American citizens to determine who might be admitted, Phelan was one with Californians. The future he envisioned was to be a homogeneous commonwealth. He wished for California the pattern that Australia had chosen for itself. In private correspondence he cited the examples of Australia, New Zealand, and even Canada.

In the Senate, his focus on Asians in California was so pronounced that few beyond the Pacific Coast congressional delegation appreciated his concerns. Americans at the time were not less racially motivated, it was just that other members of Congress failed to share Phelan's sense of alarm. The Pacific Coast seemed remote and, surely, the slight number of Asians living there hardly imperiled America. The south did not take the "yellow peril" as seriously as it took its own racial relationships. In the major Northeastern urban industrial centers, the national immigration policy was of concern, but the representatives from these states lacked Phelan's West Coast perspective.

Phelan composed Woodrow Wilson's 1912 campaign statement opposing Chinese and Japanese immigration. He had initiated this action because the Hearst newspapers were using Wilson's academic writings from his days as a Princeton political scientist against the Democratic candidate for president. Wilson seemed to favor the Chinese as workers over the second wave of European immigrants from Southern and Eastern Europe. This was a significant Phelan contribution to the Governor's first campaign for President. Because California opinion was so solid, the candidate's recantation was a practical requirement and Phelan's draft became Wilson's official position statement on Asian immigration.

Phelan's Public Statements

Phelan's public statements were frequent and broadly distributed. As California's most popular orator Phelan spoke at an unending list of historic, patriotic, and memorial events. He regularly campaigned for himself and most other Democrats throughout the state and he was exceedingly well published. He believed in public education, particularly on the Asian question. Among the popular and scholarly outlets in which he placed his views were the *Overland Monthly*, *Atlantic Monthly*, *North American Review*, and *Annals of the American Academy of Political and Social Sciences*.

Phelan's own California agricultural dream was of the children of Europeans cultivating the land. In a type of transplanted Jeffersonian agrarian ideal, farm labor would retain a dignity Phelan wished to attribute to agricultural work. He never directly addressed the differences between field labor versus leasing, owning, or sharecropping, and in 1920 welcomed Mexican labor as a solution to the insufficiency of the American farm labor pool.

From Phelan's premise that the citizens of the nation rightly determine the nation's own membership, he moved to an extreme conclusion. He

Minority Report

The community's only politically significant minority report came from the old and cantankerous John P. Irish. A long-retired federal office holder form the Grover Cleveland administration, Irish addressed the Commonwealth Club, much to Father Yorke's disgust. If Asians were given half the chance as the Irish in California, he said, they would do twice as well. Years later Irish personally leafleted Market Street at the Phelan building on behalf of Japanese immigration.

Phelan did his best to discredit the eccentric Irish with ridicule, rather than connecting him to the commercial agriculture industry of the San Joaquin Delta or Central Valley which sought inexpensive field labor.

To Yorke's anti-Asian editorials, Phelan made no objection. He covered the same grounds in a more refined manner. A classic presentation of Phelan's Asian views appeared in his 1901 *Address*, "Debate On The Chinese Question." Phelan's presentation took place at San Francisco's Unitarian Club and took the form of an exchange of views with the Imperial Chinese Consul Ho Yow. Phelan's views prevailed and Federal law made the previous ban on Chinese immigration permanent. At this point Phelan considered the Chinese immigration question closed. Thereafter, he pursued the question of Japanese immigration with even greater intent. Every conviction he held concerning Chinese immigration he applied to the Japanese. Besides, the Japanese were backed by a world power of increasing strength.

Threat of Asian Immigration

With unfailing decorum, Phelan even summarized his views for individuals and shared them in personal letters. To N. Masaoka, a pro-immigration activist, Phelan wrote the following on May 12, 1914:

California was pioneered by the white race, which now occupies the soil. The Japanese are largely agriculturists, and are ingenious and industrious, especially when working for themselves; that they prefer to take a share of the crop or a lease of the land from the owners and develop it to its utmost capacity. They are capable, in a fierce competition of this kind, to displace the white population, and ultimately overrun the agricultural lands of my State. I do not believe that the creation of wealth is the exclusive or even important business of the country; I believe the preservation and development of the white race in California is of first importance, and the character of that population will determine the success or failure of the American republic. The history of the world shows that race problems are the most difficult of solution, and I fear that there would be an irreconcilable race conflict between the Japanese and Americans, because the Japanese, unlike the Europeans, do not assimilate with the white race. This does not imply any inferiority on the part of the Japanese, but a fundamental difference.

If you concede that the Japanese are capable of driving out the white population in a competitive struggle, in the development of agricultural lands, which you may regard as creditable to the skill and industry of your race, then you will understand my position, as opposed to the encouragement of the immigration of Japanese agricultural laborers and that there is nothing further to say.

introduced an amendment to the Constitution that would deny U.S. citizenship to persons of Asian ancestry and exclude all Asians from the Fourteenth Amendment's definition of citizenship. This was his ultimate, and unsuccessful, effort to end the influx that existed around the edges of the immigration laws that were in the process of becoming exclusionary. He did not expect such an amendment to the Constitution to make actual progress through the formal amending process, but his official proposal displayed the harmony between Phelan and public opinion in California. On this subject with his fellow Californians, he was indeed, intense. And that intensity found its full release in his reelection campaign in 1920.

Changes in 1920

In 1914 the Republican-Progressive split in California that mirrored the national political picture, allowed Phelan's victory against an overwhelming Republican voter registration. Circumstances allowed Phelan to associate himself with a Wilson administration that was near the apex of its domestic prestige. With this advantage and with his campaign resources and energy, Phelan won the election.

By 1920, not only had the world changed, but virtually all of Phelan's political advantage had changed as well. Wilson's popularity had disappeared. Worse, to be associated with him was a political handicap. Equally foreboding, the Republican-Progressive split in California had mended. In fact, Hiram Johnson gathered the support of both wings to himself, aided by his outstanding success as governor and the subsequent demise of national progressivism with the advent of World War I.

As the election year advanced, the Senator's political advisors recommended what he already knew. He needed a reelection issue that was broad in nature, not party-specific, and that would bring crossover votes to him. Phelan needed all the votes he received in 1914 plus the majority share of those that went to the third candidate. This time he expected only a two-way contest—himself and the Republican nominee for Senate.

Who that nominee might be concerned Phelan. He and Hiram Johnson were the most noted Californians in politics. The third Californian of prominence was Herbert Hoover. A member of Stanford's first graduating class, Hoover made an independent fortune as a mining engineer around the world. In World War I he earned a solid reputation in American relief efforts for Belgium and later as the wartime food administrator at home. Phelan had defended Hoover's reputation on the floor of the Senate and was personally well disposed toward him. Yet, Phelan felt anxiety about him as a potential Republican rival for the Senate in 1920. Hoover relieved Phelan by conveying that he did not intend to seek the Republican nomination for the Senate.

From this most cordial expression, Phelan assumed that Hoover was at least neutral. After that, Phelan toyed with the idea of Hoover for President as a Democrat. His reputation for successful administration, his clean political record, and his California residence all would be of help to Phelan as a candidate on the same ticket. Despite Phelan's initial efforts, no Hoover boom materialized. Hoover declined his premature political opportunity. To Phelan's ultimate disgust, however, Hoover was hardly out of politics. For the moment, though, Phelan seemed well enough off. His only formidable competitors for position were accounted for. Johnson already was California's junior Senator; Hoover was not yet interested in political position.

Reelection Campaign

Senate business, including debates and numerous votes on the Paris Peace Treaty and the League of Nations, kept Phelan busy at his official tasks in Washington. Being unopposed in the Democratic Party primary allowed his organization additional leisure. The first mention of plans for the full reelection campaign actually appeared in Fay's correspondence file for August 26, 1920. Phelan's opponent who received the Republican Party nomination for U.S. Senator was Samuel M. Shortridge. He had been the runner up for the Republican nomination six years earlier, and his nomination could actually be of profit to Phelan. Shortridge was popularly associated with reactionary political views, corporate corruption, and the perjury and graft of those whom he defended in the San Francisco graft trials of 1906-07. Shortridge was not admired by the state's progressive activists for the company he kept. So, in terms of his civic record, Shortridge was in trouble.

Over the issues with which the California voters were concerned, Shortridge and Phelan agreed and disagreed. The anti-Asian mania infected popular elements in California life: the press, organized labor, California's small farmers, veterans, local governments, and innumerable business

Single-Minded, but Playful

So clearly was Phelan associated with the movement to end Asian immigration and the curtailment of the rights of Asians, particularly in California, that for years into his retirement he was assumed to have remained single-minded. But his humor never deserted him. Once, after attending an animal play at the Bohemian Club in which "The sunfly wooed the beetle — clearly a case of miscegenation," a "serious gentleman" asked Phelan his opinion of the production.

Recounting the incident in his letter to Gertrude Atherton, Phelan wrote, "I observed that it was obviously a piece of 'Japanese Propaganda,' which he carried to his neighbors, with much earnestness, as an evidence of my intolerant spirit and the obsession which possesses me of reading everything in the light of the Japanese menace!" Certainly this playfulness was not the view that he shared with the public.

groups, as well as both candidates. The two candidates, during the election campaign, cooperated in the organization of the Japanese Exclusion League. Shortridge, like almost everyone else, placed himself on the popular side of the race issue. His position was clear and established, even though Phelan dominated the field. Phelan had, in fact, been the one who gathered the League into existence from among the local and diverse exclusionist groups through the state.

The two candidates differed over the question of the League of Nations. The Senate had rejected the League and Wilson's Paris Peace Treaty. However, the question remained a live one, stirred public debate, and constituted a major issue in the upcoming national election. The debilitated President himself insisted that the election of 1920 be a solemn referendum on the Treaty and the League.

Shortridge's position was clear and easy to identify: he opposed the League of Nations. He had established his position as an opponent of the proposed international organization quite early and had separated himself from his Republican primary opponents. He opposed foreign entanglement and said so to the California voters.

During the late days in December 1919, when the League was still before the Senate, Phelan had worked through Senator Gilbert M. Hitchcock, the Democratic Minority Leader, to "…get the President to agree to certain reservations." Senators Lodge and Johnson would not back down and accept a League without reservations. Phelan's intent was to help persuade the sick President to do so. Striving for the ideal, accepting what was possible, and formulating the settlement so that greater advances may be achieved later — this was Phelan's standard political practice. He learned once more that it was not Woodrow Wilson's.

Phelan was himself convinced of the necessity of a League and believed that such a necessity was "seeping into the consciousness of the people." As an old fighter against the public apathy that had allowed special interests and corruption to control local government, he always had warmed to the challenge of public education. Phelan grasped easily the value of an international organization as a mechanism to cope with the new and more interdependent postwar world. In his reelection campaign, Phelan tailored the issues for California. He campaigned throughout the state for a League of Nations and the Senate reservations to the Treaty that Wilson rejected.

Though Article X of the League guaranteed the territorial integrity of member nations, this would not require the United States to intervene on behalf of established nations such as Britain against Ireland. Phelan stood for broad latitude for the U.S. Government to determine its commitments to the world organization. This reflected his position on the Irish question.

As with perhaps too many other matters, the issue sooner or later brought him around to the Japanese implications. Phelan was more conscious than other American political leaders of the growing power of the Japanese military within Asia, accompanied by Japan's perceived population pressures and industrial and market needs. He viewed the League of Nations as potentially a very useful mechanism for monitoring Japanese militarism and expansionism and as a world organization through which the other world powers might restrain Japanese ambitions.

Phelan saw the Hawaiian Islands, already with a large and growing Japanese population, as a target for Japanese expansion. Phelan's wish was to redirect what he perceived as Japan's expansive impulses away from Hawaii and California and toward other parts of Asia. Further, he wished to keep the friction alive between Japan and China so that Japan's aggressive impulses not be directed to the West.

As part of the post war settlement, Phelan was in agreement with President Wilson's position that Japanese hegemony over the Chinese province of Shantung not be interfered with. In fact, Japan should be encouraged to look to China to provide for a population outlet and economic expansion. If that was difficult for China, then Phelan felt that the resulting friction would distract Japan from American interests.

On the same ballot with Phelan and Shortridge in 1920 was a state initiative measure designed to prevent Japanese from leasing agricultural land in California. Phelan's political organization assigned John T. Waldorf, a campaign worker, the tasks related to the organization and promotion of this initiative campaign. Phelan's reelection campaign then focused upon the Japanese at two levels. At the national level the League of Nations should be approved, with appropriate reservations that would guarantee America's freedom of action. At the state level, the Alien Land Law Initiative should be approved.

Phelan, of course, believed fully in both. He did not have to convince Californians on anything anti-Japanese. Disillusionism and isolationism

Because James Duval Phelan was such an easily identified ethnic himself, his position on Ireland and the League of Nations is fascinating. Elsewhere in Irish America Woodrow Wilson's League was denounced as a hindrance to Irish independence, the work of a President uninterested or hostile to Irish freedom. Phelan, an educated, integrated, and sophisticated second generation Irish American, reflected a California perspective. Ireland's needs, Phelan felt, could be addressed by a specific reservation to American acceptance of Wilson's League. (America would determine what would be the business of the League and what would not.) This reservation, Phelan felt, was necessary because of Japan! Certainly more militant Irish Americans and the Irish themselves would have a difficult time appreciating the Californian's orientation. In two generations a Phelan absorbed and blended the values of contemporary California and his ethnic heritage. But he could not believe that the same could be possible for other peoples from differing cultures.

were on the advance, however, so his pro-League position was more of a political risk. Except for the political burden of an increasingly unpopular federal administration, Phelan's strategy of running an independent campaign way out in California might have succeeded. He declined the offer of Senator Thomas Walsh of Montana to send in nationally known Democrats. He did accept telegrams of endorsement from Treasury Secretary William G. McAdoo and from Frank P. Walsh of the War Labor Conference Board, an activist in Irish American nationalist circles. Beyond that, he toured the state once again in his own automobile, and he loved it. Nineteen-twenty was his last big chance to see the California landscape he so loved while pursuing a higher purpose. His experienced campaign staff lined up the California press, submitted a steady flow of favorable publicity, and received its advertising money's worth. Even by 1920, Phelan felt best delivering three speeches per day, but was capable of as many as eight.

Had Phelan been ignored by outside influences, victory could indeed have been his. His own party was in national disarray. Leaderless, with Wilson remaining a semi-invalid, the Democratic administration was lashing out at its own members. At least that was Phelan's view. On the eve of the fall harvest, the U.S. Attorney General, A. Mitchell Palmer, initiated a suit

During his senate years, James Duval Phelan regularly offered Montalvo's hospitality to touring politicians. Unlike his treatment of his inner circle, Phelan wined and dined the office holders, but he normally moved them along to their next stop rather quickly. There was always time, however, for a parting photograph on the front steps of the villa.

against the California Raisin Growers Association, a major constituency. In his telegram to Tumulty in the White House, Phelan said that even if Palmer backed off he had damaged Phelan's chances as well as those of the national ticket of James M. Cox and Franklin D. Roosevelt.

Further, the State Department issued a statement the day before the November election that placated the Japanese and countered Phelan's position on the Alien Land Law. Furious at a cabinet level department headed by a Wilson appointee, Bainbridge Colby, Phelan asked "…why did the Department interfere in our state elections at the behest of … [the Japanese] to the detriment of a Democratic Senator. I will be elected on this issue tomorrow."

Dénouement

Phelan was not reelected though. Hoover had broken his silence, as well as what Phelan believed was his word, and appealed along with Hiram Johnson for a Republican Congress. What Wilson attempted and failed to do in 1918, the forces of reaction succeeded in doing in 1920. They argued that the Republican nominee for President, Warren G. Harding, would need a supportive legislature in order to succeed as President. The election returns were a Harding landslide which, likewise, dislodged Phelan from the United States Senate, replacing him with a man of questionable associations, more limited vision, and identical views on racial matters.

Phelan's postmortem analyses to William Randolph Hearst, Joseph Tumulty, Senator Key Pittman, and personal friends were accurate and without rancor. Hoover and the federal departments were important, but "The landslide was overwhelming…." "Shortridge was swept in by the sentiment of 'Down with Wilson and in with everybody except Wilson'."

Actually, Phelan did not do badly in the popular vote. California voter registration favored the Republican Party by nearly 650,000, yet Shortridge won by 70,000 votes. The heart of the explanation was the coattail effect. Republicans Harding and Coolidge defeated Democrats Cox and Roosevelt in California by 360,000 votes where, four years earlier Wilson had captured the state by 4,000. Phelan was accurate in writing "…had Harding not run more than 150,000 majority…, I would have been elected."

Incapable of depression, Phelan playfully idled away his time awaiting the final returns. In a fondly composed get-well note to Mrs. Rudolph

Spreckels, he lamented that he was "politically sick. My opponent leads me by fifteen thousand." His concluding line was one he used often: "Condemned for my sins to live in California." He actually welcomed his fate.

Cora Older, wife of the editor of the *Bulletin*, offered her sympathetic analysis and advice: "You hardly need to be told how sad Fremont and I were … your defeat is the last gasp of the Progressive past in California.… Your great showing makes clear that only in a year of political madness and reaction could you possibly have been defeated." As a perpetual health faddist, Cora Older advised Phelan to live out of doors in order to "develop new physical strength for another contest." Like many others she looked to Phelan to seek the California governorship or retake a senate seat.

Phelan had other plans. Perhaps taking the cure at a comfortable and fashionable European spa could be endured, but only if undertaken with good company and without the new health fanaticism which was becoming so trendy. Outdoor dining? He had always enjoyed that. Certainly horseback riding and swimming would be fine. But Phelan did not build Montalvo to sleep on the ground. Now, there would be time for all of life's enjoyments, too. He had worked hard through his Senate term and had felt obligated to his constituents. Now, he could indulge his travel interests. And perhaps his old friend Franklin Lane, ill with heart disease, had the right advice. Another four or six years in office would go fast. Life was abundant, but it was not forever. Now was the time to look to himself.

James Duval Phelan (fourth from right) tried to schedule himself into his own encampment at the Bohemian Grove each summer. He enjoyed the plays, the conviviality, and the contacts. As the years passed, however, the membership became less artistic and "bohemian" and more power-centered. Towards the end, John Downey Harvey became Phelan's personal encampment manager-in-resident and who emplored Phelan to come to the Grove to let loose. Phelan did — less often.

Chapter Fifteen
Retired Life and Travel

Through the decades since James D. Phelan's death in 1930 visitors to Villa Montalvo have repeated the same question: Why did the Senator never marry? The great variety of responses until now were determined less by the results of historical research and more by a docent's prudence, playfulness, or as often as not, defensiveness. Through most of Phelan's life those who were close enough to know him personally found the question useless. Gertrude Atherton, four years his senior, had no interest whatsoever in remarrying and would hardly think that her best and most loyal friend should spoil their own relationship by doing so. Maude Fay, like Atherton, pursued her own career, only in opera, and with Phelan's patronage. Her brother, Charles, was Phelan's political manager and lifelong personal friend. Their mother, in fact, had been matron of honor in the wedding of Phelan's parents in 1859. Charles Fay knew Florence Ellon and disapproved of her relationship with his patron and friend. For Fay not to have known of Agnes Tansill was impossible and for him to have kept his sister in ignorance of such a public secret was, indeed, remote. From her older brother's point of view, Maude Fay's knowledge could inform her behavior.

Given the sensitive social, cultural, and economic relationships that existed between Phelan and his inner circle, no one was sufficiently innocent to wonder why he would never marry. When the young Washington civil servant, Agnes Tansill, pressed him on the subject, Phelan merely brushed her off. Her awkward pressure on Phelan to marry her, accompanied by her lack of both stature and leverage, irritated Phelan and provided him with the occasion to end the relationship as politely as she would allow.

James Duval Phelan drew Gertrude Atherton and Helen Wills into his Montalvo circle during the 1920s. Atherton was California's most commercially successful writer; Wills was the world's celebrated tennis champion. His patronage was befitting each woman's needs. To Atherton he gave friendship, understanding, and respect. To Wills he provided recognition, guidance, and alternate career development. En route, he never intruded.

James D. Phelan and Helen Wills

During the nineteen-twenties, James Duval Phelan addressed the marriage question in a response to the most commanding and desirable woman he had encountered during his lifetime. Helen Wills, the world tennis champion, embodied Phelan's idealized California girl: in spirit, in form, in talent, and in promise. As Phelan was approaching seventy, California's world-acclaimed champion was hardly past twenty-one. Too young and too peripheral to understand the Senator's established relationships, America's beautiful and most admired sports queen may have posed the question without having to ask it. Her radiant presence constituted the question. For her part Wills had always responded positively to Phelan's public demonstrations recognizing her championships. She and her mother inconvenienced themselves in the hope of additional encounters with California's patron. And in later life Wills shared her regret with Atherton that so many years had separated her from her patron.

In any case, the realistic, reflective, and forever rational Phelan offered Helen Wills his answer to the question posterity has persisted in asking. Without mentioning his single state as such to Wills, Phelan cited the "wonderful hours" of intellectual activity he was able to enjoy, the hours of "calm reflection since I am permitted to live my own way...." His well-ordered single state resulted in a life he found eminently fulfilling. He sought cultural refinement in solitude or in the company of accomplished and loving friends. Throughout, he was intent on remaining the one who exercised the choice between the luxury of solitude or the enrichment of select personal association. His sense of family was an extended one. His parents, Alice and James, were difficult for him to forget. Obligation and service mixed with brotherly love controlled his relationship with his surviving sister, Mollie. Pride and satisfaction, mixed with occasional dismay, controlled his affections with his sister Alice's children. His own choice not to marry foreclosed, of course, the continuation of the family name — a matter that, surprisingly, never elicited his apparent concern.

The Arts

The satisfaction Phelan derived from the arts and from his relationships with those who created art were his replacements, filling what others might consider the void within his private life. Once the incumbency of public office ceased, the arts, their creators, and their aspirants occupied Phelan's intellectual preserve. This capturing of the patron's attention, though, was not through default. The time was right and Phelan merely moved them closer to the heart of his idealized personal environment.

Phelan's chronic optimism helped greatly in 1920. Defeat in his bid for reelection to the United States Senate became a threshold, not a conclusion. Previously his primary commitment of time and labor had been to political service. Beyond politics now stretched the most culturally engaging, final decade of his life. Certainly no other Irishman in American political history stepped away so easily and assuredly from a calling within "the art of the possible" in order to embrace the gracious and exciting world of the arts — fine and performing, classical and popular. For that matter, no other Californian, regardless of heritage, contributed at such an elevated level to public service and offered such cultural refinement to the American West.

To punctuate his transition from intense political engagement to genial patronage and appreciation of the arts, Phelan took two steps that for him were natural and symbolic. First, at a profit, he disposed of his embassy-row mansion in Washington. Selling it to the new Swedish Ambassador, Phelan relocated jointly in his sister's fashionable post-earthquake San Francisco residence and his own Villa Montalvo. Second, and with equal enthusiasm, he arranged for an around-the-world tour the quality and extent of which would befit a man of his interests, means, and disposition. Concurrently, Phelan agreed to repeat the work that had initially brought him to public attention in San Francisco. He arranged to write his travel observations for the San Francisco press. Following the trip he gathered his articles, including some from 1883, and published them as *Travel and Comment* (1923). His route in 1921, however, brought him to Hawaii first and then through Asia and the Middle East in order to reach Europe from the east.

Phelan, a consummate product of Western Civilization, brought with him through Asia the burden as well as the perspective of his European culture. His prior exposure to Japan, China, and South Asia had not been through reading and study, but rather through the partisan dynamics of the California conflict between Phelan's dominant culture and the state's Asian immigrants. His detailed itinerary demonstrates his intent to expose himself to Asian art, culture, architecture, and the landscape. His writings betray the internal struggle between his esthetic desires and his political and racial convictions. In Hawaii, for example, he became preoccupied by what he considered the silent Japanese invasion that convinced him that ultimately America would have to forego democratic institutions in order to protect the island from the subversion of its own future majority.

Oahu in the fall of 1921 was pristine, certainly from the perspective of late-century environmentalists. Yet Phelan omitted any mention of the island's scenic grandeur. Even investment opportunities escaped his commentary though he was well acquainted with Walter F. Dillingham, one of Hawaii's magnates. Instead, military, diplomatic, and geopolitical considerations drowned out all competing thoughts. Phelan's assessment of Japan's growing strength in the Pacific, the progressing militarization of its government, the quality of its industrial leadership and work force, as well as its limited raw materials and food supply, all caused Phelan to predict the worst. Because of his clear identification with what other Americans recognized as

James Duval Phelan (fourth from left) at the Bohemian Grove with Noël Sullivan (left), John Downey Harvey (third from left), Charles W. Fay (right), and two other friends.

Phelan's personal relationships were as interesting as his public associations. Here he is sharing center stage with his friend from school days, "Downey" Harvey. Harvey's sparsity of letters leaves him an ever-present, two dimensional figure in Phelan's life. Always well-turned out, Harvey became dependent upon Phelan after 1906. Phelan behaved toward him just the same as if Harvey were an independent, accomplished success. He took no advantage. Downey's own emotional life remained masked by resignation and good cheer.

Beauty Beyond Culture

Throughout a six-hour train ride from Yokahama to Nikko he observed "an exhibition of simple manners and good behavior" among those who shared the second-class car, the best available. Phelan contrasted what he considered a better class of Japanese who remained at home with a peasant class that had immigrated to unfriendly American settings. Those he observed in Japan he considered "urbane, proud, and ... kindly and considerate."

In Nikko Phelan visited the temples in the company of large numbers of Japanese pilgrims who were celebrating the emperor's birthday. He ascended Mount Nantai-zan as part of the holiday throng, enjoying en route the sensations associated with the "raging gorges fed by the eternal snows melting into Lake Chiuzenji." He even added his own informed approval to the Japanese saying: "Do not use the word 'splendor' until you have seen Nikko." Splendidly shaped by nature and enhanced by human artistry, the temples held his gaze. They offered beauty in their form and added grandeur in their setting, the extended groves of crytomaria (Japanese pine).

California's anti-Asian fixation, Phelan's warnings of Japan's military threat, likewise, went unheeded. What else might midwestern senators or southern Democrats expect from him?

Japan

Phelan's intention was to visit Japan as a private citizen, "desiring to efface myself in order that my investigations might be unembarrassed by publicity...." The centers for the arts and culture ranked high on his itinerary. Nonetheless, the presence of Japan's most ardent critic did not go unnoticed. When he disembarked the Pacific Mail line's *The Hoosier State*, in Yokohama, ten journalists and their accompanying photographers greeted him. The vigor with which the recently retired politician actually resisted notoriety is questionable. What is certain is Phelan's directness. His sense of personal security, perhaps inviolability, sprang from his observations of the American Japanese as well as his perception of Japanese culture. As a result, Phelan, in his words "decided to pay them the best compliment I could by telling them the truth without fear." Such directness may have been more culturally acceptable to Phelan than to the Japanese. When Tokyo's *Nichi-Nichi* proclaimed that "The great enemy of Japanese arrives and opens his mouth hatefully," Phelan believed that he had provoked the "right reaction." The contents of his interviews were widely printed in the metropolitan press, complete with photographs. Phelan concluded from the headlines that he "left no doubt in the minds of their readers as to my hostility."

His "hostility" was ideological, of course, rather than personal. In traveling through the Japanese countryside Phelan found the people to be "cheerful and courteous."

Phelan attended the popular theatre and saw a historical drama he characterized as "unreal and bombastic.... There was the powerful shogun and the fierce men-at-arms in a mock battle...." He seems not to have witnessed a performance of kabuki, the highly stylized traditional drama that may have appealed more to his tastes. Kamakura and a viewing of the great Buddha "whose benignant face is universally known" satisfied another of Phelan's interests. The industriousness and sobriety of the citizenry distracted him from his artistic and cultural mission; he viewed this effective citizenry as an international threat.

His personal observations of the Japanese at home augmented his California-inspired prejudices. He felt that the "Japanese are witty and cheerful, and never lose a chance to exhibit merriment." Reflecting as much upon his fixed views of human nature as upon his observations, Phelan added, "This is surely indigenous and spontaneous, because humor is not an accomplishment — it is a gift." He saw "the potentialities of the Japanese more vividly," he wrote, "because of their training and intelligence." His conclusion, nonetheless, remained fixed: "We can treat them as an outside power, but we cannot incorporate them in our body-politic for reasons which affect the purity of the races and the perpetuity of our institutions."

Phelan, on three occasions, enjoyed mingling socially with Japanese men and women, the settings and agendas fixed by well-to-do hosts. Officially, he recorded that "the delicacy of their home hospitality made a most pleasing impression." He felt that their efforts to assume European and American ways of hospitality was quite unnecessary: "I am disposed to believe…that they need no stimulus to quicken the gladsome character of their welcome." His first social opportunity came by chance. Aisahu Hyishi, the manager for the Imperial Hotel in Tokyo, had been educated in San Francisco. He told the former mayor that he had seen him in San Francisco during his own student days at Lowell High School. Now successful, he invited Phelan to a traditional Japanese dinner, not at the hotel, but at a remote private club. For Phelan, a person of cultivated tastes, the evening was magic.

Rather than a restaurant, Phelan described the building more accurately (in appearance as opposed to function) as a "house — a light and airy structure with almost diaphanous partitions." Charcoal braziers warmed guests who had entrusted their shoes to the care of two young women. Either as a cultural discovery new to himself or for the education of his San Francisco readers, Phelan repeated the analogy that "it would be no less a breach of etiquette to walk in your boots over the sofas and chairs of a European drawing room than to tread rough-shod on the matting in these dainty houses."

This seems to have been the first time James Duval Phelan reclined upon a cushioned floor attired in evening dress. Of the twenty guests all the women wore traditional costumes while all but two men joined Phelan in western formal attire. Phelan's insights did not extend deeply enough to cause him to wonder why Japanese women were present as guests at an entertainment held beyond a private residence, contrary to polite custom.

James D. Phelan's party (Noël Sullivan, Soffie Harvey, and Genevieve Harvey Barron) shared local transport in Jaipur, India, in 1922. The foursome was completing the Asian phase of their around-the-world tour. From India, their itinerary brought them through the Middle East and on to Europe.

Soffie and Downey Harvey's daughter Genevieve had been invited around the world, in part, in the hope that travel would improve her mental health. It did — greatly. Only typhoid almost claimed her life.

Phelan appreciated the artfully prepared and delicately presented Japanese foods. "The viands," he wrote, "were of extraordinary flavor, and very deliciously cooked." Having fought and lost California's fight against American prohibition he was even more demonstrative regarding the saki that accompanied the foods, all of which to him seemed so exotic. "A small glass of warm Saki — an ardent liquor — was not forgotten, nor was it rejected by the Americans. The Japanese could hardly have known that abstinence had become our established national religion, otherwise, always thoughtful, they might, alas, have shunted the Saki!"

The evening concluded with a company of very young geishas entertaining with music, singing, and dancing after which "the guests silently slipped away, pursuant to an ancient custom, which saves the host, theoretically, from the pangs of parting." Phelan rated the evening "a perfect entertainment." He had prepared himself by reading about the prevailing etiquette and then allowed the evening to unfold. He accepted it as an enriching gift, the sharing of culture, and he welcomed more. Next came the tea ceremony at the home of the mayor of Tokyo, Baron Gato.

Before attending this artistic ritual, Phelan prepared himself by reviewing the Japanese poet Okakura-Katuzo's "Book of Tea." Heightened anticipation was to enhance consummation. Mentally prepared, Phelan sensed first the penetrating influence of the atmosphere itself, "an unearthly spirit of gentleness and beauty seemed to pervade the spot." Informed by the poet of the cult of teaism, Phelan drew unto himself the "dream of evanescence," and followed the esthetic command, "linger in the beautiful foolishness of things." Baron Gato enacted the ceremony in a special room where "Not a color was permitted to disturb the tone … nor a sound to mar the rhythm." The Baron's family surrounded him in a half circle. The younger generation, Wellesley and Harvard educated, conversed in English. "A young girl, skilled in the art, began to prepare the revered beverage. The bowl was of rare beauty and great value....It was elaborate as a rite … poetry and tradition still have loving devotees in a transformed, if not perverse generation."

Phelan's last cutting remark, of course, despoiled his own cultivated pleasure of the moment. Despite his dedicated devotion to the beautiful and the sublime, he could not release himself from the grip of his cultural and personal imperatives. His third encounter with Japanese society required no such release. Phelan accepted luncheon and the invitation to address the

Tokyo Chamber of Commerce on his personal views of "the Japanese Problem in California." Phelan did so in his refined, but direct and comprehensive manner, and he followed up with an extended elaboration in the form of a letter published in the *Japanese Times*.

Most unfortunate from the vantage point of Phelan's transition from politics to art and culture was the assassination of Premier Takashi Hara. Phelan visited Kyoto and recognized the city of culture and refinement as the "art center of Japan." His impressions, this time, were destroyed not by the intrusion of his own cultural preconceptions but by the political terrorism that was so very much alive within Japan. Premier Hara was murdered on his way to Kyoto where Phelan had planned to witness his address before the convention of Japan's governing party.

The viciousness of Hara's assassination turned Phelan's mind from the art of Kyoto to the tragic fate of liberal government in Japan. The result was article five in Phelan's series to the San Francisco press. From Japan's center of artistic refinement, rather than write of culture Phelan assessed Japan's crisis in government and industry. Penetrating enough, the article responded to a tragic event that distracted him from his interest in Japanese history and culture. It allowed him to depart Japan with the same convictions he brought with him upon his arrival.

Traveling Companions

The articles Phelan composed for the San Francisco press did not reveal the private aspects of his traveling arrangements. Even in his summary, *Travel and Comment*, which he published as a public report and offered as a personal gift to his extended circle, only the accompanying photography revealed that Phelan had traveling companions. Phelan, despite his commitment to the single status, hardly enjoyed extended solitude. In order for him to spend eleven months traveling around the world, he required suitable company and his selections were reflections upon himself.

Besides Charles Fay and Gertrude Atherton, Phelan's closest friends who were unrelated to him were Soffie and John Downey Harvey. Phelan and John Downey Harvey had been friends since school days. The guest list for Alice Phelan Sullivan's wedding in 1881 included young Harvey's name. When Phelan's post-fire correspondence resumed, Soffie Harvey was an

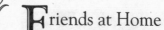

Friends at Home

James D. Phelan would meet Charles Fay in Europe at the tail end of the year abroad and together they would visit civil-war-torn Ireland. Until then and particularly during the period when Phelan was away himself, he needed Fay to remain in San Francisco to oversee the enlightened and integrated management of Phelan's personal and public interests.

Gertrude Atherton, of course, was enjoying her own professional success and always set her own social agenda; her workaholic approach to writing and publishing hardly lent itself to a year off, even if she justified it as research or inspiration seeking. Besides, Phelan seemed to derive great satisfaction from correspondence with Atherton, providing her with comfortable working space at Montalvo when she would accept, and simply sharing her company on literary occasions. Traveling together might not have enhanced their altogether satisfying, established relationship.

James Duval Phelan always sought the most comfortable and efficient transportation available. In the Chinese countryside, this was it. "It is a strange sensation to be drawn by humans," Phelan wrote, "but they consider it play work, and they think only of the remuneration they receive."

In Peking, Phelan considered the Grand Hotel "a pretentious hostelry, with spacious halls and an excellent orchestra....It is all very modern."

established member of Phelan's inner circle along with her husband. John Downey Harvey had enjoyed, as Phelan had, a comfortable upbringing. His widowed mother, Eleanor, remarried into great wealth and enjoyed, as Mrs. Edward Martin, being the social arbiter of San Francisco until her death in 1928 at age ninety-eight.

Downey, as Harvey was called, had one insurmountable handicap. He lacked wealth or adequate income. His mother all but lived forever and her fortune came from the line that ran directly to his half-brother, Peter Martin. Phelan assisted Harvey in railroad construction and the associated financing that had created other large fortunes. Harvey's Ocean Shore Railroad scheme, connecting San Francisco and Santa Cruz, was faltering when the 1906 earthquake and fire reduced him to bankruptcy. Thereafter, Phelan moved into the breach, actually paying Downey's life insurance premiums on the policy he held as collateral against his friend's overwhelming debt. Phelan saw the couple through bankruptcy proceedings in a way that protected Soffie as well as he could. Thereafter, Downey became a permanent Phelan retainer. True to himself, Phelan kept the Harveys with a dignity that never wore thin and never exploited the power this relationship conveyed upon him.

As the next generation of Harveys appeared Phelan smiled upon them as well as their parents. The growing correspondence shows Soffie to have been the more compelling of the couple, seemingly better able to face their plight with honesty, understanding, and simple gratitude. She repaid Phelan with the only coin available to her. She enriched his life by her effective management of his large and frequent entertainments at Montalvo. Social secretary, domestic supervisor, interior decorator, and hostess — Mrs. Harvey filled all these roles. She did so out of love for the man she married and to whom she remained faithful and out of love for their wonderful friend, their family's benefactor, the man who enjoyed their company and seemed never to notice that she and Downey had become his virtual dependents.

In 1921, Genevieve Harvey Barron, Soffie's and Downey's young married daughter, suffered an emotional collapse. Phelan's experience with his sister Mollie encouraged him to offer his own generic prescription — supportive companionship in a stimulating and novel environment. Whether insufficient prudence or overly abundant enthusiasm carried the day is undocumented. Whichever, Soffie and her daughter Genevieve agreed to accompany Phelan around the world. The trip nearly killed the younger woman physically, but it seemed, until a 1925 relapse, to have been the permanent emotional cure for which all had hoped.

Besides Soffie and Genevieve, Phelan included his sensitive, thirty-one-year-old bachelor nephew, Noël Sullivan. Highly religious, accomplished, and noted as a liturgical singer, Sullivan enjoyed respect and popularity within his uncle's social circle. Always supportive, never threatening, he embodied the final symmetry to Phelan's party and purpose. With his guest list complete, Phelan directed Thomas Cook and Son through the details of itinerary construction, paid the $18,000 fee, and the party departed.

Phelan's natural concern for his guest-companions increased when the foursome reached China. Yet, despite the discomfort of inferior accommodations and abundant evidence of smallpox, the party remained healthy enough. Hardly in jest Phelan wrote that "Peking dust is so deadly that … it should alone be capable of disinfecting itself, but it does not." His own vaccination did not take so he concluded that he should be immune anyway.

Typhoid, not smallpox, finally overtook the party and from Egypt, not China. It attacked the weakest member, Genevieve Barron. By the time the incubation period elapsed they had landed in Italy and there the party was to remain. Phelan set his itinerary aside, refusing to abandon the critically ill young woman who remained confined to bed under medical and nursing care throughout the summer of 1922. Not until her long-in-doubt survival was assured did he feel free to complete his tour through Western Europe. Genevieve Barron did not recover sufficient strength to return to New York until the following spring; her confinement and convalescence required eleven months in Rome. Phelan, regretting the cause for the delay, nonetheless fully enjoyed its location — Italy, home of the cities, the landscapes, the architecture and the art he appreciated and understood.

Phelan's paramount concern was for the well being of Genevieve. Bonds of family and love aside, she did contract the life-threatening disease as his guest. Its intense fevers, profuse sweating, and complete exhaustion reduced the young woman to invalidism. But rather than in a hospital, Phelan chose to provide for treatment and convalescence in a first-class (clean) hotel, augmented by medical and nursing care that he could directly monitor. Beyond his own sympathetic and supportive bedside attendance, Phelan consumed the weeks that grew into months pursuing the artistic satisfactions of Rome.

James D. Phelan posed before the Sphinx and pyramid near Cairo. While being shown the interior passages, he regretted having left his hand gun at his hotel. A local ruffian threatened him, demanding his wallet when Phelan became separated from the group. It was in Egypt that Genevieve Barron contracted typhoid fever. Her critical condition halted their tour in Italy.

Flea Market Treasures

Phelan's insatiable quests for esthetic experiences brought him as far afield as Rome's flea markets that offered objects stolen from the wealthy as well as those being peddled by those of former, pre-war wealth. Old families on the margin were exchanging occasional pieces for ready cash. These markets Phelan found interesting and exciting, but hardly the place for personal purchase.

Equally curious, certainly provocative, was the Capuchin Order's display of the remains of their own departed members; bleached, dismembered, and, in Phelan's view, composing "a picture of beautiful designs."

Leg and arm bones, he noted, were configured into "fancy chandeliers, and the skulls look down upon you from an elaborate cornice." Hardly upset, Phelan tossed off these lines:

> You are bones, but what of that?
> Every face, however, full,
> Padded round with flesh and fat,
> Is but modeled on a skull!

Searching for Art in Rome

He sought art everywhere. Retracing his steps from prior visits to the eternal city, Phelan reviewed his favorite monuments and revisited the classical buildings they complemented. The museums, galleries, studios, and academies each consumed his now-extended allocation of days, then weeks and months. He devoted more critical attention to the landscapes beyond the city. He studied the urban-rural relationships. And he indulged his enhanced interest in landscaped gardens, particularly Villa D'Este in Tivoli.

Phelan concentrated his attention disproportionately upon two works. He was quite taken by the Cyrene Venus that had been unearthed in an American dig near Tripoli five years earlier, in 1917. The sculptor was unknown, but the work was attributed to the Greeks and dated about 500 B.C. Exhibited in Rome's Museo Della Terme, the work's flesh-like realism fascinated the critics. Agreeably, Phelan accepted contemporary criticism that ranked it above both the Venuses of Medici and Milo. The beautiful rendering of the human figure ranked second in Phelan's personal appreciations of statuary he studied during his enforced Roman spring and summer. His personal prize went to The Laocoön: violent, sensuous, and heavily laden with a historical message that Phelan had made a hallmark throughout his political life. He even acquired a full-sized copy of the Vatican pre-Christian treasure, which he left to the Palace of the Legion of Honor in his will.

Phelan and his nephew, Noël Sullivan, expanded the range and duration of their trips beyond Rome as Genevieve Barron's crisis passed and her condition stabilized. By midsummer Phelan felt free to resume the original itinerary through Germany and France and on to England and Ireland. Barron's severely weakened, but now hopeful, condition allowed their departure though it still required her to remain in Rome with her mother for an extended convalescence. By this point, Phelan looked ahead to rendezvousing with Charles Fay and his son Charles, Jr., in Paris, thus creating an all-male foursome for the final leg of the journey into civil-war-torn Ireland.

Ireland

Until his approach to Ireland, Phelan had met with a chain of notables from the mayor of Tokyo to the newly elected Pope Pius XI. In between the list remained more political than artistic, particularly as outposts of the British Empire constituted most ports of call. Ireland, always different, was in this respect as well. Artists, particularly writers and poets, were in power— though not securely. Phelan's long delay in Italy resulted in his arriving in Dublin during a violent, culminating phase of the Irish Civil War.

His parents had initiated his Irish network early in life and Phelan extended it through broad correspondence, frequent trips, and a lifetime of lavish hospitality and gifts for the Irish who visited California (usually fund raising) and for many in Ireland as well. Cultural interests that drew him to poetry, literature, and history attracted him to Irish writers. He was a major California bibliophile who cherished autographed works and personal contact with men and women who created literature and circulated ideas. These cultivated relationships, plus extraordinary timing, allowed the Californian, coincidentally, to play a significant cameo role in Irish history. But for Barron's illness Phelan's party would have arrived and departed Dublin between episodes of civil unrest, thus reducing his visit to a pleasant social event. Such, though, was not the case.

After World War I, he had watched England and Ireland spar their way through to a treaty which, from England's point of view, successfully partitioned Ireland, and thereby, divided Irish opinion and leadership into warring camps. Phelan's sensitivity to the tragedy of the civil war was acute. The loss of life appalled him. That Irishmen should kill one another over their own political disagreements, he found to be even worse; it was unnecessary.

Those Irish who rose in revolt against British rule at Easter 1916 sacrificed their lives so that the spark of revolution could live. They earned Phelan's praise. "Patriot" was Phelan's highest rank of nobility. Without such Irish idealists no treaty with Britain would have been possible. Because Ireland never defeated Britain, any expectation of complete freedom in 1922 was unrealistic. According to Phelan's formula for political change, Ireland was at the compromise point. The Anglo-Irish Treaty, he felt, should be accepted and Irish leaders and citizens should unite to make it work. Ireland's struggling Free State government, he believed, was the duly constituted agency through which this stage of development should be concluded. Further, Phelan reasoned, dramatically effective and stable government under the Treaty would allow the Irish to advance themselves for full self-government in the future.

James Duval Phelan had appreciated the art of western civilization since his postgraduate residence in Europe forty years earlier in 1882. Except for young Genevieve Barron's illness, Phelan would have welcomed his forced extension in Rome. The Cyrene Venus and other recent archeological finds captured his attention and enthusiasm. He tried to acquire suitable copies of what he liked. In this case, he was forced to content himself with photographs, one of which he shared with his friends by including it in his book, Travel and Comment.

Advancing Political Change

James D. Phelan's own approach to political change was by formula. First, he preferred to identify the objective and define it in idealized terms. Next, he organized the available resources (including heavy emphasis upon education of the electorate) and advanced as if complete achievement of the goal were possible. When the inevitable obstacles of inertia, opposition, and pleas for compromise blocked his advance, he was prone to accept the best of what was possible. If he could, Phelan structured compromise so that subsequent efforts could move more promisingly toward the original ideal. Even though his own political experience was entirely different from civil-war-torn Ireland, that Phelan applied his process to Ireland was quite natural. It was how he thought.

Few Irish Americans, particularly Californians who helped vote Phelan out of office, shared his thinking. Phelan, though better informed than most of his former constituents, had never focused his political interests on Ireland. Militant Irish Americans, such as Father Peter C. Yorke, did. As long as the Irish fought England, the Irish abroad knew who to support. Once the Irish started fighting one another, confusion spread. Phelan's position was prominent, but it reflected the minority Irish American opinion. The majority opinion encouraged direct opposition to the Free State government in Ireland. The Free State was a creation of England. Majority views advocated complete freedom from England and a republican form of government throughout the island. That difference of opinion divided the Irish in America and fomented the Civil War in Ireland.

Ireland: Trying to Help

No longer accountable to the California Irish, James Phelan attempted to moderate the war. Interestingly, his literary and social connections, not his political ones, provided his entree to the Irish power brokers.

When Phelan arrived in Dublin those Irish leaders whose point of view he shared were in power, and their legitimacy was being challenged by their former comrades in arms against Britain. Phelan's well-placed personal contacts, included Dr. Oliver St. John Gogarty, Sir Horace Plunkett, and P. A. O'Farrell, who was the brother-in-law of the Minister of Finance W. T. Cosgrave. These men brought Phelan to the center of power and provided him with the historical distinction of being the last person to interview both General Michael Collins and President Arthur Griffith, the negotiators of the Treaty with Britain and resolute leaders of the Free State Government which that Treaty brought into being.

Phelan's intention was "to meet the cabinet, Arthur Griffith and General [Michael] Collins ... in the vague hope that some suggestion might be made ... for Irish unity under a liberal constitution." The Collins-Phelan interview took place on the evening of July 31. Phelan believed that he found in the General the proper "combination of gentleness and strength that is probably characteristic of all potentially great leaders." Phelan did not consider Collins to be eloquent, but remarked upon his fluency. Phelan asked Collins what message he wanted delivered to the American people. Collins's ready reply, certainly agreeable to Phelan, was: "Give them our kind regards and say that when all this is ended we'll come over and explain it to them."

Twenty-one days later the death of Collins, Ireland's most promising and charismatic revolutionary leader, forced Phelan's reassessment. Collins died directing Free State troops. Hindsight compelled Phelan to downgrade his estimate of Collins as a military leader. Harshly, he concluded, "the amiability of his character was inconsistent with military success."

President Arthur Griffith's physician was Phelan's literary friend, Dr. Oliver St. John Gogarty. Gogarty brought together the distinguished American and his famous Irish patient for what was to be Griffith's last interview (he died soon after from a brain hemorrhage). As experiences go, this was a depressing one for Phelan.

Phelan's respect for Griffith emanated from the stricken leader's organizational skills and his inspirational role within Ireland's revolutionary movement. Phelan urged a peaceful solution to the war, but the dying President rejected it as impossible. "No — it is too late," Griffith said. "Every door has been closed to conciliation, and it must be fought out to the end." Although speaking was a painful task, Griffith remained resolute. His final proclamation to the world was through James D. Phelan who judged him to be "embittered by the ingratitude of his countrymen, after a life of service."

Farewells

Phelan's role was a traditional Irish American one. He radiated hope and good will. Reconciled to his own limitations as a friendly observer of another's tragedy, he moderated his intensity and cushioned his disappointment. To his credit, he understood and accepted the inflexibility of Collins and Griffith and, by his California formula for political change, would await other opportunities for the Irish to formulate their own solutions to their own problems.

Phelan's farewell gesture was a dinner in honor of Sir Horace Plunkett, admired by Phelan because of his practical, enlightened, and generous approach to Ireland's problems. Phelan's guest list included those who had befriended him in Dublin, augmented by prominent men of letters. Most noted at his Shelbourne Hotel banquet were the Irish poet George "A E" Russell and Douglas Hyde, the Irish language revivalist whom Phelan and Frank

James Duval Phelan and his nephew Noël Sullivan culminated their 1921–1922 world tour in Dublin, here pausing before the Vice-Regal Lodge, Phoenix Park. Always attentive to the promptings of their Irish heritage, both men followed closely the civil war then ablaze in Ireland. Phelan, through his personal contacts within literary circles, sought resolution of the violence and disorder. He was the last person to have interviewed the opposing leaders of the war in Ireland. Phelan was received with respect, but his efforts at reconciliation were set aside.

Departing. Uncharacteristically, James Duval Phelan neither identified the place nor recorded the date. His vehicle's vintage, the monument's base and style, the street lights, and the building's facade — all offer their hints. Wherever, Phelan was at his ease.

Sullivan had hosted in 1906, and who was to become the first President of Ireland under the constitution of 1937.

That evening and that company marked the gracious conclusion to a journey begun around the world a year earlier. In keeping with the heritage to which he was a distant heir, Phelan presided over a celebration rich in talk, abundant in food, powerful in drink, and emotional in spirit. Despite, or perhaps because of, Ireland's chronic distress, the ranking poet at table, A E, offered his own "prose-poem breathing of hope and comforting with consolation." Noël Sullivan responded with his compliment to Ireland, fondly rendered Irish vocal compositions. His uncle, California's most accomplished and gracious host, concluded their evening and his world tour with the lines from William Butler Yeats:

> The wrong of unshapely things, is a wrong too great to
> be told,
> I hunger to build them anew, and sit on a green knoll
> apart
> With the earth and the sky and the water, remade, like a
> casket of gold,
> For my dream of your image that blossoms, a rose in
> the deeps of my heart.

Chapter Sixteen
Patron of the Arts

Though James Duval Phelan was unable to purge politics fully from his heart when he turned homeward to California, he had drawn art's expressions closer to the center of his life.

Patronage came early and easy to Phelan. He studied and indulged himself in each of the fine and performing arts, except music which he accepted as support and complement to theatre, dance, and opera. Phelan acted throughout life on his own axiom: "art cannot exist where artists are not remunerated....and art cannot live without patronage." His first close observation of the artist-patron relationship was in sculpture.

Douglas Tilden

Local patrons whose tolerance for the peculiarities of artists was rather low allowed the financial panic of 1893 to terminate their support of Douglas Tilden. Phelan, one year beyond his assumption of full control over the family enterprises, stepped forward into active patronage. In doing so, he demonstrated both commitment to talent and tolerance of personal behavior he could not understand.

Tilden contracted scarlet fever at age five which resulted in his total loss of hearing, and loss of speech as well. His parents were able to provide for his education at Berkeley's Institute for the Deaf, Dumb, and Blind where he distinguished himself as a student and remained as an instructor. Tilden received a traveling scholarship at age twenty seven. In New York and Paris he perfected his skills as a sculptor. En route he exhibited before the *Société des*

Phelan's Patronage

James D. Phelan's patronage of Douglas Tilden's work took many forms and extended through Tilden's productive career, ending with Phelan's death in 1930. Phelan even arbitrated the artist's insensitive encounters with critics, selection committees, and Tilden's own family. Phelan commissioned Tilden's work, introduced the artist's designs to private and civic awards committees, and provided Tilden with a stipend when intervals between major commissions exceeded the man's modest capacity for financial management. Phelan did so over the artist's wife's opposition.

Admission Day sculpture by Douglas Tilden. James Duval Phelan's attention to California history — the Spanish missions, the story of '49, admission to the union — and his promotion of the Native Sons of the Golden West sprang from a profound impulse. Phelan intended that his generation secure as a permanent commonwealth the government and culture superimposed upon the land his father's generation had occupied. That mission required the popularization, if not creation, of a history. The artistry of Tilden helped.

Artistes Francais and *Société National des Beaux Arts*. Coveted recognitions came in the form of honorable mention from the Paris Salon in 1890 and the bronze medal at the Paris Exposition of 1900.

When Tilden returned home from Paris and found himself without a patron, he resumed teaching and began advocating the rights of the deaf. Phelan went directly into Tilden's classroom at the Hopkins Institute of Art on Nob Hill (then part of the University of California), introduced himself, and commissioned their first joint public monument. It was best known as the *Admission Day* monument or as the *Native Sons* monument. By the time of its San Francisco dedication at the intersection of Market, Mason, and Turk Streets in 1897, the young art patron had become mayor of San Francisco. Phelan presented Tilden's work to the public as his gift and thus began the lifelong relationship between artist of talent and patron of means.

Phelan's follow-up commission was for a monument commemorating the discoverer of the Pacific Ocean, the Spanish explorer Vasco de Balboa. Phelan intended to demonstrate the place of monumental statuary as an integral part of urban planning. These efforts foreshadowed his contributions to Burnham's City Beautiful. This particular monument was to be located at the west end of Golden Gate Park appropriately looking toward the Pacific. Tilden completed the model, but world events intervened. The timing of the Spanish-American War and San Francisco's role as a supply point in support of the war effort in the Philippines arrested the project.

Phelan's permanent interest in the history of California's Spanish heritage reasserted itself instead in alternate artistic expression, a monument whose subject was noncontroversial politically and, at that time, culturally as well. For that he once more turned to the gifted Tilden. Tilden's rendering of *Padre Junipero Serra,* a nine-and-a-half foot bronze atop a twelve foot pedestal, is perhaps the Phelan-Tilden contribution to San Francisco's adornment that is encountered by more interested viewers than any other Tilden creation. Its location in Golden Gate Park immediately south of the main Kennedy Drive (at the entrance to the oval drive to the de Young Museum) has assured its continued visibility and impact.

Tilden recognized the larger importance of Phelan's backing in his bid for the *California Volunteers* monument commission. Phelan was central to the project, which celebrated the conclusion of the Spanish-American War and memorialized California's volunteer soldiers who had, in the Philippines,

Football

The internationally acclaimed *Football Players*, which Tilden exhibited in the Paris Salon in 1894 and for which he received the bronze medal in 1900 at the Paris Exhibition was Phelan's only ready-made purchase. The American players constituted a larger-than-life bronze. Phelan, even though he never participated in sports himself, was taken by the work and offered it as a permanent recognition for either Stanford or California athletes. The splendid Tilden was to be Phelan's prize for the victorious footballers in two of the next three contests at Berkeley and Palo Alto. The concept behind Tilden's striking creation is now standardized in presentation trophies awarded to the winners in sporting events — the sports figure's image atop a pedestal rather than the traditional loving cup.

Surprisingly, given Berkeley's total failure against Stanford through the universities' formative years, California's eleven (no substitutes) swept the Big Game series, in 1898 (22-0) and again in 1899 (30-0). California accepted its striking prize in May 1900; the names of the heroes and their coach cut deeply into the stone base. The game, its players, and its impact on American life have changed, but Phelan's patronage and Tilden's art remain in place gracing the southwest corner of the Berkeley campus. The magnitude and strength of Tilden's creation continue to honor the sculptor as the bronzed heroes rest in the shade of the sheltering trees.

won that war for America. Phelan was the disburser of the $25,000 fund that supported Tilden's work for the two years he labored to create the monumental group. The twelve-foot bronze was being cast in Chicago at the time of the San Francisco earthquake. Four months later, in August 1906, it was dedicated in its first location at Market Street and Van Ness Avenue.

A far greater contribution to the world of art resulted from Phelan's earlier intervention on behalf of Tilden. The trustees of the estate of James Mervyn Donahue accepted the responsibility for erecting a suitable public memorial to the memory of Donahue's pioneer industrialist father, Peter Donahue. The elder Donahue created San Francisco's first foundry and print-

Donahue Monument by Douglas Tilden. Fittingly, the work survived the earthquake and fire of 1906 and offered a secure reference point for photographers of the disaster who chose graphic examples of contrast amid the ruins of the once great city. The Mechanics has also endured in popular appeal beyond that of its contemporaries.

Tilden's chronicler, Mildred Albronda, comments: "The graceful movements and gestures of the Mechanics create an art form in space....The interplay of ... mass and space, the articulation of planes and curves, the sense of movement, create a unity of concept that belongs to the present day. And yet, the sublime expressions on the faces plunge one's imagery back in time...."

ing press, its first gas lighting and street railway system. His son bequeathed $25,000 for a public fountain as permanent recognition of Peter Donahue's contributions to the founding of San Francisco. The trustees commissioned Tilden to create the memorial, but they lacked sufficient faith in his ability to transform his unorthodox design into tangible reality. Rather than installment payments as the delicate and costly process of modeling and casting advanced, they insisted on reserving full payment until delivery. The massive and strikingly angular work of art appealed to the committee, but they refused to ascribe to the Donahue estate the risks associated with its gestation and birth.

To Tilden metals constituted the unifying factor among the Donahue family's contributions to California's initial economic and industrial development. His artistic inspiration was simple and forceful. Tilden intended to place a group upon a massive granite pedestal within the center of a forty-foot stone fountain. The idea sprang from his observation of a worker straining to put holes through sheets of metal. The tool was an angular punch, large and strange. From the metal worker's inspiration, Tilden developed a design that placed five semi-naked mechanics exerting their collective strength, agility, and precision to compel the larger-than-life punch to do their bidding.

Phelan's contribution to the creation was simple, enlightened, and critical. He told the executors of the Donahue estate that he would make good any losses sustained in the various stages of modeling and casting. Phelan signed a contract with the four executors and Tilden and Phelan signed one as well. Once in place at the convergence of Market, Bush, and Battery Streets, the compelling group awaited dedication by President William McKinley in 1901.

In his relationship with Tilden, Phelan demonstrated his full commitment to art when a great artist was difficult to endure. Phelan perceived Tilden as erratic and inconsiderate when, for example, he offered spontaneously support for Phelan in his first U.S. Senate campaign and publicly opposed Phelan and endorsed his opponent during the reelection campaign of 1920. In a remarkable letter to his friend Fremont Older, Phelan reviewed his relationship with the sculptor and concluded that not only did he not understand Tilden's political behavior, he doubted that he should try to understand it. "As a general proposition, I think it is a real mistake to hold personal idiosyncrasies against a real artist. They are all freaks anyhow!" Not only did Phelan not hold Tilden's political about-face against him, he simultaneously enlisted Older's help for a new commission that would once more serve all the interests Phelan advanced, including Tilden's.

Uncharacteristically, though, Phelan drew a social line between the artist and himself. The patron never welcomed the artist to his social events, neither within his small circle of intimates nor his larger circle of friendly associations. Tilden's special communication skills would have been perceived as exciting, as an added and recommending accomplishment within the circles. Phelan's own interest in the problems associated with deafness was enhanced after the death of his secretary George Welch. Welch's young child was deaf too, and Phelan concerned himself with the educational options then being advanced for children with hearing disabilities. The degree to which Phelan's observations of Tilden's interpersonal problems as an adult may have influenced his convictions remains unknown. Yet, permeating Phelan's generous and unfailing assistance to Marguerite Welch and her children was Phelan's strong preference for educational options that were based on firm (not cruel) discipline. Perhaps he felt Tilden's had been lacking.

Gertrude Atherton

James D. Phelan's relationship with California's novelist Gertrude Atherton was altogether different. He admired her work and respected her independence. He provided her with emotional stability and solace within the elegant, though highly transient, world she created for herself. He gave and accepted friendship as further enhancements enriching his abundant life. For her part, Atherton cherished the weekends and special occasions that brought them together. She proclaimed him to be California's most refined and accomplished citizen, and she pondered abandoning California at the time of his death and would have but for her own family's presence there.

These two special California children first met in 1902, the year that Phelan concluded his third term as mayor and Atherton chose to return to the birth city, having successfully established her international reputation as a writer. The Bohemian Club, the locale of frequent Phelan-arranged literary parties, celebrated her return by organizing a banquet. Phelan's role in Atherton's homecoming recognition is unclear because of the destruction of

Douglas Tilden's California Volunteers *escaped destruction during the 1906 earthquake because of timing. James Duval Phelan's committee had selected Tilden's drawings and commissioned his work in 1904. When the earthquake struck, Tilden's bronze was in the casting stage — fortunately in Chicago! Tilden's* Serra *commission celebrated California's Spanish heritage. This one, the* California Volunteers, *celebrated America's victory over Spain. For Tilden's patron, history meant progress.*

Phelan's papers by the fire four years later. Atherton's biographer, Emily Wortis Leider, quotes an Atherton letter to her Macmillan publisher crediting the *Bulletin's* editor and others for the welcoming. Where Fremont Older became active in literary affairs his friend Phelan, the Bohemian Club's former president and its leading literary enthusiast, was close at hand.

In 1902, Atherton was forty-five years of age, four years older than Phelan. She was always cautious about revealing her age, and sensitive and attentive to her appearance as well. By all accounts, Atherton remained a striking figure even though she manifested inordinate concern over her aging. So great was Atherton's youth fixation that she underwent experimental medical treatments in order to maintain her productive energy (for writing).

In that same year Phelan was forty-one, but never evidenced any preoccupation whatever about his age. His appearance did concern him, at least to the extent of always being neatly groomed and finely tailored (including custom-made undersuits and shoes). He required fine foods — tastes cultivated and delineated by his European experience. The enthusiasm with which he also proffered select California wines and fine champagnes amid

San Jose State College's poetry society enjoyed a fall outing at Villa Montalvo in 1926. The student chapter, named for Edwin Markham, received James D. Phelan's steady encouragement. With him at the luncheon on the east terrace are (to Phelan's left) Helen Wills and Fremont Older. To Phelan's right are Gertrude Atherton and Cora Older. Profession Henry Meade Bland, seated with the full view of the Santa Clara Valley and facing Phelan, is flanked by his poetry students. The day was September 18, perhaps warm.

elegant dining, identified Phelan quite naturally as a refined advocate of gracious, if caloric, living. Though only about five feet seven inches tall, he was at his ease in evening attire, effective and compelling as master of ceremonies, and graciousness personified as host whether at Montalvo, the Shelbourne in Dublin, or the Ritz in Paris. As the years advanced, his cultivated mind and attractive manner heightened his popularity as an after-dinner speaker. He was the best informed and most engaging of his contemporaries. When the occasion allowed, he was also quite amusing.

By 1906, when the Phelan-Atherton post-fire correspondence commenced, California's daughter and San Francisco's favorite son were well acquainted. Atherton developed as loving an attachment to Phelan as her own emotional repressions allowed. In time, this fondness expressed itself in her great concern over Phelan's good health and well being. When he habitually retired to European watering spots to take fashionable "cures," Phelan did so because he found the experiences to be amusing, and he normally shared the good times with friends — Rudolph Spreckels or his devoted cousin George Duval. When Gertrude Atherton learned, as she put it, that he was "finally taking a thorough cure," she projected into the event a seriousness that Phelan hardly associated with such excursions. Quite seriously she asked, "I ... only hope you will continue to obey orders when you are dismissed! Will you???" Less alcohol was an integral part of such regimes, a great enhancement in Atherton's eyes.

When Florence Ellon, on the other hand, learned from a "cured" Phelan that he was "eschewing the juice of the grape" she assumed that he was merely depressed and needed cheering up. So she did her best: "Life is beautiful!" she wrote to him from Paris. "I love it and so do you! I can see the fire and flash in your eyes when you said 'Au Revoir'....I am feeling well and am told [I] look so." She responded to his rambling talk about grapes and vines as decoration by refocusing this attention. She wanted to know how his "big tree" was doing! Because the ground shared by these two ardent admirers was so limited, Phelan never introduced Ellon to Atherton. They meet only in his correspondence file.

More pertinent are the artistic comparisons between Atherton and Tilden and the quality and extent of Phelan's patronage. Before Atherton died at age ninety-one she produced more than fifty novels. Many were huge commercial successes, almost all were notable, and some brought her into the

Phelan's Exercise

Because James Duval Phelan's idea of exercise was limited to horseback riding and ballroom dancing, his weight increased ever so gradually from young adulthood in the one-hundred-and-fortyish range to one-hundred-and-seventy-four at his portly maximum. His tailors responded by adding quarter-inches, then halves, to his waist bands. Unlike Atherton and other friends who espoused health fads, particularly later in the twenties, Phelan relied upon standard medical practices that emanated from scientific investigations. He accepted the aging process as irreversible and concluded that life was to be enjoyed as fully as possible within the bounds of moderation. Of course, moderation should be taken as pleasantly and moderately as possible, too.

General Grant

With Gertrude Atherton, James D. Phelan shared his reminiscence of being seated across the table from General Ulysses S. Grant at a San Francisco wedding banquet in 1878. The former President had arrived from the Orient at the conclusion of his culminating world tour. Rather than touting to Atherton his family's position in local affairs, which allowed his attendance, Phelan humorously compared Grant with the incumbent in the White House. "I remember his stolidity and silence; he was as bad as Coolidge."

competitive arena with lastingly great American writers of the twentieth-century. She enjoyed widespread public recognition, an achievement she cultivated intensely and valued highly. She had mastered her craft, but her massive literary output would not withstand the test of time.

Tilden's artistry was, indeed, monumental in every way. The artist lived for his art and could not fathom why his celebrity did not remain uniformly evident between dedications. He was as incapable of cultivating mass opinion as he was unaware of emerging public relations methods that Atherton utilized in her relentless campaign for name recognition. Unlike Atherton, Tilden was financially dependent. When the demands for his art neared their apex he relinquished his teaching position with the University of California. The nature of his medium necessarily set uneven income as the standard, one aggravated by economic cycles and shifting interests and trends in public art. Atherton, conversely, recognized clearly that earning money through publishing was her only escape from intellectual bondage in her husband's family. Tilden, perhaps because of his disability, came of age within a protecting, special environment. In a sense, it was a tailored environment containing aspects of both dependency and freedom. Tilden's needs were chronic: financial and psychological. Atherton's early financial independence and her international social mobility helped greatly. They did not liberate her from the personal need for companionship, appreciation, and sustained emotional support. James Duval Phelan recognized and met that need. He was the sculptor's financial patron and interpersonal arbiter. He was the novelist's emotional patron, the most significant man in her mature life who understood her art and respected her person. He helped her and he even instructed her, but Phelan never attempted to impose his will or his desires upon her.

Correspondence

Within Phelan's correspondence the Atherton collection is the second largest — 201 letters from the author to Phelan. Atherton's prodigious output is exceeded, between the years 1906 and 1930, only by the regular letters of George L. Duval. Phelan's cousin and confidante from childhood penned 298 letters. His record was established with an advantage. Besides the social interplay, he and Phelan coordinated family business arrangements, and they lived a continent apart most of their lives. After Duval's early days in San

Francisco business, the two met mostly when Phelan passed through New York on business or en route to Europe. Occasionally they toured Europe together, but mostly Phelan tried to convince Duval to spend less time making money and more time enjoying it.

Phelan's outgoing correspondence to Duval and Atherton was different. He did not advise Atherton on the quality of her lifestyle. Phelan revealed himself more freely to Duval, a man who was also of great means (derived from business) and who retained the subcultural values both cousins imbibed in their youth. To both Atherton and Duval, Phelan was playful, supportive, understanding, and always a font of practical help and, occasionally, inspiration. But most of all, Phelan was always there, as close as the other side of a stamp, for whatever concerns weighed upon these special loved ones. Duval and Atherton were appreciative; Phelan was enriched.

Phelan loved dividing his time between the California sunshine and corresponding, particularly to Atherton. He could be nostalgic or amusing as the fancy struck him. Always engaging, and never a bore, Phelan undoubtedly found silence uncomfortable. With Atherton he enjoyed a warm rapport. Both shared racial views that were so prominent throughout America, including Phelan's California anti-Asian fixation. They exchanged popular, pseudoscientific books lamenting the passage of the white race. Although Atherton's work, unlike Phelan's, provided far less a forum for the expression of racism, her biographer, Leider, makes her one in the spirit with Phelan.

Even when Phelan felt compelled to instruct Atherton in politics his letters exuded charm and good humor. Atherton, as a famous writer, enjoyed access to the media and took advantage of her opportunities, frequently through letters to *The New York Times*. During World War I, for example, before America became a participant and when Senator Phelan was attempting to advance President Wilson's neutrality policy, Phelan chided Atherton for publicly allying herself with a more pro-British, interventionist position. A British correspondent, Phelan thought, was nudging her to favor war for Americans. Phelan characterized her actions: "You give him bread and he demands roast beef — something with blood in it!"

Atherton, expectedly, enjoyed corresponding too. Reporting from New York's Algonquin Hotel where she had established residence to write, she shared with Phelan her surprise party with eight men. A mutual friend, Joseph Redding, actually read his new opera to the gathering — a forgettable

Phelan on Bryan

Gertrude Atherton believed that Wilson's first Secretary of State, William Jennings Bryan, was a traitor. He opposed the President's increasingly forceful responses to the German provocations. James Duval Phelan perceived the aging Democratic stalwart as benign. When Bryan resigned from the President's Cabinet, Phelan wrote Atherton that "the Administration has been strengthened,..." Bryan "is essentially an evangelist or propagandist ... holding idealistic theories...." In fact, "the strength that has come to the Administration by the withdrawal of Bryan may, by properly interpreting our attitude to foreign governments, avert war....If the rest of the world was as benevolent as Bryan, the lion and the lamb would lie down together in perfect security, and the lamb would not be on the inside...."

Playfully Phelan closed: "If Bryan were cast away in the icy regions of the North and ... driven to a choice between cannibalism and death, he would try to convince the lone survivor by a powerful argument that it would be necessary for the peace ... that they should arbitrate, and that it was the Divine's ordination that the fittest survive. Failing of arbitration, I believe he would enter into a suicide pact. That, I believe is his character. When I see him, I will put this question before him, and let you know whether I guess aright."

Gossip Paid Off

One 1910 Gertrude Atherton letter to James D. Phelan was exceptionally rich in gossip, making Phelan privy to the private life of an otherwise esteemed member of the British Parliament, T. P. O'Connor, leader of the Irish Parliamentary Party.

O'Connor's wife visited Atherton after the O'Connors separated. Atherton never particularly liked Mrs. O'Connor, but found her to be "entertaining." Perhaps Atherton's reservation was that the woman named her dog "Mr. Phelan." According to Atherton, Mrs. O'Connor "has evidently conquered the doldrums and was very funny about Tom. It seems that this Greek lady has had him in chains for twenty years, and has had three others besides — to which, apparently, he made no objection. Far from it, indeed." When one of the three, 'Uncle Teddy,' died, T. P. "went in mourning for him, as one of the pall bearers! Then the lady got lonesome and insisted that 'Tom' come and live in the house with her. So Tom moved over and never returned. But he has settled some shares ... on Mrs. O'C, and she came over as soon as he departed."

When the periodically touring "Tay Pay" (T. P.) appeared in Washington and San Francisco, Phelan dexterously stood aside and allowed Garret McEnerney, dean of the California Bar, introduce and vouch for O'Connor before Father Peter Yorke and the San Francisco Irish. Yorke verbally executed both O'Connor and McEnerney — ostensibly for their international politics. Phelan had the inside story from Atherton much earlier and wisely watched from the sidelines.

experience. Rather than his opera, she discussed Joe. He was an Algonquin resident as well, and Atherton pretended to need Phelan's guidance: "Do you think he would be a safe person to ask to unhook me, at a pinch?" The hotel maids went home at ten o'clock, so when Atherton returned from social events, if she did not knock on Redding's door, her only recourse was "the elevator boy!" Chat such as this found its way onto her manuscripts, which contained a panorama of people, plots, and occasional politics. En route Atherton offered Phelan her personal reviews in miniature of the New York theatre and opera, the productions as well as the performers — alerting him about what to see next.

Elsewhere, but with less lightheartedness, Atherton promised to introduce her bachelor patron to a real beauty she encountered at her publisher's office. Elizabeth Jordan was "a beauty and very clever and amusing." Changing the subject, and as was the custom between them, Atherton concluded by sharing. In this case, it was her experience at the recent Columbia University commencement and President and Mrs. Nicholas Murray Butler's post-commencement luncheon. All the women in attendance were appendages of their husbands whose fields were education and the arts. "I was the only person on my own."

Almost as an after thought she appended, "I long to hear that you have been elected." The reason why her interest in her friend's primary campaign for the United States Senate ranked so low may be a combination of her disinterest in politics generally and her focus on her own life. She was supremely interested in Phelan, but she never shared his interests the way he shared hers — spontaneously. Certainly if he required her comprehensive attention to politics (as he requested specific campaign help occasionally), he would not have been the James Duval Phelan whose company she so loved. Phelan simply gave more than he received. That was the role of patron. That he never noticed, and she occasionally did, only added to his stature in her eyes.

Sensitivity was Phelan's hallmark, but he understood substance as well. He commented occasionally on the peripheral merits of Atherton's work or he compared one of her novels with another. In that context, of course, one of the writer's successes merely exceeded another. He read her *Crystal Cup* in serial form and correctly advised her that it would not receive the popular acclaim (sales) she enjoyed with *Black Oxen*. Delicately and obliquely he characterized the theme of *Black Oxen* as "a message to the public, which cannot be found every day." That novel, according to Atherton's biographer, Leider, was "one of her most powerful and accomplished efforts and her biggest commercial success...." Also, in great measure, it was inspired by Atherton's personal subjection to the 1920s Steinach Treatment which "consisted of mild X-ray stimulation of the ovaries." The subject and the inspiration hardly remained separate in the book.

Knowing, yet restrained, Phelan continued: "The 'Crystal Cup' has not the same dramatic force, and, to my taste, is too conversational....I am sure the book will sell on the prestige which you have so deservedly won by your other books." And softening even further his criticism, Phelan observed that they were in the new "age of Jazz. I think the movie pictures have corrupted the public taste for works that are essentially literature." Without classifying the *Crystal Cup* within any hierarchy of literature, Phelan still offered an excuse for what he considered limited sales potential. It was the corruption of public taste, not the limitations of her literary expression.

Being even more supporting, and even a bit directing, Phelan commented upon her highly successful *Conqueror*, a glorification based upon the life of Alexander Hamilton. He had just completed reading the *Glorious Apollo* by E. Barrington, a work he characterized as "substantially a true biographical sketch [of Lord Byron], amplified by the imaginative art." Her own use of Hamilton, Phelan wrote, "was so successful, that I am now surprised that you did not follow up that line, and meet what is apparently a popular demand for 'glorified biographies,' in novel form."

Phelan's more substantive work on Atherton's behalf extended down to basic research as well as commissioning expert secondary accounts of historical events which he then conveyed to her during the research phase of her writings. Phelan's tangible assistance stood behind her early historical romance *Rezanov*, the story of a Russian nobleman-adventurer on the California coast. Tradition had it that Count Nikolai Rezanov had fallen in love with Concepcion Arguello, the young daughter of the Spanish commander of the Presidio of San Francisco. Phelan hired Ina Coolbrith, former editor of the *Overland Monthly* and librarian-tutor to Jack London, to research the subject and convey her typed report to Atherton. Thus, Phelan assisted both the declining poet of California's past and its novelist of the future.

In 1914, Atherton dedicated her *Story of California* to Phelan. Its publication was timed to coincide with his first campaign for the United States

James Duval Phelan appears here with Mary Pickford and Douglas Fairbanks. Phelan declined to invest in the new and growing film industry because he felt that he knew little about it as a business enterprise. Also, he rejected the motion picture as an art form. Most of the luminaries whom Phelan entertained, beyond politics, claimed their distinctions from high culture. Film stars could be beautiful, sensitive, and even creative and intelligent. Their product, Phelan believed, was debasing the standards of American culture. This conviction, among so many others, differentiated Phelan's guest lists at Montalvo from William Randolph Hearst's at his enchanted castle, San Simeon.

Reincarnations

Gertrude Atherton's apparent belief that she was the reincarnation of Aspasia, the intelligent and beautiful consort of the ancient Pericles, at best humored Phelan. According to Atherton's biographer, Leider, the novelist did not originate the idea of her own reincarnation. She received it from a former actress, Cora Potter, who had turned to the occult and became captivated with mysticism. Atherton met Potter in Monte Carlo in 1925, at the time Potter was convinced that she herself was an incarnation of Mary, Queen of Scots.

As was his way, James D. Phelan encouraged Atherton in her literary enterprises, particularly in the inspiration and research phase. In this case he brought to her attention obscure, foreign language works on the relationship of Aspasia and Pericles. Phelan's familiarity with the bibliography of the subject rested upon his lifelong reading in the classics.

Phelan's interest in Atherton's life as Aspasia seems not to have been motivated by burning concern over who her real-life counterpart for Pericles was. The occultist Potter said it was Lord Northcliffe, editor of the London *Times*, who died in 1922. Leider disagrees. Her guess is that Phelan, not Northcliffe, filled the role of Pericles "as leader, husband, and soul mate" for Atherton. At Phelan's own death in 1930, Atherton "felt orphaned, outcast. Like Aspasia bereft of Pericles she stood 'alone in the path, her arms hanging listlessly'."

Senate. He had cooperated by providing photography to illustrate her chapter on the California missions and had lent her books from his library collection on California history. Phelan himself clarified her portrayal of the rehabilitation of San Francisco following the earthquake and fire. Further, he assisted her by providing research he had been independently subsidizing.

Phelan and Rudolph Spreckels had underwritten a book-length manuscript by progressive journalist Franklin Hichborn. When the highly regarded investigative reporter published his work the following year it appeared in limited edition entitled *"The System" as Uncovered by the San Francisco Graft Prosecution*. Phelan and Spreckels did not reveal their subventions for the pro-prosecution book by the knowledgeable and attentive Hichborn. Phelan did make its essence available to Atherton, however, for her prior use, with Hichborn's permission.

The most historically significant use of Hichborn's Phelan-supported manuscript had to await the prize-winning book by Professor Walton Bean of the University of California, *Boss Ruef's San Francisco*, which did not appear until 1952. Bean's reliable and readable account accepts the Hichborn theme but, like Atherton, failed to note San Francisco's unique ethnic factor in the city's social and cultural life. Phelan's own diminished ethnicity denied even him that insight. His currency in the field of California history did allow him to offer Atherton the results of Stanford Professor E. D. Adams' archival research relating to English designs on California prior to American acquisition.

The time he lavished on Atherton's work reveals Phelan's unrestrained generosity. When he spent this time says even more about the importance of their relationship. On *election day*, 1914, the day he stood for the Democratic nomination for U.S. Senator, he composed for her literary use a comprehensive review of both the earthquake and fire as well as the graft prosecution. In the de-emphasized mid-portion of his letter, he noted

> I closed my campaign....Saturday night I spoke to four thousand people....
> I expect to survive the primary, after which the real battle will begin ... for
> the final election on November 3rd. The primary held today is an elimina-
> tion contest, as you are aware.

His last clause was generous too because he could not be sure that she did understand the system through which he sought his own fulfillment. After all, what could he assume of a literary artist, yet citizen-friend, who had him mark her sample election ballot so that she would know how to cast votes?

Phelan's literary and cultural sophistication allowed him to share, even enjoy Atherton's imaginative flights into antiquity. At the same time his common-sense approach to this life and his skepticism about the next allowed him more than perspective and detachment. With the complete discretion of a gentleman he pursued Atherton's Aspasis fixation for private amusement. He obtained a letter of introduction from Atherton and took it upon himself to meet the actress Cora Potter in Europe during his 1926 trip.

Phelan and Colonel Harry S. Howland sought Potter out in Monte Carlo and Howland noted in a diary the mystic's fixation on Atherton as Aspasia. He quotes Potter's flattering portrayal of Aspasia and the intellectual and physical attributes she likened to Atherton's. Potter had told all this to Atherton the year before and repeated it to the undoubtedly straight-faced Phelan and Howland. Recording what Potter told them, Howland added that Atherton was to achieve even greater perfection as a writer and that Aspasia was the "'opportunity to reveal herself and give the world a great picture of an extraordinary woman.'"

The humor with which the retired soldier and the insatiable experience-seeker received Potter's message and its acceptance by Atherton is muted but evident, even in the sanitized diary. Phelan and Howland concluded: "'Mrs. A. went away [from Potter] promising to dig into her inner consciousness and find her soul as it existed five hundred years before Christ.'" What they exchanged over brandy and cigars either never found its way into the diary or the more sensitive nephew, Sullivan, expunged it.

Phelan's patronage of artists allowed him to share their excitement and their inspiration. Through personal association Phelan enjoyed greater intimacy with the artists than the artists shared even with their intended audiences. That, of course, remains a major benefit and motivator for patrons. Being a patron, however, hardly required Phelan to believe whatever fantasies inspired the artists. In the case of Atherton and her identification with Aspasia, he succeeded in restraining his impishness and Holland's comedy, because of his respect for Atherton herself, even without regard for her literary and commercial success that he so admired.

By the eve of the First World War Atherton was already quite comfortable and open in sharing family problems with Phelan. She solicited his help

Colonel Harry S. Howland, who had taken up residence in one of Phelan's guest cottages at Montalvo, amused himself at writing or, as Phelan explained to Atherton, "driving his own typewriter." Phelan provided the retired officer shelter and provisions augmented by liberal amounts of spending money. For his part Howland speculated in oil stocks, served as the fourth on double dates with Phelan and various ladies, and offered lively male company on other occasions.

When the two toured Europe in the summer of 1926, Phelan's last visit to the culture he so loved, Howland kept their diary. The intent seems to have been its publication, but only after the two gentlemen and their intimates enjoyed all the uncensored belly laughs in private. Phelan, in fact, circulated the lively parts through Noël Sullivan and asked him to rewrite pages that reflected poorly upon women of their acquaintance.

Outdoor dining upon the broad east terrace was James D. Phelan's favored mode for luncheons. The gathering normally honored Californians for their achievements. Celebrities and friends from more distant places were always made to feel at ease as well. Following the meals, Phelan's guests gathered at the outdoor theater located west of the pool for entertainments or awards.

Guests at a luncheon on April 29, 1921, honoring Edwin Markham included George Sterling and Cora Older.

in obtaining a position for her son-in-law after supporting him, her daughter Muriel, and their three children for nearly a year. Unburdening herself somewhat, she told the man with the unlimited attentiveness, "I do not resent this … and I love to write and never feel any ill effects from it, still I think that a man should support his family." The next generation appeared even more unorthodox. Her granddaughter Florence's marriage seemed to be concluding in 1928, but for different reasons. Atherton confided in Phelan:

> Her story is a strange one, and very modern … [her husband] seems to have been possessed with a morbid desire to possess her mentally, experiment and … analyze her to death. Try to force her to have affairs and then carry on like a madman if he thought there was any danger. In other words a swollen itching ego. This trying to make something new and very modern of marriage has been a failure in every case I have witnessed….Florence was fascinated at first but she … has had enough of it.

Always true to form, Phelan maintained his independent interests in Atherton's grandchildren and did what he could for them unobtrusively.

Sterling and Others

Phelan's artistic understanding, tolerance, and compassion was displayed most fully in his relationship with George Sterling. The San Francisco poet laureate truly suffered unto death, agonies so commonly assumed as side effects of a bohemian life and creative mind. Sterling's letters to Phelan reveal the innocence of a boy despite the riotous indulgences of his adult life. Too strongly influenced in his formative years by Ambrose Bierce, the overshadowed Sterling failed in his attempt for national recognition as a poet and writer. In an unburdening and revealing letter to his patron, Sterling confessed the utter collapse of his once-hopeful New York literary career. Unlike Atherton, Sterling was unable to succeed beyond California, and unlike Tilden he was unable to extract satisfaction from his California accomplishments. He admitted to Phelan that never had he been more diligent and more sober and for so long, yet the eastern publishers rejected his best but accepted his worst. "Marooned" in the East, he respectfully appealed for cash sufficient to cover his debts, a ticket home, and camping equipment. As collateral the poet-bohemian offered patron-capitalist the copyrights on an unwritten 100 page ode to Yosemite. Phelan loved Sterling as a troubled artist, and he helped him without violating Sterling's own sense of integrity. Beyond financial patronage, Phelan's generosity of spirit was monumental.

Sterling responded as his fluctuating condition allowed, expressing gratitude for Phelan's steady recognition and encouragement. Throughout his years of physical and emotional torment, to the very eve of his suicide by the cyanide he habitually carried, Sterling offered his own poems, at Phelan's suggestion, for incorporation into the souvenir books commemorating Montalvo's annual best. Sterling's cameo appearances at the Villa became interludes during which he shared recognition and appreciation. Confronted with a failed career and a tattered personal life, Sterling captured the beautiful less often and less well. Unfortunately, he could claim no other reason for being.

Throughout his lifetime, Phelan offered support and encouragement to a vast array of individuals and institutions, beyond the arts as well as within. The exact form of his patronage among artists followed upon his perceptions of the individuals' specific situations. Tilden needed income and recognition. Atherton need acceptance, comfort, and appreciation. Sterling needed more than Phelan was capable of giving. And in each case the patron stepped forward and gave of himself and of his treasure. He did so for the enhancement of beauty, the refinement of culture, and the gratification of self. Phelan was kind, sensitive, and enduringly solicitous.

In Tilden's case, Phelan patronized first-class talent. Atherton had her competitive moments and remained a writer of international consequence in her own time. Then there was Sterling, promising at first, unfulfilled, then dead. Phelan stood by him to the very end. In 1926, San Francisco put its poet Bohemian to rest in style, in state in the majestic rotunda of the classical new City Hall. Like Phelan, Sterling had been born into Catholicism and even had entered the seminary for the study of the priesthood. When he abandoned Catholic practice, Sterling did so with a vengeance, ultimately to his own earthly destruction and death. The prudent and refined Phelan was the one who stood at the casket's edge, hand upon the pall, offering the world's final appreciation. Those who shared his words concluded that the patron wordsmith-orator had outshone his poet. No wonder that Phelan remained San Francisco's choice for articulating the city's deepest feelings. In the midst of loss the community turned to him for expression, as at the deaths of William McKinley, Warren G. Harding, and Woodrow Wilson. Phelan was their San Francisco eulogist.

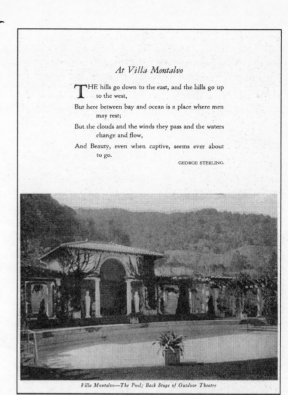

At Villa Montalvo

THE hills go down to the east, and the hills go up to the west,
But here between bay and ocean is a place where men may rest;
But the clouds and the winds they pass and the waters change and flow,
And Beauty, even when captive, seems ever about to go.

GEORGE STERLING.

Villa Montalvo—The Pool; Back Stage of Outdoor Theatre

Villa Montalvo was a haven during George Sterling's troubled years. He lived for the poetic expression of beauty and love, but failed to earn critical acclaim. Yet, James Duval Phelan sustained and encouraged Sterling, without reserve.

Maude Fay

The historical connection of Phelan to opera most often noted is his attendance with his sister at the great Caruso's last San Francisco performance on the evening before the great earthquake and fire of 1906. Phelan had enjoyed the performance greatly and undoubtedly regretted the star's hasty departure from the shaken city. Phelan's interest actually began earlier and in a manner that is both expected, yet different. In 1902 Phelan became the patron who stood quietly behind the operatic career of Maude Fay.

Fay, nineteen years of age at the time, was the young sister of Phelan's confidant, Charles W. Fay. Together she and Charles were but two of the four boys and three girls in the Fay family. The Phelans and the Fays had been close from their family beginnings in gold rush San Francisco. James Duval Phelan was eight years older than Charles Fay and twenty-two years older than Maude. Charles had done well in the street paving business (which James D. Phelan may have helped establish) and graduated into political management by the time his sister was but thirteen. Unlike Phelan, Fay remained closer throughout life to the doctrines of their parents' religion.

In 1902, Charles Fay was earning a respectable $300 per month as clerk to the San Francisco board of supervisors. He and his brothers could not provide for their talented and promising young sister's expenses, those associated with serious pursuit of a career as a prima donna. They could hardly be expected to visualize what manner of life stretched before her. Phelan understood. Maude required voice training, wardrobe, travel, even regular living expenses. The gifted youngster possessed a gloriously clear voice and extraordinary good looks. Over the next twenty years Maude Fay relied upon Phelan for continuing financial and moral support and encouragement. Under his patronage she began her serious study for the operatic stage in Dresden. Her early success took place in Munich where she secured a place as the leading soprano at the Munich opera house. Dutiful to her patron, she regularly reported the progress and recognitions she encountered. By 1909, Phelan was replenishing her expense account, taking a businesslike approach to the matter. Fay had established herself as a professional artist and Phelan, in essence, extended her $5,821.77 against her earnings at five percent. Her brother Charles co-signed with her. In the summer of 1910, Phelan witnessed her London debut. His letters home revealed as much about his candor as they did about his protégée. To his chief secretary Thomas Mahony, Charles Fay's colleague, Phelan offered an unqualified statement of Maude's success. To Soffie Harvey his reserve was evident.

Back in Munich, Fay continued performing to filled houses and highly appreciative audiences, sparkling at times with the German nobility. The king of Saxony, she wrote, presented her with a gold medal. She had enjoyed Phelan's visit, updated him on the activities of Bavarian royalty, and regretted that he had not seen her refurbished and attractive apartments. Her goal, certainly comparable to Atherton's in literature, was a triumphal return to America. Her hope was to open San Francisco's projected new Opera House in the role of Elisabeth, the soprano lead in Richard Wagner's *Tannhauser*. In 1913, however, the young artist's hopes were considerably in advance of Phelan's reorganization of the opera house scheme. Once war with Germany erupted, Fay's Bavarian recommendee for director of a San Francisco opera company not only became unacceptable, Fay's very association with Germany was to become a personal and, therefore, professional handicap.

If Gertrude Atherton was ever guilty of an unpublished thought, she made up for her omissions via personal correspondence. She even took the questionable liberty (in Fay's case) of publishing what was private. The record of Atherton's relationship with the younger, more attractive, and less experienced artist began somewhat less positively than Atherton's biographer suggests. Atherton, in fact, began on a negative note. As early as 1906 Atherton assured Phelan that she would "keep Maud [sic] Fay up to the mark…," offering gratuitously that Fay was level headed and would not need discipline. In her letter back to San Francisco, Atherton played opera critic to Phelan, who read a decidedly mixed review of the protégée.

Atherton explained, "She looked extraordinarily young and appealing and acted well, although she has not yet learned the rudiments of gesture, and she sang … remarkably well considering that a Wagner role must fit like a glove before an artist can do it and herself full justice….after a few years of training here she will become [a] great artist and develop a great voice…." The critical flaw, according to Atherton was Fay's voice, "as sexless and coldly sweet as a choir boy's soprano. It is almost remote…." Atherton's automatic access to the media of the day and her relentless need for subject matter placed in jeopardy the privacy of everyone she knew, Phelan excepted. The

Maude Fay's clear and lovely voice matched the innocence and charm of her handsome good looks. Together the combination promised, with training, operatic success. Her misfortune was her identification with German opera during America's World War I period of intolerance for all things German. Her own political innocence and Gertrude Atherton's unkindness all but terminated Maude Fay's promising career.

Helen Wills drew James D. Phelan in charcoal during their Atlantic crossing in 1926, Aboard the Majestic *bound for New York, she sketched while he composed — poetry to California's sun child.*

result caused Fay great distress and caused Phelan considerable imposition. Fay, however, hardly helped her own cause.

Fay's identification was with Wagnerian opera. As her career in Munich attracted greater acclaim, her appreciation of German culture and nationhood grew as well. She had become a respected artist within a society that valued her talents and encouraged her aspirations. To reject the society that accepted her so fully would hardly be easy. Not yet secure enough to return to America in triumph, Maude Fay found herself on the wrong side of both World War I and Gertrude Atherton. Determining which was more devastating is difficult. Together, though, their result was clear. Gertrude Atherton and World War I reversed the trajectory of Fay's promising career.

In the fall of 1914, the contending European powers were decimating each other's best regiments across the broad western front. Using the U.S. State Department's diplomatic pouch, Fay wrote to Phelan the news of her upcoming opera season. With this she began including her commentary of life and morale behind the German lines. She recognized the horrors of war but added that "here in Munich were it not for the sad faces and mourning one would not know that the most horrible war the world has ever known is going on now...." Approvingly she continued, "...Germany has success & her enthusiasm, marvelous patriotism, unity & trust in her Kaiser ... assure her a victorious outcome."

Phelan's campaigns for the Senate distracted him through the fall. He answered her letter only after his successful general election. His answer was rather light, perhaps just trying to regain command over his abundant correspondence. He expressed his gratitude to her brother, Charles, for the successful management of the campaign. Her other brothers, as well, constituted "a tower of strength." Phelan continued, "so all the Fay family are rejoicing in my victory." Signaling his own international views, he concluded, "It is well for America that its battles are battles of ballots." Her enthusiasm for Germany's victory in war evidently overran the implications of his subtlety.

By the spring the Senator reported on his personal lobbying on her behalf with the Metropolitan Opera. Success would have meant her leaving Munich and returning home to America. Quite guardedly he wrote to Fay that "the roads of the Metropolitan seem very hard, but I believe by perseverance you should make an impression." He had talked with Otto Kahn in

New York but made no apparent progress. He promised Fay that if another opportunity to help presented itself, he would try again.

This paragraph was the significant one for Fay. Sensitive to her anxiety, Phelan buried it (bad news) in mid-letter, between California events and a concluding, perhaps again too-subtle paragraph of far greater importance. As an illustration for Fay, Phelan summarized his own behavior relative to the mounting foreign policy crisis between Germany, at war with England and France, and the United States, holding as best it could to its policy of non-belligerency. Had the protégée followed her patron's example of personal restraint, her career objectives may have been reached. Certainly, her career would have been more serene.

"Following the attitude of the [Woodrow Wilson Democratic] Administration," Phelan made clear to Fay, "I have maintained strict neutrality, so leave to the more ardent the discussion of war prospects." The artist's response remained ardently pro-German. She noted the popular German feeling that England was dictating American policies which, under the guise of official neutrality, allowed the United States to provide munitions for the withering Allies. Fay even defended Germany's sinking of the *Lusitania*, which with Germany's subsequent declaration of unrestricted submarine warfare goaded President Wilson into his call for America's entry into the war against Germany. "About the *Lusitania* … England must take the entire blame.…And to think England armed her & let the passengers believe they were on a passenger ship.…It is more than humane what [Germany] has already accomplished."

Phelan, now a U.S. Senator kept Fay's confidence, but the other female artist in his life did not. Atherton received Fay's equally unguarded correspondence and reacted publicly. The novelist had reversed her position from German sympathy to her own verbal belligerency. In her state of militaristic excitement, Atherton published in *The New York Times* one of the personal letters Fay had sent to her. The letter was pro-German and in it Fay defended her decision to remain in wartime Germany. Fay shared with Atherton her unrestrained joy at having done her part for the German war effort through one charity performance after another. "My coffers are empty," she wrote to Atherton, "but I feel I've put a good load into my experience box — and enriched my ideals and belief in humanity. For this I must eternally thank these good Germans.…"

Phelan shared traditional views on the subject of marriage. For ordinary persons the demands of domesticity were arduous enough. For artists they could be overwhelming.

On his way to the Bohemian Grove play during the summer of 1925, Phelan took time out to explain to Atherton that the production "Wings" was to have an original score "by a man named Edwards, who was so highly sensitive, poor soul, that he commit [sic] suicide … just as his work was completed … he had to give up his young son to a vixen of a wife, who could not understand his artistic yearnings. Art," Phelan concluded, "is a jealous mistress, and I think that great artists should not be embarrassed by baggage."

Softening Disappointments

In 1921, when she was 38 and James D. Phelan was 60, Maude Fay rethought her strategy. "I have eaten the dust of humility in my own country," she confided in her patron. "I must return to N.Y. through Italy & Europe....I cannot believe that a woman in my years-strong & healthy—in excellent voice & filled with ambition for my career alone—is meant to sit back & go to seed." She sought renewed patronage that would enable her to study new roles in Italy, reestablish her European pre-war reputation and return home to an enhanced American career. As ever, the patron responded. Only this time Fay dallied in San Francisco as Phelan set off for Asia in the early stages of his round-the-world tour. By then a new character had entered her stage, one who was to soften and grace her decision to relinquish her quest for American recognition. She announced her intention to marry Navy Captain Powers Symington. Instead of directly stating the end of her professional career (and no longer needing Phelan's recent, generous subvention), Fay wrote that she would reserve his check to keep up her music. "It will be my fund for my art life."

True to himself, Phelan responded with additional benevolence: wedding gifts of a Steinway piano from San Francisco's fashionable Sherman Clay, an elegant tea service, and instructions that Downey and Soffie Harvey's gift be selected by Downey and paid for by Phelan's office. Montalvo, of course, was readied for the exclusive honeymoon use. Phelan's secretary Thomas B. Doyle closed off the Villa to visitors and left the housekeeper on call for the bride and groom. Fay wrote to Phelan in gratitude, "Of course I am the happiest woman in the world....Surely one woman you have made happy!"

Fay's naivete, extraordinary indeed, was betrayed by Atherton's act of public exposure. With absolute disregard for Fay's rights to privacy, Atherton published the text of Fay's personal letter in *The New York Times*. Atherton added her own self-righteous lecture on President Wilson's conduct of foreign affairs. The significant difference between the literary and the performing artists whom Phelan patronized was not their severely limited understanding of the dynamics of politics. It was the assuredness with which one assumed that the world required her to expose the other's presumed lack of patriotism or, worse, treason. Presumably, Atherton's attempt at character assassination had no ulterior motivation, such as the destruction of an ascending rival for Phelan's attentions.

Atherton continued in her own correspondence with Phelan, advancing the interests of her friend Marcia van Dresser over Fay for an opportunity with the Metropolitan. "Maude Fay will never be an artist to her dying day," Atherton persisted, "because she is not a musician....No doubt, however, she can pull many more wires ... and has immense magnetism off the stage. It is a remarkable fact that she has none on....I have wiped her off the slate."

Now as a United States Senator Phelan found himself stuck between the two California women whose extraordinary indiscretions created a public embarrassment. In character, he remained the gentleman peacemaker. Fay agreed to bury the hatchet because Phelan would be appreciative. She did not do so with good grace. In New York, having returned from a Germany that was showing the increasing stress of total war, Fay expressed her views. "Mrs. A. is the *only* person ever claiming to be a friend to me who has persistently *hurt* me in the Press. I have been bored with her vulgar & stupid write-up about me ever since my appearance in London....I have no respect for her whatever—no ill will either—just rarely ever think of her." Despite all this, Fay agreed to abide by Phelan's wishes and let the Atherton matter die.

Fay noted in a companion letter that with the departure of his sister Mollie and his niece Gladys Doyle from his luxurious Washington residence, the Senator was left to his "Bachelor freedom." She announced her own scheduled arrival and playfully said that she should stay with friends. Otherwise, "we might not be able to convince Washington that ours is a brother & sister friendship!" Their social contacts continued through the years of her professional disappointments at home.

She was scheduled to have opened as Elsa in Wagner's *Lohengrin* at the Chicago Opera only to have the entire season cancelled on the eve of America's entry into war against Germany. Not pleased with the quality of her own work, she suffered great anguish — on hold at the breakthrough point of her career. She wished to persevere, feeling that to do otherwise would guarantee a life of doubt and regret. She asked Phelan privately (he should not tell her brothers) for support, adding: "If you feel I am a poor speculation I beg of you not for a moment to consider friendship in anything." When she asked, Phelan provided. A "Thousand thanks," she offered, "for the note & check — Real chance may come to me.…Words express very little of what I feel in appreciation of your kindness — I shall try to give proof of it." And she did her best, spending the next three years endeavoring to overcome the pro-German classification that haunted her career.

Phelan persisted in character through the years doing all he could to heal the personal injury between these California protégées — Atherton and Fay. For her part, Fay remained forever grateful to the patron who created for her "a dream career and life." She even graced the transfer of Phelan's patronage to a performing artist in what was to become a revolutionized field, women's athletics. On the occasion of Helen Wills' stunning series of tennis victories on the Riviera during the spring of 1926, Phelan celebrated the American girl's accomplishments by hosting a banquet in her honor. His primary guests included all Californians who happened to be in Paris at the time of the young beauty's European triumphs. His banquet program blended high and popular culture. Maude Fay shared her cultivated talents with her patron, his banquet guests, and his new protégée. Thereafter Phelan signaled for the lights to dim. The new machine flickered, the silver screen came alive, and the overpowering young Helen Wills took command.

Fay quietly withdrew from that special after-dinner screen performance and stole away to the happiness she shared with her husband who had entered private business in Paris. She had had her day. Helen Wills, beginning her own career, would go on to dominate world tennis competition throughout Phelan's lifetime and continue through the 1930s. She was a first-class talent and the last one to whom California's patron extraordinary was to offer recognition and encouragement.

Phelan's support of a sculptor, a writer, a sports star, and a failed poet merely represents the most dramatic salients within Phelan's broadly

James D. Phelan was most comfortable in the role of mentor to talented people. His highly cultivated tastes in poetry and literature, art and music, and finally even gentile sports like tennis, all brought out the best of his generosity and encouragement. The success and recognition of his protégé was the only reward he sought.

James Duval Phelan delighted in the public presence of Helen Wills — his ideal California woman. Because her celebrity was so great, Phelan considered her even above the natural envy of here contemporaries. Free too, perhaps, from the contentiousness among protégées. To recognize her French tennis victories, Phelan hosted this formal banquet in Paris. All Californians were invited. Though close to Phelan (sharing the head of the table to his left), Wills may not have noticed the quiet, early departure of Maude Fay whom she had supplanted.

distributed patronage. These are the most easily isolated cases, and they clearly display a direct relationship of talent to critical acceptance. Phelan's patronage of the prima donna was not so clear, and her equation of talent to acclaim is far more difficult to establish. Phelan enjoyed being a patron. Evaluating progress and determining ultimate artistic worth was not pleasing so Phelan deferred that task.

More lastingly significant than the individual careers that Phelan enhanced is his institutional patronization, which culminated in his ultimately successful extension of the San Francisco Civic Center. His political insights, financial acumen, and his comfortable associations within the cultural and economic elites of San Francisco resulted in the creation of the city's Opera House and War Memorial concert and arts center. Harmoniously designed and located in accord with the principles of the City Beautiful plan, the two neoclassical structures complemented in style and location the imposing post-fire City Hall. Phelan's personal generosity assisted, as well, in transforming disputed options into functioning realities of beauty and grace. This legacy has enriched generations.

Chapter Seventeen

Host of Montalvo

James D. Phelan conceived of Montalvo not as a hideaway for Gertrude Atherton or a station where a debilitated magnate might recoup from the ardors of business and political life. He intended that Montalvo serve him in exuberant celebration of beauty and refinement. Each celebration was to be enjoyed in the company of those whose tastes appreciated the beautiful. Given Phelan's temperament and refinement, Villa Montalvo simply extended logically from his gracious personality and cultivated lifestyle.

Gertrude Atherton in her own celebrated autobiography, Adventures of A Novelist, *proclaimed Montalvo the possessor of the finest view of any country estate in America. Always pursuing the refinements life offered persons of her self-assured station, she awarded Montalvo her top mark. Having lodged virtually everywhere and having seen most everything, her ranking at least was informed. She enjoyed her friend's estate when he gathered and banqueted hundreds of citizens whose service to the nation he recognized; she also partook of Phelan's intimate evenings among his closest friends.*

James Duval Phelan lived the popular California outdoor lifestyle. With or without noted guests such as Ethel Barrymore (middle of lower photo) the urbane bachelor enjoyed splashing in the water with his "rubber duckie."

Just when Gertrude Atherton began staying over in Phelan's homes is unclear. As soon after the fire as he was able to rent a San Francisco residence for himself and his sister, Phelan sent Atherton the new address. Thereafter, she apologized for having left her bags behind in Mollie's room and promised to have them collected. Once Montalvo was complete, Atherton was a secure member of its inner circle. She and her daughter received invitations to the special events that California's host extraordinary staged, as well as encouragements to remain. On occasion, Phelan even offered Atherton the opportunity to take up residence. "Why not ... go into seclusion at 'Villa Montalvo'," he wrote. "You could sit in the Spanish court and dream the days away...you are welcome to it as a workshop, with the only danger of weekend interruption and disturbances." Sometimes she accepted; sometimes she declined. Phelan understood both responses; neither required an explanation.

She had settled into the old Lyndon hotel, down the road in Los Gatos, during the winter of 1928. She did not tell Phelan. When he learned of her proximity, he thought of her comfort and naturally offered Montalvo's use. Comfortable enough as she was and dreading repacking, she remained in the lovely country town. Never one to miss an opportunity, though, she took advantage of the invitation to instruct Phelan, who was having her portrait done. "Tell [Josef] Sigall to take off that sprawling signature of his from my bust. He should work a little more on the neck and dress, but does not need me. He seems to have no idea of flesh tints...."

Contrary to Montalvo tradition and Atherton's own adept promptings, Phelan did not maintain in reserve a suite for the author, although she always occupied the same pink room at the head of the spiral stairs whenever she remained over. Atherton's own nomadic lifestyle allowed her only occasional visits, not extended residence. This pattern made it easier for Phelan to establish as a rule that when he was absent only his sister Mollie and his friend Soffie Harvey could reside in Montalvo and only they were free to include their guests. He broke his own rule only at the request of Maude Fay for the opera star and her groom's honeymoon in 1922.

Phelan's entertaining often began in the California sunshine lounging at poolside (sometimes Phelan even cavorted in improvised water ballet with visiting starlets). Then he would retire to soak in his own tub and end up napping through a formal dinner's first courses. Honored but infrequent visitors would toy with salads nervously in the presence of Phelan's empty chair.

But when their gracious host descended the staircase and appeared at last, the mood rose with the good-natured Bronx cheer from his intimates.

California's Honorary Host

Phelan served as California's honorary host to touring mankind and as such set the social and cultural tone by the size of his parties and the distinction of his guests. He hosted the California Regiment for supper when the officers and men returned from World War I. The Notre Dame football team, the officers of the American fleet, aristocrats, poets, authors, public men, and the children from the San Jose junior high schools; all enjoyed their recognitions and their steaks or hot dogs as the event required. For his mature guests, he always offered alcoholic beverages. His liquor stock, laid in on the eve of prohibition, might conceivably have supplied the entire American Expeditionary Forces in the Great War.

The menu he offered the 110 Democratic politicians he brought down from their San Francisco national convention in 1920 is unknown. Presumably, they were less interested in Montalvo's grandeur than in their host's stock of Novitiate, Masson, or his recently-acquired fifty-eight cases of imported dry gin. Franklin Roosevelt and New York Governor Al Smith were Phelan's most noted political celebrities to partake of Montalvo's delights. Young Roosevelt and his wife Eleanor arrived as part of the substitute delegation when President Woodrow Wilson had to cancel and remain in Washington because of World War I. Phelan's other presidential invitee, his former colleague in the Senate, Warren G. Harding, was unable to schedule Montalvo into his San Francisco visit — just as well for the Senator's reputation as a host. President Harding died that evening at the Palace Hotel.

Yet, many lacked cultivated aesthetic appreciation. The world of the masses would have objected to Phelan's tastes, particularly in the visual arts. The sculptured nudes that graced his temple of love and embraced before the cypress grove violated prudish popular standards. Though Phelan was closer both by blood and chronology to the immigrant past than contemporaries such as Smith, Phelan's wealth, education and most of all California's Mediterranean environment molded a different person with far different perspectives. During his numerous foreign travels Phelan selected art judiciously and when unable to locate exactly what he deemed appropriate for an alcove or

James D. Phelan's interest in home photography began early and remained with him throughout his life. He upgraded his cameras as soon as improved technology reached the market. When he was not snapping pictures, his friends were — often with his camera and encouragement.

Edwin Markham, James Duval Phelan, and George Sterling.

The most significant criticism levied against James Duval Phelan as a patron of the arts was offered by Professor Benjamin Lehman of Berkeley's English Department, a friend and ultimately the literary executor of Noël Sullivan. Lehman, at the conclusion of an oral history interview in Berkeley, 1969, maintained that Phelan could not differentiate between first-class talent and talents of inferior grades.

Emily W. Leider, Gertrude Atherton's biographer, accepted the academic criticism and focused its impact through the assertion that Phelan even placed the poetry of William Butler Yeats on a par with Edwin Markham's. At a Montalvo lecture, however, Leider pointed out that Phelan's judgement in the visual arts was far superior than in the literary arts. Lehman, indeed, did overlook Phelan's patronage of Douglas Tilden. Tilden constituted a case in which Phelan recognized genius and persevered in its patronage, a clear case where Phelan never confused polite association for artistic talent. As to equating Yeats with Markham, first, no documentation is offered to support this surprising assertion. And second, even though Phelan boosted most things of value from California, he did understand the limits of credibility. When he bade farewell to revolutionary Ireland in 1922, he recited Yeats, not Markham.

a fountain, he commissioned original work and replicated classics. He appreciated discussion and he sought expert opinions, but no agents made his decisions and in the end no one told him what was art.

Amidst his inner circle Phelan talked of books, poetry, art, travel, and the ideas of the day. On the broad east terrace, between sparkles in the conversation, his guests drank in the horticultural beauty that separated them from the statuary garden below. As Montalvo evenings fell, only the select few shared the intimate confines of his softly-lit library. Atherton recalled with pleasure the frequent presence of Noël Sullivan. In his mid years, the heir apparent and future patron of artists his uncle sometimes overlooked, charmed and delighted the seasoned novelist as they warmed themselves at the fire and talked of authors they had read and places they had visited. Edwin Markham, California's most noted poet, shared his corner with a less well known, but locally popular George Sterling. Sterling's career and life were becoming disappointments, especially to himself. Even though Phelan did not guess the depths of Sterling's growing illness and depression, the patron's standard behavior offered California's once-so-promising poet the solace, recognition, and encouragement he received only at Montalvo.

Phelan articulated the promise of a California paradise. Architecture, landscaping, sculpture, drama, literature, poetry, and the multitude of other fine and performing arts each took its place.

Poets and Poetry

From young manhood when his father had redirected him into banking, finance, and property ownership and management, James D. Phelan's heart already contained its own poet's dreams. Through advancing years and increasing responsibilities, he took pleasure in writing and sought the company of the more accomplished. He recited his own sonnets when encouraged by those who were sensitive, appreciative, and certainly understanding. He even turned graceful lines upon the demand of public occasion such as the 1919 St. Ignatius College (now University of San Francisco) alumni banquet. The Irish tenor, John McCormack, sang and Phelan recited.

At Montalvo those who understood included Markham, Sterling, and the more academically inclined Henry Meade Bland. Bland was the Professor of English and Poet Laureate of California. He served as chair of the Edwin

Markham Poetry Society of the State Teachers College, San Jose, and became an intimate of Phelan due to the Senator's patronage of the Poetry Society and the encouragement of the college students.

Phelan enjoyed serving as honorary chairman of the college society and avidly supported the poetic aspirations Bland shared with his enthusiastic students. Each year when the wisteria blossomed at Montalvo, the Senator invited the San Jose student poets for luncheon and a program of verse, music, and song. The student readings of their original poetry served as the program nucleus, interspersed with Spanish singers or Hawaiian musicians. When the mood struck him, and only after all others had been encouraged and recognized, Phelan joined in, sometimes from works of the college's nationally prominent, distinguished poet, Markham, sometimes with a verse of Phelan's creation. Before the lovely afternoons concluded, Phelan bestowed laurel crowns on the best of the student poets, with the respected Atherton and the admired Wills actually placing them upon the victors' heads.

Phelan's patronage was a worthy gesture in itself and, as in so many of his activities, he simply liked the experience. For Atherton such afternoons with aspiring youth became sufferable because of the obvious enjoyment of the

Following poetry readings at Montalvo, Professor Henry Meade Bland addressed his appreciative thanks "To James D. Phelan, Poet and Believer in the Beautiful." With practical follow-up Phelan requested background information and critical opinion of the students whom he thought possessed talent worthy of further encouragement.

Phelan recommended one student, Dorothy Bendon, to Markham who, as ever, was compiling original works for publication. Phelan also published her Montalvo contribution in a lovely leather-bound annual volume, A Day In The Hills. Thereafter the young woman's poems appeared beyond his patronage and she ultimately turned to literary criticism.

The San Jose State College poetry society received Phelan's support and encouragement. Each spring he hosted them and their professor. Gertrude Atherton and Helen Wills placed small wreaths of laurels upon their heads. More lasting were the memories and the bound volumes of the students' poems.

Helen Wills, just past her majority, tried to please her social and cultural patron. Her tennis career had already been well launched toward her ultimate seven U.S. titles, eight at Wimbledon, four French crowns, two Olympic gold medals, and her concluding victory in Dublin capturing the Irish Championship. The far-sighted Phelan gloried in the fame she gathered to California through her prowess on the court. Yet, he knew too well that youth so quickly vanishes, requiring then a dexterity of mind in order to retain place in a forgetful world. Wills was less than a third Phelan's age and, he hoped, still malleable. He toasted her at Montalvo, witnessed her triumphs in France, and feted her in Paris. Under his patronage she labored mightily to develop as a painter and a writer. Youthful and insecure even in her international fame, she considered her visits to Montalvo as "the most delightful experiences of my life...."

man whose friendship she most valued. Phelan held her unrestrained admiration and could enforce her attendance merely by wishing it. His enjoyment and her fond affection even prompted Atherton's outward display of pleasure when she undoubtedly would rather have been alone writing.

Phelan's poetry sessions were not restricted to students and teachers. When Edwin Markham, whose early recognition came from his gripping "Man with a Hoe," returned home to San Jose from New York, Montalvo's host feted him before an admiring inner circle, augmented by local literati of the day. Markham's playful mood met Phelan's in spontaneous poetic gratitude. His guest-book signature adjoins this quatrain to Phelan:

> Outwitted
> He drew a circle that shut me out,
> Heretic, rebel, a thing to flaunt.
> But love and I had the wit to win.
> We drew a circle that took him in!

Helen Wills

By 1926 few American men who read the newspapers could have been unaware of Helen Wills. Her biographer, Larry Engelmann, portrayed her as an all-American girl: supremely talented, extraordinarily attractive, and refreshingly moral. She symbolized everything that the jazz babies of the 1920s were not, and she became the immensely popular counter model for those repelled by the age of excess. Besides all of this, Wills possessed an aura of mystery. Her nick names, "Little Miss Poker Face" or the "Ice Queen," suggested that her placid exterior masked a deep emotional life.

Phelan was not a sportsman himself. He dabbled at golf, but mostly as a social activity, certainly not for competitive expression — never for exercise. He had offered Tilden's magnificent football monument as an athletic prize, and he hosted the Notre Dame football team at Montalvo on its victory tour home after defeating Stanford in the 1925 Rose Bowl. But his interest in football hardly surfaced between the Stanford and California "Big Games." Likewise, Phelan's interest in Helen Wills was not sports centered. The primary reason for his attention and patronage was the clear association of the youngster's great talent with California. The secondary reason, which was to develop during their relationship, was the aging patron's public satisfaction and private excitement. The gifted young athlete's personal presence stimulated him; her victories gratified him.

In his role as patron, Phelan enriched Wills' life. He enhanced the quality of her public recognition and established the tone for celebration of her success as a star performer. He introduced her to a broader world of culture and celebrities. He provided career guidance and encouragement to develop beyond what he considered to be sport's confining limits. And he allowed her an exciting place beside him amidst his circle of talent and friendship. Wills was undoubtedly the most satisfying of Phelan's protégées and certainly the most accomplished performer.

Wills was different from each of the others. Her youth, command, focus, reserve, and her early and limitless success separated her certainly from Tilden, Sterling, Atherton, and Fay. Forty-four years Phelan's junior, Helen Wills was the only child of a medical doctor and an educated and sensitive homemaker. Dr. Clarence Wills guarded his child's privacy during her formative years and Catherine Wills remained Helen's constant companion and best friend. The relationship of mother and daughter was a healthy one that generated a warmth and support that was quite sufficient and rewarding for both women. Phelan's correspondence file on Wills commences only after his celebrated Paris banquet. In early June, Helen had been stricken with acute appendicitis that compelled her to withdraw from further French tournament play. Phelan was with Catherine Wills at the time when she was reviewing the diagnosis and deciding upon surgery for her daughter. After his experience with Genevieve Barron in Rome, Phelan was a sound and practical, if nonmedical, consultant.

Following her easy and quick convalescence, Helen and her mother sailed for New York aboard the S. S. *Majestic*. Phelan was among the prominent passengers as well. He and the celebrated athlete idled away the crossing together by dabbling in the arts. He glorified the new world champion in poetry and she responded with a charcoal rendering the Senator. Her autographed drawing was a worthy effort, accurate yet kind, particularly sensitive and prudent for a twenty-year old whose lessons and practice hours had not concentrated upon art. Her work encouraged Phelan in his conviction that drawing and writing would be the fields for her lasting success. Success at sports, Phelan knew, was gratifying, but very temporary. In California, Phelan extended his personal hospitality to Wills and her mother, including

James Duval Phelan (shown here with Helen Wills and James "Sunny Jim" Rolph) was never at a loss for proper and engaging words, no matter the occasion or the circumstances. Wills' unforthcoming personal manner was something Phelan attempted to grace over, particularly with the well placed and powerful whom he enlisted in her development beyond tennis. When, for example, she seemed not to have thanked the banker-financier A. P. Giannini, Phelan's friend, for arranging a secret screen test, Phelan covered for her. "Helen Wills is a very young woman, about 21, and probably has much to learn. But I do not think she is unappreciative of the kindness done for her....I enclose you herewith the last letter I received from her, which shows a certain degree of warmth which you would never suspect … [I] desire to encourage her in her work, which ultimately will be art and literature."

Forever prudent, Phelan came close to open indiscretion in his own verse "To Helen Wills" when he warmed to his own theme of California's new generation of sun children, the new Olympians. In rapture's flight Helen's lips became "impeccable," her totality "delectable."

Florence's Pond

Florence Ellon enjoyed only one drive-through of Montalvo, and that was during its construction phase. She followed up by suggesting "an artificial lake or waterfall" that might be placed "on the hill slope to the left" of the Villa. "A bit of water does add such a touch of life," she suggested to Jimmy. Phelan liked the idea of water in motion, a symbol of vitality. He also liked the proposed location. He blended Ellon's ideas, however, with his own tastes and the realities of the terrain. On the hillside beyond the southeast corner of the villa he constructed the lily pond. Rather than featuring the falls to generate its cycle of life, Phelan added his own inspiration to Ellon's original idea. Their pond's focal point became an emerging mermaid, amply provided for in stone and approvingly monitoring the playfulness surrounding her. To provide for her modesty without obscuring her beauty Phelan planted a grove which offered the mermaid warmth in sunlight or privacy in shadows. He allowed nature's seasons forever to choose.

A view of Villa Montalvo from the Love Temple in the 1920s with Cora Older's suggested pink geraniums in full bloom.

them within his inner circle. Montalvo stood ready to shelter mother and daughter from the unwanted attentions of fans and to offer seclusion and rest following Helen's repeated European triumphs throughout the 1920s.

Phelan modified his plan of Montalvo in but two particulars, both in the interests of women. For Wills, his modifications were less creative than Florence Ellon's pond. Phelan ordered a tennis court cut into the hillside to the northwest, diagonally across the villa from Ellon's pond. Characteristically, Wills never offered any suggestions to Phelan. He constructed the court for her amusement when he offered the villa's comforts and solitude for her and her mother's recuperation following her European triumphs of 1927. "My role," he wrote Wills, "is that of proud Californian...! Command me!" "You must need a rest, and could ... come to 'Montalvo,' where you and your mother will be very welcome, — live in the open, play and swin [sic] in the pool, and no one need know you are home until you decide to make an 'official arrival.' You could get off at San Jose, where I would meet you."

Phelan feted Wills at banquets from Paris to San Francisco to Montalvo. He had San Francisco tennis courts named for her. He staged an official reception for her in the grand rotunda of City Hall. And he commissioned her portrait and her sculpture. As only a man of his urbanity could, he wrote: "We were all of one mind that your Bust is a success. I examined it very critically, and like it well." Phelan trailed off, "It is still in clay, and the sculptor says he has a few things to do." To his credit Phelan persisted in encouraging

Wills in writing and art. He introduced her to Jules Pages, a French artist who had been associated with the Julien Academie. Phelan intended that Wills study with him. Phelan included her poetry along with Markham's, David Starr Jordan's, Sterling's and others in a privately printed edition he brought out in 1927. He indulged and promoted her ambitions for a film career, this time through his personal contacts with Will Rogers, Douglas Fairbanks, A. P. Giannini, and acquaintances within the management side of United Artist and Metro-Goldwyn Studios.

Health Problems

As his years passed and the Twenties roared closer to the Great Depression, age and good times (enjoyed in moderation, but perpetually) started to take their toll on California's favorite son. He built Montalvo, in part, because of Santa Clara County's glorious sunshine, an escape even from his garden banquet room atop the new Phelan Building in the city. Sunbathing, nude and in the privacy of the loggia aside his personal apartment, became his habit. Each winter bronchitis gripped him earlier and held him longer into the spring. Sunshine was his preferred medication. At times he even abandoned Montalvo, searching southward for the warming rays of winter's sun. When Palm Springs promised restoration, he planned an alternate villa. When the California desert failed as well, he extended his search into Northern Mexico. The fads of nuts, all fruit, extract of peppermint, and x-ray therapy — these he felt were about as effective for Soffie Harvey, Cora Older, and Gertrude Atherton as the "cures" he took at fashionable spas — all were medically worthless at best. Worse, the health fads of the Twenties, unlike stays at European resorts, were not even socially pleasant. What faith he had, Phelan placed in "nourishing food, fresh air and sound sleep," augmented when needed by the best medical care he could command.

Recurring lameness in his left ankle hardly handicapped Phelan. His discomfort, he wrote to his cousin Duval, "prevents me from running races, but does not deny me dancing. I can throw my weight on my partner when I dance, and she interprets it only as excessive affection." He did not elaborate. Instead, he beckoned Duval west: "come ... and rest at 'Montalvo,' as long as you like. We could make trips to the Desert or Agua Caliente during the bad season, if there is one." And of course Duval should feel free to bring

James Duval Phelan loved dogs from his earliest childhood. Among his favorites was Boz, who attended all Montalvo functions, in the villa and outside. Phelan commissioned the artist Joseph Sigall to paint Boz. The artist had previously done the portrait of President and Mrs. Calvin Coolidge.

To Boz, Phelan wrote "A Tribute to a Dog."

> *Dear Boz, you know not Christmas Day.*
> *It's just the same, you sleep and play.*
> *No special kindness do you ask,*
> *No respite from a daily task.*
> *It's Christmas always where you live.*
> *You dinna ken the Pleiades,*
> *The meaning of the Magi's Star.*
> *Nor do you bend upon your knees*
> *And pray for light that shines afar.*
> *You little know the way of sea,*
> *Of God or women — nor do we!*

James Duval Phelan with Rowena Mason and Boz in the middle garden of Montalvo. Phelan had befriended Mason and her father at the time of her mother's death. Phelan had enjoyed the mother's writings.

Sixty-five years later, Rowena Mason Myers recalled those days. Phelan had attended the mother's funeral and rather than leave them at the grave, he invited Rowena and her father back to Montalvo where he elevated their spirits. "He placed a lovely flower on me, and I felt happier."

Later Phelan encouraged Rowena's career in journalism while her boyfriend, Robert Myers, completed law school. Once while staying over at Montalvo, the young woman was harassed by another weekend guest, a member of Congress — the Speaker! She mentioned the incidents to Phelan. The next morning she saw Phelan's car leaving the grounds with the older man.

along his own doctor or his valet if he wished. "I think you ought to add a little weight, at your time of life, and get back your appetite...." If his hard-working and deeply religious bachelor cousin could just enjoy life's kindnesses, then he too could ride the trails at Montalvo, plunge into the bracing pool, and luxuriate in the California sunshine.

Concerned about his health, Phelan took special precautions. He engaged a team of specialists at The Johns Hopkins Medical School who identified a long-contained prostate infection, but otherwise gave him a sound bill of health. Perhaps more notable than his medical report was his traveling party. He had entrained for Baltimore in the late spring with his own San Francisco doctor and the doctor's wife, Phelan's secretary, and chauffeur. Phelan even included his Mercedes as baggage.

Phelan stayed at The Hopkins for a full medical examination. He was pleased enough with the results and his letters home to his nephew Noël Sullivan included lighthearted descriptions of the medical regimes to which he was subjected. Sullivan's reputation as an advocate of the underprivileged in American society seemed already fixed, at least in his uncle's mind. Phelan wrote what Sullivan would appreciate — ill health was no discriminator among the classes. Phelan was required to sit and wait his turn between those who appeared without means, but whose cases interested the specialist-teachers. Likewise, wardrobe meant nothing. No hospital gown was tailored; none was cut from fine cloth. Failing health became the great equalizer.

Closing Years

During this period his exchange of letters with Helen Wills became more intense. The old patron was indulging himself. Clearly, he wrote, "one of my pleasures is to exchange thoughts freely with you." He gloried in her athletic success which, by 1929, left all American and European competitors in her wake. "You are young and so far in many ways above others that you do not excite their jealousy...." The compliments she received from the well placed and the noted enhanced Phelan's pride.

His faltering handwriting ended with advice to "Keep up your game," by which he meant the game of life as well as her play before the net. Life, too, "has its rules and its rewards." His semi-legible script terminated in verse which painfully harkened back to his youth, sweet times, only to seek again final solace and comfort: "And be soft as a mother, tired body of mine." If the twenty-three year old star felt puzzled by the letter's meaning and intent, her quandary had no impact upon her game. Wills continued her absolute dominance in the world of women's tennis.

With Atherton, Phelan shared the esteem he felt for Wills. The young star "…holds an unique place as a type of American womanhood uncontaminated, and she should be very jealous of that position.…" Sensitive to the possibility of jealousy on the part of the senior protégée, Phelan characterized Wills' early literary efforts in a way that Atherton could accept. Wills, Phelan continued, is "more an admired personality, in the eye of the reading public, than a literary producer." Nonetheless, when the San Francisco Opera season opened, Phelan invited the young star to accompany him. Only when the conflict of her Eastern tennis commitments became clear did he turn to Gertrude Atherton as his alternate guest. Still, Phelan persevered.

Before Christmas, Phelan wrote a letter of encouragement to his great nephew, Fred Murphy, Jr., who was studying literature at Georgetown University and having some difficulty settling on a permanent college major. In the finest of humor, Phelan declared himself fully restored to good health, "except my feet which 'lag superfluous on the stage'." That same evening he had tickets for the San Francisco opening of "The Taming of the Shrew." And who was to be on his arm this time, but Helen Wills. He had succeeded in arranging a foursome which included his companion's mother and his rather permanent house guest, Colonel Harry Howland. The latter, Phelan proclaimed, was to serve "as chaperon and bodyguard, because 'the prettiest girl in America'— according to Mrs. Atherton — ought not be exposed to the dangers of Metropolitan life." Phelan understood the boundaries that propriety established, and he extracted as much pleasure as he could, even during a period of declining health.

When the impending marriage of Wills to a cosmopolitan young stockbroker, Frederick S. Moody, became common knowledge, Phelan understood that as well. He had anticipated their marriage even though he had not been privy to the couple's secret three-year engagement. Indeed, he had encouraged Wills to be among her own generation. Regrettingly, nonetheless, he wrote to the artist he had commissioned to do Wills' portrait, that "I suppose a celebrity like Helen cannot wed without losing something of her individuality.…Perhaps the world is jealous that anyone should presume to take a

Phelan's connections guided Helen and her mother into the American diplomatic circuit in Europe and hastened the star's presentation to England's Queen Mary (wife of George V). Perhaps unsurprisingly, the tennis champion required two sets of long gloves for the royal encounter. One matched set would not correctly fit both hands and forearms, the muscular structure of her racket hand being so developed.

James Duval Phelan with Helen Wills and Fred Moody before Wills and Moody announced their engagement. Phelan had hoped to save Wills from the institution of marriage

This Montalvo lawn party of the 1920s is typical of the events James Duval Phelan hosted for the young and the talented — those who were to bring California to its next stage of development. Often he invited organizations of college women to come, bring their friends, and have a day in the sun — luncheon, dancing, and swimming. Faculty mentors from Mills College accompanied their students and discussed poetry with Phelan. His central concern on days such as this was that the younger generation enjoy their own company.

well beloved champion off her pedestal…." Then blending his mild criticism of Catholicism with his own rendering of its doctrine he added: "The Universal Church has set an example of virginity and, at the same time, of maternity, to show the super excellence of both." For one who was equally unimpressed by maternity and virginity, Phelan recognized the inevitable. Even in his decline he opted not to play the old fool.

The stock market had already crashed and he had taken considerable paper losses. Speculative investments had always made Phelan nervous, in any case, and he was in the process of reducing them anyway. Loss, though, was not his preferred method of doing so. His diversified portfolio and his father's conservative example left Phelan in far better financial condition than many of his overextended friends. As ever he was philosophical in money matters. In the winter of 1929, he was quite sound financially if somewhat reduced physically. He declined to accept the collapse of the stock market as sufficient reason for him to curtail his social and cultural life.

Phelan hosted his last reception for Helen Wills in early December, 1929. "Last night," he wrote fancifully to his nephew Noël Sullivan, "she was

like a woman of another race— so superior to the average in carriage, height, line & form—classic & statuesque in white satin a la mode." On her arm this time was young Moody, her fiancé. Phelan continued to Sullivan, "I fear we shall lose her (nominally) before the New Year. She is drawing closely to the vortex."

Then in an utterly telling line, Phelan revealed much of himself. His sentence gathered the pleasures and the aggravations of his forty-two year relationship with Ellon, as well as his lifelong aversion to marriage. Then he weighed them against the physical, psychological, and social appeal so dramatically displayed by his idealized California woman. On the eve of the marriage of the American icon to a personable stockbroker, California's most cultured gentleman concluded: "If I were thirty & courageous I would save her!" Not from Moody — he would save her from the institution of marriage. And he presumed that he could do so. Only to his sensitive nephew did Phelan make so personal a revelation.

In reviewing the correspondence among Phelan, Wills, and Atherton, the biographers of the latter two (Larry Engelmann for Wills and Emily W. Leider for Atherton) leave little room but to conclude that Wills looked upon Phelan so fondly as to have been welcoming of greater attention. Her professional focus and her inability to convey emotional warmth, however, didn't advance such an objective. Retrospectively, the best Wills could articulate was a regret that her life and Phelan's had not been set more closely together within adjoining time frames.

When Larry Engelmann interviewed Fred Moody, Moody told him that he agreed, at Wills' request, to keep their promise to marry a secret even though he had no idea why Wills wished it so. Even Engelmann, an intrepid biographer, found no good reason. Wills had turned twenty-one in 1926, and both were, of course, free to marry. And besides, Wills' mother was fully understanding and always supporting.

One perhaps unflattering explanation is the possibility that the champion's attraction to Phelan was stronger than her antiseptic statement on life's parallel time lines suggests. Also, the three years of her secret engagement were the three years of her increasing association with Phelan. And as the end of this three-year period approached, Phelan felt moved to explain to Wills why he would not marry.

James Duval Phelan maintained appearances for as long as he could during the early summer of 1930. He had his automobile modified to accept his wheelchair and he travelled locally. At his side throughout was his nephew Noël Sullivan. Sullivan would be incapable of carrying on the family enterprises and Phelan had for his father, but Sullivan's presence was comforting to Phelan.

Sullivan, Phelan's heir apparent, had no reason to become anxious about his uncle's enthusiasm for Wills. Immediately upon Phelan's enraptured description of the world champion followed the uncle he had always known and loved so well. "Did I tell you," Phelan continued in his letter to Sullivan, "I am in love with a white lady & nightly salute her as I pass to my room. She stands in Miss P[helan]'s patio. You will like her & may even recognize her as an old young friend…. I am, indeed, Pygmalion-like and yearn for her incarnation." Phelan chose "a draped and beautiful Spanish lady of Carrara marble, life-sized," rather than pursue the Ice Queen, Helen Wills.

Along with his mother's beads, Sister Agnes of Jesus sent James D. Phelan this note: "I am enclosing a token [the rosary beads] that conveys an assurance of the prayers of many years….It seems to me that it would please… [your mother] at this moment, when she & our dear ones Above are praying for you, that I would send them to you, a little chain connecting the radiant intercession of Heaven with the hope-laden pleas from earth's dark exile!"

Salvation according to Catholic doctrine was her objective and would become her offer. And her stricken uncle need not even believe, just hope. Perhaps his hope to see his mother would suffice for him to see the Blessed Mother too, even though the latter was the nun's wish and not his. At this stage, Agnes of Jesus needed the help of others to advance her God's will; she needed those who enjoyed physical mobility beyond the convent walls, like her brother Noël.

Final Seasons

The spring of 1930 was to be Phelan's last. He hosted his final Montalvo event on April 23, a celebration in poetry on the occasion of Edwin Markham's seventy-eighth birthday. Twelve days later, on May 5, Phelan suffered his first stroke, a briefly debilitating experience. Charles Fay assisted him to the lounge, offered him an aromatic and called Doctor Louis Mendelsohn, a neighbor and friend.

Over the course of the next three months, until the late afternoon of August 7, 1930, Phelan and his army of physicians, friends, and health professionals fought death with all the resources known to medical science, all that were available to the wise and the wealthy. Remaining at Montalvo, Phelan first presided over its conversion from garden paradise to an intensive care facility augmented by a new Cadillac built to accommodate his wheelchair. During this period of hope, alternately dashed by recurring and progressively more severe strokes, Phelan underwent physical and mental changes.

At first he continued his cherished personal correspondence with those with whom he had long established bonds of love. These reflective moments became even more precious. Jokingly, he wrote to Duval that his gardener circulated the word that Phelan was limited now to chopping down three trees per day. Other light moments contained kernels of grim inevitability.

When his personal secretary, Belle Driscoll, was unable to reach by phone the President of the Metropolitan Life Insurance Company, she gave up in acute frustration. Turning to Phelan, she said, "What do you wish with him, anyway?" Phelan responded, "I want to get my life insured." To which Driscoll blurted out, "He won't insure you for fifteen cents." Phelan forgave her outburst because of the fondness he always felt for her too. "But," he concluded, "it was no joke."

When he gathered for one grand consultation all of his physicians, their consultants, and all their spouses at a champagne and filet mignon dinner in the dining room below, Phelan appreciated their enjoyment of his hospitality, but privately wondered if the Irish wake was a bit premature. The laughter, conversation, and good times shared by the living should, he thought, at least await the arrival of the corpse. Even George Duval's neurologist had arrived by train from New York, dispatched as a token of the cousin's love and solicitude. The noted specialist was able to affect the situation little beyond accepting Montalvo hospitality. Actually, Phelan preferred to share it with Duval himself.

Through these weeks rest, consultation, and increased medication were interspersed with more frequent and more debilitating seizures. James Duval Phelan's decision-making powers gradually diminished. Instead, he became a captive of those loyal and attentive family members, employees and friends who formed a conspiracy around him, a conspiracy of love. Their agreed-upon objective was the recapture of Phelan's immortal soul and its guidance into the heaven so firmly believed in by these loving co-conspirators.

Final Rites

Phelan's niece, the cloistered Carmelite nun Sister Agnes of Jesus, made the first move — a brilliant one given her uncle's devotion to his nuclear family. Upon receiving word of his early seizure Sister Agnes pulled upon the family cord, literally and symbolically. She sent him the actual rosary beads that his mother, her grandmother, had given to her on the day of her own first communion, May 8, 1899. Undoubtedly, Phelan had witnessed his invalid mother's bestowal of the religious token upon the little girl. The beads now had become the tangible object connecting three generations whose members stood on each side of life's great divide, one member being about to leave the world of the flesh to join that of the spirit. The young girl herself (a second generation heir to the original Phelan and then Sullivan fortunes) had subsequently dedicated her adult life to poverty and self-denial. By 1930, Sister Agnes had touched each bead daily — prayer, over and over again for 31 years, every "Hail Mary" honoring the Blessed Mother of God. Her "Uncle Didden" (her childhood effort at "Uncle James" which stuck) was not interested in the Blessed Mother; privately he even had made sport of the doctrine of a Virgin Mother. Phelan's compelling interest was his mother, not God's. The result, though, was clear. Sister Agnes's first step of her comprehensive spiritual envelopment captured the dying man's attention.

Independently, at first, came the inquiring Catholic priests. Father Richard Collins, pastor of St. Joseph's Church in San Francisco initiated the clerical contact. He and Phelan had a long-established relationship dating back to the turn-of-the-century when Phelan advanced him money to buy

James Duval Phelan awaited death as graciously and properly as he had awaited guests. His preparations for this final caller were more intense, though. Through his will, he wished to recognize and encourage those whose love and service had contributed to the California culture he had celebrated. Next, his orderly mental review brought him to Florence Ellon; the pleasure of his youth, the responsibility of his concluding days. Strangely, in the summer of 1930, Phelan was carrying out his own instructions, penned in the winter of 1894 to his brother-in-law. Frank Sullivan was now immobile; Phelan himself was dying; Ellon — who was to know? Perhaps off to Paris yet again!

Saving Phelan's Soul

James Duval Phelan's niece Sister Agnes of Jesus extended her best effort to save Phelan's soul. Bound to her cloistered grounds and working through her co-conspirators of love, she shared herself and her faith for the last time with her uncle:

Rest all you can, your mind, your heart! I wish that I could say to you, & that you would understand me, rest them in God who created them, Who only knows their wearyness, their need! Come to Him in thought, ever most fleetingly, such thoughts are heart cries, are real prayers, they will bring you rest & peace as nothing here below can for a contact is formed between Strength & weakness, between Power & dependance, and a Word between the Creator & the creature. He who lives, who knows all, & he who cries and hopes all!

Think these days dearest Didden of the one Source of help & blessing, and I know that your body & soul will respond! The great St. Augustine whose mind is one of the loftiest known, cried out after finding rest & peace at last - 'O God the human heart was made by Thee & for Thee, & finds its rest not until it rests in Thee!'

uniforms, guns, and supplies for a Catholic paramilitary organization, the League of the Cross Cadets.

Collins was the right cleric to make the final approach to Phelan. "He is a genial, companionable person, without any affection of sanctity, I was glad to receive him." Phelan wrote to Duval, adding that the priest "was discreet enough not to engage me in controversial subjects." Phelan encouraged the diocesan priest, whose conversation seemed to revolve around golf and poetry, to call again at Montalvo. Phelan's reaction to the local Jesuits was hardly so benign. "My Jesuit friends, who live in this neighborhood," he shared with his cousin Duval, "inquire repeatedly here for me, but I have not personally admitted them to my presence." To Phelan their interests in the endowments of their institutions seemed to be as great as their interests in his comfort and well being.

Father Collins was the one who pursued the advantage — in two ways. First, he wrote to Phelan and included what he believed to be the last poem, the original, penned by Phelan's friend, the late George Sterling. The letter contained the realistic touch Phelan undoubtedly appreciated in the priest. Collins observed that once the poem was completed: "Very soon after poor George blazed his own trail … into the bosom of God forever.…" Still, Collins ended softly, if by formula: "God bless you & spare you long for very many love you." Phelan liked Collins personally and remained open to his spiritual ministry.

Next, and inevitably given their shared calling and culture, the Irish priest and the cloistered nun broadened their conspiracy to extend their network to the other insiders — Phelan's indulgent and religious nephew Noël Sullivan and the ever present, devoted secretary Belle Driscoll. Once this was accomplished, Collins and Sister Agnes planned their next move, but before they could implement it, Phelan made one of his own: Florence Ellon.

As he spent his evenings alone upon the east veranda counting his dwindling nights, he saw "everything pass before me … in orderly review." Flo, as part of that orderly review, held a special place all to herself. He intended that her place at his death be just as it had been through his life — officially absent. Intentionally, he excluded her from all of the numerous renderings of his will. Instead, he chose to take care of her personally, privately, and finally.

In Ellon's own review of their relationship she had concluded even before his illness that, "For the Past I've no regrets, a beautiful dream. It was wonderful." Confronted now with the serious illness of the man who had provided for her and her family for forty-two years, Ellon made no final claims or requests. She, too, offered her own prayers for the recovery of the man she knew so well. Upon his own initiative, Phelan called his executive secretary, Thomas B. Doyle, down to Montalvo from the Phelan Building in San Francisco. Doyle's Sunday visit was strictly business, business he only alluded to in his own letter to George Duval. Phelan, he wrote, directed him "to attend to certain matters which were bothering him." The prime, if not singular, matter was a final conveyance of financial independence upon Mrs. Ellon. Doyle managed the details (property and additional funds that would provide for a comfortable home and maintenance for her through her own advancing years). Ellon's final thank-you letter in French, arrived at Montalvo five days later. Phelan was destined to fail once again in his final effort to convert the passion of his youth from consumption to conservation and investment. But thereafter the problem was not to be his.

As his health deteriorated Phelan became incapable of initiating his own correspondence or actions. First, he stopped writing. Next, he ceased dictating and Mrs. Driscoll comfortably filled the gap by personalizing his fond appreciations mingled with news to his inner circle. Mrs. Ellon, however, was not among the Irish Catholics Mrs. Driscoll favored with the inside communications. Driscoll's reaction to Ellon's last expression of solicitude written in English may only be guessed at: "All the time I'm thinking of you and yes, You're always in my prayers. How I'm hoping with all my heart that you'll be well again _very_ soon....I am waiting to see you when You tell me that I may." Phelan by then was incapable of any written response and close to being incapable of any whatsoever. To this letter Mrs. Driscoll refrained from offering a response. Delicacy and propriety, Phelan hallmarks, prevented her from answering what she may have thought should be in her beloved employer's heart. The last of Ellon's 194 letters to her man went unanswered. Doyle had provided and Ellon understood and looked ahead.

Given the mores of the Irish Catholic subculture that the insiders shared, that Father Collins and Sister Agnes of Jesus may have been compartmentalized by Driscoll and Doyle is likely. Neither the male nor the female Irish secretary would have been comfortable discussing Ellon with a priest or a nun under any circumstances. In this context such an initiative by them would likewise have demonstrated disloyalty to Phelan as well. The

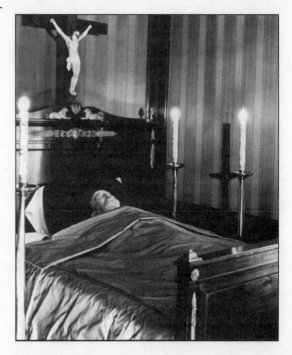

The large crucifix, the liturgical candles, and the meaning they conveyed all arrived at Montalvo from the Carmelite Monastery, compliments of James Duval Phelan's cloistered niece Sister Agnes of Jesus. They were not the symbols by which Phelan had lived. But the symbols were those of a powerful heritage that a California lifestyle had not displaced.

James Duval Phelan lying in state in the rotunda of the San Francisco City Hall.

San Francisco had no other public figure of Phelan's stature and accomplishments. That his lying in state took place amid the splendor of the marbled hall symbolized and brought closure to Phelan's life of service and celebration. The Jesuits of his youth welcomed his mortal remains back within their new St. Ignatius Church (which Phelan had helped pay for). Quietly though, they said the mass and said but few words.

likely result was that Collins and Agnes of Jesus may never have fully appreciated the timeliness of their competition with Ellon for Phelan's remaining attention.

In fact, Phelan, for all his physical and mental reduction, still maintained his personal dignity and ultimate authority. Ellon represented his temporal life, one he had fully indulged during the days which had been allotted to him. And Agnes of Jesus represented an eternal life he doubted. His last well-considered act was to gratify the needs of both women. Simultaneously and symbolically he satisfied his worldly debts while he projected hope, if not faith, in rejoining his mother and father, (if need be) in God's presence. To Ellon he bequeathed temporal freedom; From Sister Agnes he accepted eternal hope.

Her uncle accepted from the hands of Father Collins the Catholic relic that Sister Agnes had conveyed. "His mind," Belle Driscoll reported, "was very confused, and I cannot say that he realized the full significance…" of having accepted the symbol. Five days earlier, and therefore more alert, Phelan had accepted the last rights of the Catholic Church including the sacraments of Extreme Unction, Holy Communion, and Confession. Exactly how hard the golfing priest who never brought up "controversial subjects," pressed for full personal disclosure as a condition of reconciliation was, of course, wrapped in the seal of confession. Father Collins' temperament as well as his professional ethics would suggest that Flo was never mentioned. That Jesus was, however, is equally uncertain.

Consummate gentleman unto death, Phelan accepted the final gratitude of both women. The salutations of their terminal letters were as diverse and as meaningful as the life of the man they loved.

Mon Cheri! Jimmy
Pax Christi! Uncle Didden

Chapter Eighteen

The Phelan Will and Villa Montalvo

James Duval Phelan was a man of business, and one of the most important acts of his career was to determine who should receive his sizeable fortune. This was no small task, since that fortune included his extensive agricultural properties in California and beyond, his banking and business assets, his commercial buildings in San Francisco and San Jose, his portfolio of stocks, and his percentage of the Phelan family corporation. There had to be, as well, the allotment of his artistic treasures that reflected a lifetime devoted to high culture in marble, bronze, and canvas. And there was, of course, his beloved home in the sunshine, Villa Montalvo. Although he was a stickler for detail throughout his life, he left this final personal obligation unfulfilled until the eleventh hour. It was not until the last months of his life that he officially signed the legal will and testament that would dispose of his earthly goods. In the company of his local physician, Dr. Louis Mendelsohn, and his lawyer, Phelan recorded his last and greatest act of philanthropy.

Although he had spent more and more time toward the end of his life at his country estate and signed his will at Villa Montalvo, Phelan remained a true son of his native city. He identified himself as a resident of San Francisco, and the city did well by his benefactions. Churches, orphanages, cultural, fraternal and philanthropic organizations, and even the public library of San Francisco were all remembered in his will. Having no children of his own, he left a legacy for the children of San Francisco. Phelan had been president of the San Francisco Playground Commission since 1919, and he now left $50,000 to the commissioners for the development of China Cove as a recreational center. He specified that if this could not be done, the money

In addition to the orchards, ornamental trees, and shrubs on the Phelan estate, three acres of sloping lawn stretching from the villa to the Italian Garden required watering. James Duval Phelan's head gardener laid out a sprinkler system and recycled water from the Senator's pool to irrigate Montalvo's gardens.

249

Son of the gardener who laid out the Santa Cruz estate of the senior James Phelan, George Doeltz was responsible for planning and landscaping Senator Phelan's Villa Montalvo. Doeltz's leisurely pose with newspaper in hand gives little indication of the demanding work required to establish and maintain the Montalvo gardens, lawns, orchards, greenhouse, and hillside trails. While the villa was still under construction in 1912, Doeltz began the task of clearing and planting. His supervision of the Villa Montalvo gardens continued for forty years.

was to be used "to encourage healthful sports for San Francisco children." A number of the city's foundling homes were left beneficences. Narrow sectarianism had never been part of Senator Phelan in life, and in death his bounty extended to Catholic, Protestant, and Jewish foundations. The San Francisco Protestant Orphanage Society and the Pacific Hebrew Orphan Asylum each received $25,000 for their work. The elderly and the sick of the city were remembered in substantial gifts to the Native Sons and Daughters of the Golden West and the University Mound Old Ladies' Home. To commemorate the deceased pioneers of California he left another bequest for the erection of a monument on Telegraph Hill. Throughout his life Phelan had a well-deserved reputation as a cultural patron, and the arts were not neglected in his passing. A sum of $60,000 was set up as an endowment to award prizes to young Californians for achievements in the fields of literature and art. The San Francisco Art Association was particularly favored: $100,000 for the construction of exhibition rooms in its new building on Jones and Chestnut Streets. The Bohemian Club, which perhaps only in its first decade could be considered really "Bohemian" in any artistic sense, was given Phelan's bronze Rodin group. The San Francisco Public Library received a substantial monetary bequest, and California's poet laureate, Henry Meade Bland, was recognized with a smaller sum.

In his will, Senator Phelan demonstrated for the last time the strong ties that bound him throughout his life to his family. Nearly a half million dollars, in carefully designated amounts, was left to relatives in California, the eastern states, England, and Ireland. Relations as far removed as the children of third cousins were not forgotten and received handsome remembrances. Naturally the largest sums went to his closest relatives. $100,000, for example, was given to his sister Mollie "to augment her estate," even though that estate ran into the millions. Noël Sullivan, Phelan's nephew, not only became a trustee of Phelan's estate, but he was given his uncle's camp and equipment at the Bohemian Grove along with other valuable property, artwork, and furnishings. In memory of his father and mother's wedding in old St. Mary's Church, Phelan gave $50,000 for the parish poor. As a further act of filial piety, he honored his father by endowing the "James Phelan Scholarships" in art and literature at the University of California.

Other institutions of higher learning profited by the Senator's last will and testament. Santa Clara University, which had conferred an honorary doctorate on Phelan after his terms as mayor of San Francisco, received $50,000 for scholarships. His own undergraduate school, St. Ignatius College, was left a like amount. Two local women's institutions, Mills College in Oakland and Notre Dame Convent in Belmont, received lesser sums. The University of California was given a sum designated to support research.

At his table at Villa Montalvo, in San Francisco, or Washington D.C., Senator Phelan had delighted in entertaining those who had brought distinction or recognition to California. Some old favorites, such as George Sterling, were beyond material rewards by the time the Senator made out his will. But to his living favorites, Phelan was characteristically generous. Helen Wills, whom even Phelan had not been able to turn into a Hollywood movie star, was left, perhaps as consolation, $20,000, "in appreciation of her winning the tennis championship for California." His intellectual companion and fellow booster of California, Gertrude Atherton, received the same amount. Long her patron, friend, host, and even humble "research assistant," Phelan paid his last honeyed compliment to "California's great authoress." Each of her children and grandchildren was also left $5,000. Old friends from his political crusade days, the Fremont Olders and Francis J. Heney, were remembered with tangible rewards. Overlooking the latter's political opposition to Phelan during his senatorial campaign, the bequest was made "in recognition of his valiant services for San Francisco."

Those who had contributed more personally or directly to Phelan's stately life were acknowledged with gratitude. Each servant at Villa Montalvo was given a small sum, and those, like his head gardener, George Doeltz, who had been in service with the Senator since Montalvo's construction, received more than a year's wages and smaller amounts for their children. Phelan's secretaries, Thomas B. Doyle and Belle Driscoll, who had become increasingly indispensable to the Senator, were far more handsomely rewarded. Soffie Harvey, Phelan's hostess for so many years at Villa Montalvo, and her husband were given $50,000. And the Senator's lifelong friend, business agent and political adviser, Charles W. Fay, and his family were not forgotten. In a gesture that reflected his personal regard for these old friends, Phelan gave Mrs. Fay a diamond inherited from his mother. Other special friends received a particular painting or statue from his personal collection.

Phelan's largest single bequest, a million dollars, was devoted to the creation of the "James D. Phelan Foundation" for charitable work in his native

The Laocoön

In James Duval Phelan's will the Palace of the Legion of Honor was singled out to get both money and one of the Senator's most prized possessions, a copy of the Laocoön. Phelan had purchased this himself during one of his last trips to Europe. Fascinated with the writhing figures of the mythical Trojan priest and his sons, when he saw the original in the Belvedere Courtyard of the Vatican, the Senator believed he discovered in it a pregnant symbol of danger to his beloved California. According to the ancient myth, Laocoön had tried to defend Troy against the seductive gift left by the Greeks — the famous and fateful wooden horse. Laocoön and his sons were attacked and killed by snakes emerging from the coastal waters. In this instance, Phelan's artistic taste fell victim to political and racial myopia. For him the statue was a powerful emblem of the threat facing California and the entire United States from Japanese immigrants and influence. By giving the statue to a public museum, he undoubtedly hoped his own persistent Laocoön-like warnings of danger to the Republic would live on after his own death.

Viewed from the wooded hillside behind Villa Montalvo, the fruit orchards that dominated Santa Clara Valley agriculture are clearly visible. In the spring during Saratoga's Blossom Festival, James Duval Phelan enjoyed a vista across tens of thousands of flowering fruit trees to the eastern hills. In this photograph taken by Phelan's head gardener, Montalvo's landscaping is still in its infancy.

city. The trustees, including Noël Sullivan, were to serve without pay, and the income of the trust was to ameliorate the plight of the poor and the sick. For more than a half century the poor have benefited from this manifestation of Phelan's munificence. The income from this endowment has paid for the visits of nurses and nurses' aides to the homes of the poor in the city's urban ghettos. James D. Phelan was born to affluence and enjoyed the luxuries and comforts of the wealthy throughout his life, but his generosity was proverbial, and the bequests in his will were in character with his life. The cartons of letters housed in the Bancroft Library requesting contributions for endless worthy causes attest to Phelan's widespread reputation as a soft touch. The imminence of death simply made the gifts larger in size and final in character. While it had been decades since his shadow crossed the threshold of his old parish church, Mission Dolores, he gave $20,000 for the poor of that parish. Other Catholic institutions and orders, such as the Sisters of the Presentation, did equally well by Phelan, who had been so often acknowledged as the leading Catholic layman of his age. The Catholic Church had not done badly from the will of its dutiful, if somewhat wayward, son.

Villa Montalvo

But what of the griffin-guarded estate in the foothills of the Santa Cruz Mountains, his particular treasure, Villa Montalvo? Once during the course of an afternoon stroll along the inviting trails through his property, Phelan had surveyed the estate and reflected on its probable future. He could imagine, he told his companion Gertrude Atherton, that after his death his estate would be occupied by a community of Catholic religious. "I suppose I'll look down on all this one of these days and see priests or nuns walking about. My family are all such pious Catholics!" As he got on in years, draped clerical figures, heads bowed in modesty or meditation, haunted the day dreams of this apostle of the good life.

Although the Catholic Church received many benefactions from the will of James D. Phelan, it was not to receive his beloved Villa Montalvo. Well read as he was, and schooled in the classics, perhaps Phelan deliberately followed the example of the ancient Greek philosopher, Theophrastus. In his will Theophrastus disposed of his property with an eye to cultured discourse as well as civic utility:

As for my garden, the walks and the house adjacent to the gardens, I give in perpetuity to my friends who desire to devote themselves in common to study and philosophy therein — it shall not belong to anyone individually but they shall enjoy it peacefully and amicably as is just and fitting.

In his will, James Duval Phelan decided to leave Villa Montalvo as his gift to the people of California for the cultivation of the arts he had loved and patronized throughout his life. The words of the will, which would become, on more than one occasion, the objects of close legal scrutiny, read as follows.

I would like the property at Saratoga, Calif., known as Villa Montalvo, to be maintained as a public park open to the public under reasonable restrictions, the buildings and grounds immediately surrounding the same to be used as far as possible for the development of art, literature, music and architecture by promising students.

The impeccable host, who so often had stood smiling before the carved Spanish doors of Villa Montalvo welcoming gifted artists, singers, actors, and literary figures to his home, was not conceding to death what he had so greatly enjoyed in life. California's great patron of the arts ensured that on the broad and inviting acres of his foothill estate music, poetry, and art would continue to flourish. Phelan's dream of California as the home of the arts would live on after his passing. Beauty would still be the reigning deity at Villa Montalvo.

As custodian of this legacy to the people, Phelan selected the San Francisco Art Association. To help maintain the estate and cultivate the arts on the premises, he specified that $250,000 be set aside for the Art Association. This would be a permanent endowment, the income from which would allow his intention of creating a center for the arts at Montalvo to become a reality.

Choosing a Trustee

The choice of the San Francisco Art Association as trustee for Villa Montalvo seemed, in many ways, perfectly natural. Phelan had long been associated with this respected San Francisco cultural institution. A life member, he had participated in its activities for decades and served as a member of its board of directors. In the mid 1890s, Phelan cut his administrative teeth as

Home for the Carmelites

Only a few years before James D. Phelan began construction of Villa Montalvo, his sister, Alice Sullivan, purchased Mrs. Robert Lewis Stevenson's home in San Francisco for the cloistered nuns of Carmel. This foundation quickly proved too small for the nuns, and the Senator's sister left a substantial legacy for the construction of a new home for the Carmelites in Santa Clara. On the site of the old farmstead of Judge Bond, where Jack London conceived the idea for *The Call of the Wild*, Alice's share of the Phelan fortune created a spiritual oasis. Behind pink walls and wrought iron fences, shielded from sight by the silvery leaves of Mediterranean olive trees, there arose an architectural and spiritual replica of 16th century Spain — the Spain of the Catholic mystics, Teresa of Avila and John of the Cross. There, in the most profound cloistered seclusion, the Carmelite sisters prayed for the souls of sinners preoccupied with the distractions of the flesh and the world. There, the body of Alice Phelan Sullivan was transferred after her death and interred in a small octagonal burial chapel opening onto the sisters' own chapel. There, Alice Phelan Sullivan's daughter, Sister Agnes of Jesus, one of the cloistered Carmelite nuns, regularly included her uncle James D. Phelan in her fervent prayers.

The Sainte Clare Club in downtown San Jose, California, was built by James Duval Phelan, who later offered it to San Jose for use as a museum. The city declined the offer, however, so the building remains a private club.

president of the San Francisco Art Association, the only elective office he held before becoming mayor of San Francisco. Phelan's fellow patrons of the San Francisco Art Association were offered, through the generous terms of the Senator's will, not only a public trusteeship, but a most attractive haven for their artistic enterprises. In the elegant surroundings of the millionaire's country estate the arts could thrive. The gift of Villa Montalvo to the San Francisco Art Association ranks among the most generous of Phelan's acts of cultural patronage to his native city.

The designation of trusteeship for Villa Montalvo to a San Francisco organization did not mean that Phelan turned his back on the Santa Clara Valley. The very location of the estate in Saratoga and the careful wording of the will indicating that the property should be "a public park open to the public," meant that the citizens of the valley would have for their pleasure the Senator's lovingly cultivated gardens, the rustic hillside paths, the impressive views of the surrounding countryside, and the cultural stimulation provided by the artistic development that would be undertaken on the premises by the San Francisco Art Association. Attached though he was to the city of his birth, Phelan's love of California was not narrowly circumscribed. His neighbors in the Santa Clara Valley, simply because of their proximity, would be its principal beneficiaries.

Without prejudice to the valley residents, Phelan doubted that Santa Clara County could provide the necessary commitment and leadership to make Montalvo into the artistic center he envisioned. Recent experience seemed to substantiate this view. Only three years before the Senator signed his will, he had witnessed the tepid and hesitant nature of the county fathers' devotion to the arts. In 1927 Phelan visited a temporary museum assembled in San Jose as part of a civic celebration. The exhibition at the Fiesta de las Rosas had been arranged by his longtime friend, Cora Older, and the Senator was impressed with the quality of the materials displayed. The collection, in his discriminating judgment, warranted permanent housing as the nucleus of a full-fledged county art museum. In a gesture of extraordinary generosity, Phelan offered to give the elegant three story building he owned on St. James Street, the Sainte Claire Club, to the County of Santa Clara as a public museum. He also promised $5000 to outfit it properly for exhibition purposes.

This unexpected offer by Senator Phelan took the county supervisors by surprise. Neither in San Jose, nor the entire Santa Clara county, did there exist a public museum devoted to the arts. At the northern edge of the county, on the campus of Stanford University, the ample, if rather eclectic collection of art and memorabilia assembled by the Stanfords was the most significant private collection available to the public. Closer to the center of population, the new Rosicrucian Museum, which would offer curious citizens a romanticized glimpse into the treasures of ancient Egypt and Mesopotamia was still under construction. No major public collection of art existed, nor was any civic building devoted to the artistic education or enlightenment of the residents of the county.

James D. Phelan found that the county was still reluctant to assume responsibility for a public art museum, even when the building was handed to it as a gift. When Phelan's offer came before the county supervisors it met opposition on a number of grounds. The building, it was alleged, was not appropriate for a museum without major modifications. It was constructed of inflammable materials that would put the valuable art objects collected there at risk. It would cost too much for monthly upkeep. In a petition less than complimentary to the cultural maturity of their fellow citizens, a Palo Alto group argued that the residents of the valley did not currently demonstrate any interest in the art collection of the Stanford Museum. They objected strongly to spending tax money on the proposed San Jose museum which, they were convinced, would be even less well patronized.

One of the major arguments advanced against accepting the Senator's offer was that there were too many strings attached to the gift. But, in fact, there were few. As a devotee of California culture, it was not surprising that Phelan wanted the proposed museum to be a showcase for regional history and art. In this, he was supported by pioneer organizations that offered their collections for exhibition in the proposed museum. Nor is it surprising that, as a successful businessman and former civic official, Phelan stipulated that the county had to appropriate sufficient funds to maintain the building permanently as a museum. He did not want to transfer title of the Sainte Claire Club to the County, only to have it used after a few years for other purposes. If the building were no longer to be used as a museum or art gallery, Phelan insisted that it should return to his estate.

The Santa Clara County Board of Supervisors unanimously rejected Phelan's offer. With appreciation for his generous proposal, the board decided that without title to the property "for any purpose which the needs of the

Reluctant Art Patron

Regional government leaders had established a history of singular reluctance to take responsibility for the construction of a gallery or museum. During the previous decades, San Jose, the county's capital and principal city, had twice allowed the art collections of prominent citizens to escape to other locations. The numerous art objects gathered by the San Jose pioneer, General Henry Naglee, were offered to the city, but the offer was met with delay and indecision. Naglee abruptly rescinded the offer and gave his collection to the Crocker Gallery in San Francisco. Like so many other treasures, his art works were destroyed in the fire following the great earthquake.

An even larger collection purchased during European travels by Myles O'Connor, head of a prominent Santa Clara Valley family, was offered to the city if a suitable museum would be built to accommodate it. After great initial enthusiasm, the city again failed to respond to this opportunity to provide Santa Clara County with an artistic center. Neither public funds nor private philanthropy were forthcoming to produce the $20,000 required for building a suitable museum. Vexed with this public rebuff, the O'Connors packed off their treasures to a private college on the East Coast, along with a $200,000 check for the construction of a gallery. Once again timidity and indifference triumphed over civic vision.

Phelan's Provincial Retreat

James Duval Phelan always identified himself with San Francisco, its cultural riches, and its lively society. Even after the construction of Villa Montalvo, when not attending to his duties as senator in Washington, he spent the better part of his time in the city. Montalvo was a retreat, but one that offered more than recreation, sunshine, and the rural beauty of the Santa Clara Valley. It was also a luminous gravitational center for the elegant celebrities who inhabited Phelan's San Francisco social and cultural orbit — a great, welcoming oasis in the semiarid cultural landscape of a still rough-hewn California.

Following in the dusty tracks of his white, chauffeur-driven Mercedes, Phelan's friends, relatives, and clients made their way up the steep gravel road of Villa Montalvo for weekends filled with brilliant conversation, genteel exercise, memorable meals, and fun. With none of the hardships of the rustic stone and wood cabins his literary friends had laboriously built for themselves farther to the south along the Carmel coast, Phelan's provincial retreat offered all the amenities of civilization. Without the damp and chill of San Francisco's fogs, the good life of the city could simply continue in the warmth of the sun.

county may require," it could not accept his gift. Phelan's building on St. James Street, therefore, continued as before to house the Sainte Claire Club. To this day it remains a sedate and exclusive men's club in the heart of a redeveloped San Jose. The local population had to wait a generation for the establishment of a public art gallery in the Santa Clara Valley's major city.

The San Francisco Art Association

As Senator Phelan sat on the veranda of Villa Montalvo during the long evenings of his last summer, he must often have pondered the future of his beautiful estate. As much as he loved the Santa Clara Valley, and as much enjoyment as he had drawn from its warmth, its natural beauty, and its people, there was no existing cultural organization or public agency that could carry out his dream for Montalvo. The possible exception was Stanford University. It was relatively close, richly endowed, and enjoyed increasing prestige as a major institution of higher learning. But throughout his life, Phelan had demonstrated no particular interest in Stanford. After all, it had been the Notre Dame football team he entertained at his estate, not their Stanford foes. While not a vain man, it was natural for Phelan to wish Montalvo to be remembered as *his* contribution to the cultural development of California, not as a mere southward extension of the Stanford farm. Stanford, in fact, was not mentioned in his will. For a proper trustee for his most treasured endowment, he had to look to his native city. No doubt with some contentment, Phelan consigned Villa Montalvo to the care of that long established and experienced cultural organization over which he had once presided, the San Francisco Art Association.

Early in 1927, about the time Senator Phelan was attempting unsuccessfully to give San Jose the gift of a public museum, the San Francisco Art Association dedicated its recently completed Spanish Colonial Revival headquarters on the flank of Russian Hill. Built around a welcoming courtyard, the building, designed by Bakewell and Brown, was the latest home of the somewhat peripatetic Art Association. Founded in 1871, a decade after James D. Phelan's birth, the Association was one of the pioneer city's most important cultural organizations. Beginning over a fish market on Pine Street, and once sharing space with the Bohemian Club, the San Francisco Art Association had a career almost as colorful as that of San Francisco itself.

It attracted to its board of directors many of the city's leading citizens and artists. These were men committed to the Association's goals: "the promotion of Painting, Sculpture and Fine Arts akin thereto, the diffusion of a cultivated taste for art in the community at large, and the establishment of an Academy or School of Design." The training of young California artists in preparation for further art instruction in Europe became one of the principal tasks of the Art Association, and, as early as 1874, it began operating the California School of Design. This enterprise, which has undergone a variety of name and location changes, was the oldest art school in the western United States and continued to be the Art Association's most significant work.

From fish markets and garrets, in the 1890s the Association moved to the posh surroundings of the mansion atop Nob Hill built by the railroading pioneer, Mark Hopkins. This extraordinary venue for an art school had been donated to the Regents of the University of California in trust for use by the Art Association. The mansion, with its fanciful towers, marbleized wooden walls, and palatial living quarters, was the gift of Edward Searles, the young architect who married the widow of Mark Hopkins and became heir to her substantial fortune. The school was rechristened the Mark Hopkins Institute. Classrooms and an exhibition gallery occupied the mansion and, perhaps more comfortably, painting studios spread over into the stables. Bernard Maybeck and Douglas Tilden were just two of the many distinguished teachers who served on the faculty of the Institute.

The opulent and fanciful mansion was destroyed in the fire of 1906. Even after this catastrophe, however, temporary buildings were constructed on the same site and the redoubtable school soon resumed art instruction and public exhibitions. For a decade following the Panama-Pacific International Exposition of 1915, the Art Association operated a museum in the Palace of Fine Arts designed by Maybeck. According to its director, the museum became "the center of the cultural activities of our city, a rallying-place for all the arts, a sort of forum where the exponents of the Seven Arts may meet and have their say on a basis of their common interests in Art...." With the sale of the Nob Hill site in the 1920s, the Art Association acquired property at Chestnut and Jones. There it established a permanent home for its art school, which by then was called the California School of Fine Arts. (Under yet a new name, the San Francisco Art Institute, the school still continues its influential role in the development of the arts on the West Coast.)

In 1893, the extraordinary Nob Hill mansion built by Mark Hopkins became the home of the San Francisco Art Association's galleries and art school. With its gothic towers, mullioned windows, and mansard roofs, the eclectic wooden structure earned its sobriquet, "Hopkins' Folly." It provided a perfect setting for the Association's annual Mardi Gras costume ball, but was less satisfactory as a teaching facility. The devastating fire following the 1906 earthquake destroyed both the building and the Association's art collection. A temporary building at the same location housed the school for a number of years, but the site was sold in the 1920s when the art school moved to its new Chestnut Street facilities.

Framed by its acres of manicured landscaping, Villa Montalvo reflected the ideal lifestyle envisioned by its builder and host. Appropriately for the home of an United States senator, the American Flag flew near the entry road. As a joke, some of Phelan's servants erected a bare pine pole at the crest of the hill behind Montalvo and topped it with an old pot. They christened it "Teapot Dome."

By the time Senator Phelan drew up his will, the San Francisco Art Association had established an impressive record of successful cultural patronage while surviving earthquake and fire, dislocation, and depression over its nearly sixty year career. The Association's impressive new building, the work of the same architects responsible for San Francisco's elegant City Hall and Opera House, was a symbol of the city's artistic maturity. The building also symbolized the San Francisco Art Association's cultural leadership, as well as its permanence and dependability. The Association had proved financially resourceful and was undeniably committed to civic and cultural improvement in San Francisco. The sculpture and paintings exhibited for the public offered San Franciscans artistic education and personal enrichment. The Art Association art school brought recognition to California. Talented young people trained there consistently won top prizes in national competitions, often outshining students of older art schools of the East. Few things were dearer to James Phelan than the cultivation of artistic talent, especially when it reflected favorably on his native state. By bestowing the trusteeship for Villa Montalvo on the well-established and competently administered San Francisco Art Association, Phelan combined responsible public benefaction and the strong promise of artistic development.

A Cautious Response

It was probably inevitable that there would not be an easy transition between the ownership of Villa Montalvo by Senator Phelan and its trusteeship by the San Francisco Art Association. Montalvo had been a cultural oasis created for the pleasure of one urbane and wealthy man and his friends. Although Phelan had watched expenditures, both in the building and in the maintenance of the estate, with surprisingly close attention, Montalvo had been the apple of his eye. It allowed him the spaciousness and freedom to live the life he dreamed of as appropriate to California. Montalvo was both his palace and his playground. One of the many obituaries noted after his passing that Phelan had been "quick to see the value of the artistic touch in beauty of design and landscaping of playgrounds." What was true of the city playgrounds Phelan administered was even more true of his personal playground in the foothills of the Santa Cruz Mountains. He had not stinted on Montalvo. With its deer paddocks, its noisy macaws, its Egyptian obelisk, Temple of

Love, shaded benches, outdoor theater, and cellars filled with the finest champagnes, wines, and liquors, Villa Montalvo had been worthy of its sociable and pleasure-loving millionaire owner. He lavished his affection and his fortune on his villa.

But if Montalvo was Phelan's most beloved creation, that was not to be the case with its new proprietor. Two problems were immediately apparent. The first was geographical. Phelan had lifelong connections with the Santa Clara Valley, and it was natural for him to think of the Saratoga foothills as merely another accessible point on the compass of his far flung holdings. The San Francisco Art Association was more circumscribed in its cultural patronage and its geographical familiarity. The blossom-carpeted acres of the Valley of Heart's Delight might offer a pleasant springtime diversion by automobile, but not cultivated ground for aesthetic development. The Association's very name, as well as its constitution, testified to its total identification with the city of San Francisco.

The second problem was financial. Despite its appearance of stability and material success, the San Francisco Art Association, like the country itself, was entering into a period of economic stagnation and uncertainty. Senator Phelan died less than a year after the great stock market collapse that heralded the beginning of the depression of the 1930s. The Association's move to its new facilities had been costly, and its executive director, E. S. Macky, soon resigned his position and returned to the faculty because of "the present financial position of the Art Association." Signs of economic downturn were already clearly visible when the Art Association learned that it had been designated in the Senator's will as the trustee of his estate. Villa Montalvo, the fair and favored child of a well-heeled bachelor, was now offered as a distant stepchild to the hard-pressed parent of other needy offspring. At a time when the San Francisco Art Association's resources were becoming increasingly strained and donations were drying up, it was called on to make a decision on the Phelan bequest.

Although the San Francisco Art Association could undoubtedly provide a much needed cultural stimulus to the communities of Santa Clara County by administering the Montalvo property, the Association's response was cautious. From its first notification of the terms of the Phelan bequest, it realized that there were many perils along the way to successful fulfillment of the terms of that bequest. The Art Association was not ungrateful or unduly

Icicles hanging from the courtyard fountain were an unusual sight at Montalvo and not part of James Duval Phelan's Mediterranean vision. George Doeltz, an amateur photographer throughout his years at the estate, captured this winter surprise.

The oval swimming pool at Villa Montalvo, shown here surrounded by potted plants and impeccable landscaping, was a center of fun for Senator Phelan and his guests. After his death, the pool was eventually drained and filled in.

suspicious of an exceedingly generous gift, it was merely being realistic. After extending expressions of sympathy to the family of Senator Phelan, "a poet and true lover of the muses," the Association board of directors began a prolonged consideration of the offer. As a prelude to that discussion, and in order to have direct contact with the trustees of the Phelan Estate, Noël Sullivan, the Senator's musically gifted nephew, was asked to finish out his uncle's unexpired term. Before the end of the year, he was subsequently elected in his own right to a seat on the Association's board of directors.

The executives of the San Francisco Art Association recognized from the beginning the problem of administering Villa Montalvo at a distance, but the paramount concern was that the endowment left by Phelan was insufficient for his intended purposes. The correspondence of the officers of the Art Association, and official reports, committee records, and minutes of meetings of the board of directors, all carefully preserved in the library of the San Francisco Art Institute, give a detailed and realistic appraisal of the difficulties presented by the Senator's legacy. The principal of the legacy, $250,000, could not be touched. Only the interest was available to spend on upkeep and cultural programs. In the depressed financial conditions of the time, the Association's financial advisors anticipated an income that was far from generous. Estimating a five percent return, the available income would be at most $12,500 and, more likely, as little as $10,000 for an entire year. Without major economies, the cost merely to maintain the villa would be more than $10,000. Little or nothing would be left from the endowment income for the promotion of the arts.

Alternatives Discussed

Curiosity and concern brought the directors to visit Villa Montalvo. The executives of the San Francisco Art Association were distinguished businessmen and artists of the city, but it is clear that they were not intimates of James D. Phelan. They had not been part of the charmed circle invited to weekend at Montalvo. Now, without the irresistible host to welcome them at the entry door, they attempted to become familiar with the property posthumously offered them. With lawyers and trustees of the Phelan Estate in tow, they motored down the peninsula in groups to inspect the griffin-guarded grounds and empty buildings in Saratoga.

Impressed, but still uneasy with the modest size of the anticipated revenue, the Finance Committee of the Art Association approached Noël Sullivan with the hope of an alternative arrangement. According to the terms of the Senator's will, if the San Francisco Art Association refused to accept responsibility for Montalvo, the property would revert to the Phelan Estate. In order to retain some advantage from Phelan's generous bequest, but to avoid the liability of administering the Saratoga property, the Association spokesmen suggested to Sullivan, in March 1931, "some other means of perpetuating Senator Phelan's memory in exchange for the property at Montalvo and the $250,000 bequest."

By a somewhat curious article of the will, Noël Sullivan was to receive the guest house on the grounds of Villa Montalvo, "with a reasonable space surrounding the same." In addition, he was made the recipient of the entire contents of the villa itself. All Phelan's books and art works that were not specifically designated in the will, and all the furnishings inside the house, likewise went to Noël Sullivan. If the San Francisco Art Association was willing to reject the offer of Villa Montalvo in return for "a personal contribution to the Art Association" from the Sullivans, Montalvo and its treasures could have been kept intact and would have remained in the possession of the Phelan-Sullivan family. The offer must have been alluring. Noël Sullivan could have become the new master of Montalvo. Surrounded by the memories of his revered uncle, he could have continued to enjoy the good life he had tasted so often and so pleasantly there. But, after consulting with his sisters, Sullivan rejected the proposal. The intentions of their uncle regarding the disposition of his estate had to be respected, and the family did not wish to break the letter of the Senator's will.

On purely financial grounds it was probably unwise for the San Francisco Art Association to accept responsibility for Villa Montalvo. But respect for Senator Phelan's wishes, a sense of public responsibility, and basic good will dictated otherwise. The constitution of the Art Association succinctly stated its objectives. In addition to operating the art school, the objectives were to maintain a museum of fine and applied arts, to hold art exhibitions, and to provide fellowship for the membership of the Association. With no clear plan for its use, and no additional resources to meet the terms of the bequest, it was difficult to see where Montalvo fit into this pattern. Before calling for a vote on the acceptance of the Phelan property at a special board meeting,

University of California

From the earliest discussions regarding the acceptance or rejection of the Phelan property, there had been a suggestion that the University of California might be willing to accept the trusteeship of Villa Montalvo. The reason for this was the board of directors' concern for the reduction of the taxes paid on the property. The annual taxes levied on Montalvo at the time the Art Association assumed responsibility were nearly $3,000.

While by modern standards this may seem virtually insignificant, it represented nearly a quarter of the income available from the Senator's bequest. It was the Association's belief that a legal transfer of title to the University of California would qualify Villa Montalvo as a nonprofit educational institution and eliminate the taxes. This fond hope was one of the arguments in favor of accepting the Phelan bequest. Despite exchange of correspondence with the Regents of the University of California, nothing came of the proposal. However, it would not be the last time in Villa Montalvo's history that the idea of a transfer of title to an educational institution occurred.

The secluded garden paths of the villa and the trails laid out on the hillside behind the main house were among the most attractive features of the estate Senator Phelan left in his will as a park open to the public.

the president of the Art Association informed the members that the income was inadequate to do anything more than maintain the grounds and building. But with a combination of resignation and hope that must have been felt by many Californians during the depression, he recommended acceptance of the bequest. He promised to do "the best possible we can at the present time, hoping that something may develop in future years so that the ideas and wishes of Senator Phelan may be realized."

At the best of times it is difficult for a nonprofit group to turn down a substantial donation from a longtime member and generous benefactor. The San Francisco Art Association was certainly not the only institution that accepted a donation whose responsibilities it was ill equipped to handle. In addition to Montalvo, Senator Phelan had left the Art Association $100,000 for its other commitments, along with two exquisite Peale miniatures of George and Martha Washington. It would have appeared ungrateful, even churlish, to accept those bequests and reject responsibility for his beloved home in the Santa Clara Valley. After careful consideration of the legal advice offered by its attorney, F. M. McAuliffe, the San Francisco Art Association formally accepted the Phelan bequest of Villa Montalvo on May 14, 1931.

Financial Struggles

The immediate problem confronting the Association was the investment of the funds left by Senator Phelan. The board of directors established the Montalvo Trust and deposited the $250,000 in the Wells Fargo Bank and the Union Trust Company. The smaller bequest for the construction of exhibition halls at the Art Association's California School of Fine Arts was entrusted to the Crocker First Federal Trust Company and entitled the Phelan Fund. The choice of banks, which were to receive a five percent commission, was not well received by Noël Sullivan. The Art Association had asked Phelan's nephew to serve as the chair of a Montalvo Committee, but he was not consulted about the financial aspects of the bequest. Soon after the funds were deposited, he wrote the directors requesting that they invest the Phelan money with the Bank of America, whose directors had been close personal friends of his uncle, and with whom Phelan had many business dealings. His advice arrived too late. Villa Montalvo had changed hands, and Phelan's nephew, who had so charmed the Senator's guests with his conversation and singing, would no longer have any special role to play in the property. Claiming the press of other obligations, Sullivan resigned from the Art Association board of directors before the end of the year.

The banks were now instructed to develop plans for investing the funds. Given the recent collapse of the stock market, the board insisted that the major concern was safety, rather than high financial return from the funds. As a result, the money was tied up in the purchase of bonds issued by utilities, such as the Pacific Gas and Electric Company, returning a meager four-and-a-half to five percent, and railroads, such as the Southern Pacific. The latter bonds, at four percent to four-and-a-half percent, produced little in the way of income, but their purchase was rich in irony. The investment of money bequeathed by the fighting progressive James D. Phelan in railway securities was singularly inappropriate, since the railroads had long symbolized the deeply entrenched economic and political interests corrupting California.

The experiences of all too many investors in the stock market certainly dictated fiscal caution, and as a public trustee, the San Francisco Art Association felt its responsibility keenly. Its own economic circumstances were so straitened that the Association had to borrow $2,500 just to pay the fees for the Montalvo bond purchases. But this conservative policy of investing Phelan's legacy produced little income, and years would pass before the property could be developed as Phelan had wished into a center of the arts. Stringent economy, not cultural enrichment, became the Art Association's principal concern. This hardened into firm policy toward Villa Montalvo.

Although considerably smaller, the secondary bequest James Phelan left to the Art Association was to prove something of a distraction from its new responsibility as trustee of his country home. Phelan realized that since the destruction of its galleries in the Mark Hopkins mansion, the Association had no appropriate space to display its art. The Palace of Fine Arts and the Palace of the Legion of Honor had been used for the annual exhibitions, but neither offered a satisfactory permanent residence. The $100,000 left by Senator Phelan for the construction of galleries at the art school was intended to stimulate the San Francisco Art Association to fulfill its long-standing obligation. But, although it was a substantial bequest, the money was inadequate for a full scale museum, and the "unsettled economic conditions," as the Art Association reported to the Judge of the Superior Court in August 1934, did not allow it to raise the supplementary funds needed. Another, and

Although a trio of French doors open onto Montalvo's terrace overlooking the Santa Clara Valley below, the more modest Spanish doorway on the north side of the house was the main entrance to the villa. Awnings could be lowered to provide shade or protection from unseasonable rain. The large stained glass window above the entrance carried out Phelan's Spanish motif, depicting Cabrillo's voyage of discovery along the California coast.

Even though Montalvo was run with businesslike efficiency, during the Senator's frequent absences the domestic staff could take advantage of amenities designed for their cultivated and urbane employer. Here, sitting by the central fountain in the Spanish patio, one of the staff is enjoying a musical interlude.

less costly, possibility opened up with the completion of the new Civic Center. As part of this cultural complex, the Art Association opened the San Francisco Museum of Art in the Veterans Auditorium.

Although Phelan's bequest could not be applied to this project, since it specified that the $100,000 was to be used for construction of new galleries, the will also provided a convenient escape clause. The income from the trust could be used for student scholarships if the galleries were not constructed within a short time of Phelan's death. The San Francisco Art Association took full advantage of this clause. The Phelan money was used to fund travel scholarships for advanced students enrolled in the school. Without suffering from the potentially edifying, but uncomfortable poverty of many struggling artists, students could now make their way to Europe to study the artistic masterpieces in the great museums. James D. Phelan, who had delighted in these treasures during his many trips to Europe, would undoubtedly have been pleased with this outcome of his secondary benefaction to the San Francisco Art Association.

The maintenance of a new museum was an additional commitment of the Art Association's time and resources and a further distraction from Phelan's estate in Saratoga. At one of the few meetings held by the Association's Montalvo Committee, during the brief chairmanship of Noël Sullivan, the committee recommended that the grounds immediately be made accessible to the public according to the terms of the will. In order to provide adequate supervision, the committee proposed that a superintendent of Montalvo be hired, even designating General C. G. Morton of Los Gatos as a suitable individual for this position. When the Art Association approached General Morton, it found his terms too dear — an automobile and $200 per month. This salary alone, for a halftime position, represented nearly one quarter of the Art Association's entire income to operate Montalvo.

Luckily for the new trustees, Dr. Louis Mendelsohn, a friend and neighbor of Senator Phelan, stepped into the breech and, for nearly a decade, looked after the interests of the Art Association at Villa Montalvo. Learning of Mendelsohn's friendship with Phelan and his reputation for civic leadership, the Art Association president contacted Mendelsohn during the summer following the Senator's death and asked him to assume the function of superintendent of Montalvo. Mendelsohn already had a brisk medical practice and many local obligations when the Art Association suggested he take responsibility for Montalvo and guard the property against vandalism. But, as a former friend of Phelan, a concerned neighbor, and a man who willingly undertook public responsibilities, Mendelsohn agreed to supervise the estate.

In outlining his duties, the Art Association implied that these would be minimal. He would merely be responsible for issuing admission passes, setting ground rules for public use of the gardens, and giving instructions to the head gardener. Mendelsohn soon found that the responsibilities were far more demanding of his time, patience and good will. It was not uncommon to find him and fellow Montalvo neighbor, Michael Antonacci, going through the villa on stormy nights putting out buckets in an effort to prevent permanent damage from leaks in the roof. In addition to warding off the elements, Mendelsohn had to try to maintain the estate in respectable condition, repair broken water mains and downed power poles, ensure proper use of the facilities by visitors, and deal with a gardening staff no longer submissive to the Olympian authority of their former employer. One of the younger gardeners even had to be routed out of the Senator's bedroom, where he had decided to take up residence. In addition, Mendelsohn had to attend to the Art Association's mandate that he "observe every possible economy in the administration of the property." Observing its own precept, the Art Association had proposed that Dr. Mendelsohn undertake these duties entirely on a voluntary basis. Subsequently it agreed to pay him a largely token salary of $50 a month. Mendelsohn was to provide for any secretarial support and use his own car for transportation.

During the first years of his supervision, Dr. Mendelsohn was constantly looking for ways to economize. In terms of expenditures, the principal cost was the salaries of the three remaining gardeners who tended the entire estate without any mechanized equipment other than an antiquated truck. Doeltz and the other grounds keepers were now pressed to undertake painting and basic maintenance tasks around the estate. The elaborate flower beds were reduced, and time-consuming and expensive gardening chores were minimized. After surveying the wages of gardeners on other properties in the area, Mendelsohn advised the Art Association that the Montalvo gardeners were, in fact, overpaid. With the effects of the depression worsening, wage cuts were commonplace, and in an analogous situation, James D. Phelan himself had reacted to economic forces with similar economies. Although generous in the extreme, Phelan had been a scrupulous businessman when it

Louis Mendelsohn

Dr. Louis Mendelsohn had been one of the last people to see Senator Phelan alive. He had been in attendance when Phelan signed his will, and, along with a San Francisco doctor, tended the Senator during his last illness. Mendelsohn was not one of Phelan's old acquaintances, having moved to California from his native Boston in 1924. The doctor quickly became active in civic affairs in the little unincorporated village of Saratoga and established a wide circle of clients and friends.

Phelan's own circle, with the exception of a handful of emigre San Francisco intellectuals like the Olders and the Norrises, had rarely extended to the residents of the foothills or the valley. The Senator was a generous patron of local charities and provided gifts of flowers and greens for special events, but he seldom had close contact with the neighboring "villagers" of Saratoga. Dr. Mendelsohn was an exception. The physician literally intruded into Phelan's life when he built a house on the hill below Montalvo, disturbing the Senator's previously unspoiled view of the valley. Despite his initial annoyance, Phelan soon discovered that the Harvard-educated Mendelsohn enjoyed similar cultural interests.

A Royal Command

Not long after the first meeting with their distinguished neighbor, Mendelsohn and his wife, Marjorie, were recipients of one of James Duval Phelan's peremptory invitations to luncheon at Villa Montalvo. Years later, Mrs. Mendelsohn recalled that the summons by Phelan's secretary for the same afternoon "was rather in the nature of a most courteous but royal command." More invitations followed, and Phelan recognized that Dr. Mendelsohn was not only a scientist, but a skilled craftsman and a gifted violinist. The Senator adopted Mendelsohn as a personal physician, summoning him to attend him by sounding a siren at the villa that could be heard throughout the whole area. Phelan enjoyed spending the evening with Mendelsohn discussing music, poetry, and drama. In his will, Phelan showed his respect for Mendelsohn's medical expertise by leaving him and a fellow physician, Dr. John Gallway, a sum of money for research and outpatient care.

came to the running of Montalvo. He had demanded of his head gardener, for example, precise weekly reports of work accomplished, and the collection of Phelan's papers in the Bancroft Library, contains stacks of these meticulous, repetitive reports. With the end of hostilities in World War I, Phelan had noted that when American soldiers returned from the trenches, there would be a surplus of labor and, as a consequence, wages of the gardeners on his estate should be reduced. Unimpressed with this recent precedent, or the venerable economic theory of supply and demand, Doeltz countered Mendelsohn's suggestions by asking the Art Association for an increase in salary.

Mendelsohn could provide a degree of supervision and basic care for Villa Montalvo, but, working under the strict economic restraints imposed by the Association's limited budget, he could not prevent a gradual decline in its condition. The richly endowed villa was soon reduced to a mere shell of its former greatness. The house, according to the terms of the will, had been stripped of its furnishings by Noël Sullivan. Now insurance on the property was reduced, the elevator in the main house was put out of service, and routine care amounted to nothing more than a monthly cleaning by a visiting charwoman. During his lifetime, Phelan had enjoyed experimenting with technological innovations, occasionally to his own cost. One of his experiments was with a "Solar System" to provide hot water. The new trustees now had to remove it. The tile roof of the main house, which had been a constant problem since the original construction, proved particularly undependable during the heavy rains of 1933. Damage was done to the interior, and the ceiling of the dining room, in particular, was badly soaked. Without furnishings, without heating to ward off the damp of winter days, and without the accustomed staff that had tended it, the Phelan mansion's doors were closed to the world it had formerly welcomed so graciously.

Mendelsohn had to reduce drastically the costs of operating the grounds. The Senator's recent plans to shore up the roads into the villa and secure an improved water system were now impossible to execute. Many of the distinctive features of Phelan's estate also had to be abandoned. The deer paddock had been a constant delight to Montalvo visitors since the building of the villa, and among his numerous employees, Phelan had a special "guardian of deer." The Senator had personally negotiated for exchanges of bucks and does. The deer were now given to the East Bay Metropolitan Park. The aristocratic blue and white peacocks that used to strut ostentatiously along

Montalvo's paths disappeared, and the macaws suffered from disease and had to be shut in pens under quarantine. Particular favorites of Senator Phelan, the macaws came to a sorry end. The last surviving bird, given to Alum Rock Park, was placed in a cage only to become a victim of a thoughtless boy with a sling shot.

The Senator's dogs had been a characteristic and lively part of life at Montalvo, at times to the peril of smaller neighborhood pets. Hardly a year after Phelan's death, one of his neighbors, apparently believing the estate virtually deserted, complained directly to the president of the Art Association in San Francisco that the dogs roamed the grounds of Montalvo untended and barked throughout the night. Mendelsohn assured the Association that the dogs were properly kenneled and tended. But the general impression was that Montalvo had been abandoned. By explicit instruction of the Art Association, Mendelsohn kept heavy chains across the entrance to exclude the curious and preserve the access lane as a private road.

A passerby would have had difficulty reconciling appearances with the idea of Villa Montalvo as a "park open to the public." As trustees, the Art Association directors were concerned about their legal obligations to allow access to the villa, and they were forcefully reminded of their responsibility by a complaint from the Northern Federation of Civic Organizations:

> We note that the grounds of the villa are barred by a chain, and, as far as they can be seen from the roadway, are in a neglected condition. We would suggest that the failure to carry out with due expedition the generous purpose of the donor is inconsistent with a proper respect for his memory or a due regard for the interests of those who he intended would benefit through his generosity.

Dr. Mendelsohn had been cautioned not to allow permits for visitors to Montalvo until a policy for general operation of the villa was in place, and in the years immediately following Phelan's death, few visits were allowed. Some neighbors were given special permission to use the grounds for afternoon walks, and a few organizations, such as the Catholic Women's Center, the Book Club of California, a class in landscape design at the University of California, the Sierra Club, and the Edwin Markham Poetry Society, were allowed to have outings at the villa. According to Mendelsohn's accounts, however, throughout 1933, no more than 750 people were admitted to the

In his Italian Garden, James D. Phelan's sense of classical proportion, his love of art, and his appreciation of the human form combined to produce this attractive vista. With no resident domestic staff after the Senator's death, and only a few gardeners remaining to keep up the grounds, security against occasional vandalism became a serious concern for the new trustees.

One of the few photographs of Montalvo during this period records the visit of the Musical Honor Society from San Jose State College. Attired in long gowns, the women of the Society are seen reflected in the Senator's pool. The former master of Montalvo, who had often entertained students from the college, and who greatly enjoyed the company of beautiful women, undoubtedly would have been pleased with such charming and intelligent young guests.

estate. Only the gardens and hillside trails were open to these visitors. The house was entirely closed. Most guests were members of the San Francisco Art Association, which held an annual picnic at Montalvo for students, faculty and friends of the art school. On these occasions the swimming pool would be filled and the villa came to life once again with conversation and laughter. A few faithful friends of Phelan also arranged to drive down from San Francisco on an annual pilgrimage to celebrate the Senator's birthday.

The Art Association gradually formulated a general policy that permitted access by permit, but excluded any group that would attempt to raise funds by sponsoring events at Montalvo. Sensitive to the legal terms of its trusteeship, the Association tried to avoid any activities that appeared to contradict the spirit of Senator Phelan's will. With a skeletal staff available to watch over the grounds, and with parking limited to fifty automobiles, it exercised caution in allowing admission permits, and steered clear of activities that it considered inappropriate to the villa. Even with such strict restraints, there were still occasional incidents of disorderly conduct or vandalism to statues around the property.

By 1936, as economic conditions throughout the country became somewhat less bleak, the Art Association's attitude toward Villa Montalvo seemed more positive. With income from its Montalvo Fund exceeding expenditures by only a slight amount, the money available for developing the estate was still extremely modest, but the San Francisco trustees began authorizing much needed repairs. In March, the president of the San Francisco Art Association told the officials of the organization that "Montalvo must now come in for a special amount of attention." Public use of the estate increased considerably as more organizations and individual visitors were allowed onto the grounds. The Art Association even staged a Spring Festival, inviting hundreds of guests to picnic in the gardens and enjoy a concert in the outdoor amphitheater. Even during such an idyllic day in this protected sylvan setting, however, the depression, which had so severely impeded progress in carrying out Senator Phelan's wishes for the development of Villa Montalvo, cast its ever-present shadow. The afternoon's musical diversion was provided by the W.P.A.'s Federal Music Project, which provided work for otherwise unemployed musicians.

Chapter Nineteen

The Montalvo Foundation of the San Francisco Art Association

The hopeful prospect of economic improvement, as important as it was psychologically, and a gradually accruing Montalvo bank balance were not the only reasons for the Association's changing attitude toward the Phelan estate. One of the most significant reasons for this change was the presence on the board of directors of a remarkable woman, Anne Dodge Bailhache. More than any individual during the period of Montalvo's supervision by the San Francisco Art Association, she had a crucial and formative role in shaping the future of Villa Montalvo according to the Senator's wishes. Once she visited Montalvo, she recognized its potential as a center for the arts. She saw in its solitude a place of quiet for contemplation and renewal, and in the beauty of its natural setting, a place for inspiration and artistic creativity. As an artist and a San Franciscan, she shared Phelan's conviction that California would be enriched by a colony for painters, musicians, and writers that would nurture their own talent and stimulate love of the arts in the surrounding community. With sufficient vision and will, she believed the San Francisco Art Association had the opportunity to transform Montalvo into that nurturing and exciting artistic center.

Anne Dodge Bailhache began her association with the San Francisco Art Association soon after the organization accepted the trusteeship of Montalvo. She had a lifelong interest in the arts and was a very capable painter, whose works were exhibited in Bay Area galleries. As a founding member of the San Francisco Society of Women Artists, she had been invited to represent that organization at meetings of the San Francisco Art Association. Within a few years she became, in her own right, an artist member of the Art

Over the ornate Spanish doors of Villa Montalvo, James Duval Phelan installed an expansive window commemorating the 1542 voyage of Juan Rodríquez Cabrillo. An adventurer who had earlier taken part in Cortés' conquest of the Aztec Empire of Mexico, Cabrillo led a small fleet along the Pacific coast, past Monterey Bay, as far as Point Reyes. Phelan, like many Californians of his era, saw the state's history as a romantic pageant peopled by heroic figures like Cabrillo.

The Guest Cottage, built on the side of a steep ravine, contained apartments in which the Senator's friends stayed during their pleasant sojourns in the country. In the basement of the cottage, James Duval Phelan once stored his treasured supply of wines, champagnes, and liquors — a careful investment against the rigors of Prohibition.

The gift of the guest cottages to James Duval Phelan's nephew allowed Noël Sullivan, his relatives, and his friends to continue to enjoy the beauty of Montalvo on holidays or weekends. Phelan envisioned the pursuit of the arts taking place around them in the gardens and in the villa itself, the presence of Sullivan and his gifted companions lending additional ornamentation to that gracious cultural setting. Not burdened with the general upkeep of the villa, Phelan's nephew would still provide visible continuity with the founder of Montalvo. His presence would be a reminder of Phelan's great public benefaction. Noël Sullivan acted generously in transferring title to his building in the heart of Montalvo to promote the development of the estate according to his uncle's design.

Association's board of directors. Articulate, clear thinking, well organized, extremely industrious, and holding strong convictions, she more than held her own with the overwhelmingly male membership of the board Within a short time Bailhache was elected secretary and, more importantly, she became chairperson of its virtually moribund Montalvo Committee. After consulting her fellow artist members about potential uses of the dormant property, she became convinced of the value of this neglected treasure. Now a believer herself, she stimulated interest in Villa Montalvo among her fellow committee members as well as the Art Association's executives. It was primarily Anne Bailhache who supplied the ideas and the energy that led to the development of Montalvo as a center of the arts. Before any plan of development could be considered, however, the physical integrity of the property had to be restored by the Art Association.

The worldwide depression of the 1930s was undoubtedly the primary reason for the delay in carrying out the Senator's wishes for his estate, but another stumbling block was found in the terms of the will itself. Phelan had left the building known as the "guest cottage" to his nephew, Noël Sullivan. Even though the property was given as a public trust for the development of the arts, it was natural that Phelan should have wanted to perpetuate the relationship between his family and his beloved home.

Except for a number of utility rooms and servants' quarters, and a few old ranch buildings that were hardly usable, the cottages were the only accommodations outside the main building. Only a short walk from the villa, these apartments were close enough to be considered integral to the Montalvo complex. Noël Sullivan also owned a piece of land around the building and enjoyed a right of way through Montalvo to reach his property. If he saw fit, he had the legal right to construct an alternate road to his apartments through the property of the San Francisco Art Association.

Noël Sullivan, in fact, did not use the Montalvo cottages. Absorbed in developing his own artistic career and the many financial responsibilities connected with the Phelan Estate, his contact with Villa Montalvo was fitful after his resignation from the San Francisco Art Association Board of Directors. His title to the cottages was a serious drawback to any development of the estate as a cultural center. Until the physical integrity of the Phelan estate was guaranteed, the Art Association was reluctant to begin any systematic planning. To develop the estate as an artistic center in any coherent fashion, it was essential to have control of these apartments. The guest cottages were needed to house students and resident artists.

San Francisco Art Association officers and Sullivan began discussing the Montalvo property early in 1936. Having little cash for outright purchase of the cottages, the directors explored the possibility of a trade. Sullivan was willing to exchange the cottages for a six-acre parcel of Montalvo land containing two gardeners' houses. The land offered in trade by the Art Association was property along the exit road from Montalvo, contiguous to land that Sullivan, and his sister and brother-in-law, Frederic Murphy, already owned. After several months of negotiations, land surveying, and discussion of water rights, the amount of land to be traded for the guest cottages was reduced to a little over three acres. In addition, the Art Association paid Sullivan a modest sum to complete the transaction.

The trustees, according to Phelan's will, were to maintain the property as a park open to the public. That provision was straightforward and unambiguous. The succeeding stipulation, however, was open to a variety of interpretations. The buildings and the grounds immediately around them were "to be used as far as possible for the development of art, literature, music and

Access to Noël Sullivan's apartments on the Phelan estate was crucial for the development of Montalvo as an arts center. After a mutually beneficial exchange of property between Sullivan and the San Francisco Art Association, Anne Bailhache began developing a residence program for artists, musicians, and writers. The cottages were converted into comfortable self-contained apartments.

Artists' Colony Model

The San Francisco Art Association solicited information from the MacDowell colony and received encouragement and support from Edward MacDowell's widow, Marian, for the creation of a similar foundation in California. During his relatively brief life, Edward MacDowell, a talented painter, a concert pianist, and one of America's foremost musical composers, had planned to turn his rustic retreat in the woods at Peterborough into a refuge for young creative artists. He invested his fortune, earned from an exhausting schedule of concerts, composition, and teaching, in his estate. The grounds included both a picturesque log cabin, where he enjoyed composing, and Hillcrest, his imposing and spacious house. After MacDowell's death, his widow devoted her life to the execution of her husband's wishes.

The MacDowell property developed into a thriving art colony with a score of studios and nearly fifty buildings scattered throughout the grounds. These provided living quarters, dining commons, and lounges for summer residents. Old East Coast money supported the enterprise, and the colony attracted to its comfortable cabins some of the brightest and most creative talent of the younger generation. Aaron Copeland, Roy Harris, Willa Cather, Stephen Vincent Benet, and Edwin Arlington Robinson were a few of the better known artists in residence at Peterborough during its first quarter century. This colony, with its six hundred acres and twenty-five to thirty summer residents, was a model and a challenge for Villa Montalvo.

architecture by promising students." Phelan was quite specific about the areas of culture he wished to cultivate at Montalvo, but the method of cultivation was left undefined. The possibilities seemed to range from founding a fine arts school for children to an exclusive colony in which composers, painters, or writers of proven merit could find seclusion for further artistic development. Not mentioned explicitly in Phelan's will was any instruction for a cultural program for the residents of the surrounding community. It was left to Anne Bailhache to mold Montalvo into an institution and offer a viable program to advance the arts according to the terms of the will, and, as her thinking broadened, fill a cultural role in the Santa Clara Valley.

The San Francisco Art Association had a wealth of experience in art patronage and education, but it had no idea how to go about developing Villa Montalvo. One of the earliest suggestions made was that it should become a refuge for the arts, modeled on America's first great artist colony, the MacDowell Association in Peterborough, New Hampshire. No such haven for artistic development existed on the West Coast. The geographical setting of Montalvo, its woods and gardens, its ordered architecture and its tranquility, and, of course, the wishes of James Duval Phelan, argued strongly for a development similar to that of the prestigious MacDowell Colony.

Artists' Colony

This model guided Bailhache when she began formulating plans for "Montalvo: A Resident Foundation in Art, Architecture, Literature, Etc." This was basically in keeping with the initial thinking of the San Francisco Art Association regarding Montalvo, since, as early as 1931, it had looked on the Saratoga property as "a country residence for art students." But, guided by Bailhache's broader vision, the Phelan estate was to be far more than a mere adjunct to the California School of Fine Arts. It was to become a West Coast equivalent of the MacDowell Colony, offering the same opportunities for reflection and creative productivity to established artists. Through its San Francisco school, the Art Association already served aspiring and inexperienced young talent by offering introductory instruction and artistic formation. Bailhache now called for the Art Association to support those who were proven artists and writers by offering them a limited period of intense work in an ideal ambience. Montalvo, according to the carefully laid out plan developed by Bailhache, would be "a bodily and spiritual refuge, where the process of gaining access to the essential mood is rendered as simple as tact and understanding make it." Only those whose work passed the discerning scrutiny of established experts would be given the opportunity for residence. For the next dozen years, this concept of Villa Montalvo as a colony for mature artists remained the primary focus of Bailhache's efforts.

In meticulous reports, Bailhache laid before the Art Association her plans and the financial and material requirements. With the guest cottages, she believed there were now enough residential accommodations to begin operation as an art colony. Since all the buildings stood glaringly empty of contents, the Art Association first had to purchase furnishings. Residence apartments, whether in the main house, the cottages, or the servants' wing, had to be outfitted to make them livable; art studios with sky lights were to be created in the old servants' quarters. Bailhache estimated, rather optimistically, that there was sufficient capital accumulated in the trust fund to make these purchases and undertake the necessary renovations. Her detailed projections took everything from box springs to bath mats into account.

With its advantage of mild weather, it was assumed Montalvo, unlike the MacDowell Colony, could be operated throughout most of the year. Heading the operation would be a resident director, who would be in charge of business and cultural affairs and serve as the link between Montalvo and the San Francisco Art Association. A cook, a housekeeper, and two housemaids would look after the comfort of eight residents, each of whom was to be charged a modest weekly fee for room and board. As in former days, the dining and breakfast rooms would be used for meals. The library and billiard room were to be outfitted and restored to their original purposes, while the main hall would be devoted to meetings, lectures, and concerts. Bailhache anticipated that the program would expand to accommodate twenty artists in residence. And, according to her projections, the greater the number of residents, the larger would be the income and the more financially secure Montalvo would become. Citing the MacDowell Association, Bailhache assured the still skeptical directors that there would be no difficulty in finding artists eager to enjoy a period of residence at the Montalvo colony.

The Montalvo Committee of the Art Association praised Bailhache for her determination, her devotion to executing Senator Phelan's vision for Montalvo, and her personal inspiration. After nearly two years of discussion,

Wrought iron lanterns and grills, sharply contrasting with the pale walls of the villa, carry further the Spanish style that dominated the ornamentation and furnishings of Villa Montalvo. James Duval Phelan considered this style appropriate because of California's historic connection with Spain. He was complimented by one contemporary architectural critic for evoking at Montalvo "a tradition purely Californian."

In the Love Temple, a chaste Venus emerges from the ferns planted in the large basin at her feet. In contrast to the pure white figure, the basin is made of variegated stone. Satyrs cling to the edge, apparently more interested in keeping their difficult perches than in the attractive figure above them. This photograph was taken in 1925. During the 1940s, this statue was vandalized and what remained was damaged in the 1989 earthquake.

in 1937 the members unanimously accepted the Bailhache plan for developing the artist colony and proposed that she be appointed resident director on the estate. But despite the long-awaited development of a plan for an art center, delay followed delay. It would not be until 1939 that Villa Montalvo was opened, and then only after substantial modification of these original plans.

Insufficient Funds and Revised Plans

The continuing problem, insufficient funds, was predictably the primary cause of delay. The fragile surplus painstakingly accumulated each year was sharply reduced soon after Bailhache presented her plan. An increased county tax rate and unforeseen financial charges against the trust fund wreaked havoc with the projected income necessary to develop Montalvo. The committee's description of the income early in 1938 as being in a "very precarious position," was hardly an exaggeration, since the net annual increase was expected to be a mere $717.85. For all of Bailhache's influence and enthusiasm for Montalvo, her development program had to be shelved to await a stronger financial position. While California and the nation were beginning to experience the heartening signs of economic recovery, on the local institutional level the progress was uneven and sometimes painfully slow.

James D. Phelan's dream for his country home had to wait still a little longer for fulfillment, but in some ways the delay was fortunate. Forced to distance herself from the original plan, Bailhache had an opportunity to question her formulation and broaden her thinking about Montalvo. Appealing as an idyllic artists' retreat was to a working artist like Anne Bailhache and to other artists connected with the San Francisco Art Association, it was a limited conception for use of the estate. Undaunted by the enforced delay, but increasingly more aware of economic realities, Bailhache now expanded her plan to include two additional programs. The first was to found on the Montalvo estate an extension of the California School of Fine Arts. The second, and critical, addition was to sponsor an association of local residents who would become financial supporters of Villa Montalvo and link the San Francisco Art Association to the community.

Both these new aspects of the Montalvo proposal were responses to immediate needs. Artists at the California School of Fine Arts and artist members of the San Francisco Art Association looked at the Phelan property as an adjunct facility to their art school. In their view, its purpose was to serve their own artistic development and provide them with an alternate, and very inviting, locale for art instruction. They were not reticent in sharing their views with the Montalvo Committee, and Bailhache was sympathetic to their argument. Accordingly, a graduate summer school in art was projected, with the intention of adding advanced instruction in music, landscape architecture, and creative writing as time went on. Within months, and for a variety of reasons, the development plan included a Montalvo branch campus of the art school that would hold classes throughout the year. Classroom and individual instruction in the arts was to be the second major dimension of the artistic program contemplated for Villa Montalvo.

One of the concepts that became increasingly important as Bailhache and her committee continued their prolonged deliberations was the opportunity to "decentralize" culture. Opportunities to hear the finest music, or see quality art works, or cultivate or enjoy literary talent were normally identified with major metropolitan centers. Bailhache was aware that Santa Clara County still retained its agricultural character and that no public art gallery existed between San Jose and San Francisco. In terms of higher culture, it was an underdeveloped area. The plan for Montalvo evolved into a cultural center that would bring the highest arts of civilization to a provincial world. An extension branch of the Art Association's school on the Phelan grounds would be a major step in that process of cultural decentralization.

The second, and far more important, step toward decentralization was the formation of a community association linked to Montalvo. In terms of the general public, a strict interpretation of Senator Phelan's will could reasonably argue that the Art Association's only obligation to the community was to allow residents access to the gardens and grounds of the villa. Until now, admittance had been given to groups or individuals only by permit. Greater public access to the grounds as a park would be possible when the Art Association began its artistic operation on the grounds in earnest. There was no necessary connection between the two functions of Montalvo as public park and center for artistic development, as there was none between the two clauses in the will. Such a narrow view, however, seemed to violate the spirit of Phelan's bequest. His interest in art and music, his commitment to refinement and beauty, his own generous and welcoming style as host at Montalvo, and his gift of the villa to the public argued in favor of a more

The solarium today has been glassed in as it was in James Duval Phelan's day. See the photograph in Chapter Eleven as a comparison.

Public Scolding

With its customary caution, the San Francisco Art Association did not rush into activity, and it received a public scolding. After visiting Villa Montalvo, John D. Barry, a columnist for the *San Francisco News,* noted that James D. Phelan's memory was not well served by the present condition of the estate. Under the caption, "Magnificent Estate Bequeathed to a Group of Artists, and Left Unused for Many Years," the journalist chastised the Art Association for its lack of progress at Montalvo. He pressed the Association to inaugurate the long awaited art center at the Phelan mansion as part of the upcoming Golden Gate Exposition.

As the Panama-Pacific Exposition had marked San Francisco's recovery from the devastating earthquake and fire a generation before, the city planned a Golden Gate Exposition for 1939 as a symbol of restored confidence and energy after the dulling years of depression. Phelan had been integrally involved in the city's recovery from that earlier crisis. "It would grieve him if he could know that so far his wish for the property he had developed so skillfully had been defeated," Barry wrote, urging the immediate opening of Montalvo. Phelan's heirs and the trustees of the Phelan Estate were also concerned and disappointed that the Art Association had not yet executed the Senator's wishes for Montalvo.

democratic interpretation. The artistic growth of "promising students," specified in the will, could be expanded to promote the artistic cultivation of a broader public. Phelan was a gifted amateur, and his concern for the "development of art, literature, music and architecture" could certainly be conceived of in terms of awareness, appreciation, and enjoyment by nonspecialists. The Art Association had demonstrated its commitment to promoting artistic education and enjoyment among the public.

The San Francisco Art Association had no intention of excluding the neighboring community from the benefits of Montalvo, but only gradually broadened its own vision to see the integration of the community as a vital and necessary part of any plan for developing the property. Financial necessity now joined with aesthetic commitment to bring a new emphasis to community participation. It became increasingly clear that the Art Association did not have the fiscal resources to develop Villa Montalvo in any significant way on its own. To succeed at all, Bailhache and her committee now realized that Montalvo must become a recognized center of the arts serving the neighboring community. Community support was indispensable for any viable program at Montalvo.

New Plans Announced

With the approval of the board of directors, Anne Bailhache publicly announced the plan in the fall, 1938, issue of the *San Francisco Art Association Bulletin.* The three components were residential units for artists, advanced level art instruction, and a program of cultural and educational community activities offered in conjunction with a local support group. The multifaceted program was to serve a variety of needs — artistic, educational, and community. Broadly defined, the plan tried to do a great deal. Montalvo's cultural benefits would embrace artists, students, and the general public. Through this plan, Bailhache believed that the Art Association could carry out Phelan's vision of Montalvo as the potential "Athens of the West."

Because of the constant problem of limited financial resources, so ambitious a program clearly ran the risk of falling short of its stated goals. But Bailhache took a pragmatic approach. She cautioned that it was imperative to grow slowly and wisely. In words that could apply to the spirit guiding the development of Montalvo at any time during the next four decades, she wrote:

To grow only as the need for growth develops is the basic principle upon which the plan has been built. Changing years with their own requirements may eventually change the pattern of the original plan. For the present, the functional relationships of the whole are interchangeable. If actual development in any section reveals its impracticability it may be abandoned without sacrifice of the whole.

The plan recognized that Villa Montalvo was not the exclusive preserve of any one group or any particular interest and allowed for growth and adaptation. The San Francisco Art Association had not won much credit during its early tenure as trustee of Villa Montalvo. Through the work of Anne Bailhache, however, the foundations were laid for a cultural institution able to survive an uncertain and rapidly changing future.

Before implementing this plan, Bailhache, the newly appointed director of the Montalvo Foundation of the San Francisco Art Association, solicited the opinions of educational and cultural leaders. President Ray Lyman Wilbur of Stanford University, Elizabeth Sprague Coolidge, a distinguished patron of music in Washington D.C., the regional president of the American Institute of Architects, the directors of the area's major art museums, and other educators, artists, and community leaders returned encouraging replies. Then Bailhache asked her fellow member of the Art Association's board, architect Eldridge T. Spencer, to design plans for the necessary renovations to the villa and the guest apartments. In addition to structural changes, Spencer calculated the cost of isolated artists' cottages that Bailhache hoped would later be constructed throughout the grounds of the estate.

Bailhache was originally allocated a mere $5,000 by the Art Association for improving and furnishing Montalvo. This represented about half of the accumulated interest on the endowment fund since its inception, after deducting expenses for maintenance. The sum proved inadequate and Bailhache came back to the Association for additional funds. Before the doors to Montalvo could be opened the following summer, virtually the entire accumulated income from the fund was spent. Bids were let out in the spring of 1939, and trucks loaded with workers and building materials were soon noisily winding their way up the narrow gravel road to the villa. From the small rooms in the guest cottage, the contractor constructed four comfortable apartments, each with a work space, bedroom, bath, dining area and fully

James Duval Phelan's appreciation for honest sensuality was clearly revealed in his choice of ornamentation for his gardens. Here the three graces huddle amidst the shrubs and flowers of Villa Montalvo.

Griffins, perched on high pedestals and standing watch over the entrance to Villa Montalvo, were fanciful recreations of the fierce creatures described by Garci Ordonez de Montalvo. They proved slight protection against vandalism during the period Montalvo was effectively closed to the public and barred by a metal chain across the entrance road.

equipped kitchenette. These were to be the first of the twenty envisioned resident artists' living units. The main building was painted and repaired, put in good working order, and modestly furnished. One of the rooms was converted into a small art gallery in which Bailhache could mount monthly exhibits. A director's suite and administrative offices were outfitted upstairs. After considering turning the main room on the ground floor into a memorial to Senator Phelan and replicating the heavy Spanish style furnishings he had enjoyed, Anne Dodge Bailhache decided this would prevent the room from being used for other necessary functions. Instead, it was left to serve for more than twenty years as Montalvo's principal lecture and concert hall. It's now used for fundraisers, rentals, and pubic tours.

Even before renovations began, Bailhache prepared a portfolio of photographs, architect's drawings, and background materials to send to philanthropic foundations. To make Montalvo the full-fledged, productive art center of the new plan, substantial funding would be required. The Carnegie, Rockefeller, and a number of other foundations received materials. Bailhache's chief hope lay with the Rockefeller Foundation. David Stephens, the Foundation's Director of the Humanities, visited California in the spring, and made a special trip to Montalvo. He was impressed with the villa's potential as an artistic center and complemented the Association on its development proposals. Bailhache was sufficiently encouraged that she considered delaying renovations, so that the Foundation would not be dissuaded from funding the entire project. Despite continuing correspondence, however, Rockefeller support did not materialize. Instead, the Foundation urged the Art Association to cultivate local support for its undertakings.

The advice confirmed Bailhache's increasing awareness of the need to develop a committee of Santa Clara County residents. The Art Association had already begun to look to the neighborhood surrounding Montalvo for allies in the effort to create an arts center, and it was soon obvious that there was substantial local support for the proposed development. Montalvo, so long dormant, could become a significant regional asset and a point of local pride. Some residents remembered the Senator, far more were aware of his exquisite country home and its legendary tradition of urbane hospitality. Most visitors who had been admitted to the grounds since Phelan's death were local people from no greater distance than San Jose.

The Montalvo Society

Louis and Marjorie Mendelsohn, who had both devoted so many hours watching over Montalvo, were among those who recognized the potential of this undeveloped neighborhood treasure. As respected figures in Saratoga and the Santa Clara Valley, the Mendelsohns were perfect catalysts for the formation of a local association of Villa Montalvo supporters. At the request of Bailhache, in early October 1938, Dr. Mendelsohn brought together a small group of selected residents to discuss an organization to support cultural activities at Villa Montalvo. Their positive and enthusiastic response led to a subsequent meeting later in the month with officers of the Art Association at a buffet luncheon at the villa. Those attending affirmed that there was substantial local support for cultural development in the area and a willingness to support it financially. One local artist was so thoroughly convinced of widespread support for Montalvo that he suggested that, instead of looking only to patrons who could afford a substantial fee, membership should be only a dollar. He predicted that there would quickly be a hundred thousand residents enrolled as members. Without following this egalitarian prescription, the group unanimously approved the Art Association's three part proposal for Montalvo and set up an organizing committee, chaired by Dr. Mendelsohn, to draw up a constitution and bylaws for the new local auxiliary, the Montalvo Society of the San Francisco Art Association. Mendelsohn was supported by five other local residents. These original organizers of the Montalvo Society — Mendelsohn, Lucy Whiting, Henry Newmark, Mabel Pierce, Gustave Epstein and George Dennison — shared a vision that Senator Phelan's wishes for Montalvo could become a reality.

As a demonstration of its commitment to local participation and to establish closer communication, the Art Association's own Montalvo Committee expanded its composition to allow an equal number of members from the local community to join the representatives of the San Francisco Art Association. Mendelsohn and his colleagues now joined Bailhache's directing group in drawing up a list of hundreds of individuals to be invited by the Art Association to become charter members of the new Montalvo Society.

Villa Montalvo once again opened its gates to the public on July 29, 1939, with walls newly painted, red tile roof patched, and four residential artists apartments ready for occupancy. As James Duval Phelan had wished, his

Montalvo Open Again

For that sun-filled afternoon on July 29, 1939 when Villa Montalvo reopened, in an atmosphere reminding many visitors of Fitzgerald's *The Great Gatsby,* the lingering effects of the depression were forgotten. Members of the Art Association, distinguished patrons of culture, and newly recruited members of the Montalvo Society promenaded along the garden paths and sipped iced drinks on the expansive terrace. Temporarily forgotten, too, were disturbing newspaper reports of the territorial demands by Germany, which within two months would plunge the world into war. So, too, were accounts of the military expansion of James D. Phelan's old nemesis, Japan.

Officers of the San Francisco Art Association welcomed guests to this place of cultural hopes and artistic promise. Dr. Stephen C. Pepper, head of the art department at the University of California, hailed the inauguration of the first refuge for artists in the Western United States. Voicing the vision that inspired the new Montalvo Society, he foresaw that, "through the cooperation of the artists and the community, Montalvo in its silence and beauty will become one of the creative forces of the world."

One of the premier musical ensembles of the world, the Budapest String Quartet, played a program of Beethoven, Schubert, and Haydn quartets in the great hall. The French doors were opened so that many of the guests could listen to the music from the shaded veranda above Montalvo's gently sloping gardens. Beyond, in the heat of the summer sun, lay the Santa Clara Valley, which that day became the recipient of Phelan's generous gift.

The Coolidge Foundation

The first artists to take advantage of Montalvo's residence program were the musicians who formed a quartet hardly less distinguished than the Budapest ensemble. The Coolidge String Quartet, through the patronage of Elizabeth Sprague Coolidge, took up residence and performed four concerts at the villa during the month of September 1939.

The Coolidge Foundation in the Library of Congress underwrote the cost of this series of concerts and allowed the Montalvo Society to inaugurate its program of events in extraordinary style. Mrs. Coolidge attended the July opening of Montalvo and for the next three years took a close interest in the development of the villa's program. She occasionally stayed as a guest of Montalvo in the main house, and, until the American entry into World War II, continued to contribute her Coolidge Quartet as one of the summer music offerings at the Phelan estate.

home had at last been transformed into a center for the development of the arts and his gardens and forested hillside into a park to be enjoyed by the public. More than four hundred people made their way to Villa Montalvo for the formal inauguration of the art center.

As had been hoped, the first artists in residence at Montalvo found the serenity and beauty of the villa conducive to concentration and serious study. The Montalvo Foundation attempted to continue the relationship between the Phelan family and the art center by inviting Noël Sullivan to become an officer of the Montalvo Society Board of Governors. Although he was already one of the principal patrons of the Bach Festival in Carmel, Sullivan does not appear to have taken any active role in directing the new association. He did not accept the Foundation's invitation to serve on its committees, but occasionally wrote the director recommending musical friends who wished to become affiliated with the art center. Soon after the official opening, Sullivan volunteered to contribute a concert to the Montalvo center. An accomplished basso, he sang a program of arias and songs before an audience of family friends and Montalvo supporters in the outdoor theater.

The Montalvo Society grew quickly in membership, and within a few months more than 250 people were enrolled as contributing members. The Montalvo Society also took financial responsibility for the small gallery, set up in Senator Phelan's library, that opened to the general public in October, 1939. It sponsored monthly exhibitions, and one of its principal purposes was to offer to visitors a taste of the most recent developments in the arts.

One of the pressing concerns of the Montalvo Foundation was instituting the promised extension branch of the California School of Fine Arts. Even more pressing was the issue of tax exemption. Repeated efforts by the Art Association had not won an exemption from county taxes. Santa Clara County assessors were unimpressed by the claim that Villa Montalvo was a branch of an educational foundation, since there had been no evidence of any educational activities during the long period Montalvo lay dormant. A further benefit of the project was that art instruction would be made available to young Santa Clara Valley residents who would otherwise have no such opportunity to develop their talents. Instructors from the San Francisco school could also enjoy a refreshing change of venue, and become liaisons between the artistic community of the city and the Montalvo Foundation.

Art School

The Art School at Montalvo began its brief career in February, 1940. Lucien Labaudt, a highly regarded mural painter and designer, came from San Francisco to lead the first program. Three days a week, he offered courses in still life and landscape painting. He was joined by another outstanding painter, William A. Gaw (soon to become the Acting Director of the California School of Fine Arts), who taught outdoor drawing and painting. The program, which continued for about two years, attracted a creditable enrollment, with more than fifty students during its summer session. The school was originally planned as a component of an art program exclusively for graduate students. Bowing to reality, the Montalvo classes quickly lowered their sights and offered instruction to beginners as well as advanced students. To supplement enrollment and provide additional advantages to the neighboring community, Saturday classes for children soon followed.

With extension art classes going forward, the San Francisco Art Association once again attempted to interest the Regents of the University of California in accepting legal title to Villa Montalvo. The Art Association was willing to retain its responsibility for Montalvo as an art center and would continue directing the art school on its grounds. The Art Association informed the regents that the Santa Clara County assessor had promised to remove Villa Montalvo from the tax rolls if the University agreed to the transaction. The Association's lawyer, Florence McAuliffe, drew up documents for a transfer of title and presented them to the regents early in 1940. Realizing that Montalvo's financial position would be far stronger if the heavy tax burden was removed, Noël Sullivan and the other trustees of the Phelan Estate agreed to this alteration in legal title to the Senator's property. The regents failed to act on the petition, however, and the Art Association had to continue to pay the burdensome taxes. The Association president informed the regents that without violating the spirit of James Phelan's will, transfer of title and the ensuing relief from its tax liability would have allowed the Art Association the opportunity to expand its educational and cultural program at Montalvo. All too soon it became clear that the art center at Villa Montalvo remained economically vulnerable.

The Montalvo Society and the resident director could be quite satisfied with the progress of the art center during the first two years of its operation.

Prestigious Board of Advisors

In order to give its work increased credibility and provide artistic guidance for its endeavors, the Montalvo Foundation decided to create an advisory board. The director invited respected artists, musicians, and educators in the Bay Area to become charter members. From the University of California alone, the heads of four separate departments — Music, Art, English, and Architecture — accepted membership on the advisory board. The director of the San Francisco Museum of Art, already a supporter of the Montalvo project, also agreed to join. Pierre Monteux, the famous conductor of the San Francisco Symphony Orchestra, who had conducted the riotous premier of Stravinsky's *Rite of Spring* a generation before, likewise accepted the invitation. Like so many illustrious corporate advisory committees, despite an impressive charter of responsibilities, this one contributed little to the actual direction of Montalvo. But the willingness of the members of this blue ribbon committee to be associated with Villa Montalvo was a clear indication of widespread support in the educational and artistic community for the concept of the art center.

More Taxes

In the years following Phelan's death the county had wanted to raise the taxes on the estate. Having heard that the villa was filled with priceless art treasures, the assessors were not convinced until they walked through Montalvo's empty rooms that the rumors were entirely false. To avoid a tax the county wanted to charge on the estate's orchards, the Art Association even had to order the gardeners to stop cultivating the fruit trees. It was hoped that a branch campus of the California School of Fine Arts could convince the county to eliminate, or at least reduce, the taxes on the property.

The charm of Montalvo's gardens, the beauty of its architecture, the memory of its former proprietor, and the distinction of its cultural programs brought increasing numbers of visitors. Expanding local support was one of the most encouraging features of these early years of the art center. Membership in the Montalvo Society continued to grow, and an annual treasury of about $2500 was available for the programs and special projects at the villa.

With growth, the Montalvo Foundation also became increasingly more complicated and cumbersome in administrative structure. Good intentions, tempered by inexperience, resulted in the creation of a whole series of confusing parallel committees and subcommittees, all having some relationship, however tenuous, to the San Francisco Art Association. Within a year of the formal opening, the director had attempted to simplify this complicated and redundant administrative organization. However, when she moved to merge the local organization's board of governors into the Montalvo executive committee, giving the neighbors equal representation with the San Francisco Art Association, her proposal was defeated by the local leadership. The Montalvo Society, far from being merely a pocket to be opened upon request, was beginning to establish its own proprietary interest in the operation of Villa Montalvo. This autonomy was of sufficient concern to the Art Association's legal counsel that he advised the board that the Foundation's administrative structure, in particular the local Montalvo Society, was illegal.

One of the influential local supporters of Montalvo, Robert Kirkwood, Jr., also recognized that there was a structural problem in the administration of the art center. Kirkwood was a respected member of the Saratoga community and a successful Republican politician, who succeeded Dr. Mendelsohn as president of the Montalvo Society. Kirkwood presented the San Francisco Art Association with a proposal which, in effect, would have relieved it of responsibility for Villa Montalvo. He was determined that the local residents should be given a more authoritative voice in the administration of Montalvo than they had received in the past. Seeing potential problems among the Montalvo Society, the director, and the Art Association because of a lack of clear lines of responsibility, he proposed a careful definition of each body's responsibility, and a shift of power among the existing bodies. Kirkwood's analysis of the administrative problems of the Montalvo foundation was insightful, and his proposed solution was realistic and sensible. However, since it explicitly removed Montalvo from control by the Art Association and implicitly undermined the authority of the resident director, it was not favorably received. The Art Association directors, distracted by other and more pressing commitments, reverted to the policy of giving only fitful attention to the Phelan estate. The board did not, and probably could not, give Montalvo the support needed. In the years after World War II this led to the failure Kirkwood had predicted, and, ultimately, to the transfer of trusteeship to other and more willing hands.

A more immediate concern to Montalvo was the continual shortage of funds. The percentage of Montalvo Society membership fees contributed to the general fund, the interest from the Phelan bequest, and occasional donations to the Foundation did not provide nearly enough money to reach the goals stated in the development program. To realize these goals, Bailhache devoted much of her abundant energy to soliciting funds from the major cultural organizations on both coasts. The director again outlined her plans in writing for the Guggenheim and Rockefeller Foundations, and the Rosenberg Estate. But she was unable to obtain institutional support.

In the first weeks after Pearl Harbor, Anne Bailhache realized that, as long as the war lasted, for Montalvo and other cultural institutions it could not be business as usual. The Montalvo Society, which had sponsored most of the presentations at the art center, suspended virtually all of its activities for the duration of the conflict. Membership in the Society declined, and only a token sum of money was transferred to the Foundation for general upkeep. Without this indispensable financial and community resource, the possibilities for Montalvo to continue its work correspondingly dwindled. Even with adequate resources, however, it is questionable whether Montalvo could have continued its operation unchanged. Long working hours, patriotic volunteer work, and public attention increasingly fixed on previously unheard of locations in North Africa, Europe, and the Pacific left little time for people to concentrate on art exhibits, lectures, and concerts. The discouragement of unnecessary travel by automobile, or even by public transportation, meant that pleasurable outings to the Phelan estate in the foothills were a luxury that most citizens had to live without. The imposition of gasoline rationing, combined with the scarcity of tires for civilian passenger cars, virtually ended public use of Villa Montalvo during the war years.

While Bailhache could not foresee all these developments, when the war began she attempted to define a new role for the art center during the con-

Art and Music at the Villa

By the spring of 1941, some five hundred people per week strolled through the grounds or viewed the art exhibits in the villa gallery. The Montalvo Society offered a distinguished program of lectures by Andre Maurois, Alfred Frankenstein, Gaetano Merola, and the British art curator, H.S. Ede. Musical programs were among the most successful presentations by the Montalvo Society. In addition to chamber groups, the society offered piano concerts and vocal recitals by singers from the Metropolitan Opera. More challenging to the traditional tastes of most of its members were the composers' forums that featured the works of the American musicians Roy Harris and Roger Sessions. For a forty cent admission charge, the terrace and lawn of the villa were opened to the public for picnicking and a concert by an eighty piece symphony orchestra and the Northern California Negro Chorus, both sponsored by the W.P.A.

Artists, musicians, and writers occupied the residential units, and, in addition to pursuing their own projects, occasionally made personal contributions to the cultural atmosphere at Montalvo by showing their creative work, performing, or lecturing. The gallery exhibited works of young Californians and, faithful to the spirit of Phelan's wish to nurture the arts, the art center sponsored a day long forum for eighty young artists, musicians, writers, and dancers living in the Santa Clara Valley. The high point of the day's many events was a dance performed in the bottom of Senator Phelan's empty swimming pool, with the spectators dangling their feet along the edge. The first theater production offered at Montalvo was also the work of young actors, three short plays by the Clay M. Greene Players of Santa Clara University.

Living Up to the Dream

In Anne Bailhache's view, even the successes the art center enjoyed at the local level were not living up to Senator Phelan's vision for Montalvo. "He dreamed of creators in the arts from distant places coming to this valley and enriching it as well as the whole world through sojourn here," she wrote in an article for the *San Jose News* early in 1941. The Montalvo Foundation was responsible for fulfilling Phelan's dream of making the Santa Clara Valley "a cradle of the future American arts." To realize this vision would take far more monetary resources than she could obtain from the Phelan trust, the Montalvo Society, or occasional local donations. For Bailhache, the real index of Montalvo's success was its development as a major artists' sanctuary. This was the part of the development plan closest to the director's heart. As she told an interviewer for *Life* magazine a couple of months later, "Our principal interest is to develop it as a place for individual creative research." For this, Montalvo needed additional residence units and detached studios scattered about the estate. It also required a music complex with recital hall and practice rooms, ateliers for large mural painting and sculpture studios, along with a little theater for experimental productions, and, for good measure, a drama school. In short, Montalvo required money, and lots of it.

flict. Inspired by the widespread public desire to contribute to the war effort, she drew up plans to convert Villa Montalvo into a rehabilitation center for wounded soldiers. She recommended that the Art Association turn the entire estate over to the American Red Cross for the duration of the war.

Bailhache believed that Phelan would have fully supported the use of his estate as a Red Cross rehabilitation center during the war. The Art Association agreed with her, taking the view that the letter of the law should not stand in the way of its spirit. However, when the trustees sought legal advice concerning the proposed transfer, their lawyer was strongly opposed. In his opinion, even though Villa Montalvo would continue to emphasize the arts, the terms of the trust ruled out any such use of the property. Without specific instructions from the court, no such scheme could be undertaken. And he was convinced that the court would never authorize this change in the terms of the trust. Bailhache's plans to mobilize Villa Montalvo for the war effort collapsed, and the art center was to sit out the war years classified 4-F.

After the War

Like the other institutions sponsored by the San Francisco Art Association, as well as colleges, galleries, and museums throughout the nation, Montalvo suffered during the war years. The most threadbare of operations was kept going, but most of its diverse cultural program simply ceased.

During the war years, Montalvo endured, if it did not thrive, but with the lifting of wartime restrictions on travel and the end of rationing it prepared to resume its activities. Emblematic of a renewed sense of confidence at Montalvo was the energetic planning for the future during the immediate postwar years. A small surplus of funds had been built up during the enforced quiet of the war, and Bailhache's fertile imagination had no trouble devising plans for its expenditure on the art center. The inactivity of the war years behind her, the irrepressible director once again churned out scores of memos, responses to letters, sketches of plans for new facilities, and reports to the trustees. The Montalvo archives preserve hundreds of these drafts, many of which she dashed off at speed on the backs of old Montalvo programs, or on government requisition forms listing the amounts of peanut butter and pickles to send to local military bases. Montalvo was a lean operation.

The local Montalvo Society did not resume its activities immediately after the war, but Bailhache sponsored her own program for the community, charging a small fee to pay for the events. Music had been a staple of Montalvo's cultural life, and she began once again the popular series of chamber concerts. The art gallery in the main building reopened with showings of some of Montalvo's guest artists and began a regular schedule of exhibits in the spring of 1946. As applications increased from interested artists, musicians and writers, guest residents accommodations were expanded to ten units. These included the "Gertrude Atherton Room" as well as others in the main house and the wing near the swimming pool.

Projects and plans scuttled by the outbreak of war reemerged, and during the first months of peace the director renewed her efforts to allow Montalvo to "take its place as one of the important cultural and educational institutions in America." Residential graduate workshops, a lecture program, and an expanded summer series of musical concerts, master classes in violin and piano, improvement of physical facilities including new studio space, and a new entry road were all called for. By far, the most ambitious undertaking planned was a new resident theater company made up of "a selected group of men and women versatile in voice, agile in body, and sincere in purpose." These would be the nucleus of a drama company that would offer an annual theater festival at Montalvo and then go on the road, bringing live drama to smaller communities throughout the state. To accommodate the anticipated crowds for its public programs, much of the lawn in front of the villa was converted into a parking lot.

Aspirations soon parted company with resources, and Bailhache had to trim most of her plans and entirely abandon the theater program because of inadequate finances. The San Francisco trustees refused to approve any expansion at Montalvo that could not be paid for with money in hand. Their reluctance to risk development without adequate financing was eminently realistic, but it also reflected the Art Association's perennial unwillingness to devote its energy and resources to the art center. Bailhache became increasingly frustrated with the situation of the Montalvo Foundation as her plans collapsed for want of support and want of funds. Perhaps in exasperation, she even toyed with the idea of leasing Villa Montalvo to a developer as a luxury hotel and using the money to build artist residences, an auditorium, studios and workshops farther up the hill in the old Phelan orchard.

Red Cross Plan for Montalvo

The Red Cross, according to Anne Bailhache's wartime plan for the art center, should then develop a rehabilitation program at Montalvo for the sick and wounded, using instruction in the fine arts and handicrafts as a therapeutic technique. Without violating the spirit of the Phelan bequest, Bailhache believed Montalvo could use art to serve the nation. Wounded soldiers would be housed in prefabricated dormitories to be constructed on the hillside above the villa. A series of small cantonments would accommodate more men on the lower level of the estate. Existing buildings would be used for administrative offices, living quarters for officers and instructors, classrooms, lecture and concert halls.

The gallery would exhibit art works produced by the recuperating soldiers, thereby providing them with incentive and giving them a sense of pride in their accomplishments. She defined her envisioned program in broad terms, with classes in gardening, ceramics, wood carving, model making, lithography, and weaving, as well as drawing, painting and sculpture. Neighboring amateur groups could provide instructors who would be given special training by personnel from the California School of Fine Arts in the use of art for rehabilitation. According to her plan, as many as four hundred soldiers could be housed at Montalvo, offered art training, and restored to productive life. Impressed with the creativity and utility of Bailhache's proposal, the president of the San Francisco Art Association immediately contacted the Red Cross to discuss implementation of the plan.

Bailhache's Legacy

Anne Dodge Bailhache devoted herself to Phelan's public legacy for nearly a decade and a half. One of those who worked closely with her in the early days of the art center, Marjorie Mendelsohn, remembered her as a woman of authority, foresight, and vision who saved Montalvo. Bailhache brought to Montalvo gifts that James Duval Phelan would have greatly appreciated. She was urbane and cultivated, a woman of unerring good taste and discrimination. According to one of her administrative colleagues, who was a close friend and admirer, she could also be arrogant, snobbish, and demanding. She was offended by mediocrity and enforced the highest standards in all she and others did at Montalvo.

She could also be extraordinarily patient and kind. Before the proliferation of word processors and photocopying machines, and usually assisted only by a part-time secretary and some very generous volunteers, she ran the entire art center. Yet, with all the demands on her, she still took time to encourage young artists and musicians who wrote her at Villa Montalvo. In response to a request for information by a local youngster composing an essay on "Estates" for a class project, she wrote a long and informative letter, urging him to visit the Phelan estate to see the beauty of the grounds and gardens first hand.

Bailhache became convinced that the Art Association would not support her efforts to carry out the mandate of Senator Phelan's will with a comprehensive program of cultural activities at Montalvo. Despite rigid economies, she felt members of the board of directors suspected her of being cavalier with finances. Given the demands of other pressing business, usually related to its San Francisco art school, the Art Association continually put off consideration of her detailed monthly reports until the very end of the board meetings. On the rare occasions they were actually considered, she complained that the directors did not take the trouble to understand issues pertaining to the art center. The disinterest in Montalvo among the board members was also reflected by the rank and file of the San Francisco Art Association. When, during the summer of 1947, Bailhache arranged a special program at the villa for the Association's five hundred members, only one bothered to attend. It is hardly surprising that the following year, frustrated and suffering from poor health, she resigned as the Art Association's director at Villa Montalvo.

Anne Bailhache's most important contribution to Montalvo was the initiation of the direction the art center was to follow for the future. She laid out her vision for Montalvo as a major community resource, bringing concerts, art exhibits, lectures, and theatrical performances to the Santa Clara Valley. Bailhache also saw it as an educational center for advanced training in the arts and for more introductory classes for residents of the surrounding area. And she remained true to her personal goal, the development of Montalvo as a refuge for creative artists from throughout the country. While she was director, Montalvo was not able to achieve the heights she envisioned for it, but in the ensuing decades, Montalvo has continued to cultivate the furrows she so carefully plowed. The harvest has been abundant. Over time, and as needs changed, the emphasis has shifted from one to another of the programs she set forth, but Montalvo has remained true to James Duval Phelan's love of beauty and to Anne Bailhache's vision of its pursuit.

Chapter Twenty
Villa Montalvo at Risk

By 1948, the San Francisco Art Association had reached the conclusion that it would be better off terminating its trusteeship of Senator Phelan's estate. The future of Villa Montalvo, as a public trust and as a center of the arts, was very much in doubt. In that year, the heirs to James Duval Phelan's Estate initiated legal proceedings to reclaim the Senator's property, and the Art Association welcomed this action as an opportunity to abandon a responsibility which had become too burdensome to tolerate any longer.

The disorientation of World War II nearly ruined the San Francisco Art Association. According to its chief financial officer, by the late 1940s it was "practically broke," and creditors had to be stalled while money was found to prevent them from bringing legal action against the Association. The Association's Art Museum in San Francisco held on under the determined leadership of Grace McCann Morley, but it was a difficult struggle as donations for cultural purposes dried up. Once the war was over, peacetime presented the Art Association with both opportunities and perils. Returning to a society in which innovation vied uncertainly with tradition, tens of thousands of veterans determined to pursue one form or another of education.

The first concern and most demanding operation of the San Francisco Art Association was the California School of Fine Arts. Having survived the rigid economies enforced by its wartime penury, the school was determined to push its way aggressively to the forefront of the radically changing art world. The school was alive, vibrant, exciting, controversial — and expensive. The expansion of the educational program and salaries of the faculty providing its dynamic and exciting new directions were paid, in large part,

The years of the great depression were hard on the San Francisco Art Association, and even harder on the Phelan estate the Association now administered. The house was stripped of its contents and remained empty for most of the 1930s. This photograph, preserved in the archives of the San Francisco Art Institute, manages to capture something of the neglect Villa Montalvo suffered after the death of Senator Phelan.

287

Avant-Garde Art

When the Art Association's school originally opened its doors in the 1870s, in the accepted method of the period, one of its first acts was to purchase plaster casts of classic works from the Louvre and the other great museums of Europe. The Association's students had carefully studied and copied the techniques of the masters. That tradition of artistic pedagogy was now passé. After the war, under its new director Douglas MacAgy, the school became decidedly and deliberately avant-garde. Clyfford Still, Mark Rothko, Elmer Bischoff, Richard Diebenkorn, and other experimental artists joined the faculty. The San Francisco Art Association's school became famous as the birthplace of abstract expressionism on the West Coast, and from within its own faculty a figurative expressionist counter movement soon challenged the abstract expressionists. Ansel Adams was hired to offer the first course in photography as a fine art to be credited in any American college. He was soon joined by Imogen Cunningham and Dorothea Lange.

by the tuition of veterans returning from the war. By contrast to the lean years of the 1930s and the nearly fatal drought of students during World War II, the California School of Fine Arts suddenly seemed flush with success. It was ill-equipped to cope with the demands of expanded enrollment, a prickly artist faculty, and, for its inexperienced staff, a Kafkaesque nightmare of governmental regulations and red tape. Worst of all, the source of the deceptive abundance was temporary. GI benefits were due to end within a few years.

At the best of times the financial base of the art school had been vulnerable, now it was perilous. In this uncompromising world of debit and credit and adverse financial balance sheets, the San Francisco Art Association's commitment to Villa Montalvo was a distraction and an embarrassment.

To the board of directors, Montalvo had never been anything but a diversion from the main obligations of the San Francisco Art Association. Its own artist members considered it a wasted resource. The terms of the Phelan bequest demanded that Montalvo's trustees keep its grounds open to the public and actively encourage the arts in its facilities, but with its own pressing financial problems in San Francisco, the Art Association had neither the time nor the inclination to invest its fragile resources in the Saratoga property. And it simply did not have the money required to make Montalvo prosper according to the plans announced a decade before. Because of mistakes made by an Art Association accountant, the modest improvements already made at Montalvo had resulted in a substantial overexpenditure. By 1949, the Montalvo Foundation was actually in debt to the Art Association, and money had to be withdrawn from the principal of the Montalvo trust to repay the hard pressed trustee organization. Nearly two decades after accepting the bequest, Montalvo had become more of a liability than ever to the San Francisco Art Association. The lawsuit initiated by the Phelan heirs now presented the Art Association with a means of escaping from the legal obligations which it could ill afford to carry out.

Contact between the art center at Villa Montalvo and the family of Senator Phelan had been sporadic during the years since the Senator's death. Montalvo would occasionally be asked to welcome one or another of the family or some other friend of Senator Phelan. Noël Sullivan had declined the invitation to serve on the Montalvo advisory board, but, according to the director, he followed the career of the art center with interest. Shortly after the war he offered a second program of songs in the outdoor theater. Both he and the Murphy family had property adjacent to Montalvo, and they could hardly have been unaware of its problems. It was probably through conversations with Anne Bailhache the year before her resignation that Sullivan became convinced of the San Francisco Art Association's failure to fulfill his uncle's wishes at Villa Montalvo.

The suit initiated for the heirs of James Duval Phelan by attorneys for the Phelan Estate claimed that the Art Association had not met the obligations toward the property entrusted to them, and that the trust was never fulfilled. They argued that access to the grounds had been so limited that Montalvo could not be considered a public park, and that the trustees had never developed the arts as prescribed by the terms of the trust. The heirs maintained that the San Francisco Art Association, although having possession of Montalvo for twenty years, had never "accepted" the responsibility of the trust. The property and the monetary endowment left by the Senator should therefore revert to the Phelan Estate according to the terms of the original will, which stated, "if this gift shall not be accepted by the San Francisco Art Association the entire property shall go to my trustees … as a part of the residue of my estate."

As much as the San Francisco trustees wanted to be freed of the responsibility of maintaining Montalvo, they were anxious to avoid any legal decision that would imply they were at fault in failing to fulfill the terms of Phelan's will. The Art Association's credibility would be seriously injured, and other donors would have second thoughts about donations or bequests to an institution that had been publicly reprimanded for its failure. Neither did they wish to see the property and grounds of Villa Montalvo, as well as the $250,000 trust, transferred to the Phelan heirs without some financial recompense to the Art Association for its years of trusteeship. The Art Association countered the argument that it was not legally entitled to retain trusteeship by contending that the income from the trust was never adequate to carry out its provisions.

The crux of the matter was the interpretation of the primary intention of Senator Phelan's will. The San Francisco Art Association held that the essential mandate of the will was the development of the fine arts at Montalvo. Operation of a park for the public, a much less costly undertaking, was only an incidental and relatively unimportant part of the work entrusted to it. If the court would accept this argument and conclude that Montalvo

As it swept past the villa toward James D. Phelan's octagonal garage, the steep driveway into Montalvo provided an admirable view of the mansion. Even during the Senator's lifetime, the trip up the twisting gravel road from the highway was a minor adventure, although Phelan's powerful chauffeur-driven automobiles made the grade with little effort. After his death the road deteriorated badly and visitors bounced over potholes, ground their gears, stalled on the last sharp turn, and breathed small sighs of relief when they reached the villa.

With insufficient funds to buy power equipment or hire additional help, the small gardening staff retained by the San Francisco Art Association was hard pressed to keep up the grounds at Montalvo. To cut down on maintenance and provide more parking for visitors to the villa, the lower portion of the lawn was turned into a car park. With the establishment of the Montalvo arboretum, the lawn was replanted and the integrity of the estate's landscaping design was restored.

Santa Clara's Loss

With an equal division of James D. Phelan's property and the trust fund agreeable to the Phelan Estate and the San Francisco Art Association, it seemed virtually certain that Montalvo as a center of the arts would be closed down. Artists would no longer find a place of beauty and contemplation for their creative work in the secluded residences at the villa. But the principal loss would be to the residents of the Santa Clara Valley who would be deprived of afternoon hikes on the estate's hillside trails and the concerts, art exhibits, and other cultural activities which had been fitfully offered during Montalvo's difficult career as an art center.

could not be operated according to the provisions of the trust, then the Art Association would request that all the assets be awarded to it for its educational work at the art school in San Francisco.

It was in the interest of both parties to the dispute to reach a mutually acceptable compromise. Before the Phelan suit ever entered the courts, negotiations between the lawyers for the Phelan Estate and the Art Association resulted in a written agreement in December, 1948, by which the assets of the trust were to be divided fifty-fifty between the two parties. These assets consisted of the Villa Montalvo property and the trust fund set up to support it. When the Phelan Estate actually filed its lawsuit against the San Francisco Art Association, it was a friendly suit, meeting with the acquiescence of the Art Association. If the negotiated arrangement were accepted by the court, Villa Montalvo would revert to the Phelan family and the Art Association would be compensated from the endowment to the extent of half the value of the estate.

With the departure of its first director, and with the lawsuit about to start its leisurely progress through the courts, activities at Montalvo slowed to a crawl. Rather than hire a new director, the Art Association retained Arlene Loofbourow as executive secretary in residence at the villa. Sponsorship of lectures, concerts, and theatrical performances by the Montalvo Foundation was abandoned. Given the art center's slender resources, it was considered too much of a financial risk to sponsor such programs. On the instructions of the Art Association board of directors, Loofbourow simply made the facilities at Montalvo available to local groups looking for a place to stage their activities. Occasionally Montalvo's great hall was filled with the sound of chamber music or a piano recital, sponsored by a public spirited individual or organization from the outside, but institutional commitment to the community appeared to be at an end. To economize, upkeep of the villa was reduced and even important repairs were made only grudgingly. As the president of the Art Association put it at a meeting of the Association officers in the summer of 1950, "the income is really not large enough to support Montalvo and therefore we have to guard against any expenditures." Accumulated bills and tax invoices sometimes went unpaid for months.

When rumors began to circulate that Montalvo was to be put on the block, the neighboring community reacted with concern and disbelief. According to local tradition, the first person to get wind of the Art Association's intentions was Hazel Pierce Hincks, who found tucked in the back of a newspaper a legal notice about the intended fate of the Phelan estate. For Villa Montalvo, it seemed that it was the end of an era. It appeared that the art center, instead of benefiting from the exciting growth taking place around it, might revert to private ownership and be lost to the community. The support of Catholic charities by the Sullivans was well known, and many neighbors believed that, as Phelan himself had once speculated, in the family's hands Montalvo would probably become a convent or monastery. If this did not happen, the villa might be sold and entirely disappear before the advance of indiscriminate progress, like so many elegant symbols of the past. The San Francisco Art Association soon began receiving letters from realtors and developers offering to buy parts of the estate.

The Montalvo Society had been inactive since the early months of the war, but interest in the Phelan estate was far from dead. The threatened loss of Montalvo as an enriching community resource provoked an immediate and impressive response. Old supporters of the art center renewed their ties to a resuscitated Montalvo Society and new members quickly joined the ranks. A number of able and articulate individuals emerged to provide leadership for the neighborhood movement, but perhaps the most formidable and effective was Hazel Pierce Hincks.

Hincks and other local leaders founded a new community organization in order to demonstrate the breadth of support for Montalvo in the Santa Clara Valley. This new group, called the Friends of Montalvo, grew quickly. For one dollar anyone could buy a ticket saying, "I am a Friend of Montalvo." The gesture was symbolic of commitment by ordinary citizens to save Montalvo and ensure that it remained a cultural center for all. The Friends of Montalvo could soon boast that their membership extended from Alaska to Mexico. The donations supported cultural activities at the Phelan estate, and, as litigation on the issue of trusteeship of Montalvo entered the courts, provided an emergency fund for legal counsel.

The hue and cry raised by the two groups soon began to produce results. A "Save Montalvo" campaign caught the attention of the press, and local newspapers wrote enthusiastically about the will of the people. Letters arrived at the headquarters of the San Francisco Art Association demanding greater use of the property for the benefit of the community, and by 1950 the

Symbols of Decline

Villa Montalvo seemed to be showing its age, as well as a lack of commitment to James D. Phelan's bequest. George Doeltz, the gardener who had supervised the planting of every tree and shrub since the property was first purchased by Senator Phelan, was nearing the end of his many years of service at the villa. The absence of the master's hand showed in a gradual falling off in the care of Phelan's prized gardens.

Another symbol of Villa Montalvo's decline was the deterioration of the stained glass window of Cabrillo's *San Salvador* above the entry door of the main house. Although the gallant ship still plowed through the Pacific waves under full sail, the window itself had bowed so badly that it was in danger of crashing to ground. The Art Association, anxious about its condition but fearful of expending any substantial sum of money on its repair, thought of simply removing this fanciful conceit of Senator Phelan's, crating it up and storing it in the basement. Luckily, the owner of the LeDeit Glass Company of San Jose was so impressed with the beauty and quality of the window, with its unusual zinc-framed panes, that he donated most of his company's work on its restoration rather than see it replaced by a plate of frosted glass.

In the late 1980s, the Montalvo Service Group funded additional repairs to re-tint the glass panes.

Community Champion

A native of San Francisco, Hazel Pierce Hincks came from a pioneering family and, like Senator Phelan, combined great pride in California with a deep commitment to its development. She had particular interests in music and art and was determined to preserve Montalvo as the cultural center its founder had envisioned. Tireless in her many civic responsibilities, Hincks was an imposing figure by any standard, and more than one of her fellow leaders in the effort to preserve Montalvo considered her the savior of the art center. In an appropriately martial metaphor, one of her closest allies later described Hazel Hincks organizing an army and girding herself for battle on behalf of Montalvo. During the next four or five years she spearheaded opposition to the transfer of title to the property to the Phelan heirs and fought to secure local control over Villa Montalvo.

resident agent at the villa was complaining that "around here Montalvo business seems to be everybody's business."

While the Friends of Montalvo rallied their forces within the community, the litigation over title to the Phelan property began to follow its circuitous path through the courts. The case entered the Superior Court in March 1949. Judge Lyle T. Jacks ruled that the Phelan heirs had no claim on the Saratoga property and refused to bring the case to trial. The plaintiffs petitioned to have the ruling set aside and asked leave to file an amended complaint. This motion was denied by Judge Frank Deasy. The Phelan Trustees next went to the State District Court of Appeal which ruled that, if the heirs wished to present the case again, it would have to be reconsidered by the trial court. The case then returned to the Superior Court, where it finally came to trial in May 1951.

In their suit, Phelan's heirs argued that the Art Association had not fulfilled the provisions of the Senator's will concerning the development of the arts at Villa Montalvo and the Art Association had certainly made no progress in that direction since the resignation of Anne Bailhache. Since the Art Association claimed that it was impossible to operate the center with existing resources, it was vital for the local supporters to reactivate a cultural program and demonstrate that Montalvo was not a lost cause. In the Montalvo Society, which had been recognized by the San Francisco Art Association as an authorized support group of the art center, the residents had a mechanism for their purposes. The Society's subcommittees, in cooperation with the Friends of Montalvo, once again sponsored concerts, plays, and exhibits for the community, and the public showed its support for the "Save Montalvo" campaign by attending in unusually large numbers. Scholarships funded by the Montalvo Society enabled a number of young artists to spend a month or two in the guest cottages. For the children of the neighboring area, the Montalvo Society resumed summer art classes, previously sponsored by the Foundation. Continuing the work done earlier, the Montalvo Society arranged exhibits of paintings by local artists and students of the Art Association's own art school. Even repairs to the physical structure of the villa became the concerns of the Montalvo Society, with Hazel Hincks personally soliciting authorization for roof repairs from the Art Association president.

The inactivity and caution of the legal trustees and the concern and enthusiasm of the local residents were frequently in conflict. Correspondence between the two, both in writing and in person, remained polite and civil, but the Art Association's willingness to comply with the terms of the Phelan family's suit was unacceptable to the local residents who were intent on keeping Villa Montalvo as a public trust and a community resource. The Art Association board of directors tried to avoid anything that appeared to give the Montalvo Society a proprietary interest in the Phelan property. When the Society turned over a percentage of its membership dues to Montalvo's general fund, as it had done in the years before the war. The Art Association returned the much needed money, on the advice of legal counsel. The Montalvo Society, like any other outside group, was charged rent when it used the kitchen or any of the rooms in the villa. As the lawsuit wore on, the Art Association's lawyer even advised the trustees to forbid the Friends of Montalvo any cultural activities at the art center.

For several years, while the ultimate resolution of the Phelan lawsuit remained in doubt, the Art Association president, Ernest Born, did not rule out closer cooperation with the Montalvo Society. He reminded the board of directors of its responsibility for carrying out Senator Phelan's intentions for Villa Montalvo as long as the Art Association remained the legal trustee. If the Phelan suit proved unsuccessful, he saw the possibility of initiating a new Montalvo Committee and harnessing the energy of the local organizations. But the members of the Montalvo Society, who respected the memory of Senator Phelan, would hardly have listened with equanimity to his proposal to his executive committee in March 1951, that the Phelan house be razed and the gardens redesigned to make Montalvo into a more efficient and less costly undertaking. To promote better understanding between the Art Association and the local residents, an amicable joint meeting took place at Montalvo. Whatever understanding was achieved there was quickly undone, however, when the trustees challenged the Montalvo Society's new arrangements for classes and residence scholarships. These actions by the local groups, according to the president of the Art Association, were "tantamount to invasion of the property inasmuch as no authorization had been granted by the Board, Executive Committee, or me."

In the midst of these institutional tensions and with the litigation over ownership of the property still undecided, the Art Association appointed a new resident director at Montalvo. After struggling with its multiplicity of problems for three years, Loofbourow resigned her awkward position as

In this photograph, the guest cottages appear to be badly overgrown. Renovated in 1939 for use as apartments by artists in residence, the facility provided comfortable accommodations for artists who participated in one of the most consistently successful programs at Montalvo.

The sunshine and warmth of the foothills, so unlike the weather in his native San Francisco, attracted James Duval Phelan to Saratoga, and he took full advantage of the climate. The oval swimming pool had been an integral part of Phelan's design and forms the centerpiece of the terrace above the patio. The pool, shown here shortly after construction, is framed by colonnaded pergolas and a small red-tiled pavilion. Here, as he had written his sister Mollie, he would be able to "bask in the eternal sunshine."

executive secretary of the Foundation in 1951. She had only just become associated with Montalvo when she was informed that the Foundation intended to close down. Disillusioned by the revelation that she was merely temporarily keeping afloat a sinking ship, without adequate authority in title or substance, and answering to employers whose single goal seemed to be economy, she maintained, rather than led Montalvo during the difficult years of litigation. "This is the only position I have ever held in which I was not expected to do my best," she wrote in her final communication with the Art Association. With her resignation, the trustees restored the position of director and appointed Frederick P. Vickery.

As the date for the actual trial of the Montalvo case approached, the Friends of Montalvo were well-prepared to represent the community's interests. The local supporters were a talented and well-connected group. Many were lawyers, professionals, and civic leaders, and they now used their own considerable abilities and their network of friends, college classmates, and business associates with energy and determination. Through one of these contacts, the Montalvo supporters gained a sympathetic hearing from the deputy attorney general, R.L. Chamberlain. The California attorney general was legal guardian of public trusts throughout the state, and the local leaders convinced Chamberlain to intervene in the suit in the interest of preserving Villa Montalvo as a community asset. By the time the case came to trial, the Friends of Montalvo had marshalled their resources and retained John J. Dailey to represent them in the court proceedings. Dailey, Chamberlain, and Herbert Wenig, another deputy attorney general, worked closely together in their joint efforts to prevent this public trust from reverting to private hands.

The alliance between the Friends of Montalvo and the Office of the Attorney General, based on a shared conviction that Montalvo served the public interest, was to prove crucial to the future of the art center. Leaders of the Friends of Montalvo and the Montalvo Society were eager to assist the lawyers and show their support for Villa Montalvo. Marjorie Mendelsohn, Michael Antonacci, and Jean Kirkwood, longtime members of the Montalvo Society, prepared to furnish background information on the estate and its operation under the Art Association. Hazel Hincks, Elizabeth McSwain Jones, Mrs. Alfred McLoughlin, and other Friends of Montalvo honed their arguments concerning the contribution of Montalvo both to the neighboring community and to the development of the fine arts in California. Representing the interests of the general public, these community champions made the journey to San Francisco daily for the three weeks of the trial. They provided abundant and impressive evidence of local dedication to the continuation of Montalvo as an art center, and the benefits that it could provide the citizens of California.

The final round in the suit brought by the Phelan heirs over title to Villa Montalvo took place before Judge Edward Molkenbuhr. For thirteen days in Superior Court, the lawyers representing the four parties involved in the litigation presented their cases, and witnesses offered pertinent evidence. Eustace Cullinan and Delger Trowbridge, counsels for the Phelan Estate and the Phelan family, respectively, argued their original positions that the trust had never been accepted by the Art Association, or, if accepted, it had fully failed in execution. Donald Falconer, on behalf of the Art Association, maintained that the trust had been accepted, but that it was now impossible to fulfill because of inadequate income to develop the arts at Montalvo. Chamberlain and Wenig, representing the attorney general, along with Dailey for the Montalvo Society, denied both these contentions and argued in favor of continuing the trust. A large number of people from the community, some of Phelan's old friends, and the president and other officers of the Art Association offered hours of evidence. Phelan's former secretary provided a written deposition, and the lawyer who had assisted the Senator in drawing up the will presented his interpretation of Phelan's intention in leaving his summer home to the Art Association. On behalf of the community, Hincks, Antonacci, Kirkwood, Mendelsohn, Jones, and the others informed the court of local opinion and cultural possibilities.

The courtroom proceedings were interrupted while Judge Molkenbuhr and the various attorneys visited the grounds of the Phelan property. For an entire day the legal retinue wandered through the premises, inspecting the condition of the house and the outbuildings and exploring the trails through the woods. Molkenbuhr was obviously impressed with the estate, which had been portrayed as virtually derelict in the plaintiff's representations. He concluded that the buildings were in good condition, and the estate was "reasonably well maintained, and in every respect suitable for maintenance as a public park."

The Montalvo suit was complex and exhausting. But from his comments, it was clear that the judge had become convinced that, whatever

Arts and Science

A geologist by training, Dr. Frederick Vickery was the son of an old San Francisco family which operated the art firm of Vickery, Atkins and Torrey, often patronized by Senator Phelan. He knew the Montalvo area well since his family owned property in Saratoga touching on the Phelan estate. During the original construction of his summer home, the Senator had once offered the Vickerys an old building on his property slated for demolition. Recently retired as director of the Crocker Gallery in Sacramento, Vickery was hired on a temporary basis at Montalvo, pending the outcome of the lawsuit. Dr. Vickery, aided by his wife, an art expert in her own right, served as resident director of Montalvo for the next three years. He enjoyed guiding visitors through the house and acting the part of host of Montalvo, and he worked more comfortably with the local support groups than had his immediate predecessor.

A photograph taken by a visitor to Villa Montalvo bears witness to the decline the Phelan estate suffered after his death. With severe economy being the policy of the new trustees, and a drastically reduced gardening staff, George Doeltz could no longer give the 175-acre property the meticulous care it required.

other conditions were attached to the gift of his home to the San Francisco Art Association, Senator Phelan intended Montalvo as a charitable trust for general public use. Molkenbuhr decisively cut through the dual provisions of the will concerning public access and development of the arts at Montalvo. He ruled that Phelan's primary purpose was that the villa be used for a public park. The use of the buildings and grounds for the development of art, literature, music, and architecture, in his judgment, was a secondary purpose. Since the grounds had been open to the public, the primary purpose was clearly fulfilled. In the judge's view, the secondary provisions of the trust had been reasonably performed since the time the Art Association took possession of Montalvo, and could continue at the same level even with limited revenue. Molkenbuhr advised the trustees to cut down maintenance expenses on things like "fussy" flowers, and operate Montalvo within the income. He also urged the attorney general to request a reduction of taxes on the property from Santa Clara County.

The trust, in short, had not failed and should continue. Since Montalvo was a specific charitable trust, the Phelan Estate had no right to the property or to the funds of that trust. As a preliminary to the main ruling, the court denied Phelan's heirs and the Art Association any right to divide the assets and the property of the trust between them. Judge Molkenbuhr disallowed their compromise agreement proposing a fifty-fifty split. According to the minutes of the court reporter, Judge Molkenbuhr's decision was colored by the beauty of Montalvo and inspired by his view of the public good. In words thousands of visitors to the Phelan estate might readily applaud, the judge summed up his own sentiments. "I just feel that … if this property was to be taken away from the public as a whole … it would be a loss for the benefit of mankind for years to come … and would be rather disastrous."

The future of Villa Montalvo as a cultural center for the public was legally secure. Now it was the task of the loyal supporters of Senator Phelan's dream to make sure that the estate lived up to his vision. In October 1952, they took the decisive step of incorporating themselves into a legal corporation that was prepared to take over the Phelan trust. The new group, styling itself the Montalvo Association, was headed by more than a score of highly regarded citizens of the Santa Clara Valley. Robert Kirkwood, the Saratoga assemblyman who had recently been appointed Controller of California by Governor Earl Warren, chaired its Board of Trustees. A few members of the governing board, like the writer Ruth Comfort Mitchell, had known Senator Phelan personally, but most were attracted to the Montalvo Association because of a sense of civic responsibility. The lawyers, architects, public officials, educators, and artists who agreed to serve recognized in Villa Montalvo an extraordinary cultural asset for the entire area. Hazel Hincks, Michael Antonacci, and Robert Kirkwood had been instrumental in blocking the Phelan suit. Other members, in particular Fred J. Oehler, Chester Root, and George E. Martin would be leading figures in the Montalvo Association for many years. The inclusion on the board of the famous violinist, Yehudi Menuhin, Superior Court Judge Byrl Salsman, Edwin J. Owens, the dean of Santa Clara University's Law School, Alex J. Hart, Jr., and a number of respected regional business leaders gave the Montalvo Association an abundance of talent and an impressive air of respectability.

In the public announcement of the formation of the Montalvo Association, its purpose was defined as one of cooperation with the San Francisco Art Association to support and develop the Phelan property. Kirkwood was more to the point, however, when he wrote the president of the San Francisco Art Association, Francis V. Keesling, Jr. Kirkwood suggested that the Art Association, with its responsibility for the California School of Fine Arts and its other endeavors, had sufficient obligations in San Francisco. It did not have the time or the necessary local connections and contacts to develop support for Montalvo in the Santa Clara Valley. The Art Association actually suffered from its responsibility for Villa Montalvo, he asserted, since it competed with the other obligations of the trustees. Kirkwood concluded by asking the San Francisco Art Association to transfer the trust itself to the Montalvo Association.

This formal request for title to the Phelan estate soon brought to a conclusion the years of uncertainty concerning Villa Montalvo. The arguments for its transfer to a regional organization that had a firm commitment to its development, as well as the financial resources to meet the expectations of Senator Phelan's will, were compelling. The San Francisco Art Association had hoped to receive a substantial financial settlement from the Phelan Estate, in return for its transfer of the property to the Senator's heirs, but this prospect had been denied by the failure of the Phelan litigation. With its own slender assets, which it was trying to bolster by a development campaign at the very time it was approached by Kirkwood, the Association could do

The gazebo on top of the Senator's reservoir was once a favorite gathering spot for Phelan's extensive staff of servants and gardeners. In this photograph, the structure appears to be near collapse.

James Duval Phelan knew well the old adage contained in a guidebook for California pioneers, "be more careful to buy water than land." He carefully secured water rights for his Saratoga estate and husbanded water for Montalvo's gardens and orchards in a reservoir behind the villa. The wooden covering of the reservoir provided the Senator's staff with an ideal terrace for picnics and dances.

no more than continue minimally conforming to the terms of the bequest, earning neither recognition nor gratitude. It was clearly time for the Art Association to retreat gracefully from its legal responsibilities.

The request from Kirkwood did not come as a surprise to the Art Association. After Judge Molkenbuhr's final decision, the attorney general had suggested to the Art Association that it consider resigning the responsibility for Montalvo in favor of a regional park district or a local administrative organization. Even before they were approached by the Montalvo Association, the Art Association's board of directors decided to find an alternate trustee and considered the possibility of Stanford, the University of California, and Santa Clara County. It was clearly not anxious to turn the property over to the Montalvo Association, but after more than twenty years of association with Montalvo, it was with a sense of relief that the San Francisco Art Association accepted Kirkwood's offer.

All that remained was the issuance of a court order substituting the Montalvo Association as the legal trustee. In October 1953, with the agreement of the San Francisco Art Association, the Superior Court consented to Attorney General Edmund G. Brown's petition for the change of trusteeship. With an enthusiasm shared by many, Judge Timothy Fitzpatrick voiced his belief that, "the individuals comprising the Montalvo Association are sincere and capable, and I have every confidence they will be able, particularly by enlisting local aid, to raise funds sufficient to implement the provisions of the trust." Villa Montalvo was at last the responsibility of the citizens who cared most about its success.

Chapter Twenty-One

Villa Montalvo: A Community Treasure

When Montalvo's future was in the balance during the legal proceedings in San Francisco's Superior Court, one of the most persuasive arguments in favor of continuing the estate as an arts center was the impressive character of community support demonstrated in the courtroom. Intelligent, articulate, and determined, the Friends of Montalvo persuaded Judge Molkenbuhr that Montalvo filled an important place in the cultural life of the Santa Clara Valley. Their testimony also convinced him that the local leaders, who had already demonstrated organizational skill and community concern, represented the kind of intellectual and cultural leadership that would make the arts center successful. These people were harbingers of an increasingly mature and culturally sophisticated population in the valley. The uncompromising standards of artistic excellence espoused by Hazel Hincks and her companions augured well for Montalvo under local leadership.

With the transfer of title to the Montalvo Association in 1953, a diverse group of professionals, united in a shared commitment to Senator Phelan's dream for Villa Montalvo, took control of the destiny of his estate. They possessed hardly any professional staff and had no longtime experience in cultural center operation. In the best sense, they were volunteers, and it would be to volunteers that Villa Montalvo owed its success during the following decades. Convinced of Montalvo's contribution to an area still sorely lacking in cultural enrichment, they had saved it for the community. Now they had to make it work.

The history of the Villa Montalvo Center for the Arts over the last forty years is preeminently the story of a successful experiment in voluntary

Many neighbors anticipated that if Villa Montalvo returned to the Phelan Estate, as the legal suit demanded, the Senator's property would become a secluded residence for a community of Catholic priests or nuns. Whatever truth the rumor might have had, with the failure of the suit and the villa's prompt transfer to local trusteeship, Montalvo became a lively community art center and public arboretum.

The two warlike Amazons flanking the spouting griffin of J. J. Mora's fountain in the Phelan courtyard hardly represented the Senator's feminine ideal. After the artist introduced the more appealing figures of crouching wood nymphs under the basin, Phelan remarked, "I think Montalvo, being a Latin, needed femininity to offset the almost masculine Amazons."

community organization. Without direct state or local government assistance, and largely dependent on the financial support generated by its own supporters, Montalvo has thrived because of the commitment and hard work of its volunteers. Most volunteers felt a sense of responsibility to the community, a personal dedication to the arts, and a love of the beauty of Villa Montalvo itself. In Phelan's magnificent home, surrounded by formal gardens and acres of unspoiled natural splendor, volunteers took part in a venture that nurtured beauty and fulfilled artistic vision.

At the head of the volunteer organization was the Board of Trustees of the Montalvo Association, the persons legally entrusted with responsibility for Villa Montalvo. Actual responsibility centered on a small executive committee of officers who supervised overall functioning and direction. Under these people, a large organization grew to operate the arts center. Association committees dealt with a variety of areas: membership, buildings and grounds, personnel, financial development, investment, and the like. Other groups, known as activities committees, with responsibility for actual operation of the programs at Montalvo, developed in response to specific needs. Later, a paid director was responsible to the executive committee and supervised daily operation of the arts center and the work of the numerous volunteer groups and small administrative staff.

Dr. Frederick Vickery stayed on as director until the fall of 1954, helping the new officers during the transition from the old trusteeship to the new. After his retirement, the arts center had no official director for the next dozen years. The time-consuming work of administering the enterprise was done by bankers, lawyers, architects, government officials, musicians, and others who served on the executive committee or chaired the volunteer committees. The executive committee decided that, if the arts center was to reach its full potential, it needed a full-time executive director to coordinate its many activities and provide direction for Montalvo's future development. In 1966 the Montalvo Association received a challenge grant for this purpose from the San Francisco Foundation, a philanthropic agency that already administered Senator Phelan's endowments to aid the poor and awarded the Phelan scholarships to young artists, musicians and writers. This grant partially funded the appointment of E. P. Humphrey as resident director. Humphrey, an administrator with a strong background in art history, stayed at Montalvo for two years, until he was replaced by the well-known musician, George

Barati, who served as executive director for ten years. Barati, a cellist, conductor, and composer, had previously headed the Honolulu Symphony and remained active as a guest conductor during his decade at the arts center. He resigned in 1978, and, after a brief interim period, Patricia (Oakes) Compton served as director until 1982. She was followed by Gardiner McCauley, a former art professor and gallery director. In 1988, Elisbeth Challener, previously in charge of development at Montalvo, became the executive director.

The Montalvo Association was soon off to a promising start and its work was watched with interest by Judge Molkenbuhr from San Francisco. He offered his congratulations to the officers of the Association. "There is no doubt in my mind," he wrote them in 1959, "that Senator Phelan would be pleased with the accomplishments of those now in charge." One index of the new organization's success was the increasing financial health of the center. While there was never enough money for all its needs, less than two decades after the Montalvo Association took control of the Phelan estate the endowment left by the Senator had doubled. Much of this success was due to the increasing numbers enrolled in the Montalvo Association, the "Friends of Montalvo," whose membership eventually exceeded a thousand.

The Service Group

Chief among Montalvo's support organizations was the Service Group. Founded by Hazel Hincks and a small band of early Montalvo supporters, this was the earliest of the committees and operated under its own constitution and bylaws. Itprovided support for virtually all activities at Montalvo. The handful of members of the original Service Group invited other women to join, and membership at one time exceeded three hundred volunteers. During Montalvo's early years under community control, the Service Group did whatever was required to make Montalvo function, including sewing curtains for the guest apartments, washing windows, cleaning floors, and serving refreshments at concerts. Willing husbands and children were recruited to help with yard work and do basic repairs. A Junior Service Group of young women, usually daughters of the senior group, assisted at functions and offered special programs for children at Montalvo. When the galleries and buildings were opened to the public, the Service Group provided hostesses to answer visitors' questions and give Montalvo a modicum of security.

Montalvo Directors

Each director of Montalvo brought a personal commitment to the arts and a variety of administrative or artistic talents to Montalvo. E.P. Humphrey was anxious to expand the residential program at the arts center along the lines laid out by Anne Dodge Bailhache. As a professional musician, George Barati became personally involved in Montalvo's music program, and wanted to expand what was already one of the most accomplished undertakings at the arts center. Patricia (Oakes) Compton focused on the artists residence program and oversaw construction of the Pavilion. Gardiner McCauley recognized the pressing need for increased revenue and tried to establish contacts between Montalvo and the expanding corporate world of Silicon Valley. Under Elisbeth Challener's direction, Villa Montalvo's programs for the public became increasingly diversified and attracted record numbers of visitors.

Montalvo Service Group

Service Group members provided many indispensable services for the operation of the arts center, and their generosity was often noteworthy. When some six hundred visitors, prompted by an article in *Sunset,* suddenly descended on Montalvo the day before Christmas, when the villa was officially closed, the president of the Service Group came down to Montalvo, key in hand, and spent the entire day showing them through Phelan's home.

In the garden near James Duval Phelan's guest cottages, an Egyptian sphinx stares enigmatically into the distance. During his world tour, Senator Phelan visited the Egyptian pyramids and the colossal figure of the famous sphinx. The face of this miniature replica combines strong Hellenistic influence with the traditional Egyptian form.

Although not its original purpose, the Service Group saw the need for new equipment, and, in 1955, raised enough money for a new stove for the kitchen. From that modest beginning, the members of the Service Group began their very successful careers as fundraisers. The principal undertaking of the year became sponsorship of Yuletide at Montalvo. Beginning with a treasury of ten dollars in 1954, the Service Group's fundraising venture at Yuletide was so successful that it was soon making very substantial contributions to the arts center's annual budget.

Other volunteer committees had responsibility for specific functions at the villa: classes, dramatic productions, art exhibits, musical performances, the artists' residence program, lectures, the library, and the like. An additional committee, called New Dimensions, undertook the sponsorship of nontraditional events and programs that did not fit any other categories. Each committee elected its own chairperson. Because of the great variety of activities undertaken, and the limited physical facilities, a coordinating council helped to ensure cooperation and scheduling.

Montalvo Grounds

When the Montalvo Association acquired trusteeship of the arts center, it also acquired responsibility for carrying out the provision of Phelan's will that dedicated the grounds to the public as a park. With a gardening staff only about a quarter the size of the Senator's, the upkeep of the 175 acre estate was a formidable undertaking. Parts of the property were in considerable disrepair, and observers noted that even the pedestals of the watchful griffins were crumbling. In some of the buildings termites, leaking roofs, and falling plaster demanded attention. The carved entry doors Phelan brought from Spain were suffering from weathering and had to be refinished for the first time in more than a quarter century. To avoid accident, the Senator's swimming pool, kept empty for years, was filled in and covered with sod.

Montalvo enjoyed strong local support and the community, aware of its needs, responded generously. Members of local rose, iris, and camellia societies contributed to the beauty of the villa by donating prize specimens and laying out new gardens. To keep up with the ever encroaching underbrush and the vigorous growth of even the most disciplined vines and shrubs, Montalvo's volunteer groups scheduled regular work days during which a frontal attack was made to counter nature's invasive strategies. Despite the assistance of these volunteer troops of all ages, the struggle to maintain the gardens, lawns, several miles of hillside trails, and, in particular the roads leading to the villa, proved to be a daunting campaign.

The San Francisco Art Association had tried to interest one or another branch of government in taking over maintenance of Senator Phelan's roads into Villa Montalvo. On numerous occasions overtures were made to Santa Clara County asking for everything from watering of the gravel surface before concerts and repair of seasonal potholes, to actual transfer of title. During the depression, Montalvo's director even approached the federal government in an effort to get the W.P.A. to repair Montalvo's perennially eroding roadbeds. The Montalvo Association proved much more adept in its solicitations and much more successful in producing results.

The virtue of local leadership was also reflected in the new policy toward the extensive grounds around Phelan's home. The Montalvo Association officers invited the county board of supervisors and the directors of the Parks and Recreation Department to visit Montalvo. Without losing any of the lands in which Phelan had set Villa Montalvo, the Montalvo Association convinced the county officials to lease all but five acres of the estate as an arboretum. The board of supervisors voted the necessary funds for the project, and, by 1961, a university-trained landscape horticulturist was working full time on the estate developing plans for the Villa Montalvo Arboretum. In addition to the improvements made to the roadway within the estate, the decision involved construction of extra parking, as well as sanitary facilities, an improved water system, and an office and information center at the entrance to the property. With county support, Montalvo's grounds could now be open virtually all daylight hours with a ranger in attendance, amply fulfilling Senator Phelan's desire that Montalvo be "a public park open to the public." With laudable sensitivity to the historical value of the Phelan estate, the arboretum restored many of the garden structures as closely as possible to their original condition, and returned the main lawn, which had been converted into a parking area, to its legitimate decorative role as a spacious extension of the estate.

During the years since the Montalvo Association took over the direction of the arts center, the surrounding community changed dramatically. Senator Phelan's gift of his estate at Villa Montalvo to the public as a park for the

Yuletide at Montalvo

This popular event offers the public the chance to buy handmade gifts, toys, clothing, intricate holiday decorations created by Montalvo's craft workshops, home baked goods, and other seasonal favorites. Every year since 1960, the villa and the Carriage House have been brilliantly decorated according to a theme selected by the Service Group Yuletide Committee, and visitors have come to purchase Christmas gifts, or simply to enjoy the splendid setting in its holiday finery. Yuletide became so successful that each year it attracted increasing numbers of visitors from throughout the Bay Area. The volunteers donated the income from this event to the Montalvo Association to help pay for specific projects, purchases, or repairs.

Montalvo's Arboretum

Besides sheer enjoyment, the major purpose of the arboretum was education. In addition to the laurel, toyon, madrone, buckeye, oak, redwood and other trees and shrubs native to the area, James Duval Phelan had planted scores of new varieties. The horticultural director of the arboretum, Glen Krueg, now began the painstaking process of identifying and labeling the plants on the estate. The grounds were also used to cultivate additional trees and shrubs for scientific purposes. Soon visitors to Villa Montalvo could walk along the trails and through the gardens, guide in hand, learning as they strolled. Schools throughout the area recognized the educational value of the arboretum, and classes for students of all ages began coming regularly to Villa Montalvo on scientific field trips. Montalvo was also an official Audubon Society bird sanctuary, and for amateur bird watchers an early morning haven for identifying Western tanagers, flycatchers, vireos, Townsend warblers, and others of the more than sixty species of birds sighted on the grounds. But most visitors simply came to ramble at their own pace, enjoying the wild flowers, the shade of the redwood groves, and the quiet of the secluded trails.

refreshment of the citizens became even more important as the surrounding area underwent its postwar transformation. From the serenity and luxurious spaciousness of the hillside estate visitors could enjoy a peacefulness that was rarely obtainable in the crowded landscape below them.

With the arboretum opening, the number of visitors to the grounds increased more than ten fold. They combed the trails and gardens, but only a small percentage took time to enjoy the art exhibitions in the galleries. Paradoxically, the appeal of Montalvo as an arboretum actually threatened to overshadow it as the home of the arts. Faced with the popularity of the arboretum, the Association continually had to assert Montalvo's identity as an arts center during the ensuing decades.

Music at Montalvo

Once under the care of local administrators, Montalvo's cultural program kept within the general framework of activities laid down by the arts center's energetic first director, Anne Bailhache. A residence program for artists, musical and dramatic programs of high calibre, classes for local residents, including children's courses in the fine arts, a lecture program, and changing art exhibitions in the villa's gallery continued to be the staple offerings at Montalvo. The arts center's mandate was broad, and the center could shift priorities to accommodate the changing needs of its constituency.

When Villa Montalvo opened its doors as an arts center more than half a century ago, a performance by the Budapest String Quartet accompanied the ceremony. The presence of the world's premier string ensemble was a clear sign of Montalvo's commitment to excellence in the arts. Perhaps in no other cultural expression did this commitment receive more consistent validation than in music. When the Montalvo Association undertook the trusteeship of the arts center, it accepted the standards already set by Anne Bailhache and worked diligently to perpetuate them.

At the time it was relatively rare to have performances by the top rank of professional musicians in the Santa Clara Valley, and Montalvo's effort to present the best musical talent available filled a void in the cultural life of the area. As late as 1969, one critic could still comment tartly, "It may be stated that … Metropolitan San Jose, and Santa Clara County as a whole, is one of the most culturally deprived areas in the country." To address this void, Montalvo undertook responsibility for its most noteworthy achievements in artistic patronage. With virtually no funds, the new Music Committee launched a Summer Festival that attracted critical attention and a limited, but loyal, community following. The committee usually consisted of volunteers who were themselves skilled musicians. For many years the committee was chaired by Ruth Payette, a gifted pianist and skilled administrator, who set demanding standards for players and performances during the Music Festival at Montalvo.

An annual feature of the music program at the arts center since the 1950s has been the staging of operatic productions. Young artists of the San Francisco Opera's Merola Opera Program travelled down to Montalvo to perform lighthearted operas, such as Strauss' *Die Fledermaus*, or Cimarosa's *The Secret Marriage*. Early in its career, the Summer Music Festival staged a coup by sponsoring one of the first performances of the new American opera, *Susannah*, by Carlisle Floyd, a work that Winthrop Sargent of the *New Yorker* called "the most moving and impressive American opera since *Porgy and Bess*." This was followed by works by Lucas Foss and other modern composers. The Lamplighters also presented lively productions of Gilbert and Sullivan in the amphitheater.

Community support for the musical offerings at Montalvo remained strong, even as other musical opportunities gradually appeared throughout the county, in halting pursuit of the rapidly growing population of the Santa Clara Valley. Chamber music continued to be the standard at Montalvo for many years, and the most distinguished string ensembles in the world visited Montalvo. The Lennox Quartet, the Netherlands String Quartet, and the Pro Arte Quartet were just a few of the notable musical groups offering programs to the community. During the late 1980s, Montalvo broadened its repetoire by offering concerts by the Dave Brubeck Jazz Quartet, Ramsey Lewis, Al Hirt, and the Modern Jazz Quartet. Jazz continues to be a major focus in the 1990s.

To encourage the best young musical talent, annual competitions were held at Montalvo and the winners were given the opportunity to perform at the villa. Montalvo also invited winners of regional competitions to exhibit their talents in free public concerts in the Carriage House. An Emerging Artists Series (now known as the Discovery Series) continues to present talented younger and lesser known musicians to audiences at Montalvo.

Chamber Music at Montalvo

The members of the Alma Trio made an enormous contribution to the musical life of Villa Montalvo. The Trio already had a well established association with Montalvo and continued to offer distinquished performances. Pianist, Adolph Baller, and cellist, Gabor Rejto, often playing as a duet, were particularly generous with their talents when their international concert schedules allowed.

In 1958, the Music Committee took the financial risk of bringing the Paganini Quartet to Montalvo to play a series of eight concerts. This extraordinary group of musicians played on four Stradavari instruments, all of which had at one time been owned by Niccolo Paganini. The viola played by Charles Foidart was the very instrument for which Paganini had commissioned Berlioz to write *Harold in Italy*.

A Winged Sextet

Musical programs at Montalvo were not without their occasional problems. The amphitheater presented a beautiful setting for outdoor concerts, but nature sometimes competed with the performers for the attention of the audience. During a chamber music concert, bees could be a nuisance, and on one occasion, during an early evening concert, the musicians had no sooner tuned their instruments than an uninvited chorus of frogs began to accompany them from the courtyard.

During a performance of a Stravinsky composition by the Kronos Quartet, a local music reviewer noted that the group was joined by two insistent jays, "turning the string quartet into a winged sextet." The warm afternoon sun was also a distraction, and, in defense, some musicians tried unsuccessfully to build a temporary shell that might also help project the sound of their instruments.

Prudence dictated that chamber performances were best enjoyed indoors, and the large hall of the mansion remained the principal concert room until the Carriage House was remodeled. The influential music critic, Marta Morgan, considered the Phelan living room the perfect ambience for chamber concerts, and many friends of Montalvo heartily agreed. In that splendid room, one could almost imagine James Duval Phelan himself sitting contentedly among the crowd listening with appreciation to the music he loved.

The arts center has become increasingly identified with music performances, and even with vigorous competition from neighboring music festivals, Montalvo has held its own. Montalvo currently sponsors concerts featuring music for all tastes and ages with a series which runs from May through September and features such diverse artists as the Midsummer Mozart Orchestra, singer Harry Belafonte, and jazz pianist David Benoit. More than 28,000 people annually attend each performing arts season.

Classes

Classes in the fine arts have been a concern of the arts center since its founding. In the 1950s, one of the earliest issues addressed by the local trustees was the promotion of courses at the villa that would stimulate public appreciation of the fine arts. Among the improvements made on the Phelan estate with donations from the Friends of Montalvo and the Montalvo Society were the addition of facilities for these community oriented classes. In the years before the war there were ambitious plans for sculpture and ceramics studios. Community generosity now allowed the arts center to realize these goals. The old barn was outfitted with a sculpture studio, and scores of students, known as the Barn Swallows, developed their skills under the direction of Arturo Fallico and other experienced sculptors. Painting classes found lodging in Phelan's capacious garage, and the Senator's kitchen was turned into a ceramics studio, complete with electric kiln. Another studio housing seventeen looms for weaving instruction was created out of the servants' dining room. No new facilities were needed for French language classes, taught by one of the residents in the artist cottages. As an augury of things to come, for want of any other appropriate space, theatrical workshops were occasionally sponsored in the villa's octagonal garage.

These classes remained a staple of the arts center's program for a number of years. However, in the late 1970s and early 1980s as the arts center shifted its priorities to other areas of cultural patronage, the number of courses offered at Montalvo gradually declined.

For a number of years joint sponsorship of classes at Montalvo was a characteristic of the arts center's educational work. The center entered into cooperative ventures with organizations as diverse as local community colleges, the Federation of Musicians and the Saratoga Horticultural Foundation. In recognition of Montalvo's many contributions to the community, local organizations reciprocated generously. They frequently made financial donations to support programs and, in some instances, their members arrived at the villa with shovels, hammers, rakes and brooms to help with the upkeep of Montalvo's gardens, buildings, and trails.

With support from Senator Phelan's bequest, Montalvo periodically awarded competitive scholarships to advanced students from throughout the West in art, literature and music. With the West Valley/Mission College Foundation, Montalvo shares sponsorship of the Olympiad of the Arts, an annual exhibition of student art that Senator Phelan and Henry Meade Bland inaugurated decades before.

Art Galleries

The Gallery Committee was responsible for arranging monthly exhibits in the villa. In order to expand gallery facilities there was a need for greater space than the walls of the original library offered. One of the first major improvements undertaken by the Montalvo Association was to the east porch of the villa. By glassing it in, the Gallery Committee restored Phelan's porch to its original condition, and christened it the East Gallery. A few years later a stairway was added to the end of the front veranda to give access from this part of the villa to the Carriage House and the nearby parking area.

From the founding of the arts center there had been ongoing interest in presenting works by well-known professional artists and travelling exhibitions. Montalvo was able to compete successfully with other institutions for some smaller exhibitions of high quality. A collection of Dürer engravings came to Montalvo in the 1960s, and works by Alexander Calder and his family came the following decade. After a two-year wait, the galleries displayed I.B.M.'s travelling exhibition, "Models of Invention of Leonardo Da Vinci," replicas of airplanes, guns, armored cars, and other devices based on designs in Leonardo's notebooks. Particularly appropriate for Montalvo's galleries was a retrospective exhibition of lithographs and paintings by Anne Dodge Bailhache, who had done so much to bring the arts center into being.

From its first exhibition before the war, Montalvo had attempted to present a cross section of contemporary art. The work was often non-traditional in technique and content and reflected the trends in the broader art

Yehudi Menuhin and Montalvo

A few distinguished neighbors were able to add lustre to the arts center's offerings, while they expressed their appreciation of Montalvo's contribution to the arts. One of these was the internationally renowned violinist, Yehudi Menuhin. Although he was usually performing in England or the Continent, he frequently visited his family home in the Santa Cruz Mountains above Los Gatos. In addition to serving as a member of Montalvo's Board of Trustees, he made a gift to the center of a benefit concert. In the main room of James Duval Phelan's home, accompanied by Adolph Baller, he performed a program of violin sonatas before an audience of Montalvo supporters lucky enough to obtain tickets. A few years later the Cuban pianist, Jorge Bolet, visited the arts center from his nearby home and agreed to perform a benefit recital for Montalvo in the Carriage House. In this way, said that large, gentle man, he might be of some small assistance to "this most worthy organization which is so important a part of my community."

Heavenly Choir

On a few occasions, Montalvo unexpectedly played host to young amateurs who volunteered their talents. In a note on her day's activities as a Service Group hostess, one volunteer reported that forty young women from the nearby Notre Dame Novitiate came to Montalvo to visit the galleries. Before they walked back up the road to the Novitiate, the novices sat down to rest on the amphitheater benches and started singing. Hearing the impromptu concert, a crowd of park visitors soon gathered around to enjoy their recital. A half hour later, the novices and their superior started their trek home, followed by the applause of their appreciative audience.

The graceful circular colonnade of Montalvo's Belvedere is a typical example of the classical style that appealed so strongly to James D. Phelan's aesthetic tastes. The Senator's guests could sit on the shaded steps or hand-feed the deer that roamed freely through the shrubs around the Belvedere. Serving no utilitarian purpose, this classical miniature was a delightful conceit that still captivates the imagination of visitors to Villa Montalvo.

world. Three-dimensional art, in particular, also became part of Montalvo's repertory.

Artist Residence Program

Of the many contributions Villa Montalvo made to develop the arts according to the spirit of the Phelan will, perhaps the one that has demonstrated the strongest continuity has been the artist residence program. This was the primary focus of the San Francisco Art Association's work at Montalvo, and it was continued without interruption by the Montalvo Association. The residence program never expanded in size to rival its original model, the MacDowell Colony, or newer colonies like Yaddo or Djerassi in Woodside. But, over the years, several hundred musicians, composers, artists, writers, poets, art historians, journalists, and scholars in a variety of disciplines were given the opportunity for a few months of intense creative work. As use of the arts center's facilities has changed, the number of apartments available for residence has also varied. From a maximum of ten guest accommodations, the number of apartments for artists, either in the guest cottage or the villa itself, was usually five or six. Some of the apartments had pianos for composers and performers, and others had access to studio space appropriate for painters and sculptors.

Each year the peer panel of professionals received scores of inquiries from interested artists, and from these selected about twenty men and women for the Montalvo program. Each artist was a professional in a particular creative area, with an established record of accomplishment. Residence at Montalvo guaranteed a magnificent natural setting, hours of concentrated work, and, except for an occasionally faulty heating system, comfortable, self-sufficient accommodations. The amount of interaction among the residents depended on the personalities and desire for social exchange of the particular artists living at the center. Montalvo never developed the communal meals or social programs for residents offered by some art colonies. It recognized the necessity of quiet and solitude for creative work, and each resident was allowed the greatest amount of privacy possible in a place alive with visitors and scheduled activities. Unlike some art colonies, Montalvo offered its residents proximity to cultural and educational activities. Artists were also invited to share their talents with Montalvo's public, and over the years many contributed actively to the gallery or concert programs. Residents sometimes made enduring friendships during their idyllic months at the Phelan estate.

Artists from throughout the United States and from a number of foreign countries have enjoyed periods of residence at the arts center. The peace and serenity at Montalvo was conducive to artistic work, and it was not uncommon for artists to write that, even during periods of residence at other colonies, they had never been as productive. Reflecting on his residence at the arts center, as well as on the environment needed for creative work, one young composer wrote, "At a place like Montalvo … the artist feels encouraged to continue at his somewhat bizarre vocation." During their time at Montalvo guests completed novels, symphonies, books of poetry, orchestral suites, piano sonatas, paintings and sculpture, and a variety of other creative works. Appropriately, in light of Senator Phelan's interests, many of the artists and writers were in the early years of their careers, and their Montalvo residence provided them with a welcome burst of creative effort to advance in their art. Others, such as Francis Hackett, the English biographer and historian; the musicians of the Paganini Quartet; Bruce Bliven, writer and editor of the *New Republic;* and the Italian painter, Michele Cascella, had long before established their reputations. Most of them would have agreed with one young writer when he reflected on his experience at Montalvo. "Unique in the Western United States, unique too in its intimacy and informality, Montalvo provides writers and other artists an opportunity to develop their talents under very special circumstances."

Theatrical Center

Among many members of the Montalvo Association there was continuing interest in realizing earlier dreams of a vibrant theatrical center at the villa. Theater productions, especially those demanding large casts and crews, were one of the best means of involving the community in activities at Montalvo. Since amateur theatrical companies had always found a warm response in the foothill communities, a theater program at Montalvo required little more than an invitation to these groups to stage their productions at the villa. The Los Gatos Theatre Workshop and other neighboring companies quickly found Montalvo an enjoyable place to perform, even before it had up-to-date theater facilities. A Montalvo drama committee began producing its own

The New Gallery

Immediately after the 1989 Designer Showcase House, the art galleries underwent a radical transformation. Villa Montalvo and the local Community College District entered into a novel joint project. Students enrolled in classes in gallery design and operation were offered the opportunity to construct a new gallery for the center in the building known as the Pavilion. In a few weeks the new student-designed gallery replaced the traditional gallery spaces in the main house. The transfer of exhibits to the new gallery allowed Senator Phelan's library to be restored to its original purpose.

The affectionate pair represents an innocent Adam and Eve before the fall.

The sloping ground behind Villa Montalvo made an ideal setting for an outdoor theater where James D. Phelan and his guests could enjoy amateur theatricals, poetry contests, and musical performances. The rear of the tile-roofed pavilion, characteristically decorated with classical momentos collected by the Senator during his European travels, provided the backdrop for the stage. Guests reclined on the grass or sat under the shade of umbrellas set out by Phelan's head gardener, George Doeltz, who is seen here sitting on the stage.

Olivia de Havilland is shown below in June 1987 at the rededication of the outdoor theatre, which was named for de Havilland's mother, Lilian Fontaine.

plays, undaunted by small budgets or amateur acting. Among the local residents who became identified with dramatic activities at Montalvo were Lilian Fontaine (mother of Olivia de Havilland and Joan Fontaine) and Claire Loftus. Both had long been active in the theater, either performing, directing, or teaching, and they brought to Montalvo technical skill and an infectious love of the theater. There was something for every taste. Modern American works vied with the old standards. Some productions, like Shakespeare's *Midsummer Night's Dream*, requiring over eighty performers and a large *corps de ballet*, were quite ambitious.

Despite its apparent spaciousness, the villa offered very limited facilities for the variety of programs envisioned by the Montalvo Association and its vigorous activity committees. The outdoor amphitheater offered a charming venue for summer programs, but could not be used in other seasons. Lectures and chamber concerts were usually held in the main room of the villa, but this would not accommodate the number of people who wished to attend many of the events. As perfect a setting for intimate concerts as the villa was on a balmy evening with the French doors opened onto the veranda, Montalvo needed a more spacious facility and more flexibility for its presentations. Theater productions, which demanded rehearsal time, scenery installation, and changing and storage rooms, were particularly circumscribed by lack of a permanent facility.

In 1962, the board of directors, urged on by the persuasive Claire Loftus, approved plans for converting the Senator's garage into a theater. This heavy beamed octagonal redwood structure, which had served a variety of functions since Phelan's day, was still equipped with its sixteen foot turntable that had maneuvered the Senator's luxurious cars to parking stalls along the walls. Most recently a painting studio, the Carriage House Theatre, as it was to be called, became a multipurpose facility for concerts, dramatic productions, and lectures. With the advice of professional theater consultants, and with funds donated by the Service Group, architects adapted the garage into a theater with tiered seating for an audience of almost three hundred. The theater could be adapted to either conventional or in-the-round productions. The turntable, now driven by an electric motor, served as the stage for the latter. Further improvements were made during the following years in the theater's lighting. While the Carriage House was not state of the art, it had its own particular charm and indelible ties to the Phelan years. With its soft wooden walls and massive timber roof, it proved to have excellent acoustics, and musical performances quickly became a staple fare in the new theater. For the first time in its existence, the Montalvo arts center had a practical and flexible auditorium appropriate to its size and multiplicity of purposes.

Theatrical productions at Montalvo, depending on the season and the demands of the play, could now be presented either in the Carriage House or in the outdoor amphitheater. The contributions to the dramatic arts at Montalvo by Lilian Fontaine and Claire Loftus were recognized by the Association when these two theaters were dedicated to them. An expanded and totally renovated amphitheater, capable of seating one thousand, was christened the Lilian Fontaine Garden Theatre in 1987, and, in 1990, the indoor facility became the Claire Loftus Carriage House Theatre.

Fundraising

In 1979, for the first time in its history, the Montalvo Association decided to launch a public fund raising drive. The twin goals were to augment the endowment and provide the capital needed for the first major building project on the Phelan estate since the Senator's lifetime. Space for the multitude of activities at Montalvo was still in short supply, and the various programs were sometimes forced to compete with each other for existing facilities. When the Carriage House was converted into an indoor theater, for example, the painting studio had to find a new home in the guest cottages at the expense of two of the residential apartments. Although the interior of the villa was not conveniently designed for the arts center's many activities, the trustees refused to alter the design of Phelan's mansion.

Only the year before, Villa Montalvo had been awarded the distinction of inclusion on the National Register of Historic Places. This recognition of the architectural value of Phelan's villa merely confirmed the obvious. At a banquet held at the villa, Dr. William Murtagh of the Department of the Interior announced this designation giving, in his words, "official status to Montalvo as a cultural property worth keeping in the United States." Without touching the villa itself, the architect Chester Root provided a plan for a new building that would solve many of Montalvo's space problems. Root was an extraordinary individuals who took an interest in Montalvo since its opening as an arts center, and devoted years of his life to its development. He

To prevent accidents to the unwary visitor, Senator Phelan's pool, long since drained and unused, was filled in and planted with grass in the 1950s. These photographs from a slightly later period show a rather hirsute pergola surrounding the oval once occupied by the pool. As the functions of the Montalvo arts center multiplied, spaces that once housed servants or served as changing rooms for bathers were converted into utility rooms or craft centers for artists, sculptors, and ceramicists.Now the rooms are used as dressing rooms for performing artists' bridal parties for the many weddings held in the Oval Garden.

The Temple of Love, shown here under construction and surrounded with well-developed landscaping years later, is one of the most impressive classical features of the gardens of Villa Montalvo. Enjoying a splendid view of the valley during James D. Phelan's lifetime, the temple served as the centerpiece of the Italian Garden. The Senator's gardeners made sure that the graceful white structure was highlighted by beds of brilliantly colored seasonal flowers.

served as third president of the Montalvo Association, and the building he proposed would ultimately be dedicated to his memory.

The new structure, a colonnade and building, called the Pavilion, was to tie together the villa with the Carriage House Theatre. The architectural plans, called for an exterior design based on the Federalist style of the Carriage House Theatre. It would provide Montalvo with a flexible space capable of being used for classes, lectures, conferences, receptions, and later, a professional art gallery. The Pavilion now houses the gift shop, art gallery, and box office.

The groundbreaking for the Pavilion marked a giant step for the arts center, and the major fundraising drive required to finance it was an indication of the success of the Montalvo Association itself. Jean Kuhn Doyle, another of the pioneer supporters of Montalvo and one who had offered evidence during the legal proceedings more than two decades before, served as campaign chairperson. Harriet Lundquist became the campaign director. When construction of the Pavilion began in 1980, the fiftieth anniversary of Phelan's gift of Villa Montalvo to the public, there was reason to celebrate.

In 1990, the relocation of the galleries from the main house to the Pavilion gave Montalvo an exhibition facility with modern lighting and flexible space for its changing needs. It also allowed the villa to be used for a wide variety of events, such as fundraisers, corporate rentals, receptions, and tours. The Senator's villa library, which for many years had artificial exhibition walls covering the richly textured bookcases, was rededicated as the James D. Phelan Library and outfitted with appropriate contemporary furnishings. The books placed on the shelves reflected, as closely as possible, the scholarly interests and reading taste of Montalvo's cultivated founder. The Library Committee is responsible for locating books containing Senator Phelan's personal bookplate, as well as appropriate titles contemporary with Phelan.

Poetry and Speakers

Among the books Senator Phelan had enjoyed collecting were many works of poetry. Of all the arts, poetry had been his favorite. He had numbered George Sterling, Edward Markham, and other major California poets among his friends. Phelan also enjoyed the company of struggling amateur poets, among whom he ranked himself. Perhaps no occasion at Montalvo reflected

Earthquake 1989

On October 17, 1989, the earth shook beneath Villa Montalvo as it had not done since Senator Phelan constructed his stately home in the foothills. The marble Hermes of the upper terrace toppled and broke into pieces. Statues, stone benches, and the Egyptian obelisk fell to the ground. Several columns in the Spanish courtyard cracked, and one, instead of holding up the building, hung suspended by its capital above the patio floor. Plaster fell throughout the villa, and the ceiling of Phelan's billiard room seemed about to collapse. The worst damage done by Northern California's most severe earthquake since 1906 was to the artist-in-residence cottage built on the edge of Wildcat Creek. It suffered a cracked foundation and had to be rebuilt.

Despite its severe jostling, however, Villa Montalvo displayed a robust structural integrity. Phelan had learned a lesson from the great quake of San Francisco and built well. Even though it was located close to the epicenter of the quake, much of the damage proved to be cosmetic. The buildings were soon reopened to the public, and the art exhibit booked for the end of October opened on schedule.

the Senator's personal cultural patronage more accurately than the student poetry reading he sponsored in his outdoor amphitheater. After his death, poetry did not command the same pride of place among the arts at Montalvo, just as it ceased to command the widespread popularity it had once enjoyed among the public. But Montalvo periodically sponsored experimental workshops and poetry readings at the villa. Nationally known poets drew respectable audiences, and, in the spirit of Phelan's bequest, the arts center conscientiously encouraged lesser known and newer poets. Every two years the Montalvo Biennial Poetry Competition grants monetary awards and public recognition to talented younger writers from the Western States. The Young Writers' Competition awards prizes for prose and poetry to high school students in Santa Clara county.

The mission of the Montalvo Association has remained consistent with the wishes of James Duval Phelan. Villa Montalvo has continued to patronize the development of the arts and to offer the public a retreat of welcome tranquility and natural beauty.

Lectures were always in steady demand, and Montalvo hosted speakers on a wide variety of topics. As with most of the offerings at the arts center, the emphasis and focus shifted over time. A glimpse at Montalvo's lecturers and their subjects provides an index in miniature of changing middle class taste over nearly half a century. During the late 1950s, Kurt Herbert Adler drew a traditional audience for a lecture on appreciating opera. A few years later, a crowd turned out to listen to "one of the greatest living saints," Swami Muktananda. A slide lecture on "Environmental Art," reflected the increasing ecological awareness of the 1970s, while interest in the role of women during the next decade was manifested in lectures such as "Women in Art: The Struggle for Recognition." Montalvo has always known how to adapt.

Villa Montalvo for the Public

The public response to the call for assistance after the 1989 earthquake is an indication of the important place Montalvo holds in the Santa Clara Valley. Damage totalled $500,000, and the staff and trustees raised the necessary funds for restoration. Despite the many claims on their attention, private citizens, local foundations and civic organizations responded generously, testifying to their commitment to this garden spot and artistic center. Villa Montalvo had established itself as a valued part of the cultural life of the valley, California, and the West. Repairs were gradually completed, and Villa Montalvo was restored to its original splendor. Once again it beckoned lovers of the arts through its griffin gates. The spirit of James Duval Phelan, that amiable host and generous cultural patron, must surely have smiled with satisfaction at this display of affection by the people he had so richly endowed with his beloved Villa Montalvo.

Chapter References

1 California's Native Son

James Duval Phelan. Correspondence and Papers. The Bancroft Library, Berkeley, California. Extensive manuscript collection, major research basis for Phelan's biography and history of the period 1849–1930.

Journals

Walsh, James P. "Among the Phelan Papers." *Bancroftiana* 94 (June 1987).

2 Creating the Fortune, Creating the Family

Manuscripts

Baptismal Records, 1794–1825. Aghaboe Parish. Clough, County Laoise, Ireland.

Maxwell, Jane and Thomas Boylan. "Report from the Manuscripts Room, Trinity College, Dublin," re non-matriculation. Undated, 1990. In possession of authors.

James Duval Phelan. Correspondence and Papers. The Bancroft Library, Berkeley, California.

Sullivan, Noël. Correspondence and Papers, The Bancroft Library, Berkeley, California.

Books

Caughy, John W. *California*. Englewood Cliffs, N.J.: Prentice Hall, 1960.

Clark, Sterling B.F. *How Many Miles From St. Jo?*. with autobiography of James Phelan. San Francisco: Privately Printed, 1929.

Diner, Hasia R. *Erin's Daughters in America: Irish Immigrant Women in the Nineteenth Century*. Baltimore: Johns Hopkins University Press, 1983.

Dowling, Patrick J. *California: The Irish Dream*. San Francisco: Golden Gate, 1988.

Kaucher, Dorothy. *James Duval Phelan: A Portrait, 1861–1930*. Saratoga, Ca.: Montalvo Association, 1965.

Lotchin, Roger W. *San Francisco, 1846–1856*. New York: Oxford University Press, 1974.

Sullivan, Noël. *Forty Years Remembered: A Letter in the Form of a Memoir to the Children of My Sister, Gladys S. Doyle*. San Francisco: Privately Printed, 1954. Written, 1933.

Newspapers

Chicago Alliance. 27 February, 1882.

Linster Express. 7 November 1987.

San Francisco Examiner. 31 December 1892.

San Francisco Leader. 22 December 1906 and 13 April 1912.

San Francisco News. 31 December 1892.

San Francisco Post. 23 December 1892.

San Jose Herald. 31 December 1892.

3 Father and Son: Educating Each Other

Manuscripts

James Duval Phelan. Correspondence and Papers. The Bancroft Library, Berkeley, California.

Quinn, Frank R. "Report on Florence (Flora) Ellon: Vital Statistics, Burial." July 17, 24, 30; August 2, 29; September 20; October 20, 22, 24; November 26, 1990. In possession of authors.

"Taylor Street Alumnae." Presentation Convent Archives. San Francisco, California.

Books

Clark, Sterling B.F. *How Many Miles From St. Jo?* With autobiography of James Phelan. San Francisco: Privately Printed, 1929.

Hennings, Robert E. *James D. Phelan and the Wilson Progressives of California*. New York: Garland Publishing, 1985.

Kaucher, Dorothy. *James Duval Phelan: A Portrait, 1861–1930*. Saratoga, California: Montalvo Association, 1965.

Phelan, James D. *Travel and Comment*. San Francisco: A.M. Robertson, 1923.

Starr, Kevin. *Americans and the California Dream, 1850–1915*. New York: Oxford University Press, 1973.

Sullivan, Noël. *Forty Years Remembered: A Letter in the Form of a Memoir to the Children of My Sister, Gladys S. Doyle*. San Francisco: Privately Printed, 1954. Written 1933.

Walsh, James P. *San Francisco's Hallinan: Toughest Lawyer in Town*. Novato, California: Presidio Press, 1982.

Newspapers

New York Times. 18 March 1916.

San Francisco News. 31 December 1892.

San Jose Herald. 14 March 1949.

Oral Interviews

Vincent Hallinan, "School Days at St. Ignatius." Interview by James P. Walsh, 1979. In possession of authors.

Benjamin H. Lehman, "Recollections and Reminiscences of Life in the Bay Area from 1920 Onward." Interview by Suzanne B. Riess, 1969. The Bancroft Library, Berkeley, California.

4 Private Life, Public Life

Manuscripts

O'Neill, Thomas P. "Extracts Translated from *Mo thurus go h Americe* by Douglas Hyde (Dublin, Stationery Office, 1937)." 24 September 1990. In possession of authors.

Phelan, James Duval. Correspondence and Papers. The Bancroft Library, Berkeley, California.

Books

Hennings, Robert E. *James D. Phelan and the Wilson Progressives of California*. New York: Garland Publishing, 1985.

Phelan, James D. *Travel and Comment*. San Francisco: A.M. Robertson, 1923.

Sullivan, Noël. *Forty Years Remembered: A Letter in the Form of a Memoir to the Children of My Sister, Gladys S. Doyle*. San Francisco: Privately Printed, 1954. Written 1933.

Oral Interviews

John A. Murphy, "Oral Review of Diary of Douglas Hyde," 1990. Tape in possession of authors.

5 Campaigning for Mayor

Manuscripts

Duraind, George J. "James D. Phelan, Statesman, An Epic of Public Service," [Unpublished] Chapter xii. Phelan Papers. The Bancroft Library. Berkeley, California.

James Duval Phelan. Correspondence and Papers. The Bancroft Library, Berkeley, California.

Swanstrom, Roy. "Reform Administration of James D. Phelan, Mayor of San Francisco, 1879–1902." M.A. thesis. University of California, Berkeley. 1949.

Tully, Jean. "Public Life of James D. Phelan." M.A. thesis. College of the Pacific, Stockton, California. 1935.

Books

Hennings, Robert E. *James D. Phelan and the Wilson Progressives of California*. New York: Garland Publishing Inc., 1985.

Issel, William and Robert W. Cherny. *San Francisco, 1865–1932: Politics, Power, and Urban Development*. Berkeley: University of California Press, 1986.

Kahn, Judd. *Imperial San Francisco: Politics and Planning in an American City, 1897–1906*. Lincoln: University of Nebraska Press, 1979.

Walsh, James P. *Ethnic Militancy: An Irish Catholic Prototype*. San Francisco: R & E Research Associates, 1972.

Journals

Walsh, James P. "Father Peter Yorke of San Francisco: From Politics and the Church to Education and the Intellectual Life." *Studies: An Irish Quarterly Review* LXII (Spring 1973).

_____. "James Phelan's Montalvo: Many Accepted, One Declined." *Southern California Quarterly* LVIII (Spring 1976).

_____. and Timothy Foley. "Father Peter C. Yorke: Irish-American Leader." *Studia Hibernica* 14 (1974).

6 Mayor of San Francisco

Manuscripts

James Duval Phelan. Correspondence and Papers. The Bancroft Library, Berkeley, California.

Swanstrom, Roy. "Reform Administration of James D. Phelan, Mayor of San Francisco, 1879–1902." M.A. thesis. University of California, Berkeley. 1949.

Tully, Jean. "Public Life of James D. Phelan." M.A. thesis. College of the Pacific, Stockton, California. 1935.

Books

Brusher, Joseph S. *Consecrated Thunderbolt: Father Yorke of San Francisco*. Hawthorne, N.J.: Joseph F. Wagner, 1973.

Hennings, Robert E. *James D. Phelan and the Wilson Progressives of California*. New York: Garland Publishing Inc., 1985.

Issel, William and Robert W. Cherny. *San Francisco, 1865–1932: Politics, Power, and Urban Development*. Berkeley: University of California Press, 1986.

Kahn, Judd. *Imperial San Francisco: Politics and Planning in an American City, 1897–1906*. Lincoln: University of Nebraska Press, 1979.

Phelan, James Duval. *Addresses by Mayor James D. Phelan*. San Francisco: Privately Printed, 1901.

Journals

Walsh, James P. "James Phelan's Montalvo: Many Accepted, One Declined." *Southern California Quarterly* LVIII (Spring 1976).

7 City Beautiful

Manuscripts

James Duval Phelan. Correspondence and Papers. The Bancroft Library, Berkeley, California.

Books

Bean, Walton. *California: An Interpretive History*. New York: McGraw-Hill, 3d ed., 1978.

Kahn, Judd. *Imperial San Francisco: Politics and Planning in an American City, 1897–1906*. Lincoln: University of Nebraska Press, 1979.

Polledri, Paolo, ed. *Visionary San Francisco*. San Francisco: Museum of Modern Art, [1990].

Journals

Rischin, Moses. "Sunny Jim Rolph: The First 'Mayor of All the People'." *California Historical Quarterly* LIII (Summer 1974).

8 1906 Earthquake and Fire

Manuscripts

James Duval Phelan. Correspondence and Papers. The Bancroft Library, Berkeley, California. Particularly, Phelan's "Personal Notes Taken At The Time of the San Francisco Earthquake and Fire." Undated.

Books

Bean, Walton. *Boss Ruef's San Francisco: The Story of the Union Labor Party, Big Business, and the Graft Prosecution*. Berkeley: University of California, 1968.

Kahn, Judd. *Imperial San Francisco: Politics and Planning in an American City, 1897–1906*. Lincoln: University of Nebraska Press, 1979.

McGloin, John B. *San Francisco: The Story of a City*. San Rafael, California: Presidio Press, 1978.

9 Graft Prosecution

Manuscripts

James Duval Phelan. Correspondence and Papers. The Bancroft Library, Berkeley, California.

Books

Bean, Walton. *Boss Ruef's San Francisco: The Story of the Union Labor Party, Big Business, and the Graft Prosecution*. Berkeley: University of California, 1968.

Hichborn, Franklin. *"The System" as Uncovered by the San Francisco Graft Prosecution*. Privately Printed, 1915.

Kahn, Judd. *Imperial San Francisco: Politics and Planning in an American City, 1897–1906*. Lincoln: University of Nebraska Press, 1979.

Journals

Walsh, James P. "Abe Ruef Was No Boss: Machine Politics, Reform, and San Francisco." *California Historical Quarterly* LI (Spring 1972).

10 Hetch Hetchy

Manuscripts

James Duval Phelan. Correspondence and Papers. The Bancroft Library, Berkeley, California.

Books

Bean, Walton. *California: An Interpretive History*. New York: McGraw-Hill, 3d ed., 1978.

Cohen, Michael P. *The Pathless Way: John Muir and American Wilderness*. Madison: University of Wisconsin Press, 1984.

Fox, Stephen. *John Muir and His Legacy: The American Conservation Movement*. Boston: Little, Brown and Company, 1981.

McGloin, John B. *San Francisco: The Story of a City*. San Rafael, California: Presidio Press, 1978.

Muir, John. *The Yosemite*. Photographs by Galen Rowell. San Francisco: Sierra Club Books, 1989.

O'Shaughnessy, M.M. *Hetch Hetchy: Its Origin and History*. San Francisco: Recorder, 1934.

Journals

Chowder, Ken. "Can We Afford the Wilderness?" *Modern Maturity* (June–July 1990).

Clements, Kendrick A. "Politics and the Park: San Francisco's Fight for Hetch Hetchy, 1908–1913." *Pacific Historical Review* XLVII (May 1979).

_____. "Engineers and Conservationists in the Progressive Era." *California History* LVIII (Winter 1979–80).

Richardson, Elmo R. "The Struggle for the Valley: California's Hetch Hetchy Controversy." *California Historical Society Quarterly* XXXVIII (September 1959).

Sayles, Stephen P. "Hetch Hetchy Reversed: A Rural-Urban Struggle for Power." *California Historical Society Quarterly* LXIV (Fall 1985).

11 Construction of Villa Montalvo

Manuscripts

James Duval Phelan. Correspondence and Papers. The Bancroft Library, Berkeley, California

James D. Phelan Materials, Huntington Library, San Marino, California

Noël Sullivan Papers, The Bancroft Library, Berkeley, California

Tully, Jean. "The Public Life and Achievements of James Duval Phelan." M.A. thesis, College of the Pacific, 1935.

Books

Atherton, Gertrude. *Adventures of a Novelist*. New York: Liveright, Inc., 1932.

_____. *Golden Gate Country*. New York: Duell, Sloan and Pearce, 1945.

_____. *California, An Intimate History*. New York: Blue Ribbon Books, 1936.

Bean, Walton and James J. Rawls. *California: An Interpretive History*. New York: McGraw-Hill, 1983.

Broek, Jan Otto Marius. *The Santa Clara Valley, California*. Utrecht: N.V.A. Ooslhoek's Uitgevers-My, 1932.

Butler, Phyllis Filiberti. *The Valley of Santa Clara*. San Jose, Ca.: Junior League of San Jose, 1975.

Cunningham, Florence R. *Saratoga's First Hundred Years*. San Jose, Ca.: Harlan-Young Press, 1967.

Garnett, Porter. *Stately Homes of California*. Boston: Little, Brown and Company, 1915.

Giffen, Guy and Helen Giffen. *The Story of Golden Gate Park*. San Francisco: Phillips and Van Orden Co, 1949.

Hennings, Robert E. *James Phelan and the Wilson Progressives of California*. New York: Garland Publishing, Inc., 1985.

Kaucher, Dorothy. *James Duval Phelan: A Portrait, 1861–1930*. Saratoga, Ca.: Montalvo Association, 1965.

Older, Mrs. Fremont. *San Francisco: Magic City*. New York: Longmans, Green and Co., 1961.

Phelan, James D. *Travel and Comment*. San Francisco: A.M. Robertson, 1923.

Pierce, Nona P. *Garden Getaways: Public Gardens & Special Nurseries: Northern California*. Palo Alto, Ca.: Tioga Publishing Company, 1989.

Santa Clara County, California: Its Climate, Resources and Industries. San Jose, Ca.: San Jose Chamber of Commerce, n.d.

Sexton, R.W. *Spanish Influence on American Architecture and Decoration*. New York: Brentano's, 1927.

Starr, Kevin. *Americans and the California Dream*. New York: Oxford University Press, 1973.

_____. *Inventing the Dream, California Through the Progressive Era*. New York: Oxford University Press, 1985.

Sullivan, Noël. *Forty Years Remembered: A Letter in the Form of a Memoir to the Children of My Sister, Gladys S. Doyle*. Privately Printed, 1954.

Withey, Henry F. and Elsie Rathburn Withey. *Biographical Dictionary of American Architects (Deceased)*. Los Angeles: Hennessey & Ingalls, Inc., 1970.

Journals and Newspapers

Bland, Henry Meade. "Prefers Poetry to Politics." *Overland Monthly* (August 1920).

Bliven, Bruce. "Senator Phelan's Legacy." *Fortnight*, Nov. 17, 1954.

Daley, Edith. "To the Master of Montalvo." *San Jose Mercury Herald*, 8 August, 1930.

Hurtabise, Mark. "James Duval Phelan, More Than Villa Montalvo." *The Pacific Historian* 23 (Fall 1979).

Mason, Rowena. "Montalvo: A Modern Poet's Monument to an Ancient Dreamer." *The San Franciscan*, April, 1927.

Madison, James H. "Taking the Country Barefooted: The Indiana Colony in Southern California." *California History* 69 (Fall 1990).

Walsh, James P. "James Phelan's Montalvo: Many Accepted, One Declined." *Southern California Quarterly* 58 (Spring 1976).

"William Curlett, F.A.I.A," *The Architect and Engineer of California and the Pacific Coast* 36 (April 1914).

San Jose Mercury Herald. 8 August 1930and 13 January 1943.

San Jose News. 24 June 1938.

Oral Interviews

Mary Doeltz, Santa Clara, California, February 7, 1993.

Sr. Emmanuel, O.C.D., Santa Clara, California, November 12, 1990.

Carolyn Hayes, Saratoga, California, December 22, 1990.

Rev. Richard Roberts, S.J., Santa Clara, California, August 16, 1990.

12 Campaign for U.S. Senate

Manuscripts

James Duval Phelan. Correspondence and Papers. The Bancroft Library, Berkeley, California.

Walker, Freda K. "Democratic Senator: Phelan of California, 1915–1921." MA Thesis, University of California, Berkeley, 1947.

Books

Bean, Walton. *California: An Interpretive History.* 3rd ed. New York: McGraw-Hill, 1968.

Hennings, Robert E. *James D. Phelan and the Wilson Progressives of California.* New York: Garland, 1985.

Morrison, Samuel Eliot and Commager, Henry Steel. *The Growth of the American Republic.* Vol. 2, 5th ed. New York: Oxford, 1962.

Tumulty, Joseph P. *Woodrow Wilson As I Know Him.* Garden City, New York: Doubleday, Page & Co., 1921.

Journals

Hennings, Robert E. "James D. Phelan and the Woodrow Wilson Anti-Oriental Statement of May 3, 1912." *California Historical Society Quarterly* XLII (December 1963).

13 United States Senator

Manuscripts

James Duval Phelan. Correspondence and Papers. The Bancroft Library, Berkeley, California.

Walker, Freda K. "Democratic Senator: Phelan of California, 1915–1921." MA Thesis, University of California, Berkeley, 1947.

Books

Hennings, Robert E. *James D. Phelan and the Wilson Progressives of California.* New York: Garland, 1985.

Tumulty, Joseph P. *Woodrow Wilson As I Know Him.* Garden City, New York: Doubleday, Page & Co., 1921.

Oral Interviews

Vincent Hallinan. "School Days at St. Ignatius." Interview by James P. Walsh, 1979. In possession of authors.

14 World War I Senate Years

Manuscripts

Consular Dispatches, Hong Kong, 1882–1884. John S. Mosby to E.L. Sullivan, May 9, 1882. Department of State, General Records (Group 59), National Archives, Washington, D.C.

Notes from the Chinese Legation, 1868–1906. Tsu Shau Pang to Frederick J. Frelinghuysen, May 29, 1882. Department of State, General Records (Record Group 59), National Archives, Washington, D.C.

James Duval Phelan. Correspondence and Papers. The Bancroft Library, Berkeley, California.

Books

Hennings, Robert E. *James D. Phelan and the Wilson Progressives of California.* New York: Garland, 1985.

Morrison, Samuel Eliot and Commager, Henry Steel. *The Growth of the American Republic.* Vol. 2, 5th ed. New York: Oxford, 1962.

Tumulty, Joseph P. *Woodrow Wilson As I Know Him.* Garden City, New York: Doubleday, Page & Co., 1921.

Walsh, James P. *Ethnic Militancy: An Irish-Catholic Prototype.* San Francisco: R & E Research Associates, 1972

Journals and Newspapers

Hennings, Robert E. "James D. Phelan and the Woodrow Wilson Anti-Oriental Statement of May 3, 1912." *California Historical Society Quarterly* XLII (December 1963).

————.and Timothy Foley. "Father Peter C. Yorke: Irish-American Leader," *Studia Hibernica* 14 (1974).

————. "De Valera in the United States, 1919," *Records of the American Catholic Historical Society of Philadelphia* LXXIII (September, December 1962).

San Francisco Leader. June–August, 1919; September–November, 1920.

15 Retired Life and Travel

Manuscripts

James Duval Phelan. Correspondence and Papers. The Bancroft Library, Berkeley, California.

Noël Sullivan Correspondence and Papers, The Bancroft Library, Berkeley, California.

Duraind, George J. "James Duval Phelan, Statesman, An Epic of Public Service." [Unpublished] Chapter iv. Phelan

Papers. The Bancroft Library. Berkeley, California.

Books

Engelmann, Larry. *The Goddess and the American Girl: The Story of Suzanne Lenglend and Helen Wills.* New York: Oxford, 1988.

Hennings, Robert E. *James D. Phelan and the Wilson Progressives of California.* New York: Garland, 1985.

Phelan, James D. *Travel and Comment.* San Francisco: A.M. Robertson, 1923.

Starr, Kevin. *Americans and the California Dream, 1850– 1915.* New York: Oxford, 1973.

Sullivan, Noël. *Forty Years Remembered: A Letter in the Form of a Memoir to the Children of My Sister, Gladys S. Doyle.* San Francisco: Privately Printed, 1954. Written, 1933.

Journals and Newspapers

Walsh, James P. "Terminal Interviews: Arthur Griffith, Michael Collins, and James Duval Phelan of San Francisco." *Eire-Ireland* XXIII (Winter 1988).

Freeman's Journal. 2 August 1922.

Irish Times. 2 August 1922.

San Francisco Leader. 26 July 1919.

16 Patron of the Arts

Manuscripts

James Duval Phelan. Correspondence and Papers. The Bancroft Library, Berkeley, California.

Books

Albronda, Mildred. *Douglas Tilden: Portrait of a Deaf Sculptor.* Silver Springs, MD.: T.J. Publishers, 1980.

Dillon, Richard H. *Iron Men: California's Industrial Pioneers.* Pt. Richmond, California: Candela Press, 1984.

Hughes, Edan Milton. *Artists in California: 1786–1940.* San Francisco: Hughes Publishing, 1986.

Leider, Emily Wortis. *California's Daughter: Gertrude Atherton and Her Times.* Stanford: Stanford University Press, 1991.

Journals and Newspapers

Phelan, James Duval. "The Growth of Municipal Art in California." *For California* (June 1904).

Walsh, James P. "De Valera in the United States, 1919." *Records of the American Catholic Historical Society of Philadelphia* LXXIII (September, December 1962).

New York Times. 2 September 1915.

17 Host of Montalvo

Manuscripts

James Duval Phelan. Correspondence and Papers. The Bancroft Library, Berkeley, California. Note draft letter by Phelan to Helen Wills (partially dated, May 27, no year), misfiled in box 13 of Phelan's outgoing correspondence, 1919. The most likely date is May 27, 1929.

Books

Atherton, Gertrude. *Adventures of a Novelist.* New York: Liveright, 1932.

Bland, Henry Meade. Ed. *A Day In The Hills.* San Francisco: Privately Printed, 1926.

Engelmann, Larry. *The Goddess and the American Girl: The Story of Suzanne Lenglend and Helen Wills.* New York: Oxford, 1988.

Josephson, Matthew and Josephson, Hannah. *Al Smith: Hero of the Cities.* Boston: Houghton Mifflin, 1969.

Kaucher, Dorothy. *James Duval Phelan: A Portrait, 1861–1930.* Saratoga, Ca.: Montalvo Association, 1965.

Leider, Emily Wortis. *California's Daughter: Gertrude Atherton and Her Times.* Stanford: Stanford University Press, 1991.

Journals and Newspapers

Walsh, James P. "Into Dust Thou Shalt Return." *Pacific Historian* 15 (Fall 1971).

————. "James Phelan's Montalvo: Many Accepted, One Declined." *Southern California Quarterly* LVIII (Spring 1976).

San Francisco Chronicle. 23 December 1929.

Oral Interviews

Benjamin H. Lehman. "Recollections and Reminiscences of Life in the Bay Area from 1920 Onward." Interview by Suzanne B. Riess, Berkeley, 1969. The Bancroft Library, Berkeley, California.

18 The Phelan Will and Villa Montalvo

Manuscripts

James Duval Phelan. Materials. Huntington Library, San Marino, California

James Duval Phelan. Papers. The Bancroft Library, Berkeley, California

Montalvo Papers, Villa Montalvo Archives, Saratoga, California

San Francisco Art Association Papers, San Francisco Art Institute Archives, San Francisco, California

San Francisco Art Institute History Collection, San Francisco Art Institute Library, San Francisco, California

Noël Sullivan Papers, The Bancroft Library, Berkeley, California

Books

McKay, Leonard, ed. *Clyde Arbuckle's History of San Jose*. San Jose, Ca., Memorabilia, 1986.

Atherton, Gertrude. *Adventures of a Novelist*. New York: Liveright, Inc., 1932.

Bean, Walton and James J. Rawls. *California: An Interpretive History*. New York: McGraw-Hill, 1983.

Cunningham, Florence R. *Saratoga's First Hundred Years*. San Jose, Ca.: Harlan-Young Press, 1967.

Kaucher, Dorothy. *James Duval Phelan: A Portrait, 1861–1930*. Saratoga, Ca.: Montalvo Association, 1965.

Mitchell, Broadus. *Depression Decade: From New Era Through New Deal, 1929–1941*. New York: Harper and Row, Publishers, 1947.

Payne, Stephen M. *Santa Clara County: Harvest of Change*. Northridge, Ca.: Windsor Publications, Inc., 1986.

Phelan, James D. *Travel and Comment*. San Francisco: A.M. Robertson, 1923.

Journals and Newspapers

Colodny, Dorothy. "San Francisco Art Association, A Survey." *Opera and Concert Magazine* (March 1951).

Dobbs, Stephen Mark. "A Glorious Century of Art Education: San Francisco Art Institute." *Art Education* (January 1976).

"James Duval Phelan." *Playground and Recreation* 24 (April–May 1931).

San Jose Mercury Herald. 9 June and 2 August 1927.

Oral Interviews

Michael Antonacci, Interview with Louis R. Bisceglia, January 15, 1990.

Sr. Emmanuel, O.C.D., Santa Clara, California, November 12, 1990.

19 The Montalvo Foundation of the San Francisco Art Association

Manuscripts

James D. Phelan. Estate Legal Records. Superior Court of the State of California, City and County of San Francisco. County Clerk's Office, San Francisco, California.

Montalvo Papers, Villa Montalvo Archives, Saratoga, California.

San Francisco Art Association Papers, San Francisco Art Institute Archives, San Francisco, California.

Books

Bean, Walton and James J. Rawls. *California: An Interpretive History*. New York: McGraw-Hill, 1983.

Cunningham, Florence R. *Saratoga's First Hundred Years*. San Jose, Ca.: Harlan-Young Press, 1967.

The Edward MacDowell Association, Incorporated. Peterborough, N.H.: Transcript Printing Company, n.d.

Payne, Stephen M. *Santa Clara County: Harvest of Change*. Northridge, Ca.: Windsor Publications, Inc., 1986.

Journals and Newspapers

Bailhache, Anne Dodge. "Montalvo Foundation Organized." *San Francisco Art Association Bulletin* 5 (October 1938).

"Montalvo Dedicated." *San Francisco Art Association Bulletin* 6 (August 1939).

Los Gatos News. 26 June 1944.

San Francisco News. 24 June and 25 October 1938.

San Jose Mercury Herald, 8 August 1930, 30 July 1939, 13 January 1943, and 14 July 1947.

San Jose News. 1 January 1941.

Oral Interviews

Carolyn Hayes, Saratoga, California, December 22, 1990.

Roberta Sweeney, Mountain View, California, November 27, 1990.

20 Villa Montalvo at Risk

Manuscripts

James D. Phelan. Estate Legal Records. Superior Court of the State of California, City and County of San Francisco. County Clerk's Office, San Francisco, California

James Duval Phelan. Materials. Huntington Library, San Marino, California.

John A. Sullivan, et al., vs. The San Francisco Art Association. Superior Court of the State of California, City and County of San Francisco. County Clerk's Office, San Francisco, California.

Montalvo Papers, Villa Montalvo Archives, Saratoga, California.

San Francisco Art Association Papers, San Francisco Art Institute Archives, San Francisco, California.

San Francisco Art Institute History Collection, San Francisco Art Institute Library, San Francisco, California.

Journals and Newspapers

Montalvo Association Bulletin, June, 1958.

Jones, Elizabeth MacSwain. "Montalvo." *National League for Woman's Service Magazine* 26 (July 1952).

Los Gatos Mail News. 21 July 1949.

Los Gatos Times. 29 August 1950

San Francisco Chronicle. 13 July 1951 and 2 October 1953.

San Francisco Examiner. 4 January and 30 December 1950.

San Jose Mercury. 14 October 1952.

San Jose Mercury Herald. 14 March 1949, 26 July 1949, and 23 September 1950.

San Jose Mercury News. 10 July 1949 and 7 January 1951.

San Jose News. 31 August and 23 September 1950.

Saratoga Observer. 30 March 1949, 27 July 1949, and 22 September 1949.

The Santa Clara. 1 March 1951.

Oral Interviews

Michael Antonacci, Interview with Louis R. Bisceglia, January 15, 1990.

Olivia Davies, Los Gatos, California, November 27, 1990.

Jean Kuhn Doyle, San Jose, California, January 10, 1991.

Margaret Dyer, Saratoga, California, March 7, 1991.

21 Villa Montalvo: A Community Treasure

Manuscripts

Montalvo Papers, Villa Montalvo Archives, Saratoga, California.

Montalvo Music Committee Records, Ruth Payette Collection, Saratoga, California.

James D. Phelan Foundation Papers, San Francisco Foundation, San Francisco, California.

San Francisco Art Association Papers, San Francisco Art Institute, San Francisco, California.

Books

Bean, Walton and James J. Rawls. *California: An Interpretive History*. New York: McGraw-Hill, 1983.

Fox, Nancy and Ed Fox. *The Santa Clara County Book*. Los Altos, Ca.: Tafnews Press, 1973.

Payne, Stephen M. *Santa Clara County: Harvest of Change*. Northridge, Ca.: Windsor Publications, Inc., 1986.

Journals and Newspapers

Los Gatos Daily Times. 2 October 1953, 2 September 1954, and 30 March 1966.

Los Gatos Times Observer. 25 June 1963 and 5 September 1968.

Metro. 24–30 May 1990.

Palo Alto Times. 8 May 1967 and 22 September 1975.

San Francisco Chronicle. 28 December 1952 and 26 May 1957.

San Francisco Examiner. 18 January 1953.

San Jose Mercury. 8 November 1953; 19 June and 27 July 1966; 15 January and 31 December 1967; 7 June 1974; 12 August and 28 September 1975.

San Jose Mercury News. 2 January and 17 April 1966; 30 May 1976; 23 December 1980; 11 August 1981; 31 October 1989.

San Jose News. 13 June 1968 and 9 August 1976.

Saratoga News. 26 January 1963 and 1 November 1989.

"The Villa Montalvo." *Westways* 52 (March 1960).

Zaleski, Jean. "Getting Away From It All: Isolation as Inspiration." *Women Artists News* 7 (April–May 1981).

Oral Interviews

Jean Kuhn Doyle, San Jose, California, January 10, 1991.

Olivia Davies, Saratoga, California, November 27, 1990.

Ruth Payette, Saratoga, California, November 20, 1990.

Caroline Hayes, Saratoga, California, December 22, 1990.

Margaret Dyer, Saratoga, California, March 7, 1991.

Helen Metcalf, Saratoga, California, November 8, 1990.

Francis X. Duggan, Santa Clara, California, August 15, 1990.

James Degnan, Santa Cruz, California, September 11, 1990.

Michael Antonacci, Interview with Louis R. Bisceglia, January 15, 1990.

Index

A

Addams, Jane 159

Admission Day monument 210
  photographs 101, 210

Agnes, *see* Sister Agnes of Jesus

Alice Phelan Sullivan Corporation 48

Alma Trio 305

American Historical Association 35

American Protective Association 57, 67–69

Antonacci, Michael 294–297

artists residence program 308

Association for the Adornment of San Francisco 35, 86

Atherton, Gertrude 134, 159–162, 195, 196, 201, 213–222, 231–235, 239, 241, 251, 252
  at Villa Montalvo 139, 148
  James D. Phelan and 40
  James D. Phelan, letters 160, 170, 189, 216
  Maude Fay and 225–229
  photographs 195, 214

B

Bailhache, Anne Dodge 269–286, 289, 292, 301, 304
  San Francisco Art Institute and 269

Ballinger, Richard 127–129

Barati, George 300

Barron, Genevieve Harvey 202–204
  photograph 199

Barrymore, Ethel
  photograph 232

Bland, Henry Meade 133, 234, 250, 307
  photographs 214, 235

Bohemian Club 18, 31, 35, 52, 57, 61, 84, 86, 142, 163, 213, 214, 250, 256

Bohemian Grove 52, 112, 141, 250
  photographs 194, 197, 227

Bonnie Brae Ranch 132, 133

Boodling Board of Supervisors 60–61

Born, Ernest 293

Broderick, David 6, 150

Brown, Arthur Page 135

Bryan, William Jennings 151, 152, 154, 161, 168, 176, 217

Buckley, Christopher (Blind Boss) 52, 54, 60
  photograph 54

Budapest String Quartet 279, 304

Budd, Governor James 60

Burnham Plan 86–92, 110, 112, 117
  photograph 89

Burnham, Daniel 66, 82–92, 110, 112, 135
  photograph 86

Burns, William 115–117
  photograph 116

C

California School of Fine Arts 257, 272, 274, 280, 282, 287, 288

California Volunteers monument 210
  photograph 213

Call Building 98
  photograph 98

Carpenters' Union 63

Carriage House Theatre 310, 312

Carriage House Theatre, the Claire Loftus 311

Caruso, Enrico 93
  photograph 93

Casey, Michael 74
  photograph 75

Caukin, Grace 158

Challener, Elisbeth 301

Chamberlain, R.L. 294

charter reform 54, 61–66

Chicago's World Fair, *see* Columbian Exposition 53

Citizens' Charter Association 55

Citizens' Defense Association 52

City Beautiful movement 81–92

City Front Federation 73, 74

Clinton, Dr. Charles 68–70

Cody Place, *see* Bonnie Brae Ranch

Collins, Fr. Richard 50, 245–248

Collins, General Michael 206–207

Columbian Exposition 53, 82, 83, 84

Committee of Fifty 97, 103, 105, 108, 111

Committee of One Hundred 62, 63

Commonwealth Club of San Francisco 34

Compton, Patricia (Oakes) 301

Coolidge String Quartet 280

Coolidge, Elizabeth Sprauge 280

Costello, John 168

Cox, James 193

Curlett, Alexander 135

Curlett, William 135

D

Dailey, John 294

de Havilland, Olivia 310
  photograph 310

de Young, Michael 104
  photograph 105

Dennison, George 279

Diamond, Joseph 55

Dillingham, Walter 197

Doeltz, George 138, 142, 143, 145, 147, 251, 259, 265, 291
  photograph 250

Doeltz, Louis 143

Donahue monument, *see* The Mechanics

Donahue, Peter 16

Doyle, Gladys 164, 228

Doyle, Jean Kuhn 312

Doyle, Thomas 4, 28, 145, 167, 175, 247, 251

Driscoll, Mrs. Belle 3, 4, 37, 167, 244–248, 251

Drum, John 103

Duraind, George 39, 55, 61

Duval, George 2, 3, 12, 38, 106, 111, 215, 216, 244, 246, 247

E

Edwin Markham Poetry Society 234, 267

Ellert, Levi 54, 59

Ellon, Florence 14, 22–32, 33, 43, 48, 57, 93, 149, 154, 159, 164, 165, 195, 215, 245, 246–248
  at Villa Montalvo 238
  education 22
  expenses 28, 29, 31
  family 22, 26, 31
  James D. Phelan and 20–32
  James D. Phelan, letters 24, 28, 29, 31, 97
  James D. Phelan, support by 4, 28, 29
  James D. Phelan, travels with 25–26
  photograph 25

Ellon, Robert 22, 27

Ellon, Vera 22, 26, 31

Employers' Association 63, 73–79

Epstein, Gustave 279

F

Fairbanks, Douglas 239
  photograph 219

Falconer, Donald 295

Fallico, Arturo 306

Fay, Charles 132, 137, 154–156, 195, 201, 204, 224, 244, 251
  photograph 197

Fay, Maude 155, 195, 224–230, 232
  Gertrude Atherton and 225–229
  photograph 225

Fisher, Walter 129

Flood Building 98

Fontaine, Joan 310

Fontaine, Lilian 310, 311

Football Players monument 211
  photograph 211

Foy, Mary 159

Friends of Montalvo 291–294

Funston, General Frederick 95, 96

Furuseth, Andrew 74, 77

G

Gage, Henry 69, 79
Garfield, James 123–127
Garnett, Porter 139
Gato, Baron 200
Gaw, William 281
Giannini, A. P. 237, 239
Gladstone, William 33, 57
Gottschalk, Charles 135, 137
Grant, General Ulysses S. 216
Griffin, Thomas 155
Griffith, Arthur 206–207
Grunsky, Carl 123

H

Harding, Warren G. 45, 193, 223, 233
Harriman, Edward 108, 109
Harroun, Philip 128
Harvey, Genevieve, see Barron,
    Genevieve Harvey
Harvey, John Downey 97, 99, 103, 159,
    201–202
    photograph 197
Harvey, Soffie (Mrs. John Downey
    Harvey) 145, 146, 164, 201–203,
    225, 232, 239, 251
    photographs 145, 199
Hearst Mining Building
    photograph 85
Hearst, Phoebe Apperson 66, 83, 85
    photograph 84
Heirs of James Phelan 14, 46, 49
Heney, Francis 115–117, 157–159, 162,
    251
    photographs 116, 185
Hetch Hetchy 81, 119
    photographs 119, 127, 129
Hincks, Hazel Pierce 291–297, 299, 301
Hitchcock, Ethan Allen 122, 125
Hoover, Herbert 188–189, 193
House, Colonel Edward 153
Howland, Colonel Harry 221, 241
    photograph 221
Humphrey, E. P. 300, 301
Hyde, Douglas 48, 106, 207

I–J

Irby, John 155, 168
    photograph 185
James D. Phelan Foundation 251
Japanese Exclusion League 190
Johnson, Hiram 108, 157, 158, 164, 182,
    188, 190, 193
Jones, Elizabeth McSwain 294, 295
Jordan, David Starr 239

K–L

Kelly, Alice, see Phelan, Alice Kelly
Kirkwood, Jean 294, 295
Kirkwood, Robert 282, 296–298
Knowland, Joseph 156, 157, 159, 162
Krueg, Glen 304
Labaudt, Lucien 281
Lane, Franklin 123, 129, 153, 161, 171,
    194
Lilian Fontaine Garden Theatre 311
Loftus, Claire 310, 311
Loofbourow, Arlene 290, 293
Los Gatos Theatre Workshop 309
Lundquist, Harriet 312

M

MacAgy, Douglas 288
MacDowell Association 272
MacDowell Colony 272, 273, 308
Maguire, James 68–72
Mahony, Thomas 23–24, 28, 31, 43, 95,
    96, 156, 225
Manson, Marsden 123–128
    photograph 124
Mark Hopkins Institute 257
    photograph 257
Markham, Edward 312
Markham, Edwin 214, 222, 235, 236,
    239, 244
    photograph 234
Marshall, Thomas
    photographs 182, 185
Martin, George 297
Mason, Rowena, see Myers, Rowena
    Mason
Maybeck, Bernard 257

McAdoo, Eleanor Wilson
    photograph 152
McAdoo, William 18, 152, 161, 192
    photograph 152
McArthur, Walter 63
McAuliffe, Florence 281
McCarthy, Patrick 63, 117
    photograph 63
McCauley, Gardiner 301
McClatchy, Charles 71
McCormack, John 234
McElroy, Robert D. 44, 45, 99, 102
McElroy, Robert M. 44
McEnerney, Garret 45, 99, 103, 104,
    110, 111, 179, 218
    photograph 104
McKinley, Mrs. William
    photograph 68
McKinley, William 45, 68, 212, 223
McLaren, John 142, 144
McLoughlin, Mrs. Alfred 294
Mendell, George 123
Mendelsohn, Dr. Louis 244, 249, 264–
    267, 279, 282, 295
    photograph 3
Mendelsohn, Marjorie 279, 286, 294
Menuhin, Yehudi 307
Merchants' Association 55, 62, 63, 80
Merola Opera Program 305
Michael, M. F. 74, 75
Mid-Winter Fair 53
Mills College 38, 251
Molkenbuhr, Judge Edward 295–298,
    301
Montalvo
    Service Group 301, 302, 310
Montalvo Association 296–298, 300,
    301, 303, 309
    takes title to Villa Montalvo 299
Montalvo Biennial Poetry
    Competition 313
Montalvo Committee, San Francisco Art
    Association 273
Montalvo Foundation 282, 284, 288, 290
Montalvo gardens 142–145
    photographs, after 1930 267, 302,
    311, 312, 314

photographs, through 1930 138, 143,
    144, 146, 148, 238, 240, 242, 249,
    262, 277, 312
Montalvo reopened 279
Montalvo Society 279, 280, 281, 282,
    291–295
Montalvo, Garci Ordonez de 137, 141
Montalvo, Villa 81
    architects 135
    art classes 306
    artists residence program 276
    arts center 270, 280, 299, 302, 304
    as art colony 272, 308
    as public park 267, 271, 289, 303, 314
    bequest of 252
    community involvement 276, 290–
        293, 302
    construction 137–138
    design of 134–137, 238
    Helen Wills at 236
    James D. Phelan at 1, 91, 120, 236,
        239, 249, 251, 256
    lawsuit 294
    Library Committee 312
    musical competitions 305
    operation of 282
    photographs, after 1930 142, 263,
        278, 287, 293, 296, 297, 299, 300,
        308
    photographs, construction 136
    photographs, through 1930 2, 4,
        131–148, 192, 223, 231, 238, 252,
        258, 260, 264, 289, 294, 298, 310
    plans for 132–137
    post-war plans 284–286
    theater 310
    trustees 253, 268, 293
    war years 283, 284, 287
    wine cellar 174, 175
    Yuletide 302, 303
Montalvo, Villa, Pavilion 312
Moody, Frederick 241, 243
    photograph 242
Moody, Helen Wills, see Wills, Helen
Mora, J. J. 141, 142, 300
Morley, Grace McCann 287
Muir, John 119–128
    photographs 125, 126
Murphy, Denis J. 26
Murphy, Fred 16, 241
Murphy, Frederic 271

Myers, Rowena Mason 145
  photograph 240

N

Native Sons monument, *see Admission Day* monument
Native Sons of the Golden West 35
Neri, Fr. Joseph 17
Newhall, George 76
Newmark, Henry 279
1900 Charter, *see* Phelan Charter
Norris, Charles and Kathleen 132

O

O'Connor, T. P. 218
O'Shaughnessy Dam 119
  photographs 127, 129
O'Shaughnessy, Michael 127, 130
  photograph 122
Oehler, Fred 297
Older, Cora (Mrs. Fremont) 116, 118, 132, 137, 147, 194, 239, 254
  photographs 214, 222
Older, Fremont 28, 84, 115–117, 132, 212, 214
  photographs 116, 118, 214
Older, Fremont and Cora 251
Olympic Club 35
Owens, Edwin 297

P

Pacific Union Club 18, 35, 57, 86, 163
Padre Junipero Serra monument 210
Palace Hotel 99, 163, 233
  photographs 60
Palace of Fine Arts 263
Palace of the Legion of Honor 251, 263
Palmer, A. Mitchell 192, 193
Panama Pacific Exposition 135, 168, 182
Paris Peace Treaty 182–185
Payette, Ruth 305
Pepper, Dr. Stephen 279
Phelan Building 8, 28, 46, 48, 57, 78, 93, 95–97, 100, 107, 132, 135, 247
  photographs 7, 23, 24, 96, 108

Phelan Building, San Jose
  photograph 107
Phelan Charter 64, 66, 67, 74, 80, 114
Phelan Estate 260, 271, 287, 289, 290, 296
Phelan family business 6–9, 19, 23, 51
Phelan family property
  business 9, 26, 44, 172
  business, *see also* Phelan Building 8
  personal 8, 10, 11, 91, 102, 133, 143
  personal, photograph 11
Phelan heirs
  lawsuit 288, 289, 292, 295
Phelan Trustees 292
Phelan, Alice Kelly 9–16, 46
  family 9
  photograph 12
Phelan, Alice, *see* Sullivan, Alice Phelan
Phelan, James
  character traits 5, 10, 19
  death of 43
  education, views on 15–16
  family 5, 9, 10, 12, 19–20
  health 7
  Heirs of, *see* Heirs of James Phelan
  photographs 5, 6, 19, 23, 42, 43
  relationship with son 19–20, 42
  Will of 5, 12, 46
Phelan, James Duval
  Agnes Tansill 164–167
  anti-Asian attitudes 169–171, 185–188
  appearance 214
  art acquisitions 96, 102, 204
  art bequests 251
  art patron 66, 81, 101, 183
  artistic interests 17, 81, 308
  as author 36, 37–38, 39
  as host 61, 130, 147, 148, 163, 232–236, 244
  at Villa Montalvo 131, 138, 231–236, 239, 286, 294, 298
  big government, attitude toward 65
  Bohemian Club 18, 31, 52, 61, 84, 163, 213, 214
  Bohemian Grove 141
  Burnham Plan, support of 91
  business practices 45
  California, views on 269
  California's heritage, interest in 36
  Catholic Church, views on 20, 36, 51, 175

  charities 48–50
  charter reform 54, 61–64
  childhood 10, 11
  City Beautiful 81–92
  clothes and 163
  club & association memberships 18, 35, 52, 86
  Columbian Exposition 53, 82, 83
  correspondence 3, 21, 78, 137, 159, 188, 216, 217–219, 243, 247
  cultural interests 26, 134, 307
  death of 248
  Douglas Tilden and 209–213, 216
  drawing of 226
  earthquake account 94, 95
  earthquake losses 96, 106–108
  education 16–18
  essays 34, 37, 40, 45
  European travel 12, 18–19, 38
  family 5, 9–16, 19–20, 27, 51, 196
  Florence Ellon and 14, 22–32, 57
  Florence Ellon, expenses 28, 29
  Florence Ellon, letters 24, 28, 29, 31, 97
  Florence Ellon, support of 4, 28, 29
  Florence Ellon, travels with 25–26
  food and 214
  Frank Sullivan and 20, 46–49
  gambling, views on 40–42
  George Sterling and 222–223
  Gertrude Atherton and 40, 216–222
  Gertrude Atherton, letters 159, 160, 170, 189
  graft prosecution 115
  health 1–3, 215, 239–240, 244–248
  Helen Wills and 21, 236–239
  Hetch Hetchy 81, 119–130, 154
  inheritance 45
  intellectual interests 17, 36, 44
  Ireland and Irish heritage 51, 175–179, 205–208
  James Sullivan, investigation of 167
  Japan, trip to 198–201
  Japanese militarism, fear of 191
  library, personal 36–37, 312
  magazine contributions 36, 37, 126, 187
  marriage, views on 21, 166, 195–196
  Maude Fay and 224–230
  mayor of San Francisco 21, 59–80
  mayoral campaign 55–58
  mayoral reelection 67
  Mid-Winter Fair 53
  newspaper contributions 34

  oil industry, support of 171
  Pacific Union Club 18, 35, 163
  Palace Hotel 163
  Peter Yorke and 56, 159, 176
  photographs, as child 13–15
  photographs, deceased 247, 248
  photographs, later years 1, 3, 45, 194, 195, 197, 199, 202, 203, 207, 208, 214, 219, 227, 229, 230, 232–234, 237, 239, 240, 242, 243, 245
  photographs, middle years 30, 42, 51, 59, 65, 68, 72, 74, 79, 81, 92, 112, 123, 130, 150–152, 171, 185, 191, 192
  poetry 25, 38, 180, 204, 239
  poets and poetry 234–236
  political values 2, 17, 53, 56
  post-earthquake role 99, 103–106
  Progressive politics and 150–155, 188
  Prohibition, views on 173–175
  pro-labor attitude 73
  public speaking 17–18, 33–36, 44, 53, 55, 58, 83, 223
  racial attitudes 169, 186
  relationship with father 19–20, 42
  relief funds, administers 111–112
  religious beliefs 1–4, 17, 18
  residences 14, 31, 91
  romance and 20–32, 164–167
  San Francisco Art Association 35
  Sullivan, Noël and 39
  Teamster's strike 72–79
  Travel and Comment 39, 197
  U.S. Senate colleagues and 34, 163
  U.S. Senate, reelection campaign 189–193
  U.S. Senator 163, 167–169, 181–189
  U.S. Senator, campaign for 154–162
  U.S. senator, election 161–162
  urban environment, and the 82
  Villa Montalvo, bequest of 81, 252, 261, 264, 274, 299
  Washington residence 197
  Washington residence, photograph 164
  Will of 3, 249–252, 261, 272, 289, 302
  wine and 172–175
  women in politics, views on 158
  women's suffrage, views on 161
Phelan, John (Junior) 5, 8, 12
Phelan, John (Senior) 5–6
Phelan, Mary Louise, *see* Phelan, Mollie

Phelan, Michael   5, 6, 9, 10
Phelan, Mollie   27, 99–103, 158, 165, 228, 250
   education   16
   family   10–14
   health   13
   photographs   46, 51, 72, 79, 151
   residence   132
   residences   91
Phelan, Mrs., see Phelan, Alice Kelly
Pickford, Mary
   photograph   219
Pierce, Mabel   279
Pinchot, Gifford   123–127
Pope Pius XI   204
Potter, Cora   220
Prohibition   173–175

R

Rainey, Sam   54, 55
Red Cross   35, 105
Reinhardt, Dr. Aurelia Henry   38
Riordan, Archbishop Patrick   33, 56, 67, 71–72, 77–78, 177
   photograph   71
Robert Emmet statue   183
Rockefeller Foundation   278
Rolph, James (Sunny Jim)   117, 130, 183
   photograph   237
Roosevelt, Eleanor   233
Roosevelt, Franklin   152, 181, 193, 233
   photograph   182
Roosevelt, Theodore   99, 103, 109, 115, 116, 118, 122–127, 151, 159, 182
   photographs   105, 125, 151
Root, Chester   297, 311
Ruef, Abraham (Abe)   93, 105, 109–112, 113–118, 122, 156
   photograph   109
Russell, George "A E"   207

S

Saint Ignatius, see St. Ignatius College   20
Sainte Claire Club   135, 254, 255
   photograph   254
San Francisco Art Association   35, 269, 297

art classes   281
art school   258, 275
   finances   259, 260, 262
   history of   256–258
   James D. Phelan and   250, 253
   James D. Phelan bequest and   264
   lawsuit   289
   Noël Sullivan, negotiations with   271
   Villa Montalvo and   287, 291, 303
   Villa Montalvo, named trustee   253
   Villa Montalvo, policy toward   263
   Villa Montalvo, trusteeship   298
San Francisco Art Institute   257
San Francisco City Hall   64, 88, 95
   photographs   95
San Francisco earthquake and fire   93–100
   relief efforts   103–106
San Jose State College   214, 235, 268
Santa Clara College   17, 49
Santa Clara University   250
Schmitz, Eugene   92, 93, 97, 109–112, 113–118, 122, 149, 159
   cartoon   115
   photographs   105, 110, 113
Scott, Irving   53
Shortridge, Samuel   156, 159, 189, 190, 191, 193
Sierra Club   124–128, 267
Sigall, Joseph   239
Sister Agnes of Jesus   1, 2, 4, 17, 154, 245–248, 253
   photographs   2, 20, 244
Smith, Al   2, 152, 233
Society for Preservation of National Parks   126
Somewhere in France (book), see Sullivan, Noël   39
Southern Pacific Railroad   108
Spencer, Eldridge   277
Spreckels, Rudolph   28, 39, 105, 113–118, 167, 215, 220
   photograph   116
Sproul, Robert Gordon   104
St. Ignatius Church
   photograph   102
St. Ignatius College   16, 17, 20, 49, 62, 180, 234, 251
St. Mary's Cathedral   10

St. Mary's Church   250
Stanford University   84, 85, 255, 256, 298
   photograph   85
Stanford, Leland and Jane Lathrop   85
Stephens, David   278
Sterling, George   222–223, 239, 246, 251, 312
   photographs   222, 234
Sullivan, Ada, see Sister Agnes of Jesus
Sullivan, Alice Phelan   2, 8, 20, 27, 99, 158, 201, 253
   death of   47
   education   15
   family   10–14
   marriage   11, 13
   photographs   20, 46
Sullivan, Alice Phelan Corporation, see Alice Phelan Sullivan Corporation   48
Sullivan, Alyce   20
Sullivan, Francis J., see Sullivan, Frank
Sullivan, Frank   11, 20, 28, 46, 97, 99, 104, 106, 208
   James D. Phelan and   20, 46–49
   marriage   13, 20
   photograph   20
Sullivan, Gladys   20
Sullivan, James   167
Sullivan, Noël   9, 203–208, 221, 242, 252, 260–262, 271, 280, 281, 288
   at Villa Montalvo   234
   family and   48
   James D. Phelan and   39, 180, 250
   photographs   180, 197, 199, 207, 243
   Somewhere in France   39, 180
Sutro, Adolph   54, 59

T

Taft, William Howard   127, 130, 151
Takashi Hara, Premier   201
Tansill, Agnes   164–167, 195
Taylor, Charles   56, 127
Taylor, Edward   117, 125
Teamster's strike   72–79
The Mechanics monument   211–212
   photographs   212
Tilden, Douglas   65, 101, 209–213, 234, 257
   Admission Day   210

California Volunteers   210, 213
Football Players   211
Padre Junipero Serra   210
The Mechanics   211–212
Tivoli Opera House   93
   photograph   100
Travel and Comment (book), see Phelan, James Duval   39
Tumulty, Joseph   153–155, 166, 172, 176, 177, 193

U–V

Union Labor Party   113
University of California   79, 104, 261, 267, 281, 298
University of California, Berkeley   35, 83, 85, 177, 250
Van Wyck, Sidney McMechen, Jr.   153
Vickery, Frederick   294, 295, 300
Villa Montalvo, see Montalvo, Villa

W–Z

W.P.A. Federal Music Project   268
Waldorf, John   155, 191
Wallace, Judge William   60, 61
Welch, George   4, 21, 28, 31, 43, 45, 50, 100, 126, 137, 155, 156, 168, 175, 213
Wenig, Herbert   294
Wheeler, Dr. Benjamin Ide   35, 104, 108
Whiting, Lucy   279
Wilbur, Ray Lyman   277
Wills, Helen   21, 196, 229, 235, 236–241, 251
   James Duval Phelan, drawing of   226
   photographs   195, 214, 230, 236, 237, 241, 242
Wilson, William   161
Wilson, Woodrow   45, 129, 156, 158, 162, 167–169, 176–179, 181, 183, 187, 190, 191, 193, 233
   James D. Phelan and   18, 39, 137, 151–153, 161, 223
   legislation and   123, 130
Yorke, Fr. Peter   28, 56–57, 62–72, 75–80, 104, 149, 156, 159, 176–179, 183, 184, 186, 187, 206, 218
   photographs   57
Yosemite National Park   119, 124

Photography Credits

Photographs by:

David Arnold: pages 210, 212 (bottom), 213

Patty Arnold: pages i, 300, 302

Sal Brunetto (Montalvo Collection): page 263

George Elliott (Montalvo Collection): page iii

Arnold Genthe (Courtesy, California Historical Society, San Francisco): page 99

Robin Gold: pages 85 (both), 91, 269, 271, 273, 275, 278, front cover

J. C. Gordon (Courtesy, The Bancroft Library): page 235 (bottom)

Lawrence Huff (Montalvo Collection): page 323

Jan Janes: page 142 (top)

Don Lorenzo (Montalvo Collection): page 23

Gabriel Moulin (Montalvo Collection): pages viii, 140

Peter Stackpole (Courtesy of Garret W. McEnerney II): page 104

Michael Vaughn (Montalvo Collection): pages vii, 126, 242, 313

James P. Walsh: page 211

Bob Weaver: page 324

The following organizations or people provided photographs:

Courtesy, Archives of the Santa Clara Carmelite Monastery: pages 1, 2 (bottom), 30, 244, 247

Courtesy, Doeltz Family Collection: pages 2 (top), 4, 133, 136 (all), 138 (both), 143 (both), 145, 146 (both), 147, 164, 192, 197, 249, 250, 252, 258, 259, 260, 262, 264, 289, 294, 298, 310, 312 (bottom)

Courtesy, Louise Mendelsohn Geiger: page 3

Courtesy, Sheila O'Day: pages ii, 5, 12, 13, 14, 46, 194

Courtesy, The Bancroft Library: pages 6, 7, 8, 9, 43, 65, 68, 72, 74, 84, 86, 95 (bottom), 100, 102, 109, 112, 116, 123, 125, 130, 134, 139 (top), 144, 148, 150 (both), 152, 171, 180, 185, 191, 207, 208, 214, 222, 225, 226, 227, 229, 230, 232 (top), 242 (both), 243, 245, back cover

Courtesy, Society of California Pioneers: page 10

Courtesy, Rowena Mason Myers Collection: pages 15, 140 (top), 239, 240

Courtesy, San Francisco History Room, San Francisco Public Library: pages 24, 45, 51, 63, 89, 93, 96, 98, 110, 113, 114, 119, 129, 248

Courtesy, Irish Library & Historical Society: page 54

Courtesy, Archives, University of San Francisco: page 57

Courtesy, The Archdiocese of San Francisco Archives: page 71

Courtesy, San Francisco State University Labor Archives: page 75

California Room, San Jose Public Library: page 61, 95 (top), 107

Courtesy, San Jose State University Library, Special Collections: pages 83, 235 (top), 254

Courtesy, University of San Francisco Archives: page 105, 179

Courtesy, California Historical Society, San Francisco: page 60, 257

Courtesy, James P. Walsh: pages 122, 127

Courtesy, Leo T. Walsh: page 151

Courtesy, Larry Engelmann: pages 236, 237, 241

Courtesy, Roberta Sweeney: page 268

Courtesy, San Francisco Art Institute: pages 287

From the Montalvo Collection: pages vi, 19, 20, 25, 37, 42, 59, 79, 81, 92, 108, 118, 131, 137, 139 (bottom), 141, 148, 160, 162, 195, 199, 202, 203, 205, 219, 221, 223, 231, 232 (bottom), 233, 234, 238, 263, 267, 268, 270, 274, 277, 293, 296, 297, 299, 308, 309, 310, 311 (both), 312 (top), 314

About the Authors

James P. Walsh

James P. Walsh first became acquainted with the career of James D. Phelan while writing his M.A. thesis in history at the University of San Francisco. Phelan remained among Walsh's research interests through his Ph.D. studies and dissertation at the University of California, Berkeley in 1970. A native of San Francisco, Dr. Walsh has written several other books, including *The San Francisco Irish*, *The Irish: America's Political Class*, *Ethnic Militancy*, and *Vincent Hallinan*. He has enjoyed academic appointments at San Jose State University: professor of History, Chair of the Department of History, and now as Dean of the College of Social Sciences.

Dr. Walsh resides in Los Gatos with his wife Ann McKinnon Walsh and their son Dan. Their daughters, Eileen and Laura, are married and reside in the area.

Timothy J. O'Keefe

Timothy J. O'Keefe is an associate professor of History at Santa Clara University in Santa Clara, California. A native Californian, Dr. O'Keefe graduated from St. Mary's College in Moraga and received his Ph.D. from the University of Notre Dame. He has written numerous articles on Irish topics for a variety of scholarly journals. Since 1965 he has held teaching and administrative positions at Santa Clara University and has received awards for teaching and research, including (with Dr. Walsh) the Spirit of Ireland Award in 1990.

Dr. O'Keefe lives in Santa Clara with his wife Julia and their four children.

Production Notes

This book was designed and created in FrameMaker on Macintosh computers. The text type is Goudy Oldstyle by Adobe Systems, and the ornamental type is Goudy Handtooled by Bitstream. These faces were chosen because they were designed by an American type designer, Frederick Goudy, about the same time Villa Montalvo was being built.

Most of the photographs in this book are old, and some were virtually unprintable. All were scanned on a La Cie scanner and retouched using Adobe PhotoShop. The border pattern at the top of the chapter opening pages is essentially an electronic "rubbing" of the border inside the arches on the front terrace of Villa Montalvo.

The cover film was produced by Metagraphics of Palo Alto, California. Digital text film was prepared at the Courier Connection in San Mateo, California. The book was printed and bound by the Courier Companies in Stoughton, Massachusetts.

Timothy J. O'Keefe and James P. Walsh upstairs at Villa Montalvo